Praise for *Organizational Climate and Cu...*

"Ehrhart, Schneider, and Macey have create(... prehensive resource for scholars and practitic ... wide range of complex issues with style and substance. You'll know a lot more about culture and climate after you read it. I know I did!" —**Daniel Denison**, Ph.D., IMD Business School, Switzerland

"This book breaks new ground regarding the integration of scholarship and practice, quantitative and qualitative methods for studying and changing organizational climate and culture, and includes a sizeable body of literature." —**W. Warner Burke**, Teachers College, Columbia University

"This volume offers a powerful and scholarly overview of the climate and culture literatures and seeks to integrate them. The authors are hugely knowledgeable about these areas and so it is just a treasure trove of information. It offers new insights about the links between strategy and culture and offers a comprehensive overview of measurement methods for climate and culture. The authors take clear positions on some of the key controversies in the field, the writing is clear, there are good summaries at the end of each chapter, and some novel methods of communicating key issues to readers. One such method is the use of a summary of key critiques of some concepts with the authors' helpful responses to critiques. The authors do not, as so many academics do, sit on the fence in relation to key controversies." —**Michael West**, Lancaster University, UK

Organizational Climate and Culture

The fields of organizational climate and organizational culture have coexisted for several decades with very little integration between the two. In *Organizational Climate and Culture: An Introduction to Theory, Research, and Practice,* Mark G. Ehrhart, Benjamin Schneider, and William H. Macey break down the barriers between these fields to encourage a broader understanding of how an organization's environment affects its functioning and performance. Building on in-depth reviews of the development of both the organizational climate and organizational culture literatures, the authors identify the key issues that researchers in each field could learn from the other and provide recommendations for the integration of the two. They also identify how practitioners can utilize the key concepts in the two literatures when conducting organizational cultural inquiries and leading change efforts. The end product is an in-depth discussion of organizational climate and culture unlike anything that has come before that provides unique insights for a broad audience of academics, practitioners, and students.

Mark G. Ehrhart is Associate Professor at the Department of Psychology at San Diego State University. His research interests include organizational climate and culture, organizational citizenship behavior, leadership, and work stress, and the application of these topics across levels of analysis and in service and health/mental health settings. He has over 30 journal articles and book chapters on these topics, including in such journals as the *Journal of Applied Psychology, Academy of Management Journal, Personnel Psychology,* and the *Journal of Management.* He is on the editorial board for the *Journal of Applied Psychology,* and is a member of the Society for Industrial and Organizational Psychology (SIOP) and the Academy of Management.

Benjamin Schneider is Senior Research Fellow at CEB and Professor Emeritus, University of Maryland. Ben's interests concern organizational climate and culture, employee engagement, service quality, staffing issues, and the role of manager personality in organizational life. Ben has been awarded SHRM's Michael R. Losey Award, SIOP's Scientific Contributions Award, the Academy of Management's HR Division Career Contributions Award, and the Academy of Management's OB Division Lifetime Achievement Award.

William H. Macey is Managing Director, Global Research Office at CEB and has more than 35 years of experience consulting with organizations to design and implement survey research programs. He served as an advisor to the Mayflower Group from 1992 to 2010 and is the co-author of several recent publications on employee engagement. He is a Fellow of the Society for Industrial and Organizational Psychology, the American Psychological Association, and the Association for Psychological Science, and is a SIOP past president.

ORGANIZATION AND MANAGEMENT SERIES

Series Editors

Arthur P. Brief
University of Utah

Kimberly D. Elsbach
University of California, Davis

Michael Frese
University of Lueneburg and National University of Singapore

Ashforth (Au.): *Role Transitions in Organizational Life: An Identity-Based Perspective.*
Bartel/Blader/Wrzesniewski (Eds.): *Identity and the Modern Organization.*
Bartunek (Au.): *Organizational and Educational Change: The Life and Role of a Change Agent Group.*
Beach (Ed.): *Image Theory: Theoretical and Empirical Foundations.*
Brett/Drasgow (Eds.): *The Psychology of Work: Theoretically Based Empirical Research.*
Brockner (Au.): *A Contemporary Look at Organizational Justice: Multiplying Insult Times Injury.*
Chhokar/Brodbeck/House (Eds.): *Culture and Leadership Across the World: The GLOBE Book of In-Depth Studies of 25 Societies.*
Darley/Messick/Tyler (Eds.): *Social Influences on Ethical Behavior in Organizations.*
De Cremer/Tenbrunsel (Eds.): *Behavioral Business Ethics: Shaping an Emerging Field.*
De Cremer/van Dick/Murnighan (Eds.): *Social Psychology and Organizations.*
Denison (Ed.): *Managing Organizational Change in Transition Economies.*
Dutton/Ragins (Eds.): *Exploring Positive Relationships at Work: Building a Theoretical and Research Foundation.*
Earley/Gibson (Aus.): *Multinational Work Teams: A New Perspective.*
Ehrhart/Schneider/Macey (Aus.): *Organizational Climate and Culture.*
Elsbach (Au.): *Organizational Perception Management.*
Fayard/Metiu (Aus.): *The Power of Writing in Organizations: From Letters to Online Interactions.*
Garud/Karnoe (Eds.): *Path Dependence and Creation.*
Grandey/Diefendorff/Rupp (Eds.): *Emotional Labor in the 21st Century: Diverse Perspectives on Emotion Regulation at Work.*
Harris (Ed.): *Handbook of Research in International Human Resource Management.*
Jacoby (Au.): *Employing Bureaucracy: Managers, Unions, and the Transformation of Work in the 20th Century, Revised Edition.*
Kossek/Lambert (Eds.): *Work and Life Integration: Organizational, Cultural and Individual Perspectives.*

Kramer/Tenbrunsel/Bazerman (Eds.): *Social Decision Making: Social Dilemmas, Social Values and Ethical Judgments.*
Lampel/Shamsie/Lant (Eds.): *The Business of Culture: Strategic Perspectives on Entertainment and Media.*
Lant/Shapira (Eds.): *Organizational Cognition: Computation and Interpretation.*
Lord/Brown (Aus.): *Leadership Processes and Follower Self-Identity.*
Margolis/Walsh (Aus.): *People and Profits? The Search Between a Company's Social and Financial Performance.*
Miceli/Dworkin/Near (Aus.): *Whistle-blowing in Organizations.*
Nord/Connell (Aus.): *Rethinking the Knowledge Controversy in Organization Studies: A Generative Uncertainty Perspective.*
Messick/Kramer (Eds.): *The Psychology of Leadership: Some New Approaches.*
Pearce (Au.): *Organization and Management in the Embrace of the Government.*
Peterson/Mannix (Eds.): *Leading and Managing People in the Dynamic Organization.*
Rafaeli/Pratt (Eds.): *Artifacts and Organizations: Beyond Mere Symbolism.*
Riggio/Murphy/Pirozzolo (Eds.): *Multiple Intelligences and Leadership.*
Roberts/Dutton (Eds.): *Exploring Positive Identities and Organizations: Building a Theoretical and Research Foundation.*
Schneider/Smith (Eds.): *Personality and Organizations.*
Smith (Ed.): *The People Make the Place: Dynamic Linkages Between Individuals and Organizations.*
Thompson/Choi (Eds.): *Creativity and Innovation in Organizational Teams.*
Thompson/Levine/Messick (Eds.): *Shared Cognition in Organizations: The Management of Knowledge.*
Zaccaro/Marks/DeChurch (Eds.): *Multiteam Systems: An Organization Form for Dynamic and Complex Environments.*

Organizational Climate and Culture

An Introduction to Theory, Research, and Practice

Mark G. Ehrhart
San Diego State University

Benjamin Schneider
CEB

William H. Macey
CEB

Routledge
Taylor & Francis Group
NEW YORK AND LONDON

First published 2014
by Routledge
711 Third Avenue, New York, NY 10017

and by Routledge
27 Church Road, Hove, East Sussex BN3 2FA

Routledge is an imprint of the Taylor & Francis Group, an informa business

© 2014 Mark G. Ehrhart, Benjamin Schneider, and William H. Macey

The right of Mark G. Ehrhart, Benjamin Schneider, and William H. Macey to be identified as authors of this work has been asserted by them in accordance with sections 77 and 78 of the Copyright, Designs and Patents Act 1988.

All rights reserved. No part of this book may be reprinted or reproduced or utilized in any form or by any electronic, mechanical, or other means, now known or hereafter invented, including photocopying and recording, or in any information storage or retrieval system, without permission in writing from the publishers.

Trademark Notice: Product or corporate names may be trademarks or registered trademarks, and are used only for identification and explanation without intent to infringe.

Library of Congress Cataloging-in-Publication Data

Ehrhart, Mark G.
  Organizational climate and culture : an introduction to theory, research, and practice / Ehrhart Mark G., Benjamin Schneider, William H. Macey.
    pages cm. — (Series in organization and management)
  1. Organizational behavior. 2. Corporate culture. I. Schneider, Benjamin, 1938– II. Macey, William H. III. Title.
  HD58.7.E384 2013
  302.3'5—dc23   2013022806

ISBN: 978-0-415-87980-4 (hbk)
ISBN: 978-1-84872-528-7 (pbk)
ISBN: 978-1-315-85766-4 (ebk)

Typeset in Berling
by Apex CoVantage, LLC

M.G.E.: For Karen and Evan, who are such integral parts of the climate and culture of my life.

B.S.: For Boaz, Gabe, CeCe, Chloe, and Gillian, who make their Poppy happy every day.

W.H.M.: For Billy, Sarah, and Brandon.

Contents

About the Authors	xv
Series Foreword	xvii
Preface	xix

1. *Introduction*	**1**
Definitions of Organizational Climate and Culture	1
Assumptions	3
Our Goals: What We Hope to Accomplish	4
What We Are Not Trying to Accomplish	5
Organization of the Book	6
Summary	8
2. *History of Organizational Climate Theory and Research*	**11**
From 1939 to the Mid-1960s: The Early Years of Climate Research	12
From the Late 1960s through the Early 1970s: The Expansion of Empirical Climate Research	32
The Mid-1970s: Major Critiques of the Climate Literature and Their Resolution	50
Conclusion	59
3. *Organizational Climate Research: The Current State of the Field*	**63**
The Definition of Organizational Climate	64
Climate at the Individual Level: Psychological Climate	70

Measurement and Levels of Analysis	*72*
Types of Climate Studied: Molar and Focused Climates	*79*
Climate Strength	*98*
Other Boundary Conditions of Climate–Outcome Relationships	*105*
Climate Itself as a Moderator Variable	*108*
Additional Approaches to Studying Climate: Antecedents and Mediators	*110*
Summary and Conclusions	*114*
4. Foundations of Organizational Culture	**117**
A Brief History of Research on Organizational Culture	*118*
Approaches to Understanding Organizational Culture	*125*
Defining Organizational Culture	*130*
Levels of Culture and Cultural Forms	*135*
Methods for Studying Organizational Culture	*138*
Summary: On Understanding and Studying Organizational Culture	*144*
5. The Emergence, Effectiveness, and Change of Organizational Cultures	**145**
The Emergence of Organizational Culture	*145*
Socialization and the Perpetuation of Organizational Culture	*153*
Organizational Culture and Organizational Effectiveness	*160*
Organizational Subcultures	*168*
Culture Strength	*173*
Organizational Culture Change	*178*
Summary: The Emergence, Effectiveness, and Change of Organizational Cultures	*192*
6. Integrating Organizational Climate and Organizational Culture	**195**
On the Relative Absence of the Integration of Climate and Culture	*196*
Similarities Between Organizational Climate and Culture	*197*
Differences Between Organizational Climate and Culture	*203*
What Organizational Climate Researchers Could Learn from Organizational Culture Research	*208*
What Organizational Culture Researchers Could Learn from Organizational Climate Research	*213*
Toward Integrating Organizational Climate and Culture	*217*

Climate, Culture, and Competitive Advantage	225
Climate, Culture, and Organizational Change	229
Conclusion	231

7. Thoughts for Practitioners on Organizational Cultural Inquiry 233
Why Executives Care: Strategy, Leadership, and Organizational Culture	234
The Bases for Cultural Diagnosis and Change	236
Talent Management and Cultural Inquiry	239
The Measurement Framework for Cultural Inquiry and Diagnosis	241
Qualitative Approaches to Cultural Diagnosis	244
Quantitative Approaches to Cultural Diagnosis	249
Blending Qualitative and Quantitative Cultural Inquiry: A Case Example	275
Summary of Key Points to Consider in Conducting a Cultural Diagnosis	279

8. Summary and Conclusion 283
Organizational Climate	283
Organizational Culture	289
Integrating Organizational Climate and Culture	296
Implications for Practice	299
Organizational Climate and Culture: A Research Agenda	301
Conclusion	304

References	*305*
Author Index	*339*
Subject Index	*349*

About the Authors

Mark G. Ehrhart is Associate Professor at the Department of Psychology at San Diego State University. He received his Ph.D. in industrial/organizational psychology from the University of Maryland. His research interests include organizational climate and culture, organizational citizenship behavior, leadership, and work stress, and the application of these topics across levels of analysis and in service and health/mental health settings. He has over 30 journal articles and book chapters on these topics, including in such journals as the *Journal of Applied Psychology*, *Academy of Management Journal*, *Personnel Psychology*, and the *Journal of Management*. He is on the editorial board for the *Journal of Applied Psychology* and is a member of the Society for Industrial and Organizational Psychology and the Academy of Management.

Benjamin Schneider is Senior Research Fellow at CEB and Professor Emeritus, University of Maryland. Ben's interests concern organizational climate and culture, employee engagement, service quality, staffing issues, and the role of manager personality in organizational life. He has published 140 journal articles and book chapters as well as ten books. Ben has won awards for his research including SHRM's Michael R. Losey Award, SIOP's Scientific Contributions Award, the Academy of Management's HR Division Career Contributions Award, and the Academy of Management's OB Division Lifetime Achievement Award. Besides the University of Maryland, Ben has taught at Yale University, Michigan State University, Bar-Ilan University (on a Fulbright), and for shorter periods of time at Dartmouth College, Peking University, and the University of Aix-Marseille. Ben joined CEB in 2003 and since then has consulted with companies and associations on projects concerning service climate, safety climate, innovation climate, and the ways potential employees experience the selection process and the consequences of those experiences.

William H. Macey is Managing Director, Global Research Office at CEB and has more than 35 years of experience consulting with organizations to design and implement survey research programs. He served as an advisor to the Mayflower Group from 1992 to 2010 and is the co-author of several recent publications on employee engagement. He is a Fellow of the Society for Industrial and Organizational Psychology (SIOP), the American Psychological Association, and the Association for Psychological Science, and is a SIOP past president. He received his Ph.D. from Loyola University Chicago in 1975.

Series Foreword

Ehrhart, Schneider, and Macey have written an important book, for it bridges the science–practice divide. It puts meat on the bones of the potentially elusive constructs of "organizational climate" and "organizational culture." Definitions, history, research, and relationships between the two constructs as well as their practical utility are dealt with in informative and actionable ways. Readers will leave the book with an impressive understanding of their scientific merits and their utility as managerial tools. You are in for a terrific read!

Arthur P. Brief
Kim Elsbach
Michael Frese

Preface

This book is about how the people in work organizations experience them. It concerns the ways people interpret and understand what happens to them at work, and how they describe what it is like to work in their organizations. That is, it addresses the abstractions and meanings people derive from their work experiences—the company is very service-oriented, the company treats us fairly, the company values profits above all—as well as the specific kinds of things that happen to employees that yield those abstractions.

There is great variety in the way these issues have been conceptualized and studied, but most are captured under the broad categories of organizational climate and organizational culture. We present how each of these concepts came to prominence and how they have evolved over time. A major goal of the book is to provide a firm foundation for integrating across the literatures on climate and culture to produce a view of organizations that is tangible and manageable while retaining the abstractions that are so useful for common conversation. The cover of the paperback, designed by Chad Smith, visually captures our goal of bridging these two well-developed literatures that for too long have existed side by side but separate.

This book is a testament to the impressive body of work that now exists on the study of organizational climate and culture, and we acknowledge all of those who have contributed to the rich foundation of effort on which this book rests. In addition, the book has profited greatly from our work with various collaborators and students in our careers and their willingness to provide the energy and insight that pushed our thinking forward. The clients we have worked with in consulting roles have also pushed our thinking and made us cognizant of the necessity to not only be academically rigorous but relevant as well. Readers will appreciate this drive for relevance in how we describe research approaches and, especially, our notion of using data as a basis for both understanding and change.

The book would not exist without the calm prodding of Anne Duffy of Routledge. Anne never pushed us overtly and never threatened us, but her role as the Jiminy Cricket on our shoulders to keep working was important. We also want to acknowledge the input we received from Neal Ashkanasy, Jean Bartunek, Paul Bliese, Warner Burke, Dan Denison, Vicente González Romá, and Michael West that not only refined our writing, but also reassured us that our efforts were worthwhile. Some say effort breeds commitment, but in our case, it was commitment to understanding and then integrating these literatures that produced the effort. Of course, writing a book like this requires maintaining that effort over a long period, and we deeply appreciate our families and colleagues for supporting us and giving us the energy to keep moving forward.

Finally, we remain good friends even after all the drafts and comments and critiques we did of each other's work. Too many revisions to count have produced, we hope, an integrated whole of a book that has a common language and proceeds logically and forcefully.

Mark G. Ehrhart, San Diego
Benjamin Schneider, Tucson
William H. Macey, Rolling Meadows

CHAPTER
1
Introduction

This book is about the emergence, nature, and assessment of organizational climate and culture and the ways in which the two may be integrated to yield improved understanding about organizations and their effectiveness. The genesis of the book lies in our writing chapters for the *APA Handbook of Industrial and Organizational Psychology* (Schneider, Ehrhart, & Macey, 2011b) and the second edition of the *Handbook of Organizational Culture and Climate* (Schneider, Ehrhart, & Macey, 2011a), as well as our articles in the Society for Industrial and Organizational Psychology's (SIOP) journal, *Industrial and Organizational Psychology: Perspectives on Science and Practice* (Schneider, Ehrhart, & Macey, 2012), and the *Annual Review of Psychology* (Schneider, Ehrhart, & Macey, 2013). We realized that we had a tremendous amount of excellent and interesting material to work with for these chapters and that our reflections on what we had written revealed that we had still more ideas that might prove useful for those interested in the topics. Therefore, this book presents a summary of what we learned in those chapters with expanded reviews of relevant research literatures, potential for their integration, and expanded implications for practice.

In this opening chapter, we introduce the reader to what organizational climate and culture are, the assumptions and goals we had as we wrote the book, some clarifications of what we intentionally were *not* trying to accomplish, and a brief overview of the chapters to follow.

DEFINITIONS OF ORGANIZATIONAL CLIMATE AND CULTURE

Our experience in teaching about organizational climate and culture and in trying to inform management in organizations about the importance of these ideas tells us that everyone has their own ideas about what they mean when they say climate and/or culture. People use many different ways to characterize these two constructs. For example, as we will see in the discussions of the history of these constructs, various terms have been used to try to capture the overall or global or macro look and feel of organizations to their members. In addition to climate and culture, terms such as organizational atmosphere and organizational character have also been used.

For now we define organizational climate as the shared meaning organizational members attach to the events, policies, practices, and procedures they experience and the behaviors they see being rewarded, supported, and expected (we discuss this definition in more depth in Chapter Three). Organizational climate is an abstraction that represents the cognitive structuring of a whole out of many observations and experiences; the whole is the meaning attached to those many observations and experiences. Thus, climate is conceptually an abstraction about the meaning of a setting for the members that experience it. There has been debate about whether climate exists primarily as an individual experience or as a characteristic of the group or organization, especially because our measurement of climate typically involves collecting individual reports of climate and then aggregating them to the organizational level of interest (e.g., group, department, or organization). That debate and how it has been resolved will be one of the central foci of the chapters on organizational climate. Climate research has attempted to capture the abstractions members experience about their unit and relate those abstractions to effectiveness indices that are important to those units. Climate has been outcome-focused and in that sense, research on it has largely been based on a predictive model—one attempts to assess climate because it helps understand important effectiveness outcomes that are conceptually seen to emerge from the climate.

Organizational culture is defined as "a pattern of shared basic assumptions learned by [an organization] as it solved its problems of external adaptation and internal integration, which has worked well enough to be considered valid and, therefore, to be taught to new members as the correct way to perceive, think, and feel in relation to those problems" (Schein, 2010, p. 18). The idea that beliefs, ideologies, and values are shared has been assumed in the organizational culture research paradigm, with culture always referring to something that exists beyond the individual member and that is transmitted through stories and rituals as well as the experiences newcomers have. Much of the theory underlying culture would suggest that the members of the collective characterized by it are not necessarily aware of the culture in which they reside but that it exists in their behaviors and the assumptions they make about what is important. Culture research has historically been descriptively focused: what is culture, what are its components, and how do people come to learn the culture of their unit. It is only in more recent guises that culture research has been focused on effectiveness outcomes, and this transition from a more descriptive to a more predictive approach to culture will be one of the central foci of the chapters on organizational culture. Thus, while management consultants and news media observers of organizations have discussed the nature of culture and its importance for effectiveness, it is more recently that researchers have also had this focus on effectiveness.

The focus on the meaning and cognitive structuring of actual experiences in climate research suggests the psychological traditions, especially Gestalt psychology, from which organizational climate emerged. In contrast, the focus on values and beliefs and the methods by which they are transmitted (myths and stories) indicates the locus of organizational culture in anthropology and sociology. Readers will find it interesting in the discussions of history that come later to see how these ideas emerged and became relevant for the modern study of organizations and how we think they together yield powerful insights for not only understanding organizations, but also for helping them become more effective.

So many issues to review to understand these complex ideas, but so little time! As we noted earlier, our collective sense after the writing of the two review chapters (Schneider et al., 2011a, 2011b) was that there was a need for a more in-depth discussion of what each of the organizational climate and culture literatures brings to the table and how the two can build on each other and be integrated in both research and practice. This book is our attempt to provide an expanded historical and practical—and integrated—treatment of these complex but understandable, interesting, and important concepts.

ASSUMPTIONS

The three of us have a background in industrial/organizational (I/O) psychology, and that background has greatly influenced our approach to this book and general thinking on these topics. One of the hallmarks of I/O psychology is its emphasis on the scientist-practitioner model. This model integrates science with practice and vice versa, suggesting the rigor that should underlie practice and the need to focus research efforts on practical problems in the work place. Thus, we deeply value the need for a rigorous, scientific approach to the study of climate and culture and we believe it important for the study of both to focus on improving organizational effectiveness vis-à-vis the employees who work in them. In short, our position is that research has little value unless it is put into practice and influences how organizations actually function. We believe that the topics of climate and culture are (or should be) highly valuable to practitioners because they deal with how people sense what is valued and important in their work place, and as the sense they make of their workplace is based on what employees actually observe and experience, this information can be useful for making improvements.

Another of our assumptions is the value we place on research excellence whether of the quantitative or qualitative variety. Early research on both climate and culture was characterized by a more qualitative orientation and that approach yielded numerous insights. Culture research persisted longer with a focus on qualitative approaches as befits its background in anthropology, while climate became increasingly quantitative in its approach to measurement. The point is not which is better but the purpose for which the research has been accomplished and its usefulness. Indeed one of us has written for many years about the need for both types of methods in both climate and culture research (e.g., Schneider, 2000). On a distinct but oftentimes related note, we emphasize and value both etic approaches (comparisons across organizations), particularly for applied research efforts, and emic approaches (studying an organization individually and in-depth), particularly for practical purposes when a specific company has sought our services. So, it is one thing to know the correlates of a climate for service across many organizations (etic approach) and it is another thing to work in a specific organization to make improvements in its climate for service (emic approach).

A final assumption is that organizational effectiveness is an expansive concept and needs to be defined broadly and not solely in terms of financial performance. Particularly, it need not be defined only in the ways that management dictates. Effectiveness is multifaceted, and it is important to think about it from the perspective of the multiple stakeholders of the organization. Our preference is not to limit our discussion by focusing on either/or thinking—for example, this stakeholder (e.g., stockholders) receives an outcome OR this one (e.g., employees) does, but not both. Rather, we favor climates and cultures that work in favor of multiple stakeholders because those solutions tend to provide the most benefit to the organization in the long run. The research we will later summarize supports this more expansive perspective.

OUR GOALS: WHAT WE HOPE TO ACCOMPLISH

1. *To stimulate thinking and research on organizational climate.* Research on organizational climate has grown substantially since the turn of the century (Kuenzi & Schminke, 2009); our goal is to help move the study of climate forward, especially via insights learned from the study of organizational *culture.*
2. *To stimulate thinking and research on organizational culture.* Some organizational culture researchers have observed that the field has perhaps lost some of its earlier momentum (Alvesson, 2011), at least in that organizational culture is more rarely the primary focus of academic researchers (Martin, Frost, & O'Neill, 2006). Our review of publications in top I/O psychology and management journals suggests that empirical research specifically focused on organizational culture in the past decade or so has been more limited than it had been in the previous two decades, particularly relative to empirical research on climate

Introduction 5

(Schneider, Ehrhart, & Macey, 2013). We think this state of affairs is neither useful nor necessary.[1] So we will address how research on organizational culture can (a) benefit from the work on organizational *climate*, and (b) help with many issues practitioners face, particularly in the area of organizational change and, reciprocally, how the practical implications of organizational culture can renew interest in the topic among organizational researchers.

3. *To put a variety of information on climate/culture in one place and organize it in a holistic way.* Although several handbooks of organizational climate and culture have appeared in the literature over the past 20 years, those that we know of are edited books with some authors focusing on climate and others on culture, with little integration between the two. By authoring a book that focuses simultaneously on both topics, we hope to be a force for more integrative thinking and communication across the two fields.

WHAT WE ARE NOT TRYING TO ACCOMPLISH

1. *To present ourselves as unbiased.* We do not pretend to be unbiased in our evaluations and conclusions of the organizational climate and culture literatures. Thus, this book offers our collective perspectives on the two topics, including our viewpoint on what the topics offer individually and collectively to both understanding and practice. We focus on what we see are the key themes and "big picture" issues in the two literatures, and we review them with sample studies. We recognize that others may have highlighted different issues or come to different conclusions, and thus we are up front that this book represents our own collective perspective.

2. *To provide an exhaustive literature review.* Our goal in writing this book was never to provide an exhaustive review of the literatures on organizational climate and culture. In our overviews of the history of these constructs (particularly climate), we have tried to highlight the articles that in our view have had the largest impact on the field, supplemented with some that have less impact but help to paint a picture of the general thinking of the time. In addressing contemporary issues related to both climate and culture, we selected articles that best highlight the general themes we identified in the literature. We have certainly had to leave out many interesting and well-done articles and chapters, but hopefully our summaries provide a good starting point for readers wishing to do a more in-depth review of particular topics.

3. *To discuss all practices that influence or are influenced by climate and culture.* As outcomes of the thousands of things that happen in organizations, climate and culture can be addressed from the perspective of all formal and informal practices that yield them. We do not do this here. The fields that serve as the primary foundations for the contemporary study of climate and culture, specifically industrial/organizational psychology and organizational behavior, are the sources for those details. Thus, while leadership and teams and pay practices and job attributes all likely contribute to and are influenced by the climate and culture of organizations, the details of basic research on each of these is not within

the purview of this book; we focus on their relationship to climate and culture.

ORGANIZATION OF THE BOOK

The chapters of the book can be grouped into three general sections, each with two chapters. Chapters Two and Three focus on organizational climate, Chapters Four and Five discuss organizational culture, and the Chapters Six and Seven address the integration of the two. The final chapter, Chapter Eight, summarizes our major points from throughout the book and highlights practical implications for organizations and recommended areas for future research on organizational climate and culture.

Of the two chapters on organizational climate, the first covers the history of organizational climate research. Although aspects of this history have been summarized by us (e.g., Schneider et al., 2011b; Schneider, Bowen, Ehrhart, & Holcombe, 2000; Reichers and Scheider, 1990) and others (e.g., Ashkanasy, Wilderom, & Peterson, 2000a), the history of climate research has not been described in the level of detail we provide here. We cover the history of climate in such depth because of its importance in setting the stage for later climate research. In fact, many of the major differences in the ways climate has been conceptualized and studied can be traced to diverging perspectives in those early years. In Chapter Two, we divide the foundational work on climate into two major periods. The first period covers the years before the formal, quantitative study of climate began in earnest, when the seeds of the construct were being planted by researchers in various outlets who shared an interest in the study of the unique environments that are created by and for people in work organizations. The second period began in the late 1960s and continued through the 1970s. This era witnessed the beginning of formal studies of climate coupled with various reviews and critiques of the construct, its conceptualization, and its measurement. Of particular importance during this early work was the design of survey measures for the assessment of organizational climate, whether climate was a generic construct or whether it should be studied with some focus, and distinctions among job satisfaction, organizational climate, and psychological climate.

The time frame from the 1980s to the present comprises what we consider to be the contemporary study of organizational climate, which is the focus of Chapter Three. This period has been characterized by the resolution of many of the early controversies, as evidenced by significant progress in the areas of levels of analysis and the study of climates focused on specific outcomes (like safety and service). As part of Chapter Three, we address how climate is currently defined and studied and its expansion into significant organizational process foci of theory and research in organizations (e.g., fairness, ethics). We describe how climate research has moved beyond just focusing on mean levels of climate

Introduction

perceptions to taking into account variability in those perceptions (i.e., climate strength), and how research on climate has taken numerous vantage points, including antecedents, outcomes, boundary conditions of those outcomes, processes that mediate the resulting effects, climate itself as a moderator, and so on. In sum, Chapter Three covers both the current state of the art in the field and also suggests in some detail areas of thinking and research where progress still needs to be made.

In the second section of the book, Chapters Four and Five, we focus on organizational culture and organize the two chapters similarly to the two chapters on climate. Chapter Four concerns foundational ideas in the literature on organizational culture, although we do not develop our discussion of the history of culture to the extent that we do the history of organizational climate in Chapter Two. Somewhat paradoxically, there are extensive books on organizational culture history, research, and theory (e.g., Alvesson, 1993; Deal & Kennedy, 1982; Denison, 1990; Hofstede, 1991; Martin, 1992, 2002; Schein, 1985, 2010; Trice & Beyer, 1993), more so than exist on organizational climate (zero such books!) even though there is a larger empirical research literature on climate. Therefore, we highlight what we see as the key developments in the history of organizational culture, with a particular emphasis on the way the roots of culture research are intertwined with those of climate research. In fact, as we note, the rise in studies of culture was at least in part a reaction to the state of the field of organizational climate and the disagreements that dominated the field over what some considered to be "technical minutiae" (Ashkanasy, Wilderom, & Peterson, 2000b). After our brief historical treatment of culture, we address three foundations of the culture literature: how it has been conceptualized, how it has been defined, and how it has been studied.

Chapter Five transitions to some of the issues we view as critical for understanding where culture comes from and its effect on organizations. We begin with a summary of some of the key influences on the development of organizational culture that have been identified in the literature, including the organizational founder, the collective learning by organizational members as a result of the organization's successes and failures, and the organization's context including its industry and the national culture of its home country. Closely related to the issue of how culture emerges is how it is perpetuated and maintained, and thus in the subsequent section we address the literature on organizational socialization. This literature informs us about such topics as the stages new employees go through as they enter and learn about the organization, the types of cultural understanding acquired by new employees as they go through those stages, and the tactics used by organizations to support the socialization process. It could be argued that the importance of how culture emerges and is maintained is tied to its relationship with organizational effectiveness, which is the topic we explore next in Chapter Five. The existence of a direct link between culture and effectiveness is controversial, with critics specifically commenting on how quantitative research attempting to address this relationship oversimplifies the culture construct and ignores numerous possible boundary conditions. Another criticism is that such research ignores possible subcultures, which we discuss along with the closely related concept of culture strength. Building on the previous sections, Chapter Five culminates with a discussion of culture change. Central to this discussion is the idea that culture is both quite stable and yet constantly changing, as well as the question of the extent to which management's attempts to change organizational culture will yield their hoped-for results.

In the next section of the book, Chapters Six and Seven, we attempt to bring together the fields of organizational climate and culture in a way that benefits both research and practice in both fields. Chapter Six integrates the preceding chapters in a discussion of the similarities and differences between the fields of climate and culture and how the two can learn from each other moving forward. In addition, we discuss three recent frameworks that describe ways that climate and culture can be integrated with each other, and we provide some specific ways that the two constructs can be studied in the future in a more integrative manner. This chapter ends with a discussion of the ways by which both organizational climate and culture can provide a competitive advantage to organizations, and how organizations may approach organizational change through an integrated climate and culture lens. Although the previous chapters include an emphasis on both research and practice in line with our value for the scientist-practitioner model, the Chapter Seven is more purely practice-focused. For practitioners especially, the topics of climate and culture are of interest because they have learned that (a) executives think easily in organizational culture terms to explain what happens in their companies, and (b) the choices among tactics for approaching cultural inquiry are difficult. This chapter provides an in-depth discussion surrounding the issue of assessment including a discussion of both qualitative and quantitative procedures for such inquiry to serve as a foundation for future efforts to improve effectiveness and implement change.

Chapter Eight is, for the most part, a summary of the key points made throughout the rest of the book. Our goal was to provide a useful reference for readers wanting to quickly see the "big picture" of the content of the book. In addition, we use this final chapter to review what we see as the primary implications for practitioners along with the major directions for future research in each area separately and in the integration of the two.

SUMMARY

We collectively have almost 100 years of experience with research and thinking on, and practical applications of, organizational climate and culture. This book documents our understanding of these topics with the hope that both researchers and practitioners would simultaneously grasp the complexity of the issues involved and the potential for using that very complexity for helping organizations become more competitive. Our hope is that by discussing in depth the issues scholars and practitioners confront when dealing with climate and culture, we both humanize organizations and make them more competitive. That is, we see the people who work in organizations as the embodiment of those organizations—they make organizations real. As such, people play a critical role in helping scholars understand why organizations are the way they are and in giving practitioners the insights they need to help organizations be increasingly competitive in a dynamic and changing world.

NOTE

1. To be clear, we are not saying that there is not general interest in the concept of organizational culture. The concept continues to have much influence in theoretical work and general discussion about how workers experience their organizations. Perhaps the issue was best summarized by Weber and Dacin (2011), who observed that researchers have shifted to studying culture more as "a broad theoretical and methodological lens rather than a distinct object of study" (p. 287).

CHAPTER
2
History of Organizational Climate Theory and Research

The study of organizational climate did not emerge out of nowhere; it emerged from the concern in psychology for understanding situational influences on behavior. The early history of psychology addressed individual behavior and the seeking of generalizations that characterized individuals. Researchers were concerned with basic sensory processes such as vision and hearing and the experiences associated with them (color, timbre) as well as basic human learning and motivational processes. Beginning in the late 1930s with work by Skinner in particular (Skinner, 1938), the effects of situations on behavior became a focus of study. Thus, in laboratory experiments on animals (rats and pigeons) and humans (especially children), Skinner and his colleagues at Harvard demonstrated that behavior was controlled by situational forces, especially reinforcement schedules.

In the world of industrial psychology (now called industrial/organizational psychology), however, the individual and his or her behavior remained the clear focus of psychological work in business and industry. Indeed, from the earliest days of industrial psychology the focus was not only on individuals (rather than situations), but also on individual differences, especially as those differences were reflected in differences in performance at work (Ghiselli, 1939). Industrial psychology was the application of the study of individual differences, especially individual differences in ability, and the ways those differences were important for behavior at work and the effectiveness of organizations. That is, the

11

supposition was that if organizations had more able workers they would definitely be the most effective organizations, so what was critical for effectiveness was the selection of more able workers.

A departure from the individual differences model of organizations emerged from what have come to be called the Hawthorne studies (Mayo, 1933; Roethlisberger, 1941; Roethlisberger & Dickson, 1939). These studies, which were also conducted by people at Harvard but in sociology, demonstrated the large influence the work situation/context had on employees and their performance. Thus in a series of in-depth case studies, it was revealed, for example, that the social situation in which workers did their jobs affected not only how they felt at work, but also their overall productivity. In fact, the studies showed that some social situations at work (where coworkers threaten newcomers for being too productive) can have considerable inhibitory effects on employee productivity. In other words, situations could have both positive and negative effects on worker productivity.

What was missing from this work at the Hawthorne plant was a convenient label to capture the effects so elegantly addressed using observations of workers. Just before and just after World War II, as we will see, there began to emerge studies of these situational influences on behavior that were rigorously applied to research on work behavior. While not all that followed used the term climate as a label to summarize these effects, enough did so that the term became ubiquitous by the mid-1960s as a convenient rubric for identifying research on the effects of situations on workers.

The rest of this chapter on the early history of organizational climate theory and research has two major sections. Within each major section, we proceed essentially chronologically as this is generally the way theory and research on climate developed. The first section of the chapter comprises the years prior to the late 1960s as researchers began to refer to the concept of climate and to discuss the role of the environment more generally in understanding behavior at work. In the second section of the chapter, the late 1960s through the 1970s, the pace of research—as well as critiques of such work—expanded greatly. We highlight key examples of climate research and the resolutions to concerns about the way climate was conceptualized and studied as a segue to the following chapter on contemporary climate research.

FROM 1939 TO THE MID-1960S: THE EARLY YEARS OF CLIMATE RESEARCH

This era was an exciting time for the study of organizational climate because there were few guidelines for how to proceed either conceptually or empirically. Researchers went hither and yon pursing the construct from numerous perspectives and in numerous ways. The goal of this section of the chapter is to provide readers with a flavor of the dynamism that existed and in fact provided for future theory and research on the construct. In this section then, we trace the roots of climate research, reviewing key contributors to the early development of the field by briefly describing their perspectives and contributions. We particularly highlight points that are most closely related to the contemporary development of the climate construct and how the authors differentiated between climate and culture, as this will form the foundation for our discussions in later chapters integrating the two constructs.

Lewin, Lippitt, and White (1939) and "Social Climates"

Lewin, Lippitt, and White (1939) introduced the term "climate" to the world of social psychology research. Their research was accomplished at a time when concerns existed globally for the effect of leadership on how people behaved. Lewin had left Germany in the early 1930s because he was greatly concerned about the effects he had observed there of Hitler's leadership style. Of particular interest to him was the degree to which the autocratic leadership style he had observed resulted in changes in the ways people behaved toward others.

In this context, he and his colleagues focused their research on the role of three different leadership styles for the functioning and performance of groups: democratic, autocratic, and laissez-faire. They varied the leadership styles within four groups of 10-year-old boys, with each group of five boys participating in a number of activities including soap carving and model airplane construction. Lewin and colleagues focused specifically on the levels of aggression within each club and how the atmosphere in the group that emerged affected the aggressive behaviors that were observed. Interestingly, although the title of their paper refers to "social climates" (their quotes), they actually use the term "climate" sparingly. Instead, they refer to the "social atmosphere" or just "atmosphere" of the group, using those terms synonymously with climate. In any case, the research revealed that the boys were more aggressive toward each other under the autocratic condition, cooperated more under the democratic condition, and were less involved in the activities under laissez-faire leadership. The boys were equally productive in the democratic and autocratic conditions but there was less chatter, less cooperation, and less smiling in the latter condition.

There are several features of this early work on climate worthy of note. First, Lewin and colleagues were interested in a specific type of climate: the social climate, as characterized by the interactions of the boys with each other. Second, the observations they made of the boys focused on the level of cooperation and aggression and smiling and chatter in the groups as a whole rather than on the individual differences among group members; the effect of interest was on the group as a whole, not individual differences, in response to the climate. Finally, they viewed the behavior of the leader as the proximal antecedent of the group's climate. In fact, their conceptual model seemed to be that specific leadership styles created specific types of climates, which subsequently resulted in specific (and generally universal) social behavioral responses from the group. These three issues—the specific nature of the climate of interest, the group nature of climate, and the influence of the leader on climate—continue to be of interest to modern climate researchers as we will see (e.g., Schneider, Ehrhart, Mayer, Saltz, & Niles-Jolly, 2005).

Fleishman (1953) and Leadership Climates

Perhaps because the research presented by Lewin and colleagues was done with groups of boys and perhaps because it was published outside of the industrial psychology world, the issue of climate lay fallow in the research literature until resurrected by Fleishman (1953) in his research as part of the Ohio State Leadership projects (e.g., Stogdill, 1968). Fleishman was the developer of the leadership behavior description questionnaire (LBDQ), empirically documenting and distinguishing between the two broad categories of leadership behavior called consideration and initiating structure.

As part of the Ohio State leadership studies, efforts were made to train leaders to be more considerate to the needs and feelings of employees rather than just giving orders (as in initiating structure). In Fleishman's 1953 article, the focus was on the transfer of the training received by trainees (foremen) at the training site to the "home" work environments. Leadership climate was defined on the first page of the article in terms of the extent to which a returning foreman's boss created conditions (climate) for the transfer of training to occur. As described by Salas, Priest, Stagl, Sims, and Burke (2007), Fleishman reported that his focus on climate was directly influenced by the work of Lewin and colleagues (1939). Fleishman's research revealed that when the boss recognized and supported the more human relations orientation (consideration) taught in training, then the training was implemented by the returning foreman. On the other hand, when the bosses themselves were less considerate and more structure-oriented, then the returning foremen were seen as behaving similarly as before the training. In short, the climate created by the boss was what the trainees followed rather than what they had been taught—and had demonstrated—in training.

There are a few highlights of this research important to note. First, Fleishman, like Lewin and colleagues, focused on a particular type of climate: in this case, leadership climate. While Fleishman also wrote about the larger context in which the leader and his boss worked—calling the larger context the culture of the setting—the focus of the work was on the climate created by the leader for the returning trainee. As a sidebar, it is interesting to note that whenever Fleishman referred to "climate," the term was in quotes, whereas the term culture was not, perhaps signifying the more common usage of the term culture at the time and the infancy of the climate construct.

Second, even though the definition of leadership climate focused on the boss's leadership behavior, a key aspect of the measurement of the leadership climate construct was that it included both the foreman's perception of what his boss expected as well as the boss's report of his expectations. Thus, leadership climate was not defined by behaviors alone, but expectations as well. How those expectations were communicated was not specified. Finally, Fleishman emphasized the role of climate in organizational effectiveness. Specifically, he noted that the leadership climate created at each level of the organization is important for the effectiveness of training to transfer back to the workplace, which ultimately is intended to increase organizational effectiveness.

Argyris (1957, 1958)

Argyris's writings were largely concerned with the "formal organization" as created by management and its implications for worker well-being. In the 1957 book, the emphasis was on the lack of alignment between the formal organization and workers' needs, resulting in negative employee adaptive behaviors such as aggression and apathy. He described the formal organization largely in terms of such generic attributes as the chain of command and specialization of production that are intended to control employees' actions. This control, he noted, is most fundamentally represented in the directive leadership behaviors on the part of management. Argyris's challenge was to suggest how management might become less directive in ways that would remove the incongruency he saw between the directive and stifling ways formal organizations functioned and the adult needs of workers. In short, Argyris argued that the typical organization infantilized workers by directing all of their behavior when, as adults, workers required some autonomy and flexibility to feel connected with their work and the workplace. For Argyris (1957) the key issue, then, was the degree to which the modern corporation facilitated or inhibited the adult personality and his conclusion was that for the most part it inhibited it.

In his 1957 book, Argyris rarely used the term climate. The use of the term was limited to his description of how employees are likely to resist employee-centered leadership because of the existing "human relations climate." Nevertheless, he did discuss similar ideas without using the term climate, particularly when he described the role of the "competent executive." By emphasizing how executives should clearly communicate to employees the "objectives, policies, and practices" of management and then should ensure that the performance evaluation system is aligned with those policies and practices, Argyris laid the foundation for future discussions of the importance of alignment for creating strategic climates and the leader's role in that process (e.g., Schneider, 1975b; Schneider et al., 2005). We will return to those issues in more depth in the next chapter.

In contrast to the 1957 book, Argyris's 1958 paper describing the development of a bank's climate and "informal culture" was replete with references to climate. Unlike later climate and culture research, for Argyris climate was a much broader construct than culture. Climate was described as the totality of the complexity of organizational life, encompassing the formal organization, its interaction with individuals, and the resulting informal organizational culture. He also described climate as the "homeostatic state" of the organization "representing many different levels of analysis" (p. 516), consistent with his broad view of the climate construct. The concept of culture, on the other hand, was used more narrowly to describe the informal behavioral norms that developed as result of employees' (and separately, the bank's officers') dissatisfaction with the formal structure.

Argyris made three observations about organizations and their climate that are worthy of specific note. First, the climate of an organization will tend to be stable as long as it satisfies the needs of the individuals in the organization. Second, he described how management could change the climate by hiring different types of employees because as long as the same "right-type" employees were hired, the climate (and culture) would remain the same. In essence, Argyris (1958) argued that climates emerge in organizations as a result of the kinds of people hired by them who then work together and over time create the climate in which they work. Many years later Schneider (1987) proposed an expanded view of this idea in what has come to be called the Attraction–Selection–Attrition (ASA) cycle.

Finally, and importantly, Argyris (1958) foreshadowed much of the later work on levels of analysis by describing how the organization is a "discrete level of analysis, resulting from the interaction of the (traditional) individual, formal, informal, and cultural levels of analyses" (p. 516) and opposing the idea that the "organization can eventually be reduced to the individual level of analysis" (p. 517). We will explore this issue in considerable detail later, but emphasize for now that Argyris identified this issue back in 1958, and yet it took almost a quarter century before the implications of what he said became clear and were studied in depth.

Leavitt (1958)

Leavitt was a student of McGregor's (who will be discussed shortly), and the thinking displayed in his book *Managerial Psychology* was clearly influenced by his mentor (who in turn was influenced by his mentor, Kurt Lewin). Although organizational climate was not a primary explicit focus in his book (it is mentioned in the next-to-last chapter), the book was in fact about the "tenor" created by management for employees. Leavitt made quite similar arguments to those of Argyris (1957), proposing that the typical organizational hierarchical structure and authority system pushes its members to be more defensive, short-term, and self-focused in their behavior, when what is needed for organizational effectiveness are the opposites of these: open, long-term, and organizationally focused. One of four strategies Leavitt mentioned to counteract these unproductive tendencies is to "change the 'climate' of the organization" (p. 277), although the section on that strategy was entitled "Changing the Organizational Atmosphere" and he used the term atmosphere more than climate. His main point was that if employees are going to contribute their energies and motivation to organizational effectiveness, management needs to make employees feel more secure and in control at work, and to do so, they need to create the right "atmospheric conditions." These conditions are created by being more open with employees, providing them a chance to learn, allowing them to participate in decision-making, and giving them room to express their feelings. Leavitt mentioned that more important than specific policies enacted by management for creating "an atmosphere of security and independence" (p. 288) is management's general attitude toward people as being intelligent, motivated, and able.

Leavitt's book was a major milestone in publishing because the book was an interpretation of psychological principles applied to the workplace written more for managers than for academics. Thus, while Argyris's (1957) book received considerable attention in the world of practice, it was fundamentally an academic treatise with numerous citations and footnotes. Leavitt's book was not so encumbered, and it was written in a style that made it easily available to practicing managers. What was important is that his book and Argyris's book served, along with McGregor's writings (to follow next), to introduce the psychology of the workplace to many managers and academics who previously had focused almost exclusively on hiring the right people (Viteles, 1932) and had ignored the climate, culture, character, and atmosphere they were creating that the researchers felt inhibited rather than facilitated the effectiveness of workers.

McGregor (1960)

McGregor was a practicing executive prior to his tenure at MIT where he produced his book, *The Human Side of Enterprise*. His book, like Argyris's (1957), focused on the ways the modern organization stifled rather than facilitated the adult intelligence and motivation of workers. He argued that the theory or philosophy managers hold about worker motivation determines their behavior toward workers, so it is critical for managers to understand what their theory about worker motivation actually is to better understand how and why they are likely to behave as they do.

The focus of McGregor's book was on two such theories or philosophies of management: Theory X and Theory Y. These theories described management's fundamental assumptions about human nature that, in turn, drive how they treat workers and subsequently how workers respond. A Theory X philosophy assumes that workers dislike work, wish to avoid responsibility at work, and have little creativity and ambition vis-à-vis working. As a result, they need to be controlled and coerced into putting effort toward the achievement of organizational goals. In contrast, Theory Y presumes that workers desire to put forth effort and be committed toward the goals for which they are rewarded, and that fundamentally they seek responsibility and to exercise their creativity. Following a Theory Y philosophy, management focuses on creating the proper conditions for workers to achieve both their own goals and the goals of the organization.

As part of his discussion, McGregor dedicated a chapter to the "managerial climate" or the climate of the supervisor-subordinate relationship. He noted that the nature of this relationship is not directly tied to a particular set of policies and procedures, but more important are the "evidences of how they are administered." He then stated the following: "The day-by-day behavior of the immediate superior and of other significant people in the managerial organization communicates something about their assumptions concerning management which is of fundamental significance" (p. 133). In other words, employees go beyond a narrow focus on the tangible practices of management and attribute to those practices what management truly believes about the employees with whom they work. Those attributions employees make about what management believes constitutes the substance of climate.

In one of McGregor's first mentions of the term climate, he stated that "many subtle behavioral manifestations of managerial attitude create what is often referred to as the psychological 'climate' of the relationship" (p. 134). Note that even though McGregor described it as a *psychological* climate, it was "of the relationship," meaning that it was shared by the individuals in that relationship. This distinction was emphasized as he explicitly described that the managerial climate is not determined by the manager alone, but is co-determined by the subordinate as well. In subsequent chapters, McGregor discussed the "climate of line-staff relationships," implying that the climate concept he described as being shared between two individuals could be expanded across larger groups. He later even described the "broader context of the climate created by company policy and practice, organization structure, and general philosophy" (p. 199) within which the more local supervisor-subordinate climates are found. This broader view aligns quite closely with Argyris's (1958) observations about levels of analysis and with modern approaches to organizational climate described later in this book. We begin to see in McGregor's writings the idea that climates nest within climates at different levels of analysis, an idea we will pursue in some detail later.

Interestingly, in the last chapter of his book when discussing distinctions between effective and ineffective groups, he described the "atmosphere" of the group that can be "sensed in a few minutes of observation"

(p. 232). This is interesting because it indicates that climate exists in the behaviors of people, and it is the nature of the behavior that occurs that forms the basis for perceptions of climate. One final point on McGregor is that at the end of the last chapter, he suggested that the managerial climate had important implications in two major areas: subordinate expectations for goal accomplishment and subordinate need satisfaction. Thus, McGregor viewed the relationships established between manager and subordinate as creating a climate for both performance and satisfaction; we will speak later to the issues of creating climates that are useful for more than one important outcome.

Likert (1961)

As may be coming through to readers, the decade surrounding 1960 was a magical time for what has come to be called industrial/organizational psychology and organizational behavior. This period formed the foundation for the study of organizational climate but perhaps more importantly the broad study of leadership, motivation, and group dynamics. Rich conceptualizations emerged about what motivated people, how managers' assumptions about what motivated people might have been in error, and how moving from an authority systems-based vantage point on the management of the modern organization to a more democratic view could produce not only improved organizational effectiveness, but also need satisfaction for employees.

Likert (1961) was at the University of Michigan when he presented evidence for a new theory of management at one and the same time consistent with the classical theories of management of the time, but applied in ways that moved away from control through authority and more toward meeting worker needs. We mention the University of Michigan because at the time Likert began his writings it was perhaps the preeminent home for the kinds of thinking and research that were at the foundation of these new fields. In addition to Likert and his work on organizational design, Katz and Kahn (1966; reviewed later) were there as were Cartwright and Zander (1960), arguably the fathers of the modern study of teams at work.

For Likert, leadership was the critical factor in determining employee motivation and organizational effectiveness. By comparing lower-level managers that led highly effective work groups to those who led less effective ones, Likert sought to identify the leadership practices that resulted in increased effectiveness. Similar to Argyris (1957) and McGregor (1960), Likert concluded that managers needed to move beyond controlling employees through the exercise of authority. For highly effective leaders, he found the following: "Reliance is not placed solely or fundamentally on the economic motive of buying a man's time and using control and authority as the organizing and coordinating principle of the organization. On the contrary . . . The full strength of all economic, ego, and other motives is generated and put to use." (pp. 98–100). Building on these findings, he introduced four systems by which organizations might function on a continuum from completely autocratic to completely participative, which he later (Likert, 1967) labeled as follows: System 1 (Exploitative Autocratic), System 2 (Benevolent Authoritative), System 3 (Consultative), and System 4 (Participative Group).

Although we could not find any direct reference in Likert's writing to climate or culture, he discussed many similar ideas. For instance, Likert stated, "The values of the group, the stability of these values, the group atmosphere, and the nature of the conformity demanded by the group determine whether a group is likely to have a positive or negative impact upon the growth and behavior of its members" (1961, p. 162). The values referenced here appear to align with later conceptualizations of the concept of culture. As for the atmosphere, Likert noted that it needed to be "warm, supportive, and full of understanding" (p. 164). Where does such an "atmosphere" originate? Likert was quite explicit that he viewed its source as the leader, who "uses group methods of supervision and which develops in the entire group a sense of responsibility for getting the total job done" (pp. 34–35). Similarly, he described how "the superior of each work group exerts a major influence in establishing the tone and atmosphere of that work group by his leadership principles and practices" (p. 167). It is important to note that he did not view such an atmosphere alone to lead to group effectiveness, but instead he proposed that the atmosphere provides the context in which "all the interaction, problem-solving, decision-making activities of the group occur" (p. 166). So although the leader was viewed as an important source of support, he was also "an important source of enthusiasm for the significance of the mission and goals of the group" (pp. 171–172). Researchers today might describe this as the need for both a generally positive social climate and a specific strategic climate for goal accomplishment within the work group. A final note on Likert was his emphasis on measurement. He specifically described how this "atmosphere" of groups could and should be measured regularly, setting the stage for later quantitative measurement of the climate construct.

Gilmer (1961, 1966) and Forehand and Gilmer (1964)

The first industrial psychology textbook references to climate appeared in the first edition of Gilmer's *Industrial Psychology* (1961). In that book, Gilmer included two sections specifically focused on climate. The first was in the chapter on "The Structures of Organizations," with a section entitled "The Psychological Climate in Industry." Gilmer equated climate with an organization's "personality or character," making the following observation about research in the area up to that point: "The idea that the character of an organization is a subject for study is a rather new concept in spite of the fact that the literature includes such terms as 'quality of managers,' 'environmental factors,' and 'leadership climate'" (p. 49). Throughout this section of his book, Gilmer used the term climate in ways that seem to capture elements of contemporary perspectives on both climate and culture. For instance, similar to Lewin and colleagues' (1939) conceptualization of climate, he contrasted the "democratic or permissive climate" with an "autocratic climate." At the same time, he included such issues as the way managers dress and the cars they drive, which now would both be considered artifacts of culture. For Gilmer, the top executive played a major role in the development of the climate/culture, as he described the company's character as "an extended shadow of the personality of its top executive" (p. 50). He also noted that one of the major ways that climate/culture can change is if the behavior of the top executive changes. At the same time, Gilmer was aware of the differential impact of leaders according to their level, as he pointed out that at a local level, the foreman may have more of an impact than the executive. Finally, he discussed the concept of fit, referencing Mayo (1945) for the idea that fit with the organization and its climate/culture may be a better predictor of success than technical skills. Interestingly, he closed this section with a subsection entitled "Wives of Men in Industry," in which he argued for the importance of the wives of the male employees to fit with the organization's climate as well!

The other section on climate in Gilmer's book was entitled "The Psychological Climate for Work," in the chapter on "Attitudes, Job Satisfactions, and Industrial Morale." Although he did not use the term climate very much in this section—he focused mostly on describing the informal social structures in organizations—he did make the following observation about climate at the beginning of the section: "The social aspects of the job-work groups, leadership, and organization of the company all add up to a psychological climate for the person to work in" (p. 205). This perspective is similar to the Gestalt perspective emphasized by Lewin and colleagues and later climate researchers (e.g., Schneider, 1975b), although with a particular emphasis on the social aspect of work. There is one other section in which Gilmer, although he did not use the term climate, referred to ideas that came to be labeled as climate in later writings. In his chapter on "Business Operating Procedures," Gilmer described how procedures and "innocuous-looking rules" have implications for the environment that forms in organizations, with some intended effects but many unintended ones. His discussion foreshadowed later distinctions made in the literature between the policies and procedures created by management and the climate those policies and procedures produce among employees. Finally, Gilmer briefly made reference to a level of analysis issue with regard to the possibility of the formation of subclimates in organizations: "Different parts of the organization see different environments, and the environments they see depend on the rules for recording and processing information" (p. 86). Thus because the policies and procedures vary across different units of the organization, the environments or climates that form across those units are also likely to vary.

Subsequent to his 1961 book, Gilmer extended his thinking on climate in a 1964 *Psychological Bulletin* article with Forehand on "environmental variation" in organizational research, as well as in the second edition of his *Industrial Psychology* book in 1966 in which he dedicated a full chapter to the topic of climate. Forehand and Gilmer (1964) observed that the climate term seemed to mean "different things to different writers," a problem that to some degree continues to persist to this day, and thus they wanted to focus on those features "amenable to specification, measurement, and incorporation into empirical research" (p. 362). They provided the following definition of climate: "the set of characteristics that describe an organization and that (a) distinguish the organization from other organizations, (b) are relatively enduring over time, and (c) influence the behavior of people in the organization" (p. 362). Gilmer (1966) also described climate as the "psychological structure" of an organization, in contrast to the physical structure. Unfortunately, such a broad view of climate captures many constructs, and Gilmer gave clear indication that he equated the concepts of culture and climate (along with company personality). He also used the terms psychological climate and organizational climate interchangeably—a clear distinction between the two did not appear until several years later (James & Jones, 1974).

Consistent with this broad view of climate, both sources (Forehand & Gilmer, 1964; Gilmer, 1966) identified a range of variables as descriptive of the dimensions of climate, including size and shape, leadership patterns, systems complexity, organizational structure, communication networks, goal directions, and decision-making procedures. Of particular note, Forehand and Gilmer (1964) emphasized that various attributes of climate can have motivating effects on workers through their direct or indirect specification of what is rewarded or punished in the organization. Forehand and Gilmer (1964) and Gilmer (1966) also discussed some methodological issues, such as the different ways climate can be measured (including case studies or other forms of in-depth description, surveys measuring worker perceptions, objective indices, and experimental manipulations in a lab setting) and how climate can have both direct effects (similar effects on all members of a unit) and interactive effects (differential effects across individuals). Although both sources generally tended to focus on climate as a characterization of an entire organization (or organizational subunit), they also pointed out that individual perceptions of climate can vary based on experience, skill, attitudes, or personality. Forehand and Gilmer (1964) closed their article with four issues that needed to be resolved to establish the usefulness of the climate construct: (1) what level of analysis is appropriate for the study of climate and the importance of ensuring comparability of level across the various organizations studied, (2) the need for homogeneity of perceptions of climate within the organizational unit being studied for there to be a climate there, (3) the relative permanence of climate beyond the effects of a particular leader, and (4) how to combine different dimensions of climate to best describe an organization (advocating particularly for approaches emphasizing the overall pattern or configuration of dimensions). Finally, although in a chapter other than the one on climate, Gilmer also foreshadowed the work on focused or strategic climates, and specifically safety climate, when he mentioned research searching for a "climatic pattern" that may be associated with low-accident environments.

The article by Forehand and Gilmer (1964) and Gilmer's (1961, 1966) textbooks were very important because they introduced in considerable detail the notion that the context was important for understanding the behavior of people at work. As we will see, it is right around the time of the second book when research on climate as we know it today began in earnest. However, the idea that context has a role to play in human behavior at work received other significant input from Schein (1965) and Katz and Kahn (1966), which we explore next.

Schein (1965)

Schein's book was one of several at the time to focus on the "new" field of organizational psychology. This field could be distinguished from industrial psychology, which dealt with "the *assessment and selection of individual workers* and ignored those questions which involve the organization as a whole" (Schein, 1965, p. 2; italics in original). In Schein's view, it was necessary to view the organization from a systems perspective; individual behavior could only be fully understood when viewed in its context of a "complex social system." This emphasis on "the behavior of individuals as with the behavior of groups, subsystems, and even the total organization in response to internal and external stimuli" (pp. 3–4) distinguished Schein's writings from his contemporaries in industrial psychology but aligned with the writings of Argyris, McGregor, and Likert, who we may consider founders of the contextual movement. Schein's book was important for many reasons. First, it was one of the first books with the title *Organizational Psychology* (Bass's book with the same title also came out in 1965). Second, it presented organizational psychology as an addition to, not a substitute for, the focus in industrial psychology on individual differences and personnel selection. Third, Schein summarized the historical perspectives that at the time had permeated ways to conceptualize employee motivation in the workplace. Thus, he showed that the scientific management notion of motivation as directed by money was no longer viable (as had Argyris and McGregor), that man had more than social needs that had to be met through and in the work environment, and that human motivation included the desire to be competent and creative at work.

Given this focus on the effects of the organization as a whole on work motivation, it is not surprising that Schein mentioned concepts related to climate and culture (e.g., environment, image, and setting) throughout his book, although he used the actual terms climate and culture very little. The most direct mention of climate and culture was when describing Fleishman's (1953) research on leadership training. Schein described how "the effects of training were intimately related to the culture, or climate, of the departments from which the men came. These climates had as much of an effect on the trainee as did the training" (p. 38). Later in that same chapter, when discussing human relations training, he described how a climate or setting (he used both terms interchangeably) in which members feel comfortable being open about their feelings can stimulate more open expressions from the members of the group. The only other direct mention of climate was when discussing the importance of management's assumptions about people (along the lines of McGregor, 1960). Schein stated, "As assumptions become increasingly realistic, management practices will begin to build the kind of climate which is needed for reliable and valid communication, creative effort, flexibility, and commitment" (pp. 104–105).

It is clear that the concepts of climate and culture as applied to organizations were not well developed at this point, and perhaps not distinguishable. What these few mentions by Schein (1965) do tell us is that there was something in the environment or context of the workplace that had an important role in determining worker attitudes and behavior. Furthermore, this climate was strongly affected by the leadership of the organization that emerged out of the assumptions leaders made about what motivates workers. Finally, there is an implication that there may be different types of climates in organizations. For example, one kind of climate might directly affect the transfer of leadership training back to the job, another might be related to the level of open expression by group members, and yet a third kind of climate had broader implications for workers' more generic motivation, adaptability, and attitudes.

Although Schein explicitly mentioned the concepts of climate and culture relatively sparingly, he discussed in many other places similar concepts that would be labeled as climate or culture by researchers today. In terms of culture, Schein discussed how leaders must adapt to a group's norms, history, and tradition to be effective. He also described how in rapidly changing environments, socialization practices (or what he referred to as "systematic indoctrination") needed to be viewed as interdependent with other organizational functions like job design and selection. Finally, he described how organizational leaders must define the values and norms that become core to the organization's basic identity.

With regard to climate, when discussing the balance between primary task completion and innovation, Schein specifically described how management's policies and procedures create climate: ". . . many of the procedures which organizations develop to maximize their day-to-day effectiveness lead to a psychological climate in which innovation and creativity may actually be punished" (p. 16). Such thoughts foreshadow later discussions of possible conflicts between, for example, strategic climates for innovation and cost-cutting in organizations. Schein also discussed how an organization is "unaware of the kind of image its practices are creating in the minds of its members" that are "determiners of how individual employees will relate themselves to the organization" (p. 33). The idea of image seems to align closely with that of climate. Furthermore, even though Schein was focusing on the image formed by individual employees and its consequences for individual behavior, there was also the implication that similar, shared images would be formed across employees.

On a final note, Schein placed a heavy emphasis on the need for organizations to focus on the "total, organizational performance rather than individual subgroup performance" (p. 105). It is not that the individual parts do not matter, but it is more important how they come together in an integrative way to understand organizational effectiveness from a human organization vantage point. This idea was foundational for the literatures on both organizational climate and organizational culture.

Katz and Kahn (1966)

Katz and Kahn's influential text focused on organizations as social systems, applying open-systems theory to the study of human work organizations. Although they discussed a number of issues with regard to organizational structure, roles, communication, decision-making, and leadership, there was little direct mention in their book of climate and culture, and little additional discussion of topics that would fall under the domain of the constructs of climate or culture by today's standards. However, they did include a short subsection entitled "Organizational Culture and Climate" within a broader section on "Subsidiary Concepts" that characterized the "overall functioning and structure of social organizations" (p. 63). Their use of the terms climate and culture is informative. There is no indication that they distinguished between the two concepts. The first mention is of "culture or climate" in the first sentence of the section, followed by "climate or culture" in the second sentence. Although they use the terms individually throughout the rest of the section, they appear to be used interchangeably. What is perhaps most interesting is the other terms used in that section. That is, the concepts that Katz and Kahn considered as either equivalent to climate and culture or falling within their domain include norms, values, roles, subculture, collective feelings and beliefs, atmosphere, history, taboos, folkways, mores, types of people, work processes, physical layout, modes of communication, and exercise of authority.

Although many of these terms have come to be more associated with culture than climate, it is clear that elements of both were included in describing the social situation of organizations. And in keeping with the more-culture-than-climate idea, they proposed these elements are "passed along to new group members" (p. 66), foretelling an emphasis on socialization common in the later culture literature. As a final note on this section, Katz and Kahn mentioned that "The climate or culture of the system reflects both the norms and values of the formal system and their reinterpretations in the informal system" (pp. 65–66). This idea that the culture or climate is not something that exists within the formal structure of the organization but in its perception and interpretation by organizational members is common to many current conceptualizations of both climate and culture. In the same way, later in their book Katz and Kahn described how the informal structures in organizations are frequently in contradiction to the goal of the formal structure, and how management's goal is to direct the enthusiasm and motivation of these informal groupings toward the accomplishment of the collective goals. This point sounds similar to later discussions in the culture literature of the need to understand the deeper level of culture to have successful organizational change, and in the climate literature of the friction between the actual policies and procedures of management and the climate that evolves based on the meaning employees associate with them.

Katz and Kahn's book had a dramatic effect on work in organizational psychology for several reasons. First, they, like Likert, were at the University of Michigan and along with others (Seashore, Georgopoulos, French, Lawler) were creating a new way to study organizations from a more social psychological vantage point in contrast to the earlier focus in industrial psychology on individual differences. Second, their use of an open systems framework in which organizations are seen as production throughput systems in intimate contact with the environments in which they operate was understandable to managers and the way they think. That is, managers must be in continuous sensing mode to understand their marketplace from both an input and an output vantage point, and Katz and Kahn showed them how intimately related people are to the input–throughput–output cycle. Their second edition of *The Social Psychology of Organizations* (1978) further solidified their status as founders of the field of organizational psychology and as important commentators on this thing called climate/culture.

Additional Work on Climate through the Mid-1960s

The people whose writings we chose for explicit review were not the only ones working on organizational climate and related concepts in this time. Early on, Barnard (1938) noted that a group is defined and understood through the system of interactions. Most importantly for present purposes, he noted how it is through the interaction of individuals that "uniform states of mind" come to exist, what today we would describe as shared perceptions of what it is and how it is that work is best accomplished. Not incidentally, Barnard's thinking in this regard was clearly influenced by the works of Mayo, Roethlisberger, and Dickson. Buchele (1955), using the concept of company character, was one of the first to write about the importance of the general nature of the context created in the workplace for employees. Buchele identified a company's character as the explanation for why similar programs implemented in different companies will have starkly differing levels of success. He aligned his concept of character with other concepts such as Lewin and colleagues' (1939) three types of leadership and Fleishman's (1953) leadership climate, among others. Included within a company's character were its supportive programs and structures, decision-making and initiative expectations, superior-subordinate relationships, managers' personalities and interests, company product and mission, relative success in terms of profitability and growth, the nature of the work and work groups, and the attributes of the surrounding community in which the company functioned. Buchele's concept of character appears to be a blend of climate and culture issues, although perhaps more similar to culture given the breadth of issues he included. Buchele (1955) is not often cited in reviews of the climate and culture literature most probably because his framework was so broad as to include virtually everything—from manager personality to the socioeconomics of the context in which organizations operated. In this way, Buchele's concept of character was very similar to early measures of climate—with their focus on almost everything that might influence people in a situation.

There were several other indicators in addition to the sources described earlier in this chapter that there was a growing interest in climate during this time. For instance, in one of Fiedler's (1962) early studies on LPC (Least Preferred Coworker), he included "group climate" as a variable, although the measure itself was labeled as "group atmosphere." The items he developed for this measure captured a general perception of whether members had a positive or negative view of the group (pleasant versus unpleasant, relaxed versus stressed, etc.). Forehand (1963) measured "perceived organizational climate" in his study of the innovative behavior of managers. Using a leadership practices scale that was adjusted to rate the typical practices in the organization, he examined bureaucratic versus democratic climate perceptions as a moderator of the relationship between innovative behavior and general effectiveness. This study was at the individual level, and thus Forehand's use of the label "perceived" climate was not only appropriate, but also indicates an awareness that simply labeling it as "organizational climate" would imply aggregate perceptions.

Another example of the growing recognition of the salience of climate comes from the Bradford, Gibb, and Benne's (1964a) edited book on T-Groups. The theme across the various chapters of this book was the importance of the climate formed in T-Groups in order for them to be successful. For instance, Bradford, Gibb, and Benne (1964b) described how a "climate supporting change" is created in learning laboratories; Benne, Bradford, and Lippitt (1964) included a "climate of permissiveness and inquiry" as part of the optimal conditions for training and learning; Bradford (1964) discussed how the T-Group trainer must "develop a group climate in which learning can take place" that includes a "norm of permissiveness" encouraging open communication (p. 211); and finally in his chapter on the "climate for trust formation," Gibb (1964) contrasted the "defensive climates" found in most organizations to the "defense-reductive climates" that T-Groups encourage.

As a final example, Pelz and Andrews published a book in 1966 on their research on "productive climates" for scientists in organizations. On page 1, their overview of the book highlights the critical role of climate in organizations: "This book is based on the premise that R & D organizations provide more than facilities for their members. They also provide an *environment* which may either stimulate or inhibit the scientists' performance" (italics in original).

Early Climate Research in School Environments

Business organizations were not the only ones receiving attention in this early period with regard to organizational climate. Some of the earliest work developing quantitative measures of climate came from research in education. Examples include Christie and Merton's (1958, as cited in Tagiuri, 1968a) research describing medical schools in terms of their "climate of values," and Michael's (1961) research on high school climates as indicated by such non-perceptual variables as class size, school size, staff quality and size, curriculum, community education levels, and community cultural resources. For the most part, it is not clear how much influence a lot of the work in education had on organizational climate researchers in industrial/organizational psychology. However, there are two exceptions where the influence was clear: the work by Stern and his colleagues (1970) and the work by Halpin and Croft (1963).

Stern (1970) described an elaborate and inclusive theory—along with the research to test it—that represented he and his colleagues' efforts to better understand the college learning environment for students. The earliest work was published in 1958 (Pace & Stern, 1958) and summarized the development of the College Characteristics Index. This measure was based on Murray's need-press model of personality and was derived from an interest measure Stern had developed that was directly tied to needs described in Murray's theory. However, instead of asking about individuals and their needs, the College Characteristics Index asked about characteristics of the college environment. A number of variations of this measure for different contexts were subsequently developed, including work between 1965 and 1969 to develop the Organizational Climate Index. As opposed to measuring the environment as perceived by students, the goal of this measure was to understand the environment experienced by the administrative staff. Using 300 items and 30 subscales that aligned with the original Activities Index, Stern reported that there was general consensus for seven common factors: intellectual climate, achievement standards, group life, personal dignity, orderliness, constraint, and practicalness. This effort was notable for several reasons, including that the measure development was based on a theory of personality, that it was one of the earliest attempts to quantitatively measure the general climate of an organization, and that it was developed to be used across a wide variety of educational settings providing a basis for organizational level comparisons. Particularly relevant for this book, the measure was later extended for use in industrial settings.

Another notable effort from roughly the same time period was that of Halpin and Croft (1963). Their goal was to measure the "personality" or climate of schools as experienced by teachers. Their measure, the Organizational Climate Description Questionnaire (OCDQ), specifically focused on the "social" component of organizational climate, which they defined as the social interaction between the principal and the teachers. Their items were derived from descriptions by education graduate students and interviews with teachers, along with other measures developed to describe leaders and groups. Their analyses revealed eight sub-dimensions (disengagement, hindrance, esprit, intimacy, aloofness, production emphasis, thrust, and consideration) that loaded on three general factors (social needs, esprit, and social control). In addition, they found that schools could be grouped into six climate profiles on a continuum from open to closed (open, autonomous, controlled, familiar, paternal, and closed). In their discussion of the development of the OCDQ, they note several issues that foreshadowed concerns with which later climate researchers would grapple. For instance, they noted the overlap between what they were trying to measure as climate and what was typically referred to as morale, noting specifically their goal to focus on the description of the climate and not an affective evaluation of the climate. At the same time, their goal was not to simply attain an objective assessment of the climate; they recognized that it is the group members' perceptions that drive their behavior, not necessarily the objective reality. They were also quite aware of levels of analysis issues. They described how their original goal was to focus on the climate of school systems as a whole, but there was too much variability across individual schools within a school system, leading them to focus on schools instead. As another example, when discussing the generation of the items for use in their surveys, they noted they had to design items that would achieve two primary criteria: (1) producing between-school variability while also (2) resulting in low within-school variability. It is almost scary to see how prescient these researchers were so early in the climate research agenda since these remain, as we will see, central measurement issues in the design of contemporary climate measures for us in the business world.

But their prescience did not stop there. The importance of the proper referent for climate items is often discussed in the literature today; that is, if a climate items refers to the external world then the specific external world to which it refers must be specified or else the resultant measure is not as tangible as it might otherwise be. Thus it is notable that they got it right in that their questions asked about the experiences of "teachers at this school" and not the respondent's personal attitude or idiosyncratic experience. A final relevant issue they addressed was the role of the leader in establishing the school organization's climate. Although they acknowledged that the principal's behavior "should be construed as a necessary but not a sufficient condition which determines the school's climate" (p. 86), they go on to describe how the climate can also limit the influence the leader may have due to structural and procedural restrictions placed on him or her as well as the nature of the school populations with which he or she is forced to deal. Similar discussions continue to this day, as we will describe in the next chapter.

Climate and the Annual Review of Psychology

As we close this section of the chapter, we illustrate the rise in interest in the organizational environment and in organizational climate in particular by tracking mentions of climate in *Annual Review of Psychology* articles in the area of industrial/organizational psychology (although it was not called that yet) during this period. The *Annual Review of Psychology* began in 1950, and although there were articles on industrial psychology from the beginning, the first mention of climate did not come until the fourth volume (Harrell, 1953). Both in that volume and in the volume 2 years later (Wallace & Weitz, 1955), climate was mentioned, but only in descriptions of Fleishman's (1953) research on leadership climate in sections on leadership (Harrell, 1953) and training (Wallace & Weitz, 1955). Climate also received a passing mention by Kendall in 1956 in a discussion about the proper methods researchers should use to understand "the climate of the company and habitual approaches to accomplishing organizational objectives" (p. 225). Recognition of climate as a variable of interest received a slight uptick in 1957 by Katzell. After bemoaning that "too much effort is still being dissipated in the pursuit either of minor refinements or of unexciting objectives," he goes on to list some of the more significant variables that were "germinating in industrial psychology" (p. 263). The first item on his list was "the ingredients and consequences of directive and permissive organizational climates . . ." (p. 263).

The first significant presence of organizational climate in an *Annual Review* article came in Gilmer's (1960) review. This was prior to the publication of his *Industrial Psychology* textbook in 1961 that we described previously, but his interest in the role of the situation and in climate specifically was clear. He devoted an entire section to "Situational Variables" and begins with this quote: "A renewed interest in the study of organizational theories and situational environments within industry appears to be in the making" (p. 337). That section is filled with references to climate, and a few are particularly of interest. For instance, he described how General Electric had been carrying out "'business climate' appraisals," referencing a 1955 manual for doing so. He also described a report by "technical manpower consultants" (Deutsch & Shea, 1958) on how to create an organizational climate to foster more creativity in engineers and scientists. In line with these references, Gilmer's view seemed to be that practice was leading research on the climate, personality, or character of organizations (he used all three terms), and that this was "an important new area for study by industrial psychologists" (p. 338).

In the years that followed, climate research continued to receive mention although without necessarily being a major emphasis. For instance, in their review of "Industrial Social Psychology" in 1961, Vroom and Maier mentioned research on "company policies and leadership climate" in their section on situational factors in leadership. In his review of "Personnel Management" in 1962, Dunnette referred to how Odiorne (1960) discussed the need to create "'climates' conducive to innovation" and to Likert's theory that included the need for a "managerial climate of open communication." However, the next major recognition of climate did not come until 1964. There were two articles related to industrial/organizational psychology that year. In his review of "Personnel Management," Sells placed climate as a part of one of the three major trends in the field. He followed by including climate as one of several "environmental factors" that were "generally accepted" as "relevant to individual and organizational behavior" (p. 410). The title of the other 1964 review by Leavitt and Bass was "Organizational Psychology"; this may have been one of the first times the term was used in print. Although the article did not have a heavy emphasis on climate, it is important to mention to signify the broader shift that was occurring in psychological research on organizations at that time. The model they proposed was characterized by "systems-oriented, dynamic approaches to psychological problems in industry dealing with the interaction of organizational and human behavior" (p. 371). The only mention of climate was in the section on superior-subordinate relationships; the term "organizational climate" is put in quotes and is described as a "diffuse concept." Nevertheless, the shifting trend toward paying attention to environmental influences on individual behavior was clear.

In a similar way, Porter in 1966 did not discuss climate extensively (beyond some acknowledgement of Forehand's work in the area), but his review is important to this overview of the history of climate nonetheless. He started by highlighting the "need to wed the mature personnel-differential part of the field to the younger, and seemingly more glamorous, industrial-social or organizational area" (p. 395), foreshadowing the combining of the two into the field of industrial/organizational psychology and acknowledging the importance of integrating research on macro issues like climate with the more typical micro issues that had been the focus up to that point. He reiterated this emphasis in his section on "the organizational and social environment" when he overtly acknowledged that "the organizational and social environment plays a key role in the relative effectiveness or ineffectiveness of many personnel procedures" (p. 413). This statement captured the sentiment of the time and why interest in the concept of climate began taking off shortly thereafter.

Summary

The period from 1939 to the mid-1960s witnessed a steady increase in understanding the environment in and environmental variation between organizations. There were many terms that were used to describe that environment (such as atmosphere, personality, or character), with climate becoming the most common and well-developed construct to capture that environment. The earliest research on climate was by Lewin and his colleagues (1939), and his influence was apparent in the work of others that followed (particularly Argyris, McGregor, and Likert). Although Lewin's perspective that individual behavior was a function of the person and the environment, relatively little was known about the environment side of the equation relative to the person side that had dominated industrial psychology. The rise in interest in higher levels of analysis than the individual that led to the birth of the field of organizational psychology was coupled with a rise in interest in the climate construct. Undoubtedly, part of the goal of the new organizational psychology was to understand worker behavior and improve worker well-being, but at the same time, a close reading of the major authors of the time makes it clear that the primary goal in studying organizational climate was to improve organizational effectiveness. Ultimately, the research revealed that the two were interconnected—that treating people well tended to increase the effectiveness of those individuals and the organization as a whole. Perhaps just as importantly, research on organizational climate through this time helped make the study of the organizational system as a whole a legitimate subject of research.

FROM THE LATE 1960S THROUGH THE EARLY 1970S: THE EXPANSION OF EMPIRICAL CLIMATE RESEARCH

Although the concept of organizational climate had been receiving increased attention by organizational scholars, Dunnette and Campbell still concluded in their 1966 review of the managerial effectiveness literature that "... there is almost no existing literature concerning the measurement and exploration of variables which meaningfully describe the organizational environment. Measures of organizational climate and other situational factors are nearly non-existent and are sorely needed" (p. 7). Their description did not prove true for long; building on the intellectual foundation of the early climate writings described above, a notable increase in quantitative climate research began in the late 1960s. Indeed, as we will see, by 1970 research on climate had developed enough for Dunnette and Campbell through their publication with Lawler and Weick to devote considerable attention to the topic. In this section we start with an overview of some of the influential research and writings on climate that helped propel the field forward, and then in the next section move toward some of the critiques climate researchers faced fairly soon thereafter. The responses to those critiques and the subsequent research in the late 1970s and early 1980s formed the foundation of much of contemporary climate research and theory.

Tagiuri and Litwin (1968)

In January 1967, a conference was hosted by Tagiuri and Litwin at Harvard Business School on the topic of organizational climate. Tagiuri and Litwin (1968) compiled the papers that were presented at that conference into book form. Reichers and Schneider (1990) point to this conference and the subsequent book as a marker of the beginning of a contemporary perspective on climate. Rather than summarize each chapter in that book, we highlight the major themes below.

Conceptualizing and defining climate. The most widely addressed topic throughout the papers was how to conceptualize and define climate. In relation to other organizational variables, Tagiuri (1968a) described climate as a summary concept outside of an organization's environment, social system, culture, situation, or setting that described the quality of these other variables. Evan (1968), noting that Argyris (1958) seemed to equate climate and culture, specifically argued that culture was too broad of a concept to form the foundation for a definition of climate. Although these authors viewed climate as distinct from culture and other characteristics of the organization, a tension remained between viewing climate as environmental and yet based in the perceptions of individuals. For instance, Forehand (1968) articulated a Lewin-influenced view of climate as the interaction between person and environmental variables; similarly, Evan (1968) described climate as a "union between an individual and an aggregate level of analysis" (p. 108). Although the authors acknowledged that climate is perceived by individuals, it was consistently discussed in terms of a shared, aggregate phenomenon. Tagiuri (1968a) perhaps addressed this issue most directly by stating the following with regard to climate: "It is capable of being shared (as consensus) by several persons in the situation, and it is interpreted in terms of shared meanings (with some individual variation around a consensus)" (p. 25).

In terms of specific definitions of organizational climate, Tagiuri (1968a) described it as a characteristic of an organization's internal environment and therefore voiced concern that Forehand and Gilmer's (1964) definition of climate did not place enough emphasis on how climate is perceived by those internal to the organization. He offered this definition: "Organizational climate is a relatively enduring quality of the internal environment of an organization that (a) is experienced by its members, (b) influences their behavior, and (c) can be described in terms of the values of a particular set of characteristics (or attributes) of the organization" (p. 27). Evan (1968) voiced some hesitations about the concept of climate—he described how "from a scientific point of view, it appears to be so gross and ambiguous as to be of doubtful utility; however, from a common-sense point of view, it appears to be useful" (p. 107)—but nevertheless offered a definition that de-emphasized perceptions of organizational members and removed reference to the outcomes of climate: "Organizational climate is a multidimensional perception of the essential attributes or character of an organizational system" (p. 110). Litwin, while perhaps not offering a formal definition of climate, described climate in terms of the "*total subjective* impact of the environment on people" (Litwin, 1968a, p. 49, italics in original) and as "the total pattern of expectancies and incentive values that exist in a given organizational setting" (Litwin, 1968b, p. 172).

Types of climate and configurations. Throughout their chapters, the authors mentioned a number of dimensions or types of climate. Litwin (1968b) used Litwin and Stringer's (1968) climate measure that had the following seven dimensions: structure, responsibility, risk, reward, warmth, support, and conflict. Meyer (1968) summarized his research on the influence of organizational climate on motivation at General Electric and described how he refined Litwin and Stringer's (1968) climate measure and ultimately found six dimensions: constraining conformity; responsibility; standards; reward; organizational clarity; and friendly, team spirit. Evan (1968) described "various dimensions of climate" and included value climate, interpersonal climate, and task climate as his examples. Forehand (1968) contrasted pairs of competing climates, including climate for rule-following versus climate for individual freedom (or innovative climate), and mastery-striving climate versus defensive climate.

Several authors moved beyond a discussion of individual dimensions or types of climate to focus on their configuration. For instance, Tagiuri (1968a) described climate as a "particular configuration of situational variables" (p. 24) and the meaning of that configuration. Forehand (1968) proposed that various "conditions" or dimensions of climate (including complexity, rules-centeredness, closeness of supervision, and work-group competitiveness) coexist, and they may "cancel, or enhance, the effects of one another, or they may cohere to create a climate with effects different from those of any dimension taken separately" (p. 77). Although most of these authors did not directly distinguish between a molar or general climate perspective versus a focused or strategic climate perspective (a distinction that we discuss later), Pace (1968) provided an early indication of how one can conceptualize and measure criterion- or outcome-focused climates. He described it in the following way: "If one approaches the task of characterizing environments in relation to some criterion measure, the resulting characterizations will be limited to those aspects of the environment related to the criterion, and other perhaps equally significant aspects of the environment in general will be by-passed" (p. 144). In other words, by focusing on a particular outcome of interest, certain aspects of climate become more relevant and others become less relevant. He gave several examples of such criterion-focused climates: "the climate for research, the climate for profit, the climate for innovation, the climate for happiness, the climate for learning, or the climate for productivity" (p. 144).

Subclimates. As opposed to different dimensions or types of climate, several of the authors referred to different climates that exist based on who is perceiving them. For instance, Evan (1968) suggested that climate is perceived differently by those internal to the organization compared to those who are outsiders. He also described how members in different roles or in different subunits may perceive the climate differently. In Meyer's (1968) analysis of the General Electric climate data, two different plants were compared (suggesting the existence of a "plant climate" within the more macro General Electric climate) as were individuals who performed similar tasks (suggesting the existence of a "job climate"). Finally, Tagiuri (1968b) summarized an investigation of the "executive climate" as a subclimate of organizations that is only relevant for the executive level.

The effects of climate. Litwin most directly addressed the effects or outcomes of climate. He acknowledged that climate has an effect on the "total organization," but argued that "it does so through its influence on individual and small group behavior" (Litwin, 1968a, p. 47). In his second chapter in the book, Litwin (1968b) described his research with Stringer on climate in which they manipulated leadership styles to create particular climates (power, affiliative, or achieving), which were then found to affect motivation, satisfaction, and performance (this research is described in more detail in the next section). Evan (1968) discussed the effects of climate in terms of its implications for change in an organization. In a series of propositions, he addressed how climate tends to be perpetuated across generations (and how difficult it is to change it), the difficulty in changing climate as organizational size increases, how climate is easier to change when the consensus about it is lower (i.e., when climate strength is low), and how there is an increased level of conflict in organizations when sub-unit climates differ more.

Summary. Readers familiar with the issues that climate researchers and theoreticians confront can only be astonished by how these same issues were so articulately presented over half a century ago. Readers new to the topic need to accept our statement that they have been introduced in this brief section to the major issues in climate research and theory: the definition of climate, the dimensions that characterize climate, the degree to which organizations have numerous climates, including subclimates, and the relevance of climate for specific organizational outcomes. These topics, as well as others, will be open for consideration as we proceed.

Campbell, Dunnette, Lawler, and Weick (1970)

In addition to the Tagiuri and Litwin (1968) edited book, Campbell and colleagues' early review of the climate literature in their book on managerial performance and effectiveness proved to be another major contributor to the rise of climate research. Campbell and colleagues discussed climate in their chapter on "environmental variation," where it was presented simultaneously with other variables like structural properties, environmental characteristics, and formal role characteristics. That they distinguished climate from these other variables was notable; not all early climate research did. At the same time, they referred to research on norms (Georgopoulos, 1965), company personality (Gellerman, 1959), and organizational values (Andrews, 1967) as climate research, suggesting a lack of discrimination in the definition of the construct at the time. Perhaps this broad view of climate was based in their fairly general definition of climate: "a set of attributes specific to a particular organization that may be induced from the way that organization deals with its members and its environment" (p. 390).

This chapter is probably most heavily cited for its review of and comments on the dimensions of climate. Campbell and colleagues viewed a "fruitful taxonomy" of climate dimensions as the "key to unraveling" the organizational environment portion of their model of managerial behavior. They identified four dimensions of climate based on research accomplished until their review: individual autonomy; degree of structure imposed on the situation; reward orientation; and consideration, warmth, and support. At the same time, they did not view the commonality in taxonomies as a "cause for rejoicing" because the relatively few dimensions implied that there was more to be discovered.

Campbell and colleagues also laid the groundwork for several debates that would continue in the climate literature for years to come. For instance, they specifically referred to climate and these other situational variables as "properties not of individuals but of environments"; subsequent researchers would struggle with this issue of climate as an individual attribute versus an organizational attribute. In their view, even if there were differences in perceptions across individuals, as long as there was a significant main effect for the environment, then an environmental attribute was present. They also described as problematic the lack of clear conceptualization of climate as a direct predictor of performance or a moderator of the relationship between other individual differences and individual performance. Although subsequent researchers continued to struggle with this issue as well, perhaps a more active debate derived from another area they emphasized: whether climate (and other environmental variables) should be measured using objective or perceptual approaches. They summarized the issue in this way: "The central issue is whether the determiner of significant effects is the situation as it actually is or as it is perceived" (p. 389). In the end, they concluded that the two are distinct and both may be important. Subsequent research on climate attempted to establish relationships between the actual and the perceived with little long-term consequences since the effects of such tangibles as organizational structure that can be measured objectively are further removed from individual behavior, and likely work through perceptual measures of variables like the perceived climate that provide a more proximal predictor to behavior. In conclusion to their review of climate, Campbell and colleagues provided the optimistic view that the area had "considerable promise for the future" (p. 414).

The review of climate research by Campbell and colleagues was important for many reasons. The first was because the book in which it appeared was written by four major figures in the established world of industrial psychology and the growing field of organizational psychology: Campbell, Dunnette, Lawler, and Weick. Second, the book reviewed what was then known about managerial performance and effectiveness comprehensively: selection, appraisal, training, leadership, as well as climate/environmental issues within the broad general framework that both individual characteristics and the environment in which managers function are important for understanding what managers do and what they accomplish. Third, the book is a model of comprehensiveness in that it reviewed hundreds of pieces of research both from academia and from the world of practice (e.g., the AT&T management progress studies, the Standard Oil of New Jersey studies, and research at General Electric on appraisal and climate). Finally, the book is a good read; it is comprehensive and readable and the "story" is told with elegance and ease of accessibility. These made the book a "hit" and required reading and study for at least a decade of graduate students just when the fields of industrial/organizational psychology and organizational behavior were gaining a strong foothold in both academe and industry; Latham (2007) referred to finding it in his graduate student days, and it becoming his "academic bible."

Examples of Early Climate Research

Climate research began to grow in earnest in the late 1960s, continuing through the 1970s. Our goal is not to provide an exhaustive review of the research during that period, but we did want to provide some examples of research during that period that was both highly cited (based on information from PsycInfo and Google Scholar) and that captured the variety of research on climate-related issues that was being performed at that time. For interested readers, we have included a listing of these and additional examples of empirical research from this era in Table 2.1. Common themes during this time included the extent to which climate moderated the relationship between individual differences and outcomes (such that a fit between the individual and the situation was thought to produce better outcomes), the extent to which other organizational variables like structure influenced the climate of the organization, and the extent to which climate was directly related to outcomes like satisfaction and performance.

Litwin and Stringer (1968). In their book, *Motivation and Organizational Climate*, Litwin and Stringer used the concept of organizational climate as a bridge between theories of individual motivation and behavior

TABLE 2.1 A sample of early empirical articles on organizational climate (1968-1977)

Article	Brief Summary
Litwin & Stringer (1968)	Development of measure and experimental study on climate, leadership, motivation, and performance
Schneider & Bartlett (1968)	Development of a climate measure in life insurance agencies
Friedlander & Margulies (1969)	Climate predicting job satisfaction as moderated by individual values
Schneider & Bartlett (1970)	Further measure development and comparison of sources of climate ratings
Friedlander & Greenberg (1971)	Effects of climate on performance and retention
Payne & Pheysey (1971)	Development of a measure of climate
Frederiksen, Jensen, & Beaton (1972)	Experimental study of climate's effects on productivity
House & Rizzo (1972)	Development and validation of a measure of organizational climate/practices
Schneider (1972)	Study of the relationships among actual climate, preferred climate, and expected climate
Schneider & Hall (1972)	Antecedents of climate perceptions among Roman Catholic diocesan priests
Hand, Richards, & Slocum (1973)	The impact of climate on the effectiveness of human relations training
Payne & Mansfield (1973)	Relationships among climate, structure, context, and hierarchical level
Prichard & Karasick (1973)	Differences in climate across subunits and the relationship of climate with satisfaction and performance
Schneider (1973)	Climate from the customer's perspective related to service outcomes
Dieterly & Schneider (1974)	Experimental study of the effects of the organizational environment on climate
Downey, Hellriegel, Phelps, & Slocum (1974)	Relationship between organizational climate and job satisfaction
Lawler, Hall, & Oldham (1974)	Administrative process and structure predicting climate and climate predicting performance
Downey, Hellriegel, & Slocum (1975)	Interaction of organizational climate and individual needs in predicting performance and job satisfaction
Schneider (1975a)	The fit of employee's climate preferences and expectations with actual climate
Schneider & Snyder (1975)	The relationship between organizational climate and job satisfaction

(Continued)

TABLE 2.1 *(Continued)*

Article	Brief Summary
Sims & LaFollette (1975)	Evaluation of the Litwin & Stringer (1968) climate measure
LaFollette & Sims (1975)	The relationship between organizational climate and job satisfaction
Muchinsky (1976)	Evaluation of the Litwin & Stringer (1968) climate measure
Drexler (1977)	Agreement on climate measures across levels of analysis
Howe (1977)	Evaluation of the construct validity of group climate
Muchinsky (1977)	Relationships among organizational climate, job satisfaction, and organizational communication

and more macro conceptualizations of organizations. Based on a fairly broad definition of climate ("a set of measurable properties of the work environment, perceived directly or indirectly by the people who live and work in this environment and assumed to influence their motivation and behavior," p. 1), they conceptualized climate as an intermediary variable that is influenced by history and tradition (i.e., organizational culture), leadership style, and physical space, and which subsequently affects the motivation and behavior of workers. They emphasized the perceptual and subjective nature of climate, distinguishing it from such concepts as management practices, decision-making processes, technology, formal organizational structure, and social structure, which are objective features of the organization that can be observed directly and which have their effect through climate. In their view, the concept of climate provided managers with accessible and manageable factors for instituting change in their work units; by paying attention to climate and the factors that influence it, they could have an effect on their employees' motivation and subsequent behavior.

After describing their model of climate, Litwin and Stringer transitioned to presenting two major empirical studies of climate. The first involved the development of a climate scale. Starting with eight conceptual facets or dimensions of climate based on their review of the research literature, they asked managers to describe their work environment in an open-ended format and then sorted the topics that emerged from the open-ended data into their proposed eight dimensions. As a result, one dimension was dropped and two were combined, resulting in the following six dimensions on Form A of their measure: structure, responsibility, risk, reward, warmth and support, and conflict. After additional revisions and attempts at improvements to the scale, they finalized a Form B of the instrument that consisted of the following nine dimensions: structure, responsibility, risk, reward, warmth, support, standards, conflict, and identity (although they cautioned use of the conflict scale due to weak scale properties). When reporting on field studies later in the book, they grouped these nine dimensions into four broader categories: structure, challenge, reward and support, and social inclusion.

Next, Litwin and Stringer described their laboratory study of the effects of leadership on climate and motivation. They created three simulated organizations with 15 members each whose job was to create various "products" made of "Erector Set" parts and who worked for 8 days at their tasks. The "president" of each organization was a confederate who was trained to implement one of three leadership styles, each of which was designed to create a climate that would arouse either need for power, need for affiliation, or need for achievement. Consistent with their hypotheses, they found that these leadership styles resulted in significant differences in climate and aroused motives, all in less than eight days. They also found significant differences in outcomes across the conditions, with leadership that emphasizes need for achievement in workers resulting in the optimal outcomes in terms of satisfaction, innovation, and productivity. Overall, their results experimentally supported their model of the relationships among leadership, climate, motivation, and behavior.

Litwin left academe after publishing this research effort and began a long-term role as consultant to organizations using various versions of the scale he and Stringer had developed. Especially in his collaboration with Burke (e.g., Burke & Litwin, 1992), a model for describing organizational systems with organizational climate as a central variable evolved. The collaboration began in 1985 and continues to this writing (e.g., Burke, 2011), having accomplished major organizational change projects at such major corporations as Citibank (as it was then known) and British Airways. We will have more to say about organizational change in later chapters but it is important to note here that it was the Litwin and Stringer research that revealed experimentally perhaps for the first time the clear implications of leadership action in worker motivation and behavior.

Schneider and Bartlett (1968, 1970). In this set of papers, Schneider and Bartlett discussed the importance of including the role of the situation to better understand individual performance. For them, the study of climate was necessary because a focus only on individual differences typical of personnel selection researchers left out another important correlate of individual performance: the situation in which they behaved. Their view was that the effects of individual difference predictors would be moderated by the climate of the organization (or subunit). That is, their hypothesis was that the climate of a situation might enhance or inhibit the display of ability at work with some climates being facilitators and others inhibitors.

It is important to understand that their work was done in an era when it was believed by selection researchers that a test had to be revalidated each time it was used in a new setting because one never knew if the validity from one situation would generalize to the validity in a new situation, even for the same job. That is, selection researchers had shown that validity was ephemeral, jumping around from one site to another with no apparent explanation. Schneider and Bartlett believed that climate was the explanation; that in some situations the display of ability differences was enhanced while in others it was depressed. Of course, subsequent research on what was referred to as validity generalization (Schmidt & Hunter, 1977) revealed that validity changes from setting to setting for similar jobs are most likely a function of the small sample sizes used as a basis for the assessment of validity. That is, when sample sizes are large these ephemeral changes in validity do not appear and, furthermore, when the validity in many small samples is examined, the mean of the distribution of those validity coefficients is equivalent to that obtained on a single large sample (~500 people).

In any case, at the time they began this work Schneider and Bartlett did not have access to a measure of climate. Litwin and Stringer (1968) were working on their measure about the same time so it was not available, and creating a measure seemed the only route to testing their idea. Across the two papers, they described the development of their climate measure on a sample of managers in life insurance agencies (1968) and then presented a follow-up study on a larger sample of life insurance agency managers, assistant managers, and agents (1970). In the papers, they address several issues that climate researchers wrestled with for many subsequent years (and perhaps even to this day). First, how broad must one be to capture the climate space? In other words, how many dimensions of climate are there? They did not provide a firm answer to the question, but after conducting a factor analysis of a 300-item survey (1968), they ended up assessing six dimensions of climate: managerial support, intra-agency conflict, managerial structure, new employee concern, agent independence, and general satisfaction. Table 2.2 shows sample items for each of these scales so the reader can get a "feel" for what items in an early climate measure looked like.

Schneider and Bartlett acknowledged that two of their climate dimensions, managerial support and managerial structure, emerged from the work of Fleishman (1953) and that two facets of leadership emerged from the LBDQ: consideration and initiating structure. The dimension labeled "general satisfaction" they had originally labeled "managerial climate attitudes"; the issue of the overlap between climate and attitudes was a target for later critics. A third dimension, new employee concern, is of interest because no subsequent measures of climate with which we are familiar have addressed the issue of new employee socialization, a topic of central concern to culture researchers. Later in the book we will suggest socialization be re-introduced to climate research.

A second question, addressed in the 1970 paper, concerned the issue of from whose perspective should one assess climate. They discussed their own tendency to focus on the manager's perspective because of the manager's larger contribution to defining the climate (including using the term "managerial climate"—a la McGregor, 1960). Today that

TABLE 2.2 Dimensions with sample items from the "Agency Climate Questionnaire" of Schneider and Bartlett (1968, 1970)

Dimension Label	Sample Items
Managerial Support	Managers take an active interest in the progress of their agents
	Managers always keep promises made to agents
Intra-Agency Conflict	There are definite "in" and "out" groups of agents within the agency
	Agents look upon managers as necessary evils
Managerial Structure	Ineffective agents are told to "get busy or get out"
	Managers give agents formal quizzes on new provisions of grade books and/or policy plans
New Employee Concern	Agents receive sufficient field training prior to being left on their own
	The cost-effective way to contract a new agent is to give pre-contract training*
Agent Independence	Agents like the commission form of compensation
	Agents feel that the job they have is more interesting than other jobs they could get
General Satisfaction	Agents keep themselves informed on many topics besides life insurance
	Life insurance agents believe their status to be high in relation to that of other businessmen

*As a sign of the times in which this work was done, this dimension included the following item: "Agent's wives, as well as agents, are interviewed prior to contract."

perspective would no longer be the one used, with modern work focusing almost exclusively—perhaps narrowly—on employee perceptions as the key approach. Their attempt to empirically address the best source of climate ratings in the 1970 paper represented an early consideration of agreement about climate. They approached consensus both within and across perspectives by looking at inter-rater agreement from different positions in agencies (manager, assistant manager, agent). What they showed was that there was little agreement across the perspectives but that within the agents' perspectives there appeared to be some agreement. Thus, rather than try to understand which view was "correct," they instead focused on how the choice of the relevant perspective may vary depending on the criteria of interest. Since the target of their study was new agents hired into the life insurance agencies, they focused on the agents' perceptions for defining agency climate.

There is an unhappy and a happy ending to the tale. The unhappy ending is that the Schneider and Bartlett hypothesis that climate would moderate the ability-performance relationship was not supported. The happy ending is that the development of the climate measure received so much subsequent positive attention as an early model for what such a measure might look like that no one noticed the failure to support the hypothesis that stimulated the development of the measure![1] The measure received considerable attention in the book by Campbell and colleagues (1970) because at the time there were not many other measures around and also because, as we have now learned, there was some overlap in the dimensions from the Schneider and Bartlett work with those of Litwin and Stringer (1968).

Friedlander and Margulies (1969). In line with much of climate research at the time, Friedlander and Margulies examined climate's role in predicting individual satisfaction, but in their case they looked at this relationship as moderated by individual values. They measured the eight dimensions of climate from Halpin and Croft's (1963) Organizational Climate Description Questionnaire (OCDQ) along with commensurate measures of three dimensions of values and satisfaction; all measures and analyses were at the individual level. They found strong relationships between climate and satisfaction; six of the eight dimensions were correlated with all three satisfaction dimensions. Multiple regression analysis showed that the dimensions of thrust (positive relationship), which captured management behavior that was active and task-oriented, and hindrance (negative relationship), which captured employees' feelings of being burdened with busy work and routine activities, had the strongest and most consistent direct effects with the three facets of satisfaction. Finally, they found that a median split based on the values measures produced a different pattern of climate predictors for those high in all the values than for those low in all the values. They conclude that climate is "a dynamic phenomenon which may release, channel, facilitate, or constrain the organization's technical and human resources" (p. 180).

Frederiksen, Jensen, and Beaton (1972). A continuing early theme in organizational climate research was the interaction of person and situation variables in understanding performance behavior. The Schneider and Bartlett (1968, 1970) work was stimulated by this issue, Friedlander and Margulies were concerned about it by studying both climate and individual values as correlates of satisfaction, and Litwin and Stringer (1968; although we did not emphasize this earlier) assessed the participants in their eight-day experiment for their own needs of achievement, power, and affiliation and then showed that the climates in which they worked "brought out" those needs when the leadership fit their needs.

Frederiksen and colleagues continued this line of thinking in their laboratory study of climate. They sought to further understand the role of both the person and the situation on performance, this time via an in-basket exercise. Their 2 × 2 design was made up of two climate treatments: innovation versus rules (encouraging innovation and creativity versus the following of rules, regulations, and standard procedures) and global supervision versus detailed supervision (providing freedom in how assignments are performed versus close guidance and instruction). Using a sample of 260 administrators in the state of California, these climates were manipulated for participants via the instructions given for the in-basket exercise. For example, participants in the rules climate condition received a memo from the supervisor describing the importance of minimizing internal conflicts through the application of rules and procedures, commenting that "Rules are the distillation of years of experience. Let's know them and follow them!" In contrast, the supervisor's memo for participants in the innovation climate condition emphasized how stagnation can be prevented by seeking out new and better ways of doing things, telling the participant, "Do it the old way only if the old way is best!" Similarly, the global versus detailed supervision conditions were distinguished in a memo from the supervisor responding to an attached cartoon. In the global detailed supervision condition, the supervisor described the need to "give a subordinate concrete, constructive criticism on specific details," whereas in the global supervision condition the supervisor emphasized giving a subordinate "plenty of room for self-expression and plenty of opportunity to perform the job in his own way."

In an unusual analytic twist, Frederiksen and colleagues explored their results not only from the vantage point of the dimensions of climate individually, but also from analyses that resulted from crossing the original 2 × 2 manipulations. So, they created what they called two conditions that constituted "consistent climates," one by crossing innovation and global supervision (both of which encourage thinking and autonomy), and a second one by crossing rules and detailed supervision (both of which restrict freedom and ask for conformity). In addition, they created "inconsistent climates" by crossing innovation with detailed supervision and rules with global supervision. Their primary finding was that consistent climates produced significantly higher levels of productivity than inconsistent climates, with the case of detailed/innovation condition producing the lowest levels of all. This unusual approach to analyses pitted messages about one form of climate with messages about another form of climate, consistent with the idea that in many settings people receive conflicting messages about the expectations on them (e.g., be innovative and cut costs, production at all costs and be safe). Unfortunately, this approach to climate research has received inadequate attention over the years (for exceptions, see empirical work by Zohar & Luria, 2004, and the model of climate presented by Zohar & Hofmann, 2012).

A side note on the study by Frederiksen and colleagues is how they defined climate:

> The climate of an organization, as we conceive of it in this investigation, is a set of expectations or understandings, held in common by most of the members of an organization, as to a kind of uniformity in behavior that is seen as appropriate in that organization; these expectations presumably result from perceptions of uniformities in behavior on the part of the organization's members, from overt or subtle declarations of policy on the part of the leaders, from a uniform background or training and experience on the part of the members, or from some combination of these. Ultimately,

the climate presumably results from manipulations of reinforcements or sanctions by people in positions of power and through policies having to do with selection and retention of personnel (p. 73).

A number of elements of this definition stand out. One is that it included the idea of consensus, at least by most of the members of the organization. Another is that although it emphasizes the role of those in power in creating the climate, it also included two other drivers of climate: (1) behavioral norms, and (2) what was later labeled by Schneider (1987) as Attraction–Selection–Attrition processes whereby organizations become internally more homogeneous over time. Specifically, Frederiksen and colleagues referenced similarities in training and experience that influence employee expectations, along with selection and retention decisions that encourage uniformity. This definition is also an example of how early climate researchers tended to mix concepts that would later be more clearly distinguished as either climate (e.g., policies) or culture (e.g., norms).

Pritchard and Karasick (1973). Pritchard and Karasick viewed climate as the "psychological atmosphere" of the organization, and defined it in the following way:

> A relatively enduring quality of an organization's internal environment distinguishing it from other organizations; (a) which results from the behavior and policies of members of the organization, especially top management; (b) which is perceived by members of the organization; (c) which serves as a basis for interpreting the situation; and (d) acts as a source of pressure for directing activity (p. 126).

The thrust of their study was to examine differences in climate across subunits (regional offices of an organization) and to test the relationship between climate and both satisfaction in and performance of those regional offices. They found that climate operated at both the larger organizational and regional subunit levels with the latter offices being not significantly different on six of the eleven climate dimensions (indicating an overall organizational climate) and significantly different on the other five (indicating subunit climates). See Table 2.3 for a complete listing of the climate dimensions and summary of these findings. Their results also revealed that individual level climate perceptions were more strongly related to individual satisfaction than to individual performance. However, in the prediction of unit effectiveness it was the variation in climate across the subunits that had much stronger relationships than were found at the individual level. We will explore later this relationship between climate and satisfaction because it has been an issue of continual debate. Suffice it to say here that they explained the stronger relationship for climate and satisfaction at the individual level of analysis in terms of climate having a more direct effect on satisfaction, whereas the relationship with performance was viewed as more indirect. Pritchard and Karasick recommended that future research address the issue of causality

TABLE 2.3 Climate dimensions from Pritchard and Karasick (1973)

Significant Differences Across Regional Offices Within the Same Company?

Yes	No
Decision Centralization	Achievement
Flexibility and Innovation	Autonomy
Level of Rewards	Conflict vs. Cooperation
Status Polarization	Performance-Reward Dependency
Structure	Social Relations
	Supportiveness

between climate and satisfaction and performance, in addition to examining patterns or configurations of climate factors and interactions between climate dimensions.

An important finding from the Pritchard and Karasick research effort was that in studying unit climate and effectiveness they uncovered the fact that some dimensions of climate are not useful for the prediction of unit effectiveness. That is, they showed that for essentially half of the dimensions of climate they assessed, there was not a significant main effect for unit on climate, meaning that there was a macro organizational climate for those dimensions. The important conclusion from this finding is that climate measures must reveal main effects at the level of analysis of interest or there can be no relationships with outcomes of interest at that level of analysis. In fact, there are at present no good rules for writing climate survey items so that this goal will be achieved, although Kozlowski and Klein (2000) did outline principles for aligning constructs and measures in multilevel research that are relevant here. One caution that has emerged: be sure to write items descriptive of policies, practices, and procedures at the level of analysis at which results will be examined. A corollary caution is to ensure items are written in ways that enhance the probability of there being variance in responses to the items across units (Klein, Conn, Smith, & Sorra, 2001).

Payne and Mansfield (1973). There always existed an implicit hypothesis that the structure and context of organizations had a role to play in understanding organizational climate. Recall, for example, that in the early writings of Gilmer (1961; Forehand & Gilmer, 1964) structural issues like size of the corporation were thought to help determine the climate of the organization. For several years in the 1960s and 1970s, a group of researchers at Aston University did a number of large-scale studies in which this hypothesis, among others, was empirically explored. The studies were very influential in early climate thinking because they were done on large samples of organizations and came to be known as "the Aston Studies" (e.g., Pugh & Hickson, 1972; see Payne & Pugh, 1976 for a review).

The goal of the Payne and Mansfield (1973) study was to examine the extent to which organizational structure (functional specialization, formalization of role definition, lack of autonomy, and chief-executive's span of control) and context (organizational size, size of parent organization, age, workflow integration, and dependence) correlate with organizational climate. Climate was measured with the Business Organizational Climate Index (BOCI), a measure developed by Payne and Pheysey (1971) based on Stern's (1967) Organization Climate Index (as reviewed earlier, this was originally developed for assessing university climate). This measure of climate had twenty subscales (see Table 2.4), with seven to eight items measuring each dimension.

Payne and Mansfield studied fourteen companies, collecting data on structure and context from the CEO of each, and data on climate from employees across organizational levels. They found that the organizations had significant differences in climate (i.e., main effects) on 18 of the 20 dimensions of climate. More importantly, they showed that across the companies studied the contextual elements of size and dependence in particular seemed to influence climate. In addition, they found that climate perceptions varied across the organizational hierarchy, with individuals at higher levels tending to have a more positive view of the organization's climate.

This study is notable for several reasons. First, it revealed that organizational climate appeared to be associated with not only perceptions of

TABLE 2.4   Climate dimensions from Payne and Mansfield (1973)

- Leaders' psychological distance
- Questioning authority
- Egalitarianism
- Management concern for employee involvement
- Open-mindedness
- Emotional control
- Future orientation
- Scientific and technical orientation
- Intellectual orientation
- Job challenge
- Task orientation
- Industriousness
- Altruism
- Sociability
- Interpersonal aggression
- Rules orientation
- Administrative efficiency
- Conventionality
- Readiness to innovate
- Orientation to wider community

policies, practices, and procedures, but also with contextual issues such as size and levels in the hierarchy. Second, and easily missed in our brief reporting of their results, is the fact that most studies at this time tended to study climate at the individual level of analysis, but Payne and Mansfield explicitly stated their goal was to link the organizational structural and contextual variables with aggregate perceptions of organizational climate. Such research (assessing links between more tangible structural variables and climate) enters the domain of macro models of organizational change (e.g., Burke & Litwin, 1992), but such thinking has not been fully developed. We hypothesize, perhaps obviously, that structural and contextual variables influence climate through their effect on the organization's policies, practices, and procedures, but that is a hypothesis that has received little attention in the literature. One early exception is research by Lawler, Hall, and Oldham (1974), which we review next.

Lawler, Hall, and Oldham (1974). Lawler, Hall, and Oldham studied both the hypothesized antecedents and consequences of organizational climate among 291 research scientists in 21 research and development departments. Based on their general definition of climate ("an employee's subjective impressions or perceptions of his organization," p. 139), they discussed climate as an intervening variable that is influenced by job attributes and organizational structure and that climate in turn influences outcome variables such as performance and satisfaction. They investigated five dimensions of climate: competent/potent, responsible, practical, risk-oriented, and impulsive (see Table 2.5).

In terms of climate antecedents, they found that organizational structure (span of control, size, levels, tall/flat, levels from the top) was not as strongly related to climate as administrative process—what we would call policies, practices, and procedures. Thus, such administrative processes as professional autonomy and the degree to which performance reviews were tied to compensation were more strongly related to the climate dimensions than were the structural variables. They argued that this finding, in the context of the few other similar projects, suggested that the actual activities and processes of organizations that have a more direct effect on employees' day-to-day organizational life were the more proximal antecedents of climate relative to more distal variables like structure. They also showed that climate was related to an objective measure of aggregated individual R&D department employee performance and a director rating of administrative performance (but not of technical performance), and also, interestingly, to aggregated satisfaction ratings (rated by same source). This was interesting because, in an era when researchers were struggling with levels of analysis issues in climate research, all of these analyses were conducted at the unit level—even satisfaction was aggregated to the department level. Furthermore, they proposed several issues for future research that continue to be of interest to researchers to this day, including additional determinants of climate (such as the personality and values of supervisors and employees) and the causal relationship between climate and performance.

TABLE 2.5 Climate factors and items from Lawler, Hall, and Oldham (1974)

Factor 1: Competent/Potent
  Inhibited-*Uninhibited*
  Shallow-*Deep*
  Unscientific-*Scientific*
  Impersonal-Personal
  Uncreative-*Creative*

Factor 2: Responsible
  Irresponsible-*Responsible*
  Moral-Amoral

Factor 3: Practical
  Realistic-Idealistic
  Unconventional-*Conventional*

Factor 4: Risk-Oriented
  Daring-Cautious
  Aggressive-Unaggressive
  Cold-*Warm*
  Weak-*Strong*

Factor 5: Impulsive
  Active-Passive
  Objective-Subjective

Note: Italics indicate which side of the continuum was associated with high levels of the factor.

Summary

To provide a summary of early research on climate, we turn to the comprehensive review written by Hellriegel and Slocum (1974). Although we will refer to this and other major reviews from the time (e.g., James & Jones, 1974; Schneider, 1975b) in the next section as we discuss the major critiques of climate theory and research and the responses to those critiques, our goal for now is to capture major themes of climate research at the time, and the Hellriegel and Slocum (1974) article is notable for its thoroughness in reviewing the 31 studies that had been conducted up that point that had climate as a primary focus.

With regard to the measures of climate that had been developed, the most common measures used in the studies reviewed by Hellriegel and Slocum were those developed by Halpin and Croft (1963), Likert (1967), and Litwin and Stringer (1968), although many of the studies developed their own measures. Their analysis of the content of those measures was based on Leavitt's (1965) typology of organizations as consisting of people, structure, task, and technology dimensions, and revealed a heavy focus on the people dimension, followed by structure and then task, with technology receiving almost no emphasis. They attributed this overemphasis on people to climate scales being based on satisfaction scales (an issue we return to in the next section) and possibly to the fact that the primary developers of the scales were psychologists.

In their analysis of the research done on climate, Hellriegel and Slocum (1974) categorized the studies they reviewed by whether they studied climate as an independent, intervening, or dependent variable. With regard to studying the outcomes of climate (i.e., climate as an independent variable), they found a consistent relationship between climate and satisfaction but less so with job performance. They concluded that "the lack of consistent relationships between performance and organizational climates" (p. 272) was likely due to the large variety of possible contingencies on that relationship. There were fewer studies in the second category (climate as an intervening variable), but they identified three major categories of independent variables that had effects on satisfaction or performance through their effects on climate: human relations training programs, leadership, and manager personality. Finally, there were a number of studies in the last category (climate as a dependent variable), which they grouped into those examining the effects of structure on climate and those examining the effects of training programs. The structural variables studied included position in the hierarchy, degree of bureaucratization, employee orientation to the environment, and degree of decision-making discretion, whereas the research on training programs tended to be focused on using climate as an indicator of the effectiveness of organizational development interventions.

In their conclusion, Hellriegel and Slocum (1974) advocated for more research on the fit between the climate and the environment, on moderators of the relationship between climate and outcomes (i.e., differences between static and dynamic environments), and on the link between climate and more objective criteria, as well as for more rigorous research in general on the construct. To this list, we would add that although there were examples of organization-level studies of climate at the time (or at least organizational subunits, like offices or departments), those studies were outnumbered by those that studied climate at the individual level. This discrepancy between the conceptualization of climate as an organization-level construct in the earliest writings on climate and the empirical study of climate at the individual level proved to be one of the major challenges the field faced as it moved forward.

THE MID-1970S: MAJOR CRITIQUES OF THE CLIMATE LITERATURE AND THEIR RESOLUTION

Early critiques began showing up in the climate literature almost as quickly as the field took off in the early 1970s. Perhaps the harshest rebuke came from Guion (1973), who called climate "one of the fuzziest concepts to come along in some time" (p. 121). (It is worth noting that he also said the construct of climate "may be one of the most important to enter the thinking of industrial-organizational psychologists in many years" [p. 120].) Two additional highly cited critiques came from Johannesson (1973) and James and Jones (1974). Below we summarize the major concerns voiced in these articles as well as in other major reviews during the early 1970s. After presenting the issue that received criticism, we then present a summary of replies to the critique.

For these replies, we relied heavily on major reviews from the era by Hellriegel and Slocum (1974), Schneider (1975b), and Payne and colleagues (Payne, Fineman, & Wall, 1976; Payne & Pugh, 1976).

Lack of Clarity Regarding Climate as an Attribute of the Individual or the Organization

Critique: This issue formed the foundation of Guion's (1973) critique. He argued that the original goal had been to focus on climate as an attribute of an organization, and if this was to be the focus then measures of that variable had to be at the organizational level of analysis and there could be no variance within the data aggregated to form the more macro climate index. Nevertheless, either because it was being studied by psychologists, who tend to focus on individuals, or out of "methodological convenience" because it is easier to study individuals than organizations, studies of the construct had tended to focus on climate as an individual perception. Powell and Butterfield (1978) summarized the problem in this way: "The fact that many studies which were described as investigations of the organizational level variable of climate actually examined the individual-level perceptions of climate indicates the state of confusion over the proper unit of analysis in climate research" (p. 153). James and Jones (1974) argued that the use of perceptual measures "introduces variance which is a function of differences between individuals and is not necessarily descriptive of organizations or situations" (p. 1103). Thus, James and Jones argued, climate confounds the organizational characteristic as a stimulus and the individual's psychological process as a response.

Reply: Guion's (1973) criticism that climate was studied at the individual level more out of convenience than for sound theoretical reasons had validity, and it forced climate researchers to more carefully think through the appropriate level of analysis for their research. Responding to Guion's criticism, Hellriegel and Slocum (1974) pointed out that the definitions of climate they used in their review specifically focused on the organization and/or its subsystems. They further stated, "While the bulk of the literature does consider organizational climate in terms of its perceived attributes, it is difficult to discern how this could be interpreted as referring primarily to attributes of people" (p. 256). Powell and Butterfield (1978), who were also critical of the number of studies of climate at the individual level, made this observation: "Although the definition of OC [organizational climate] has changed over the last 15 years, it nearly always has been regarded as a property of the organization, as its name suggests" (p. 151).

An important beginning of the resolution of the levels of analysis for climate research was proposed by James and Jones (1974). They noted that it was necessary to distinguish between psychological climate (when climate is studied as an individual attribute) and organizational climate (when climate is studied as an organizational attribute).

Although some later researchers in this same era (e.g., Drexler, 1977) questioned whether the construct of psychological climate was meaningful given the large percentage of variance in climate perceptions explained by the organization, the research on climate continues to have both psychological climate and organizational climate proponents. Either way, Schneider (1975b) emphasized that for the study of organizational (or subunit) climate it was important to frame climate survey items in terms that were descriptive of activities at the level of analysis of interest rather than anything about the individual and his or her feelings or affect.

Lack of Validation of Organizational Climate Against "Objective Measures"

Critique: Guion (1973) argued that to know whether perceptions of climate were accurate, it was necessary to compare them against "an objective measure of the reality being perceived" (p. 122). James and Jones (1974) allowed for the notion that consensus within the unit could also be evidence for the validity of the climate measure but conceded that it was not as strong as evidence relating perceptions of climate to objective measures. Therefore, they advocated for dropping the requirement that climate be measured perceptually, an idea that was also advocated in later reviews by Payne and Pugh (1976) and Woodman and King (1978). These authors mentioned specific examples of how this might be done, including measures that presumably passed through fewer perceptual lenses like organizational size, lateness, absenteeism, turnover, behavioral descriptions of critical incidents, labor disputes, and accidents.

Reply: This critique was not useful because it implicitly proposed that it is not what actually happens in a setting that is climate but that it is the "objective" facets of the setting that are the climate of the setting. Clearly this was a definitional issue, but the focus on the "objective" missed the point that even the choice of what to focus on was a subjective decision and, further, unless the activities of the setting that were tied to those objective indicators were also measured, the result would not be a climate measure at all.

What is interesting about this criticism is that the examples cited in terms of studies that had used objective measures of climate were often not climate studies. For example, Evan (1963) is cited in multiple places as an example of a study employing so-called objective indicators, but his focus was on correlates of bureaucratic structure and the word "climate" was never used in his manuscript. Furthermore, most of the examples cited by Payne and Pugh (1976) and Woodman and King (1978) as potential objective measures of climate (organizational size, lateness, absenteeism, turnover, behavioral descriptions of critical incidents, labor disputes, and accidents) would best be categorized as either predictors or outcomes of climate, but not climate itself.

As noted earlier, at the core of this debate was the issue of whether climate was inherently a subjective perception or not. Litwin and Stringer (1968) were among the earliest researchers to explicitly distinguish climate as a construct based on perceptions of other objective organizational variables like structure, management practices, and technology. Although some subsequent authors, like James and Jones (1974), argued that the requirement that climate be perceptual should be removed, others disagreed. Hellriegel and Slocum (1974) made the following observation about the lack of "objective" measures of climate: "To the extent a climate researcher has a strong interest in understanding and anticipating the human component within organizations, it is probably desirable to employ perceptual measures" (p. 260). Schneider (1975b) echoed this view, noting that climate perceptions are the result of a cognitive process in which individuals organize and provide structure to the information they take in about their organization so that they can adapt to their environment more effectively. Once those perceptual structures are formed, they are not easily changed, and thus climate perceptions will not necessarily have a direct correspondence to actual policies and procedures. Thus, he concluded that climate perceptions are the result of a psychological process and not something that can be inferred based on the presence of external "objective" measures.

Lack of Uniqueness from Other Existing Research on Important Organizational Variables

Critique: One of the major critiques from James and Jones (1974) was that it was unclear whether climate added anything beyond other group or organizational variables like organizational structure, processes, system values and norms, leadership, and group processes. They specifically were critical of Forehand and Gilmer's (1964) definition of climate for being too broad, noting that "almost any study focusing on organizational or group characteristics would be included in the general area of organizational climate. In this respect, organizational climate appears synonymous with organizational situation and seems to offer little more than a semantically appealing but 'catch-all' term" (p. 1099).

Reply: James and Jones (1974) were correct about this and in fact the issue has not been fully resolved. Clearly leadership style and practices are part of and/or related to climate as are structure, systems, values, norms, and group processes—and other variables as well. As we have seen, definitional issues have plagued climate research from the earliest days. Our take is that researchers and commentators sensed that there is something "in the air" for people in a setting, that the something is being perceived, that it likely has multiple interacting causes, and that it is difficult to wrap one's arms around methodologically. Fortunately scholars kept at it and practitioners found it useful (more on this later) so work continued.

Marketing scholars speak about bundles of attributes that constitute a product or service, and those bundles can be summarized with terms that capture the meaning of those bundles for those experiencing them. For example, the bundle of attributes that comprise a Cayenne (an SUV by Porsche) yield a different impression and a different experience than the bundle of attributes that constitute a CRV (an SUV by Honda). The Cayenne is described as forceful, elegant, masculine, and so forth and the CRV is described as cute, utilitarian, and affordable. We think of climate as a construct that captures a particular configuration of attributes associated with human behavior in a setting. James and Jones were correct that it is very difficult to delineate and measure the bundles of attributes that make for different kinds of climate but we continue to believe that climate is the meaning attached to a bundle of attributes and that settings differ in the climates they present to members based on how the bundle is configured. This is a measurement issue with which we will deal more directly later, but for now it is important to identify the fact that climate is a packaging or a bundling of attributes and the meaning attached to the bundle.

Overlap with Research on Job Attitudes, Specifically Job Satisfaction

Critique: This issue of course fits with the just prior issue and the definition of climate. The proposed overlap between attitudes and climate was a central issue for climate critics with Guion (1973), Johannesson (1973), and James and Jones (1974) all emphasizing it. Guion likened studying climate as individual perceptions to the "rediscovery of the wheel" based on the idea that "perception can be used to infer attitude" (p. 123). Johannesson (1973) empirically studied this issue by comparing measures of climate and job attitudes. His argument was that affect cannot be distinguished from description, specifically noting that the idea that "feelings influence descriptions" is "the implicit assumption underlying the job descriptive index (JDI) of satisfaction" (p. 119). Based on his research findings, he concluded that climate added little beyond what was already covered by measures of satisfaction. James and Jones (1974) voiced similar concerns, although they did concede that "job satisfaction and perceived climate *may* be dynamically related and still provide somewhat different sources of related information" (p. 1107, italics in original).

Reply: Of all the early criticisms of the climate literature, the one that generated the most immediate reaction was this one. The responses were both conceptual (e.g., Hellriegel & Slocum, 1974; Payne, Fineman, & Wall, 1976; Schneider, 1975b) and empirical (e.g., Downey, Hellriegel, Phelps, & Slocum, 1974; LaFollette & Sims, 1975; Schneider & Snyder, 1975). Conceptually, it was argued that climate is a *description* of the work environment in the organization or subunit. Satisfaction, in contrast, is a personal *evaluation* of one's job situation. Whereas climate is a direct perception of the situation, satisfaction as an evaluation is filtered and processed by the individual according to some internal standard (Schneider & Snyder, 1975). The goal of climate measures is to characterize the organization (or organizational subunit); the goal of satisfaction measures is to characterize the individual's affective state (Schneider, 1975b).

Arguments along these lines led Payne and colleagues (1976) to conclude that "the concepts of organizational climate and job satisfaction are different, and no amount of empirical similarity makes them conceptually the same" (p. 46). Going a step farther, Payne and colleagues (1976) classified climate and satisfaction measures along three dimensions or facets: the unit of analysis (i.e., level of analysis, individual, or organizational unit), the element of analysis (i.e., the referent of the items, job or organizational unit), and the nature of the measurement (i.e., affective or descriptive). They argued that climate and satisfaction would be related the least when they differ on all these dimensions, and the relationships found between the two could, at least in part, be attributed to the overlap of the measures on these dimensions.

Others argued that climate and satisfaction should be related, likely because organizational climate affects individuals' job satisfaction (Hellriegel & Slocum, 1974; LaFollette & Sims, 1975) or because of overlap in survey item content (Payne et al., 1976). Empirical investigations supported the idea that climate and satisfaction were related but not redundant. LaFollette and Sims (1975) found that individual-level climate perceptions were more strongly related to a measure of organizational practices than to satisfaction, and that the pattern of relationships with performance differed such that satisfaction was more consistently significantly related to performance than climate. Schneider and Snyder (1975) argued for the distinction between the two concepts based on their findings that (a) responses to two measures of satisfaction (including the JDI) were more strongly related to each other than to climate; (b) employees tended to agree more within units on climate than satisfaction; (c) the relationship between climate and satisfaction varied across position in the organization; (d) neither climate nor satisfaction were strongly related to productivity; and (e) satisfaction was more related to turnover than climate perceptions. In addition, they pointed out that these findings were based on measures that were not developed specifically using the evaluation/description distinction as a criterion, and thus future measures developed along those lines should result in even greater distinctions between them. Downey and colleagues (1974) also supported the climate-satisfaction distinction by showing that the relationship between the two was significantly affected (not only reduced in magnitude, but often changing sign) after controlling for performance and structure.

Going back to the original critiques by Guion (1973) and Johannesson (1973), part of the issue was that the most common satisfaction measure of that era and the one used by Johannesson (1973) was the JDI. The JDI was developed by identifying those items that distinguished satisfied from dissatisfied workers. It was not developed using a content validity approach in which only items that specifically tap satisfaction would be included in the measure. As a result, the measure could include items that actually measure antecedents or outcomes of satisfaction. Researchers have demonstrated that a factor analysis of the JDI revealed two factors, one evaluative and one descriptive (Smith et al., 1974). Therefore, the concerns about the overlap may have been more a result of the satisfaction measure being used than the climate measure. In their conclusion, LaFollette and Sims (1975) argued that just as other researchers had been too quick to assume climate caused satisfaction, Johannesson (1973) had been too quick to assume that they were redundant based on correlational analyses.

It is useful to note that this issue of the overlap of satisfaction with other related constructs is alive and well in the contemporary research literature. Most prominently, Harrison, Newman, and Roth (2006; see also Newman & Harrison, 2008) have proposed that all individual difference measures of job-related attitudes assess a common facet they refer to as the A factor—A for attitude. They showed that measures designed to assess job satisfaction, organizational commitment, job involvement, and employee engagement intercorrelate at about 0.70 and they claimed this indicates they all assess a common factor. But some (e.g., Schneider et al., 2011a) have not agreed that a 0.70 correlation indicates that two constructs are the same, showing that height and weight are correlated 0.70 but are obviously different features of physiology—with different implications for both antecedents and consequences. The debate continues.

Mixed Findings for Climate's Relationship with Performance

Critique: The most thorough analysis of the relationship between climate and outcomes in early climate research was performed by Hellriegel and Slocum (1974). Although their very detailed and extensive review revealed consistent relationships between climate and satisfaction, they concluded that the results for performance were "not as easily understood, or as persuasive" (p. 271). They reviewed a large number of studies to that time and reported a wide variety of findings, including, for example:

- The consistency of climate facets with each other was related to organizational performance (Frederickson, 1966).
- Particular types of climate (e.g., high in supportiveness or emotional control, low in dominance) were related to performance (Friedlander & Greenberg, 1971; Hall & Lawler, 1969).

- Different types of climate were related to performance for employees in different types of jobs at different levels in the organizational hierarchy (Cawsey, 1973).
- Relatively few dimensions on an overall climate scale were related to performance (Pritchard & Karasick, 1973). Subsequent research reinforced this concern by finding no or weak relationships with performance (LaFollette & Sims, 1975; Schneider & Snyder, 1975).

Reply: In response to this issue, Schneider (1975b) noted, "we have not reached the stage of sophistication required to be able to specify which kinds (dimensions) of practices and procedures are relevant for understanding particular criteria in specific collectivities (work groups, positions, functions, etc.)" (p. 471). Thus, Schneider (1975b) suggested that there were two explanations for the inconsistent or lack of findings for the relationship between climate and performance. One was that measures of climate at the time (which captured what we will refer to as molar climate) were too conceptually amorphous. Schneider pointed out that the large number of dimensions of climate that had been uncovered by climate researchers indicated a lack of focus of measurement, leading him to advocate that "omnibus climate measures should not be indiscriminately used in hopes of 'finding something'" (p. 471). Instead, he argued that decisions about what climate or climates to study should be driven by the criterion of interest; climate correlates or predictors should be conceptually and operationally linked to specific outcomes. For example, if organizational turnover rates were the criterion of interest then policies, practices, and procedures of the organization that might be conceptually linked to turnover in companies should be the focus of the survey items used. Pritchard and Karasick's (1973) decision to focus on the seven (of a possible eleven) dimensions of climate that were expected to show differences in organizational effectiveness was given as an example of this approach. Schneider's admonition to focus on a "climate for something" led to the focused/strategic approach to climate, which is the dominant approach used today and one that we will explore in detail later.

The second explanation suggested by Schneider (1975b) for the inconsistent findings between climate and performance was the level of analysis used in particular studies. In the same way he proposed that the content of climate should be driven by the criterion of interest, the level of analysis of that criterion of interest should drive the decision of the level of analysis at which the data should be collected and examined. For example, if turnover rates in organizations were the criterion of interest then the climate data must be aggregated to the company level of analysis for predicting turnover rates. In addition, some variables may be more relevant at one level of analysis than another. Once again, the study by Pritchard and Karasick (1973) illustrates how the level of analysis can make a difference in the climate-satisfaction relationship. In that study, at the individual level of analysis, climate was more strongly related to satisfaction than performance. However, at the subunit level of analysis, climate was more weakly related to satisfaction and more strongly related to effectiveness.

Lack of Consensus in Ratings of Organizational Climate

Critique: Although this issue was not a primary focus of climate's strongest critics, it did receive attention by many during this period. Payne and Pugh (1976) highlighted several studies that found differences in climate perceptions across levels of the hierarchy, and they concluded that "mean climate scores may have masked important variations" (p. 1167). Johnston (1976) specifically addressed this issue in an interview study of a small consulting firm where he found that there were two climates based on the employees' level of tenure in the company. He concluded that "if there are multiple perceived climates, the measures used would produce an average perceived climate that perhaps did not exist in any of the subunits or levels of the organization" (p. 101). Building on the previously mentioned criticism regarding climate's relationship with outcomes, Johnston also concluded that the finding of multiple climates within one organization "may account for much of the failure of climate studies to show a strong link between perceived climate and productivity" (p. 101).

Reply: Different from the issue of studying climate at the individual versus the organizational level of analysis, this criticism had to do with whether it was appropriate to study an overall organizational climate if there were intra-organizational differences in climate perceptions. Although some researchers tended to focus only on the organization as a whole, other researchers specifically allowed for climate to exist at multiple levels within organizations (e.g., group, department, subsystem, etc.; Hellriegel & Slocum, 1974; Schneider, 1975b). The main purpose of Powell and Butterfield's (1978) article on levels of analysis issues in climate research was to argue that climate differences can exist at *any* subsystem level. Their review produced findings of differences in climate perceptions across a number of levels of analysis including organizational level, line or staff position, department or subunit, biographical influences, personality characteristics, and tenure. They argued that the individual was the lowest level subsystem and the organization was the most macro subsystem, and climate can be a differentiating property of these subsystems and all levels in between. In addition, they asserted that subsystem climates may or may not be related, and that climate can operate at different levels in different ways in different organizations. Subsequent empirical research by Drexler (1977) using data from 6,996 individuals in 1,256 groups from 21 organizations demonstrated that there was significant variance explained by both the organization and subunit levels, although the effect was larger for the organization level.

What emerged from this criticism and debate about where consensus did or did not exist within organizations on climate perceptions was an acknowledgement that climate could be studied at more than just the organizational level of analysis and a general acceptance that the level used in any particular piece of research needed to be empirically justified. Although the need for a homogeneity in climate perceptions had been recognized since the mid-1960s (e.g., Forehand & Gilmer, 1964), Guion (1973) was one of the first to advocate for a specific level of agreement that had to exist prior to saying an organization (or subunit) had a climate. He argued that agreement not significantly different than 100% was needed for the mean to be a valid indicator. Payne and colleagues (1976) cited Pace (1963) as the only researcher known at that time to have applied a cutoff for consensus as part of a scoring procedure; he used 66% agreement as a criterion. Payne and colleagues (1976) argued that means with less than 100% agreement could still be valid, and even a lack of agreement could be meaningful if it was linked to existing structural or political dimensions of the organization. This line of thinking laid the groundwork for later work on the statistical standards for justifying aggregation and analyses to identify the appropriateness of aggregation; we will have much more to say about this later.

Summary

The decade of the 1970s was a critical time in the development of the climate construct. Just as quickly as the construct was adopted by the field of industrial/organizational psychology, major critiques were published from several different authors. For the most part, the major concerns were about defining exactly what climate was and whether it offered something unique to the field. Looking back, such critiques and the responses to them by climate researchers were vital for the future development of research in the area. Climate researchers were forced to reflect on how they were conceptualizing climate, whether their measurement was consistent with their conceptualization, and how climate research should proceed if it was to survive. A comparison of the responses to the critiques of climate and contemporary research on the topic (which we summarize in the next chapter), makes it clear that those responses were setting the foundation for the field for years to come.

CONCLUSION

In some ways, research in the area of organizational climate was slow to develop, especially considering it was almost two decades between the classic studies of Lewin and colleagues in 1939 and when the construct started to gain more attention in the late 1950s. The period from the late 1950s through the mid-1960s and especially highly influential publications by Argyris (1957, 1958), McGregor (1960), and Likert (1961) laid the groundwork for the rise of the field of organizational psychology and with that, research on the topic of organizational climate. The rising interest in the role of the situation on organizational behavior resulted in an explosion of research on organizational climate starting in the late 1960s. However, the nature of that research was somewhat scattered, and critics were quick to point out the shortcomings of that early research. In our view, some of the problems that were identified in that early research were a direct result of researchers moving away from some of the foundational ideas from the decades prior. For instance, early writings on climate clearly communicated that the primary usefulness of the climate construct was in understanding organizational effectiveness, but early climate researchers tended to study it as an individual-level construct, creating confusion about its overlap with other individual-level variables like job satisfaction. Other problems were much-needed growing pains as the scope and measurement of the construct needed to be refined and better articulated. By the close of the decade of the 1970s, many of the major critiques had been addressed.

The downside of the controversies surrounding the climate construct during the 1970s was that they turned off many researchers, and interest in climate research declined to some degree (coinciding with a rise in interest in organization culture to be addressed in later chapters). Nevertheless, some researchers persisted, and throughout the 1980s they continued to work out the resolution of some remaining conceptual (e.g., the etiology of climate; Ashforth, 1985; Schneider & Reichers, 1983) and measurement (e.g., levels of analysis; Glick, 1985, 1988; James, Joyce, & Slocum, 1988) issues, in addition to moving the field forward in new ways to further develop the construct. We do not provide a separate review of climate research in the 1980s, although we have provided a listing of some of the major publications in the area from 1979 to 1989 in Table 2.6 for interested readers and discuss many of them in the next chapter. From our perspective, the contemporary study of climate began around 1979–1980 with the publication of three highly influential and highly cited articles: Jones and James (1979), Schneider, Parkington, & Buxton (1980), and Zohar (1980).

The key distinction among these three articles was their concern with describing the overall work environment, or the molar climate, versus climates with a specific focus (consistent with Schneider's, 1975b, conceptualization). The goal of Jones and James's (1979) article was to create a "comprehensive measure of the perceived work environment" (p. 202) that captured the aspects of the situation that had the most direct relevance for the individual's experience of the organizational environment. That instrument became foundational for future research using the molar climate approach to studying organizational climate, although Jones and James viewed their measure as one of psychological climate (an emphasis that James has continued throughout his research on climate). Although not the first research articles on focused climates, the Schneider and colleagues (1980) article on service climate and the Zohar (1980) article on

TABLE 2.6 A sample of climate articles during the 1980s (1979-1989)

Article	Brief Summary
Jones & James (1979)	Development and validation of a measure of psychological climate
Schneider, Parkington, & Buxton (1980)	Service climate as a predictor of customer perceptions of service quality
Zohar (1980)	Development and validation of a measure of safety climate
Welsch & LaVan (1981)	Participative climate as a predictor of organizational commitment
Burke & Descza (1982)	Preferred organizational climates of Type A individuals
Field & Abelson (1982)	Theoretical model of organizational climate
James (1982)	Discussion of how to assess agreement when aggregating climate perceptions
Joyce & Slocum (1982)	Discrepancy between organizational climate and psychological climate
Schneider & Reichers (1983)	Review of climate literature and theoretical discussion of its etiology
Schnake (1983)	The effects of controlling for job satisfaction on the dimensionality of climate
Joyce & Slocum (1984)	Study of collective climates, or climates defined by where there is agreement among employees
Keenan & Newton (1984)	Organizational climate as a predictor of environmental frustration
Glick (1985)	Discussion of multilevel conceptual and methodological issues in climate research
Miceli & Near (1985)	Organizational climate as a predictor of whistleblowing
Ashforth (1985)	Theoretical discussion of the formation of organizational climate
Schneider & Bowen (1985)	Service climate and perceptions of HR practices related to customer perceptions of quality
Angle & Perry (1986)	Labor-management climate as a predictor of dual commitment to the union and the organization
James & Tetrick (1986)	The nature of the causal relationship between psychological climate and job satisfaction
Solomon (1986)	Organizational climate differences between public and private sector employees
Kozlowski & Hults (1987)	Development and validation of the construct of a technical updating climate
Victor & Cullen (1988)	Multidimensionality and antecedents of ethical work climate
Glick (1988)	Response to James et al. (1988) emphasizing climate as an organizational attribute

(Continued)

TABLE 2.6 *(Continued)*

Article	Brief Summary
Jacofsky & Slocum (1988)	Stability of collective climates over time
James, Joyce, & Slocum (1988)	Response to Glick (1985) emphasizing the individual as the basic unit of climate theory
Kozlowski & Doherty (1989)	Focus on the relationship between leadership and climate
James & James (1989)	Support for a general factor of psychological climate underlying other dimensions

safety climate proved to be the most influential in transitioning the field to that approach. We will describe the research that was spurred by these three articles, in addition to other research that is associated with the contemporary study of climate, in the next chapter.

NOTE

1. For students in Ph.D. programs about to do their dissertations, the following story might be of interest. The Schneider and Bartlett (1968, 1970) research was actually supposed to be Schneider's dissertation. We say "supposed to be" because the research took six years to accomplish! The last publications associated with the original ideas were published by Schneider in 1972 and 1975. Midway through the second year of the research, it became clear it would take "forever," so Schneider proposed a new dissertation, a laboratory study of leadership, which was subsequently also published (Schneider, 1970). This dissertation took six months, not six years!

CHAPTER
3

Organizational Climate Research: The Current State of the Field

Having provided an in-depth review of the history of the climate construct in the last chapter, we now turn to summarizing the current state of research on organizational climate. Although the focus of this chapter is how climate is studied today, we also attempt to make explicit connections between current research and the early writing and research on the topic. In so doing, we can see how the field has evolved, what exciting and interesting approaches to climate have emerged, and how some ideas that continue to frame research on climate have their roots in what was written about climate many decades prior. Our goal is to give the reader a clear idea of how organizational climate is currently being studied while also showing how we got to where we are.

The chapter begins with a discussion of the definition of organizational climate, including the key themes that are common in definitions of climate and the working definition of climate that guides our own research and writing. From there, we address issues of levels of analysis, including how some study climate at the individual level (i.e., psychological climate) and transitioning to how organizational climate researchers grapple with justifying the study of climate at higher levels of analysis than the individual. Within organizational climate research, there are two primary approaches: molar climate and focused climate. We describe the literature on both, and give a particular emphasis to some specific focused climates that have received substantial recent attention. The next topic we address is variability in climate perceptions, or climate strength, and how it has become a more common topic in the literature, studied both as a moderator of the effects of climate and as an important predictor and outcome in its own right. The last sections of the chapter describe different ways climate researchers have approached the topic, including moderators of its effects, climate as a moderator, antecedents of climate, climate as a mediator, and mediators of climate's effects on outcomes.

THE DEFINITION OF ORGANIZATIONAL CLIMATE

Our review of the history of the organizational climate literature in the last chapter revealed extensive variability in the aspects of climate that were emphasized in definitions of the construct. Some attributes of these early definitions included, for example, that climate distinguishes organizations from each other (Forehand & Gilmer, 1964), is relatively stable over time (Forehand & Gilmer, 1964; Pritchard & Karasick, 1973; Tagiuri, 1968a), is perceived by individuals within the organization (Litwin & Stringer, 1968; Pritchard & Karasick, 1973; Tagiuri, 1968a), and influences individual worker behavior (Forehand & Gilmer, 1964; Litwin & Stringer, 1968; Pritchard & Karasick, 1973; Tagiuri, 1968a). As we discussed in Chapter Two and build on in this chapter, the construct has been refined, critiqued, and refined some more, resulting in clarification on how these climates come about, the content (facets or dimensions) of climate, climate's psychological relevance to people, and the importance of climate for organizational effectiveness. In Table 3.1 are five key themes that summarize these definitional issues in the literature—below

TABLE 3.1 Key themes in the definition of organizational climate

Theme 1: Organizational climate emerges through numerous mechanisms including leadership, communication, training, and so forth.
Theme 2: It is not the mechanisms that are climate but rather the experiences those produce and the meaning attached to them.
Theme 3: Organizational climate is a property not of individuals but of units/organizations; it is based on shared experiences and shared meaning.
Theme 4: Shared experiences and the meaning attached to them emerge from natural interaction in units/organizations; climate is shared in the natural course of work and the interactions happening at and surrounding work.
Theme 5: Organizational climate is not an affective evaluation of the work environment—it is not satisfaction—but rather a descriptive abstraction of people's experiences at work and the meaning attached to them.

we provide a more in-depth discussion of each theme and the way it contributes to our definition of organizational climate.

Theme 1: Organizational Climate Emerges Through Numerous Mechanisms Including Leadership, Communication, Training, and So Forth

One theme from the many proposed definitions of climate over the years has been that it is created and maintained through a number of different mechanisms. Early on, Fleishman (1953) viewed leadership climate as emerging not just from leaders' behaviors, but also from the expectations leaders had for subordinates. McGregor (1960) emphasized how climate is based on the day-to-day behavior of managers, in addition to the policies, practices, structure, and general philosophy of the organization. Litwin and Stringer (1968) emphasized leadership's role in climate as well, while also emphasizing the role of history and tradition, as well as physical space. Frederiksen, Jensen, and Beaton (1972) brought in even more possible mechanisms for the creation of climate, including the behavioral norms of workers, both direct and indirect communications from management, the training and background of employees, the organization's reward system, and the policies surrounding selection and retention. In our definition of climate, we refer to these various mechanisms and elements as the events, policies, practices, and procedures employees experience and the behaviors they see being rewarded, supported, and expected.

Theme 2: It Is Not the Mechanisms That Are Climate but Rather the Experiences Those Produce and the Meaning Attached to Them

Although all of these mechanisms have been described as important in establishing an organization's climate, there has also been a consensus that these individual pieces are not the equivalent of the climate itself. For instance, Argyris (1958) pointed out that climate was the totality of organizational life. Tagiuri (1968a) described it as a summary perception of the quality of various pieces of the organization (e.g., its environment, social system, or setting), and Evan (1968) as "the essential attributes or character of an organizational system" (p. 110). Along the same lines, Litwin (1968b) noted that climate is "the total pattern of expectancies and incentive values that exist in a given organizational setting" (p. 172). Pritchard and Karasick (1973) put it more simply by describing climate as the "psychological atmosphere" (p. 126) of the organization. This idea that climate is a way of summarizing the totality of the experience of these individual pieces was framed by Schneider (1975b) in terms of gestalt psychology. Consistent with the basic idea of the word gestalt (meaning whole), Gestalt psychology proposed that the whole is greater than the sum of its parts. Similarly, Schneider proposed that employees attempt to create order from their experiences of the many cues in their environment, that they "create perceptions of totalities consisting of inferred as well as actual practices and procedures" (p. 449). Using the terminology we used in the first chapter, we would describe climate as an abstraction that captures the meaning employees attach to configurations or bundles of experiences they have (James, James, & Ashe, 1990; Reichers & Schneider, 1990).

Theme 3: Organizational Climate Is a Property Not of Individuals but of Units/Organizations; It Is Based on Shared Experiences and Shared Meaning

In addition to the idea of climate as a meaningful abstraction of experiences by people, climate researchers have consistently emphasized that climate is important beyond the individual level of those experiences. If we return to the earliest climate research by Lewin, Lippitt, and White (1939), climate was not approached as an individual-level variable, but as something experienced by and shared in common by the whole group: the social atmosphere of the group. Other notable early climate theorists had a similar perspective. Argyris (1958) viewed climate as an organizational-level variable and placed a heavy emphasis on how the organizational level of analysis could not be reduced down to components at the individual level. McGregor (1960), even when using the term psychological climate to describe the climate of supervisor-subordinate relationships, emphasized that it was something that existed in the *relationship* and was co-determined by both parties. He also expanded his discussion to include the climate of groups and organizations. Gilmer (1961) emphasized climate as something that characterized the organization as a whole, its personality or character, and later defined it in terms of "the set of characteristics that describe an organization" (Forehand & Gilmer, 1964, p. 362). Tagiuri (1968a) noted that climate is "interpreted in terms of shared meanings" (p. 25), and along the same lines, Frederiksen and colleagues (1972) emphasized the shared nature of climate in their definition, viewing it as "a set of expectations or understandings, held in common by most of the members of an organization" (p. 73). Similarly, both Litwin and Stringer (1968) and Campbell, Dunnette, Lawler, and Weick (1970) viewed climate as a property of the organizational environment and not a property of individuals. Pritchard and Karasick (1973) viewed climate as a "relatively enduring quality of an organization's internal environment" (p. 126). We repeat here from the last chapter what Powell and Butterfield (1978) concluded about organizational climate: "[It] nearly always has been regarded as a property of the organization, as its name suggests" (p. 151).

Theme 4: Shared Experiences and the Meaning Attached to Them Emerge from Natural Interaction in Units/Organizations; Climate Is Shared in the Natural Course of Work and the Interactions Happening at and Surrounding Work

If climate is a property of an organization—or at a minimum a property beyond the individual level of analysis—the question becomes one of how this comes to be. In 1983, Schneider and Reichers expanded on the general notion that climate is a shared property by discussing climate through the lens of symbolic interactionism (Mead, 1934; Blumer, 1969). Perhaps most critical to the current discussion was this statement: "... meaning (which includes perceptions, descriptions and evaluations) does not reside in any particular thing in itself, nor does it reside in the individual perceiver. Rather, the meanings of things arise from interactions among people" (p. 30). This emphasis on the emergence of meaning from social interaction distinguished organizational climate from an approach that focused on organizational structure, which emphasized the primary role of individuals' common experiences of such organizational features as size, levels in the hierarchy, and so forth. A symbolic interactionist approach also distinguished organizational climate from the attraction-selection-attrition (ASA; Schneider, 1987) approach, which emphasized the role of homogeneity in the types of people in organizations as the primary driver of climate and differences between settings. Although not denying that these processes do affect climate, Schneider and Reichers (1983) asserted that as individuals in the same work unit interact and communicate about and share their experiences, they "respond to, define, and interpret" (p. 33) the situation in ways that create unique climates for the units/organizations in which the interaction occurs.

To a large degree, subsequent research on organizational climate continued this emphasis on the unit level. Glick (1985) characterized it this way: "Organizational climate is the result of sociological/organizational processes. Thus, it should be conceptualized as an organizational phenomenon not as a simple aggregation of psychological climate" (p. 605). James, Joyce, and Slocum (1988), in response to Glick's article, argued the alternative view that the attribution of meaning requires the cognitive appraisal by individuals, and that "it is individuals, and not organizations, that cognize" (p. 130). They therefore concluded that climate is the result of a psychological process and is thus a psychological variable; its basic unit of theory is the individual. Glick (1988) responded by drawing on theory from anthropology and sociology (Geertz, 1973; Krippendorf, 1971; Mayhew, 1980) to argue that meaning is not just a property of individuals, but also emerges from natural social interactions and systems and, as an emergent property of a social system, it cannot be reduced down to its constituent elements. In other words, even though individuals do cognitively process climate cues and attach meaning to them, it is through the very natural process of sharing experiences and meaning that these perceptions in organizations come to characterize the larger groups in which people work and interact.

Theme 5: Organizational Climate Is Not an Affective Evaluation of the Work Environment—It Is Not Satisfaction—but Rather a Descriptive Abstraction of People's Experiences at Work and the Meaning Attached to Them

The final element of climate definitions that we view as essential is that climate is a description of how employees view their work environments, not a personal affective evaluation of the work environment. The debates over the relationship between climate and satisfaction in the 1970s that we reviewed in the last chapter clarified that the descriptive-evaluative distinction was important for ensuring the uniqueness of the climate construct beyond the more traditional job satisfaction literature. Researchers have generally been cognizant and supportive of this distinction, though those who study climate through the individual lens of psychological climate (see James, Choi, Ko, McNeil, Minton, Wright, & Kim, 2008) are an exception. They propose that at a minimum satisfaction and psychological climate are most likely reciprocally related (James & Tetrick, 1986), but this is an issue at the individual level of analysis and not relevant for our discussion of organizational climate.

At the same time that climate is not an evaluative or attitudinal construct, the idea that it is descriptive does not mean that it simply captures the mere presence of the policies, practices, and procedures in organizations. As we described in the last chapter, one early critique of the climate construct by Guion (1973), James and Jones (1974), and others was that it needed to be validated against "objective" (i.e., nonperceptual) measures. As Schneider (1975b) and others emphasized, the perceptual aspect of climate is critical to capturing the meaning employees attach to the policies and practices in their organizations. As a result, there may not be a perfect correlation between the presence of individual policies and practices and the climate that emerges from them (see Klein, Conn, & Sorra, 2001, for an example of this) because there are a number of variables that also influence how members of the unit assign meaning to their experiences of those policies and practices.

Our Definition of Organizational Climate

In line with these key themes surrounding the conceptualization of climate, our definition of organizational climate is the following:

> *Organizational climate is the shared meaning organizational members attach to the events, policies, practices, and procedures they experience and the behaviors they see being rewarded, supported, and expected.*

This definition integrates across the themes just illuminated and thus is generally consistent with previous definitions of climate. In particular, this definition makes explicit the central role of the meaning assigned by people to their perceptions and experiences—the meaning *is* the climate.

It is useful to see how others have recently defined climate and compare those definitions to ours—because not everyone agrees with ours! Ashkanasy, Wilderom, and Peterson's (2000a) *Handbook of Organizational Culture and Climate* reveals some examples of these differences. In their introduction, Ashkanasy, Wilderom, and Peterson (2000b) noted that the term climate "is currently being used to describe configurations of attitudes and perceptions by organization members that, in combination, reflect a substantial part of the context of which they are a part and within which they work" (p. 8). Wiley and Brooks (2000) also included attitudes under the climate label. Michela and Burke (2000) stated, "Traditionally defined, organizational climate involves people's perceptions and experiences of the workplace in terms of warmth, trust, dynamism, ambiguity, and other affect-laden dimensions" (p. 234). Thus, despite the problems we have identified with this "affect-laden" view of climate and efforts to move the field away from this perspective, the association between climate and attitudes/affect persists. Although some authors emphasize climate as an individual-level construct (i.e., psychological climate), most recognize that it can still be shared and thus aggregated to the unit level. Nevertheless, some de-emphasize the importance of climate being shared across unit members and emphasize why it is not shared. For instance, in Virtanen's (2000) chapter, he writes, "climate is based on individual perceptions that are transparent to individuals themselves, but that they do not necessarily share with or reveal to other members of the organization" (p. 349). This description is reminiscent of Rousseau's (1990a) earlier description of climate as deriving from "the individual's potentially idiosyncratic experience of the organization" (p. 159) or perhaps even Ott's (1989) view that climate is transient. That some of these conceptions of organizational climate persist is discouraging to us. We will explore some of the sources of these varying views throughout the rest of this chapter.

Summary

Because the organizational climate construct has the potential for astonishingly diverse meanings, it has had astonishingly different definitions—when defined at all. All of these have been attempts to capture what employees make of their global experience(s) of their surroundings—in Lewin's terminology, their life space—and, in turn, relate those shared meanings to outcomes of interest. The themes we identified here represent both the key historically identified aspects of climate as well as the key developments in clarifying the construct over the years. Before moving forward from the definition of climate to the latest advancements in its measurement, we briefly return in the next section to an earlier topic, psychological climate, that continues to receive research attention despite persistent problems with its definition and measurement, as well as drawing less interest from management because of its individual rather than unit focus.

CLIMATE AT THE INDIVIDUAL LEVEL: PSYCHOLOGICAL CLIMATE

To this day, two relatively distinct threads of research exist in the climate literature: research on organizational climate that characterizes climate as a shared, unit-level phenomenon, and research on psychological climate that characterizes climate as an individual-level and personal perception. Although one could argue that both have merit and should be able to co-exist in the organizational research literature, there are some key differences in how they are defined and studied that make that challenging.

As a quick reminder of the history of the climate construct that we covered in the last chapter, the earliest roots of the climate literature through the mid-1960s almost without fail characterized climate as a property of the unit and its larger (organizational) environment. Such a focus was consistent with the state of the field of what we now know as organizational behavior (OB). Argyris (1957) and McGregor (1960) had set a foundation for such thinking, and Bass's book on *Leadership, Psychology, and Organizational Behavior* in 1960 may be the first book with OB in the title. As described in the last chapter, both he and Schein (1965) subsequently released the first books with the title *Organizational Psychology*. So, "organization" was on people's minds. In the mid to late 1960s and early 1970s, however, climate became a focus for psychologists interested in including the role of the environment in their industrial psychology research. The predominant researchers of the time were people trained in industrial psychology (it was not "officially" called industrial/organizational psychology until 1973), and business schools were hiring such people to come teach and do research. Not surprisingly, as psychologists they tended to approach climate as an individual-level variable because, at the time, industrial psychology was the study of individual differences. This focus on individuals in climate research was a major criticism from Guion (1973) and others.

James and Jones (1974) first made the distinction between psychological and organizational climate, and initially it appeared that the choice between the two was a decision that depended on the criterion of interest. As described by Schneider (1975), "The choice of a unit for analysis is then not an either-or problem but one of carefully defining the problem and then making the choice" (pp. 469–470). Nevertheless, as time passed through the 1980s, the differences in these approaches became more and more apparent. The clearest summary of the differences can be found in the very illuminating exchanges between Glick (1985, 1988) and James and colleagues (1988) that we described in the last section. The basic argument by James and colleagues (1988; see also James et al., 1990) was that climate is at its core an individual perception because the attribution of meaning occurs within the individual's cognitions. Individuals may share in these perceptions, in which case there may be a "shared psychological environment" (James et al., 1990, p. 62), but aggregates of climate perceptions are merely that—aggregates—and not a meaningful construction that exists separate from the individuals themselves. Based on earlier work by Schneider and Reichers (1983), Glick's (1985, 1988) view was that climate emerges out of shared social interactions, is a property of the system, and cannot be reduced to merely being a mean of uniquely individual perceptions.

Our view is similar to Glick's; even though climate is in fact an aggregate, it emerges out of interactions among people, and there is no research of which we are aware that teases out "pure" individual perceptions from those that emerge out of natural interactions as we have described them. The purest such research would have people work with others in a setting but never speak to them and compare their perceptions to those of people in the same settings who do speak with each other. Our prediction is that those who do not speak with others will have less sharing of their perceptions (there will be more variability around the mean) and that those who do speak with each other may well have different perceptions but will certainly show less variability around the mean. It follows from this logic that we would further predict that the degree of interaction with others that characterizes a work group and/or organization will be a direct correlate of the variability around the mean (we later report research to substantiate this hypothesis when we discuss climate strength).

Perhaps of equal importance to keeping these two research approaches quite separate has been the focus on the different criteria used as outcome variables for research in these domains. Psychological climate researchers tend to focus on affective individual outcomes (well-being, satisfaction, stress, job involvement, and so forth; see the meta-analyses by Carr, Schmidt, Ford, & DeShon, 2003; and Parker, Baltes, Young, Huff, Altmann, LaCost, & Roberts, 2003), whereas organizational climate researchers focus on more external unit and organizational-level outcomes (accident rates, customer satisfaction, and so forth; Kuenze & Schminke, 2009; Schneider, Ehrhart, & Macey, 2011b). Because of these differences in how climate is conceptualized and assessed as well as the outcomes of interest, there has been very little middle ground identified, and research from both perspectives continues to this day (e.g., James et al., 2008).

We have several concerns about research on psychological climate. One is that it is subject to many of the same criticisms that have been leveled at climate research since the early 1970s. In particular, the emphasis on the individual's personal perspective and the individual's affective processing of information leave open to question how much psychological climate can be distinguished from other job attitudes. The finding of a general psychological climate factor (PC_g; James & James, 1989) seems to suggest that much of the psychological climate literature can be reduced to an individual's general attitude toward his/her organization, similar to Harrison et al.'s (2006) "A" factor. Such overlap makes it difficult to see the usefulness of a psychological climate construct separate from research on individual attitudes toward work and working in organizations. Research on psychological climate also diverges in many ways from the early development of the construct by organizational researchers (e.g., Argyris, 1958; Lewin et al., 1939; McGregor, 1960). They clearly viewed climate as something beyond the individual and not limited to an individual's peculiar assignment of meaning to what happens around them. Climate for them was in the shared, common experience of employees and was considered useful because of its ultimate effect on organizational effectiveness. Even when individuals do not all agree, it is not necessary to reduce climate to the individual level of analysis; instead, researchers can take a dispersion approach (Chan, 1998) and focus on the role of climate strength in addition to climate level. So our conclusion is that *climate is an attribute of the work unit (e.g., group, department, or organization), and thus the appropriate level of theory and analysis for climate research is the unit*. Research on psychological climate has limited usefulness for understanding organizational functioning and effectiveness, the foci of the present book, so we will not consider it here.

MEASUREMENT AND LEVELS OF ANALYSIS

Based on the definition of organizational climate we have presented, along with some of the criticisms of climate research discussed earlier, how then should researchers go about measuring organizational climate? Glick (1985) provided some clear guidance on this front. He noted that the goal is to ask descriptive questions that summarize the unit's characteristics rather than affective questions that reflect an individual's unique experiences. Further, he emphasized that the referent for the questions should be specific, not generic, and should be aligned with the level of theory (e.g., department, organization). These two issues go hand in hand; by drawing individual respondents' attention to what happens in their setting and the common experience they most likely share with their coworkers, their responses are less likely to reflect only their personal affect or opinion. In surveys of this sort, the frame of reference is part of the item. For example an item to assess the support for service might read: "In my work unit we have the resources necessary to deliver excellent service."

This approach to climate measurement is consistent with Chan's (1998) referent-shift consensus model in which the referent of the items is the unit and the construct of interest is believed to be shared by unit members. Perhaps not surprisingly, researchers who emphasize the individual as the primary unit of theory for climate research (Glisson & James, 2002; James et al., 2008) assert that the appropriate aggregation model is Chan's (1998) direct consensus model. Using that model, the referent for measurement remains at the individual level ("I have the resources I need to deliver excellent service") and if one wishes to aggregate such psychological climate perceptions, the aggregation is of individual personalized experiences. We have already discussed the problems we see with this approach, and thus emphasize the importance for using descriptive items with a unit referent to best capture a unit's climate. The importance of using the unit as the referent was verified by a meta-analysis on justice climate conducted by Whitman, Caleo, Carpenter, Horner, and Bernerth (2012). They showed that the corrected correlation between justice climate and unit effectiveness was significantly stronger when the referent for the justice climate items was the unit ($\rho = .53$) versus the individual ($\rho = .23$).

When it comes to practical implications of measuring climate, one important issue is the level of specificity in the climate items. When conducting research on the overall climate in a work unit, it may not be necessary to use many items because it is the gestalt meaning of the similarly focused items that is the target of assessment. The idea, then, is that a sampling of the broad issues associated with a particular climate can be acceptable. When working with organizations, however, having specific items within the broad construct has clear benefits. For example, there may be items having to do with training, staffing, tools, equipment, space, leader support, and so forth, all framed as facets of the unit's resources needed to deliver excellent service. Although organizations may be interested in their general level of climate, once they have that information, they are also going to want to know particular areas to which they might make changes to effectively improve their climate. And that is where specificity in items can come in handy. By capturing a broad variety of specific facets that may affect the unit's climate and analyzing their relationships with the overall climate and key outcomes, consultants can provide organizations with specific information about areas that may be better (or worse) to target for intervention. No one area is likely to make THE difference, but that level of detail may help in narrowing the field to the few areas that may provide the most effect.

Once data have been collected, climate researchers need to address whether there is justification for aggregating individual-level data to the appropriate unit level (consistent with the level of theory; Kozlowski & Klein, 2000). Early climate researchers recognized the need for some level of agreement prior to actual aggregation; as described previously, Pace and Stern (1958) set the bar at two-thirds agreement and Guion

(1973) argued that there needed to be sufficient agreement such that it was not significantly different from 100%.

The primary progress in clarifying the issue of consensus did not come until the 1980s with the work of James and his colleagues (James, 1982; James, Demaree, & Wolf, 1984) and the development of the $r_{WG(j)}$ metric. This statistic has become the most commonly reported indicator of agreement for contemporary climate researchers in the organizational sciences, usually coupled with intraclass correlations (usually ICC[1] and often ICC[2] as well). Other less commonly used approaches for justifying aggregation include statistics such as the average deviation (AD) index (Burke, Finkelstein, & Dusig, 1999) and a_{WG} (Brown & Hauenstein, 2005), or WABA analyses (within and between analysis; Dansereau, Alutto, & Yammarino, 1984; Dansereau & Alutto, 1990). Although we will discuss some of the highlights of the issues surrounding aggregation statistics, Bliese (2000) and LeBreton and Senter (2008) are excellent sources for more information.

One important distinction when discussing aggregation statistics is between interrater agreement and interrater reliability (Kozlowski & Hattrup, 1992). Interrater agreement addresses the extent to which raters provide the same absolute ratings of climate. If all raters provide the same rating, then there is perfect agreement and their scores are interchangeable with each other. Alternatively, interrater reliability addresses the extent to which the rank ordering of the ratings is consistent across raters (Bliese, 2000; LeBreton & Senter, 2008). Most measures that are typically thought of as indicators of interrater reliability actually assess both agreement and reliability (LeBreton & Senter, 2008). ICC(1) is one such measure; it is interpreted as the percentage of variance that is explained by the unit. High ICC(1) scores will result when there is low variability within units and lots of variability across units; however, it will be negatively affected when either of those is not achieved (i.e., when there is more variability within units or less variability across units). ICC(2) as an index of the reliability of group means is also a measure of interrater agreement and reliability and is closely related to ICC(1). Specifically, ICC(2) is related to ICC(1) as a function of group size (Bliese, 2000) such that the more respondents per group, the higher the ICC(2) value will be.

There are a number of complexities that researchers will have to consider when calculating and interpreting aggregation statistics. First, they must determine which statistics to calculate. Although $r_{WG(j)}$, ICC(1), and ICC(2) are probably the most common statistics reported in the industrial/ organizational (I/O) psychology and management literatures, there is certainly disagreement on the issue of whether all of those are necessary or whether other statistics may be better. For instance, George and James (1993) have argued that within-group agreement is the primary criterion that should be used for justifying aggregation, noting that "aggregation per se is conditional on there being agreement within groups, not differences across groups" (p. 799). A second issue is how to deal with variability in within-unit response rates. In other words, some units will have better response rates than others, and for those with lower rates, questions may arise about whether the group is adequately represented (receiving responses from five of eight unit members may be acceptable, but what if it is five of 30 or 40 unit members?). Based on their analyses related to this issue, Newman and Sin (2009) concluded that researchers should attempt to understand the nature of the missing data and its effect on agreement statistics rather than deleting units with low response rates. A third issue that emerges when calculating $r_{WG(j)}$ specifically that has received recent attention is the choice of the null distribution against which the results are framed. LeBreton and Senter (2008) pointed out that the use of a uniform null distribution (i.e., an equal likelihood of all response options being chosen) is only appropriate if responses are not affected by any sort of cognitive or affective bias. Because that is not very likely to occur, they recommended calculating $r_{WG(j)}$ in multiple ways using distributions that reflect potential respondent biases (e.g., slight skew, normal distribution, etc.). They provided a more detailed discussion of these issues, including the expected variances using various response scales, in their article.

Once researchers calculate these statistics, they must then interpret them. Although there has been a tendency in the past to apply strict cutoffs with aggregation statistics, there is growing recognition that such cutoffs have been set based on arbitrary criteria (Lance, Butts, & Michels, 2006) and are overly simplistic (LeBreton & Senter, 2008). Thus, rather than setting a firm cutoff of 0.70 for $r_{WG(j)}$, for instance, LeBreton and Senter (2008) have argued that it may be better to think of agreement as existing along a continuum from no agreement (values of 0.00 to 0.30) to moderate agreement (0.51 to 0.70) to very strong agreement (0.91 to 1.00), and that the acceptable level of agreement for any given study should depend on the context of the research, the measures being used, and a number of additional issues. Along similar lines, they suggest that ICC(1) values should be interpreted as an effect size, with 0.01 being a small effect, 0.10 a medium effect, and 0.25 a large effect. Although ICC(2) is more straightforwardly interpreted in the same way as typical internal consistency reliability values and thus similar cutoffs can be applied (typically 0.70; Klein et al., 2000; LeBreton & Senter, 2008), it is not quite as straightforward as it may seem. ICC(2) values are strongly affected by unit size, and it is particularly difficult to achieve adequate ICC(2) levels when ICC(1) values are lower (Bliese, 1998, 2000; LeBreton & Senter, 2008). Therefore, it is our experience that it is quite common to see climate research studying smaller units to have ICC(2) values in the 0.40–0.60 range. As Bliese (2000) noted, there are many judgment calls involved when interpreting aggregation statistics.

Of course, the complexities do not end there. Researchers could still have to deal with nested data structures, contradictory results across the various aggregation statistics, and variability in agreement across organizational units. At the end of this section, we will return to these issues and others as we try to offer some specific, practical tips to climate researchers when faced with the challenges of aggregation and levels of analysis issues. Before doing so, however, we wanted to take a step back and encourage some self-reflection within the field of climate research.

We fear that the issue of data aggregation has become in some quarters more important and received more attention than issues about the conceptualization of climate and its role in predicting organizational performance. Of course, such a focus on measurement is very much in the blood of climate researchers as early climate researchers in the late 1960s and 1970s became distracted with measurement issues over more substantive issues on the role of the organizational environment in organizational effectiveness. It might even be said that the levels of analysis issue stultified climate research during the 1980s as scholars pursued the statistical issues that they thought required solutions. This tendency led to the following observation from Pettigrew (1990, p. 415): "The early climate researchers were not comfortable wringing their hands and biting the carpet over definitional issues. They were more likely to be driven by the maxim 'if you can't measure it, it doesn't exist.' So, off they went to measure, and the . . . definitional issues emerged for them when they had to make sense of the mass of data collected in such an atheoretical fashion." And try to make sense they did, culminating perhaps in the Klein and Kozlowski (2000) volume on levels issues in organizational research. Let us be clear: We are not saying that these developments have been negative for the field, nor are we saying that organizational climate research was the only arena in which levels issues emerged and required attention. However, it was clearly climate research that played a major role in bringing the data aggregation issue to the forefront and determining the effort lavished on the issue; therefore, this should be considered an accomplishment of the climate field.

However, scholars in other areas of research, while concerned with levels and data aggregation issues, have not let those issues dominate their thinking and research. Having worked with colleagues from other disciplines, it is interesting to compare the approaches taken to justifying aggregation. In brief, it appears to be true that organizational researchers require much more in the way of evidence to justify aggregation than is common in other fields. For instance, in other areas of psychology besides I/O psychology, or in the fields of public health and education, it is common to report the ICC(1) (based on a one-way ANOVA) and move forward with the analyses. The logic is that if the ICC(1) is significant then it has been demonstrated that there is enough between-unit variance relative to within-unit variance (i.e., a large enough unit effect) to support the reasonableness of aggregation (a view contrary to that of George and James, 1993, as discussed earlier in this section).

The question becomes, then, whether climate researchers should view themselves as being on the cutting edge with regard to these issues or whether the pendulum has swung too far and we as a field have gone too far in our emphasis on aggregation statistics. In our view, we have wrung our hands enough over the aggregation issue (or as we have sometimes referred to it, the "aggravation" issue) to state that one should be sufficiently sure of the reasonableness of data aggregation prior to doing it. This approach to justifying the study of unit or organizational climate is reasonable and avoids us continuing to be enamored with solving the aggregation problem of how best to demonstrate adequate interrater agreement and reliability that we have forgotten about the (more) important substantive issues of the effects of organizational climate on organizational behavior and outcomes.

Our thinking on this issue leads us to propose some specific recommendations for climate researchers (as well as for editors or reviewers who may be faced with these issues):

- It is our view that researchers should pay more attention to developing a strong *theoretical* justification (rather than just an *analytical* justification) for the level of climate being studied. As we reported earlier, Pettigrew (1990) clearly suggested that more attention should be paid to the justification given for the level of theory in a particular effort and the relationship of that level to the units being studied—and we agree! How units within the organization are currently organized and structured, as well as how the work within those units is accomplished, should be important elements in the conceptualization of the research.
- These issues are complex enough and our understanding of them mature enough that we should avoid the simplistic application of cutoffs with aggregation statistics. As outlined by LeBreton and Senter (2008), there may be some contexts in which a lower standard (average $r_{WG(j)}$ values of 0.60 or higher) is reasonable, whereas there may be other contexts when a higher bar (average $r_{WG(j)}$ values of 0.80 or higher) may make more sense.
- Aggregation statistics that are not as strong as typically desired (e.g., average $r_{WG(j)}$ values of 0.70 or higher or ICC(1) values greater than 0.10) should not mean that analyses at the unit level are inappropriate, especially if the level of theory and the units being analyzed are well-justified (e.g., consistent with the way the organization is structured). Instead, researchers should attempt to determine the cause of the "problem" and potentially account for the variability in agreement in the analyses. For instance, it might seem reasonable to conduct additional analyses in which the units with low agreement are removed to see if their inclusion has an impact. However, we concur with LeBreton and Senter (2008) in discouraging the practice of completely dropping units with lower within-unit agreement. Instead, agreement should be assessed based on the overall pattern of agreement across all units in the dataset. If the variability in agreement is viewed as problematic or is conceptually of interest, then the analyses can consider those. To that point, climate strength can be included as a moderator of the effects of climate level (see section on climate strength later in this chapter), thus considering level of within-unit agreement as an additional important variable of interest.
- There may often be cases when climate is operating at multiple levels of analysis, and thus there may not be a "correct" level of analysis, at least from an analytic perspective (George & James, 1993). If there are

concerns about whether the unit climate being studied is dictated by issues at higher levels of analysis, then it should be tested whether that is indeed the case (if possible) by calculating ICC(1) values at both levels (accounting for the nested structure). For example, if the theoretical level of interest is the unit and ICC(1) values at the unit level are 0.10 or better and below 0.05 at the corporate level, then it would seem appropriate to proceed with analyses at the unit level. If the ICC(1) for the corporate level were to be higher (say, over 0.05), then the analyses should likely account for the nested structure, and it may be worth reconsidering the target level of analysis because the larger number of respondents contributing to the corporate level should result in higher ICC(2) values. See Zohar and Luria (2005) for an example of these nested analyses, as well as Snijders and Bosker (1999) for a discussion of how lower levels "inherit" upper level variance.

- In line with the idea that climate may operate at multiple levels of analysis, the researcher should recognize that lower levels of within-unit agreement do not mean that there is a complete lack of consensus. Specifically, for certain kinds of climates, subclimates may be expected within which for at least some of subgroups there may be quite significant agreement. This might occur, for example, because of different levels of both contact and familiarity between employee and supervisor, or in units formed through merger of different organizational entities. By anticipating these types of issues, pertinent variables can be included in the data collection and proper multilevel analysis techniques employed to best understand how climate operates in these situations. From a practical perspective, examining variability in agreement between and within units in the organization can provide insights into why certain units are functioning differently than others. In line with our discussion of the practical usefulness of including specific items capturing the breadth of climate, examination of within-group response distributions and agreement statistics at the item level can provide insights into specific issues may be useful targets for intervention (see Bliese, 2006, for an example regarding ratings of work hours in military units).

- The issue of variability in within-unit sample size is complex, and researchers should thoughtfully and thoroughly address it. Low response rate units should not necessarily be discarded outright, but then again a minimum standard for within-group response rate (perhaps 20%–30%?) would seem reasonable. At the same time, if agreement is relatively high among those respondents in a unit where the response rate is disappointing, and the choice of unit is well-justified, it is likely that those few respondents are providing a meaningful representation of the views of the unit. It may be useful to include within-unit response rate in preliminary analyses to empirically evaluate potential effects on the results. Another approach would be to try to understand the nature of the missing data along the lines recommended by Newman and Sin (2009). Whatever the approach, these issues should be addressed from both a conceptual and analytical perspective to ensure that the decisions made are conceptually meaningful, reasonable, and defensible.

Progress along these lines would help the climate literature provide more balance between justifying the level of analysis and focusing on more theoretical and more substantively interesting issues.

Summary

Data aggregation and levels of analysis issues occupied many organizational climate researchers for much of the 1980s. The issue is clear: If climate is shared meaning then some demonstration of the meaning being shared is necessary. The problem has been that we seem to create new indicators of sharedness with relative abandon and fret over the minutiae of calculating and interpreting those indicators, and it is not necessarily clear that these efforts have improved our research or our understanding of climate. Further, in some cases it feels like researchers have become more concerned with quantitatively demonstrating consensus than with conceptually elaborating the research in the first place. Are we still, as Pettigrew put it, measuring first and thinking later?

TYPES OF CLIMATE STUDIED: MOLAR AND FOCUSED CLIMATES

As we outlined in Chapter Two, there have been two general categories of organizational climate research: the generic or molar climate approach and the focused or strategic climate approach. The molar climate approach was an attempt to capture the generic or overall sense of the experiences people had at work, while the focused approach obviously focused on a specific issue or outcome. In what follows we provide readers with an overview of the history of both approaches to the study of climate and reach some conclusions about what we have learned from them. Perhaps most interestingly we conclude that both approaches have merit and that the focused climate approach might best be conceptualized and studied as one that rests on the more molar climate foundation.

Molar Climate

Although the earliest climate researchers were more likely to refer to a specific type of climate (e.g., Lewin et al.'s, 1939, social climate; Fleishman's, 1953, leadership climate; and McGregor's, 1960, managerial climate), there was a shift in the late 1960s and early 1970s to trying to capture the totality of an organization's climate in all of its dimensions. Examples can be found in Litwin and Stringer's (1968) and Schneider and Bartlett's (1968, 1970) early climate measures, as noted earlier. Campbell and colleagues' (1970) review of the climate literature reported four consistent dimensions of climate that had been found across various studies to that time but implied that there was more work needed to identify those dimensions that had not yet been discovered. This shift from specific climates to climates that contained everything but the kitchen sink (Schneider, 1975b) can at least in part be attributed to the fact that those doing this research were largely psychologists.

Thus, their implicit focus was on the assessment of those attributes of the work environment associated with employees feeling good about where they worked, coupled with the also implicit hypothesis that individuals who experienced more of such a climate would be superior performers. That emphasis on employees feeling good is what resulted in Hellriegel and Slocum's (1974) conclusion that there was an overemphasis on the people dimension of organizations in climate research relative to other dimensions like structure, task, and technology—not too surprising for a bunch of psychologists!

Not all early climate researchers were convinced that a molar climate approach was appropriate or desirable. Even Litwin and Stringer (1968), whose scale was one of the most commonly used in early climate research (and is still used today; see Burke, 2011), acknowledged that capturing the entire content domain of climate may not be a reasonable enterprise, noting that "Because of their subjective and perceptual nature, there may be an infinite variety of organizational climates" (p. 45). Schneider and Snyder (1975) framed the issue in terms of how climate was conceptualized and questioned whether it made sense to think about organizational climate in a generic sense separate from a particular focus (climate for something) linked to a criterion of interest. They opined, "Unfortunately, there appears to be a trend among several researchers to think of organizational climate as being analogous to the concept of global job satisfaction when, in fact, such a conceptualization may be illogical" (p. 327). Schneider and Reichers (1983) were harsher in their assessment, as they asserted, "To speak of organizational climate per se, without attaching a referent is meaningless" (p. 21). Their criticism of this unfocused molar approach was because it was too general to make "fine distinctions between units nor to correlate with any specific organizational criterion (such as turnover) across units" (p. 22). Despite some of these concerns, research on molar climate continued.

Taxonomies of molar climate. A number of taxonomies of climate were proposed as empirical research experienced its rise in the late 1960s and 1970s. A rough summary sketch of the results of a few such research efforts is presented in Table 3.2 and summarized in more detail in what follows. Litwin and Stringer (1968), for example, started with six dimensions (structure, responsibility, risk, reward, warmth and support, and conflict) and then expanded to nine dimensions (splitting up warmth and support into separate categories and adding standards and identity) that reflected four broader categories (structure, challenge, reward and support, and social inclusion). Schneider and Bartlett (1968, 1970) focused on six dimensions (managerial support, intra-agency conflict, managerial structure, new employee concern, agent independence, and general satisfaction). Campbell and colleagues' (1970) review found four consistent dimensions across the climate literature of that time: individual autonomy; degree of structure imposed on the situation; reward orientation; and consideration, warmth, and support. Payne and Pugh's (1976) review of the climate literature in general and particularly in the

TABLE 3.2 Concepts used in describing molar climate dimensions

Dimension Label	Litwin & Stringer (1968)	Schneider & Bartlett (1968)	Campbell et al. (1970)	Jones & James (1979)	James & James (1989)
Structure/standards	X	X*	X*	X	
Consideration/Facilitation			X	X*	X*
Warmth	X		X	X	X
Support	X	X*	X	X*	X*
Reward	X		X		
Conflict/stress		X		X	X
Autonomy/Independence	X	X	X		X
Satisfaction/spirit		X		X	
Challenge/variety				X	X
Cooperation				X	X

Note: *indicates that the dimension label was accompanied by the word "leadership" or "managerial"

UK and Europe led them to conceptualize climate in terms of risk-taking, warmth, support, and innovativeness.

Some level of consolidation in the number of climate dimensions occurred by the late 1970s because of research on psychological climate by Jones and James (1979). One of the primary goals of their research was to create a "comprehensive measure of the perceived work environment" (p. 202) that captured the aspects of the situation that had the most direct relevance for the individual's experience of that environment. Their assumption was that there were likely a relatively small set of dimensions that could capture individuals' experiences across multiple work settings. To achieve their goal, they created a measure with 145 items divided across 35 composites (or subscales). Those composites were subjected to a factor analysis, resulting in six components that were generally consistent across three samples: conflict and ambiguity; job challenge, importance, and variety; leader facilitation and support; workgroup cooperation, friendliness, and warmth; professional and organizational esprit; and job standards. James and James (1989) later built on this research with a hierarchical model of a general psychological climate factor and four major dimensions of climate (role stress and lack of harmony; job challenge and autonomy; leadership support and facilitation; and work group cooperation, friendliness, and warmth), each of which subsumed between three and six more micro issues.

Ostroff (1993) organized the various climate dimensions that had been identified in the literature into three categories: affective, cognitive, and instrumental. The affective dimension was defined as those aspects of climate related to interpersonal and social relationships among workers and included participation, cooperation, warmth, and social rewards. The cognitive dimension was defined as those aspects of climate related to the self or individual involvement in work and included growth, innovation, autonomy, and intrinsic rewards. Finally, the instrumental dimension was defined as those aspects of climate related to task involvement and work processes and included achievement, hierarchy, structure, and extrinsic rewards. Ostroff found these climate dimensions to be correlated at a median level of 0.61 and also demonstrated that the climate dimensions contributed independently to the prediction of individual attitudes (e.g., satisfaction, commitment, adjustment, stress) and performance independent from individual-level preferences, values, and beliefs.

A more recent development in the literature on molar climate has been the work by Patterson and colleagues (2005) in developing the Organizational Climate Measure (OCM). The OCM was based on the competing values framework (CVF; Quinn & Rohrbaugh, 1983). Although this model is more commonly associated with organizational culture (as we will describe in detail in later chapters), Patterson and colleagues argued that the managerial ideologies and values of culture form the basis for the decision-making and actions of management that lead to climate. Thus, they reviewed past climate taxonomies and aligned the dimensions of climate with the four quadrants of the CVF that result from crossing the dimensions of flexibility versus control and internal versus external orientation (described in terms of approaches for organizational effectiveness: the human relations approach, the internal process approach, the open systems approach, and the rational goal approach; Quinn & Rohrbaugh, 1983). The result of the survey development process was a 17-dimension measure; the dimensions and their descriptions organized by the four quadrants of the CVF are shown in Table 3.3. The connection of the OCM to the CVF suggests ready connections between climate and culture, an issue we will focus on in depth in Chapter Six. In addition, although the number of dimensions in the OCM may seem overwhelming, Patterson and colleagues did acknowledge that it might be useful to focus on a subset of items that are most relevant for the work of researchers or practitioners in a particular setting and vis-à-vis a specific outcome.

Molar climate as a climate for well-being. Given the strong correlations among most dimensions of molar climate (e.g., Ostroff, 1993), it is perhaps best described as capturing the general sense employees have about whether their organization provides a positive environment for employees. Returning to Hellriegel and Slocum (1974), molar climate can be thought of as how people-oriented the climate is, or consistent with Burke, Borucki, and Hurley (1992), it could be labeled as the organization's concern for employees or its climate for employee well-being. Consistent with this view, James and colleagues (2008) described the general factor underlying psychological climate dimensions (PC_g) as "the degree to which the environment is personally beneficial or detrimental

TABLE 3.3 Dimensions of the organizational climate measure (OCM; based on Patterson et al., 2005)

Human Relations Model
- Autonomy (employees having a wide scope for how to perform their jobs)
- Integration (employees experiencing trust and respect)
- Involvement (employees having influence in decision-making)
- Supervisory Support (managers demonstrating concern and empathy for employees)
- Training (the organization showing concern for employee development)
- Welfare (the organization valuing and caring for employees)

Internal Process Model
- Formalization (the organization having many rules and procedures)
- Tradition (the organization operating in a established way that rarely changes)

Open Systems Model
- Innovation & Flexibility (employees and managers accepting new ideas and being willing to change)
- Outward Focus (the organization prioritizing customers and being aware of the marketplace)
- Reflexivity (employees and managers being open to evaluation and process improvement)

Rational Goal Model
- Clarity of organizational goals (employees and managers clearly understanding the direction and long-term plans of the organization)
- Efficiency (the organization being structured to maximize the effectiveness of time and money)
- Effort (employees working hard and being enthusiastic about their work)
- Performance feedback (the organization measuring and providing feedback on performance)
- Pressure to produce (managers communicating high expectations for employees)
- Quality (the organization emphasizing the importance of quality for organizational success)

to one's sense of well-being" (p. 11). The question is, how useful is such a generic view of climate, either theoretically or practically?

Theoretically, molar climate captures a number of constructs that have very well-developed literatures on their own. For instance, James and James's (1989) taxonomy included role stress (role ambiguity, role conflict, role overload), job design (job challenge and variety, job autonomy, and job importance), leadership (leader trust and support, leader goal facilitation, and leader interaction facilitation), and work group processes (work-group cooperation and work-group friendliness and warmth), all of which have been the focus of decades of research in the I/O and OB literatures. Assessing the general molar climate across these dimensions simplifies things and gives a sense of employees' overall view of their organization, but by doing so important nuances and important distinctions that have been discovered in those individual literatures are perhaps glossed over. Thus, it is our sense that a sole focus on molar climate leads to generic thinking and oversimplified theorizing.

From a practical perspective, Reichers and Schneider (1990) argued that a sole focus on molar climate and its generic dimensions is not very useful for promoting change in organizations toward the accomplishment of specific strategic goals. Nevertheless, there are at least a few ways that research on molar climate may have more of a practical impact. Research in the area of service climate by Schneider, White, and Paul (1998) investigated the extent to which the foundation issues of leadership, participation, computer support, training, and inter-department service provide a context or foundation on which service climate can be built. The support for their model indicates that an organization's communication of concern for employees through a positive molar climate facilitates employees' willingness to adopt a focus on specific strategic goals of their organization (Macey, Schneider, Barbera, & Young, 2009). It is important to be clear that molar climate is not causally linked to focused or strategic climates but that it provides a foundation such that employees are more willing to adopt the strategic focus promoted by specific policies, practices, and procedures. That is, just because an organization shows support for its employees does not mean the organization will effectively create a climate toward the accomplishment of its strategic goals. At the same time, the presence of such a foundation makes it more likely for management to be able to build a strategic climate.

Molar climate dimensions in profile. A second way that molar climate may offer more useful practical insights is through more fine-grained analytic techniques involving the dimensions that constitute a molar climate. Most studies of climate use the dimensions one at a time in trying to understand outcomes, usually in some form of multiple regression analysis. An alternative has been suggested and this concerns the study of the *configuration* of climate dimensions. Recent research by Schulte, Ostroff, Shmulyian, and Kinicki (2009) suggested that not all dimensions of climate need to be high for positive outcomes to occur. Although they found that overall climate level (or climate elevation in their terminology) was the primary predictor of internal outcomes (employee attitudes, intentions to stay, and perceptions of service quality), it was the configuration of climate that related to the external outcomes of customer satisfaction and financial performance. In particular, organizational units with climates that emphasized both employee support and service to customers had higher customer satisfaction than units that emphasized service alone. In a second study, they showed that units with climates that emphasized high levels of service to customers and moderate levels of employee support had higher financial performance than units that emphasized primarily employee support. What is interesting about this line of research is that it was the two general approaches to climate, molar and focused, that tended to separate out and distinguish the climate shapes that were found. The utility of general climate for well-being for predicting external outcomes was only found when examined in tandem with strategic climate. At the same time, the overall level of climate was almost redundant with employee attitudes (the two were correlated at 0.86 in their first study and 0.73 in their second study), harkening back to early critiques about whether climate can be distinguished from job satisfaction (e.g., Guion, 1973). Nevertheless, this research suggests that the examination of configurations of climate can help organizational management understand how best to distribute its limited resources to maximize its desired outcomes and, further, that the creation of a climate for well-being may well pay off because it provides a foundation on which a strategic climate may be built.

Summary. Molar climate research was a tactic adopted by early researchers to try to capture the total meaning of organizations to people. It seems that researchers took all of what they knew about contextual issues that might be important to people at work and measured them simultaneously, submitted those measures to factor analysis and, voilà, a measure of the dimensions of molar climate was evident. There was nothing inherently wrong in this approach, we suppose, except that (a) it lacked a conceptual foundation and (b) did not correlate well directly with important organizationally relevant outcomes. Later work suggested that such a molar climate and its dimensions might represent a climate for well-being and as such could serve as a foundation for more focused work on climate, a topic to which we turn next.

Focused Climates

Although Schneider's (1975b) essay on climate is perhaps the most often cited as beginning the push toward studying climate with a particular focus, the conceptual roots of the idea go further back. We already mentioned these in the previous chapter, but it may be instructive to summarize the various instances of this notion of focus for climate research and practice here in one place. Starting with the earliest pioneers in the field, there is evidence of interest in specific climates; for instance, Lewin and colleagues (1939) studied the social climate created by various levels of participation by leaders, Fleishman (1953) was interested in how the leadership climate affected the extent to which training was transferred to the job, and McGregor (1960) described how the Theory X or Theory Y assumptions of management create a managerial climate for the supervisor-subordinate relationship. In addition, Argyris (1957) used the term "human relations climate," and in his 1958 paper, discussed how management can create the particular climate it desires by hiring the "right type" of employees who would contribute to such a climate. Christie and Merton (1958, as cited in Tagiuri, 1968a) discussed a climate of values, and Pelz and Andrews (1966) focused on productive climates. Among the chapters in the Bradford (1964) edited book on T-Groups can be found references to a climate of permissiveness and inquiry, a climate for trust formation, defensive climates, and defense-reductive climates. Pace (1968), when discussing how climates can be focused on a particular criterion of interest, noted a variety of climates that researchers could study, including "the climate for research, the climate for profit, the climate for innovation, the climate for happiness, the climate for learning, or the climate for productivity" (p. 144). As a final example, Frederiksen and colleagues (1972) studied two specific types of climate: innovation versus rules (what we might call a climate for innovation), and global supervision versus detailed supervision (what we might call a climate for autonomy).

In 1975, Schneider made the most concerted argument for the benefits of the focused climate perspective, describing how a number of the criticisms of the climate construct are resolved when climate has a focus. For instance, when climate has a focus, it is less similar to attitudinal measures because the questions are more clearly a description of what is going on in the organization with regard to a specific strategic goal, and less about the individual's personal level of affect toward the organization. Furthermore, whereas research on molar climate can sometimes come across as a compilation of various other organizational and group processes, studying focused climates creates a stronger distinction between the climate literature and those other literatures. The questions in focused climate studies involve how those processes (e.g., leadership or teamwork) relate to a particular strategic outcome, which also narrows the dimensions of climate to those that are most relevant for prediction of the outcome of interest—and are perhaps most useful in practice. Finally, the relationship between climate and outcomes is substantially strengthened. Instead of trying to link the general positive or negative response individuals have about their organization to specific outcomes, climate items are created that ask about the policies and procedures as they relate to those specific outcomes. As a result, the relationships between focused climate and those outcomes are generally stronger, both conceptually and empirically—and practically more useful, too, because of their specificity.

Perhaps an example or two will make the issue more tangible. A molar climate item representing the support dimension might read: "The manager of my unit provides us the support we need to do our work." An item focused on a specific outcome, also representing support, might read: "The manager of my unit provides us with the tools, equipment, and resources we need to provide excellent service to customers." So, the item goes from molar generic "support" to focused specific kinds of support. As a result, the responses give more information about how the employees perceive that the organization is addressing specific strategic objectives, rather than how they are being treated in general.

At its core, the focused climate concept is about alignment. If the various facets of the organization in terms of its policies, practices, procedures, reward systems, and so on, send a consistent message about a particular issue of interest (e.g., fairness, ethics) or outcome (e.g., service quality, safety), then employees have a greater chance of receiving a clear message about what is valued in the organization (Bowen & Ostroff, 2004). In other words, it is not one single practice or policy that makes the difference, but instead the alignment of many practices and policies that sends a gestalt message to employees about what is important to the organization's success. Because of this alignment, employees will be more likely to behave in ways that are consistent with that climate, resulting in improved outcomes.

The two focused climates with the most developed literatures are service climate and safety climate. In addition to those two, a number of other focused climates have been proposed and studied in the literature. Examples include climate for innovation (Abbey & Dickson, 1983; Anderson & West, 1998; King, de Chermont, West, Dawson, & Hebl, 2007), justice climate (Colquitt, Noe, & Jackson, 2002; Ehrhart, 2004; Naumann & Bennett, 2000), ethical climate (Mayer, Kuenzi, & Greenbaum, 2009; Victor & Cullen, 1987, 1988), diversity climate (Herdman & McMilan-Capehart, 2010; McKay, Avery, & Morris, 2008; Mor Barak, Cherin, & Berkman, 1998), climate for initiative (Baer & Frese, 2003; Michaelis, Stegmaier, & Sonntag, 2010), equal opportunity climate (Walsh, Matthews, Tuller, Parks, & McDonald, 2010), climate for sexual harassment (Fitzgerald, Drasgow, Hulin, Gelfand, & Magley, 1997; Gettman & Gelfand, 2007), climate for transfer of training (Rouiller & Goldstein, 1993; Tracey, Tannenbaum, & Kavanaugh, 1995), climate for burnout (Moliner, Martinez-Tur, Peiró, Ramos, & Cropanzano, 2005), climate for industrial relations (Dastmalchian, 2008), emotional climate (Levine, 2010), leadership climate (Chen & Bliese, 2002; Schyns & Van Veldhoven, 2010), and technical updating climate (Kozlowski & Hults, 1987). Although we do not provide a review of the literature on each of these specific focused climates, we have selected a few as exemplars and provide a more in-depth review of them below. In addition, we draw from the literatures on some of these specific focused climates as we discuss some of the major themes in climate research throughout the rest of this chapter.

Before doing so, we make some more general observations about the literature on focused climates. One issue that we have emphasized in previous writings (Schneider, Ehrhart, & Macey, 2011a, 2011b) is that focused climates can be divided into two general categories of strategic climates and process climates. Strategic climates involve the extent to which the organization's environment emphasizes a specific strategic outcome that can usually be measured by external criteria. Examples include service climate, safety climate, or innovation climate. Process climates, in contrast, are focused instead on internal processes that occur in organizations as a part of daily organizational functioning. Examples include procedural justice climate and ethical climate. Kuenzi and Schminke (2009) have also categorized various focused climates. They used Katz and Kahn's (1966) types of motivational patterns to create four general categories of focused climates: climates focused on behavioral guidance (e.g., ethics and justice), climates focused on involvement (e.g., participation, support, and empowerment), climates focused on development (e.g., innovation and creativity), and climates focused on core operations (e.g., service and safety).

Regardless of whose classification scheme one adopts, these attempts at organizing the focused climate literature should be useful to better understand how focused climates can function in different ways and toward different processes and outcomes in organizations. For instance, we have argued that process climates like fairness and ethics and diversity may contribute to employees' perceptions of the molar climate for well-being, which in turn form a foundation for strategic climates that are more proximal predictors of key organizational outcomes (Schneider et al., 2011a). In other words, policies and practices in organizations create the process climates that serve as a foundation on which the policies and practices necessary for strategic climates can be built. This makes process climates mediators in producing important organizational outcomes as shown in Figure 3.1.

Figure 3.1 is another variation on what we noted earlier with regard to molar climate serving as a foundation for strategic climates. We proposed there that molar climates might represent a climate for well-being and that such a climate could offer a foundation on which organizations might build a strategic climate. Recall that this climate for well-being was not the cause of strategic climate but a foundation on which such a climate might be built. Figure 3.1 proposes that process-focused climates (like fairness and ethics and diversity) similarly offer a foundation on which more strategic climates can be built—the process climates do not cause the strategic climates but provide a (receptive) foundation on which they can be built. In other words, when employees experience

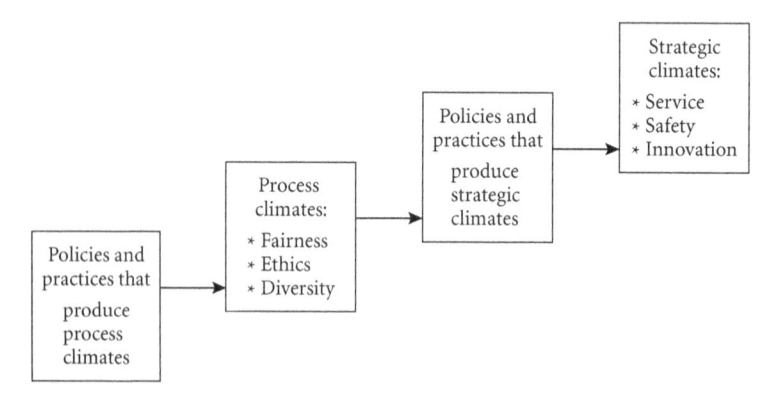

Figure 3.1 The mediating role of process climates in producing strategic outcomes

their environment as fair and ethical and as valuing diversity, they may be more receptive to management's attempts to create and maintain a strategic focus for employee effort and behavior.

To give some insight into how research on focused climates has developed over the years, we next give a brief overview of research on four focused climates—two strategic (service and safety) and two process (justice and diversity)—that have arguably received the most research attention.

Service climate. The first research explicitly on service climate from the employee's perspective was by Schneider, Parkington, and Buxton (1980). However, two prior studies by Schneider laid the groundwork for that 1980 study. One was Schneider (1973), in which service climate was studied from the customer's perspective, with customer account switching being one of the primary outcomes of interest. The second was a paper by Parkington and Schneider (1979); though it was not framed as a climate study, one of the primary variables was employees' views of management's service orientation, and held many similarities to contemporary focused climate measures. They found that the larger the discrepancy between employees' service orientation and employees' perceptions of management's service orientation (in effect, the fit between the employees' service orientation and the service climate), the more employees reported role ambiguity and role conflict.

Those studies formed the foundation for the research by Schneider and colleagues (1980), which examined the usefulness of employees' perceptions of service-related practices and procedures (i.e., service climate) for predicting customer perceptions of service quality in a sample of 23 bank branches. Their research included three primary dimensions of service climate: managerial function (the extent to which management emphasized service through its planning and goal setting), effort rewarded (the extent to which employee efforts to deliver quality service were rewarded), and an emphasis on retaining customers (the extent to which there were active efforts within the branches to retain its customers). At the branch level of analysis, correlations between these dimensions of service climate and customer perceptions of service quality ranged from 0.54 to 0.71, providing strong support for the validity of studying climate with a specific focus (in this case, service) for predicting outcomes related to that focus (in this case, customer experiences of service quality). This study also set the groundwork for later service climate research by also investigating the extent to which employees reported receiving support from the extra-branch systems within the banking system as a whole. They found that personnel support and equipment/supply support were two systems that were significantly related to customer perceptions of service quality, although not as strongly as the branch service climate dimensions (0.46 and 0.50, respectively). Later research on service climate would characterize these support functions as providing a critical foundation for the development of a service climate (Schneider et al., 1998).

Another interesting finding by Schneider and colleagues (1980) was that employee satisfaction, and particularly employee job satisfaction, had weaker and for the most part nonsignificant relationships with customer experiences of service quality compared to the service climate dimensions. These findings point to the distinction between descriptive reports of climate and affect-laden satisfaction scales, and to the stronger validity for climate for predicting outcomes. Methodologically, this research set the standard for much of the service climate research to follow. First, items were worded with the branch or branch manager as the referent. Second, scales for the dimensions of service climate were aggregated to the branch level of analysis, and the service climate items themselves all referenced service as a focus of the climate. Third, the authors reported an analysis of variance across the branch level data revealing a significant branch effect, supporting their aggregation to the branch level. Finally, the outcome data came from a different source (customer experiences also aggregated to the branch level of analysis) than the predictor data (employee experiences of service climate).

Subsequent research by Schneider and colleagues replicated and extended these findings. For instance, Schneider and Bowen (1985) were able to replicate both the role stress findings from Parkington and Schneider (1979) and the service climate findings from Schneider and colleagues (1980) for the dimensions of branch management and customer attention/retention. They were also able to show that human resource practices, and in particular the removal of obstacles that prevent workers from performing effectively (or work facilitation), were significantly related to customer service outcomes. Schneider and colleagues (1998) explicitly labeled work facilitation (including leadership, participation, computer support, and training) and interdepartment service as foundation issues that serve as a necessary but not sufficient condition for the presence of a service climate. They were able to show that those foundation issues had indirect effects on customer perceptions of service quality through their relationship with service climate. In addition, using a cross-lagged panel analysis, they showed that not only does service climate seem to have a causal effect on customer perceptions of service quality, but customer perceptions of service quality also have a reciprocal effect on service climate.

Following up with a study of grocery store departments, Schneider, Ehrhart, Mayer, Saltz, and Niles-Jolly (2005) found support for a mediated path model with service leadership predicting service climate, which then predicted customer-focused organizational citizenship behavior (OCB), which then predicted customer satisfaction, which then predicted unit sales. Their research indicated that, along with a focused climate (in their case, service climate), focused leadership (in their case, service leadership) was important to establish a service climate. In addition, the inclusion of customer-focused OCB demonstrated that it is through the behaviors of employees, specifically their efforts to go above and beyond the call of duty, that service climate has its effects on customer satisfaction and, ultimately, sales. More recently, Schneider, Macey, Lee, and Young (2009) extended some of these key findings to the organizational level of analysis. On a sample of 44 companies over a three-year lag, they demonstrated that organizational service climate was related to customer satisfaction, and that service climate had an indirect effect on company financial performance (market value) through customer satisfaction.

One might get the impression that only Schneider and his colleagues have studied this relationship, but that would be incorrect. Numerous other researchers have contributed to the service climate literature and, at least in what has been published, the link between service climate and customer experiences/satisfaction appears robust and reliable (Cooil, Aksoy, Keiningham, & Marytott, 2009; Dean, 2004; Yagil, 2008). Research on this connection between service climate and customer experiences and satisfaction was labeled as "linkage research" by Wiley (1996), and he has extended the linkage idea to all manner of links between employee survey data and outcomes of interest in and to companies. For example, in a recent book, Wiley (2010) revealed not only links between employee surveys and customer satisfaction, but also to employee turnover and to corporate performance. Other research has examined the strength of service climate's relationship to service performance relative to other variables. For instance, Way, Sturman, and Raab (2010) contrasted the effects of job satisfaction and service climate on supervisor ratings of group service performance behaviors (group task performance and OCB) vis-à-vis service quality. They found a significantly weaker connection between job satisfaction and job performance than for service climate and job performance. In addition, Liao and Chuang (2004) found that service climate predicted individual-level service performance above and beyond the personality of service providers. Research examining the antecedents of service climate has expanded the leadership variables shown to predict service climate to include transformational leadership (Liao & Chuang, 2007) and servant leadership (Walumbwa, Peterson, Avolio, & Hartnell, 2010). Further research has revealed that service climate fully mediates the effects of organizational resources and work engagement on employee performance and customer loyalty (Salanova, Agut, & Peiró, 2005), and that service climate mediates the relationship between high performance work practices and service performance (Chuang & Liao, 2010).

A meta-analysis by Hong, Liao, Hu, and Jiang (2013) provides a nice summary of some of the key findings in the service climate literature and reinforces many of the themes we have emphasized up to this point. In terms of antecedents, they showed that both leadership and human resources (HR) practices (in line with the foundation issues discussed above) predicted service climate, with the important twist that service-oriented leadership and service-oriented HR practices were stronger predictors than more general versions of either antecedent. Service climate was found to predict service performance (including task performance and OCB) as well as employee attitudes, which subsequently predicted customer satisfaction and financial outcomes (although they found a direct path from service climate to financial outcomes as well). Finally, the type of service moderated the relationship between service climate and outcomes, such that there was a stronger relationship for personal services (e.g., salons or restaurants) than nonpersonal services (e.g., banking or insurance).

In sum, service climate at both the unit (e.g., bank branches, supermarket departments) and organization levels of analysis has repeatedly revealed significant relationships with customer experiences/satisfaction as well as unit and organizational performance and financial indicators. There are also studies that show (a) service climate is a stronger predictor of performance than is job satisfaction or service provider personality, (b) service climate is a stronger predictor of customer satisfaction than are indices of HR practices, and (c) service climate mediates the effects of a number of organizational processes (e.g., leadership, engagement, high performance work practices) on service-related outcomes. Thus, focus seems to work in climate research; additional support for that conclusion comes from the work on safety climate to be considered next.

Safety climate. Research on safety climate began with a study by Zohar in 1980. Based on a review of the safety literature at the time, he developed a 40-item measure that covered eight dimensions of local safety practices: importance of safety training programs, management attitudes toward safety, effects of safe conduct on promotion, level of risk at the workplace, effects of required work pace on safety, status of the safety officer, effects of safe conduct on social status, and status of safety committee. As in the service climate work, the focus of the items and dimensions was on the outcome of interest—in this case safety. So, it is not the importance of training programs that is the issue but the importance of *safety* training programs. On a sample of 20 factories across multiple industries, Zohar showed that safety climate was significantly related to the overall safety level across the factories based on independent ratings of safe behavior by safety inspectors.

The literature on safety climate was relatively quiet for most of the 1980s and into the 1990s, with some exceptions in journals specifically focused on safety issues (e.g., Brown & Holmes, 1986; Dedobbeleer & Béland, 1991). However, as interest in multilevel issues was gaining momentum in the late 1990s, research on safety climate began to appear in top journals in I/O psychology and management. For instance, Hofmann and Stetzer (1996) found that safety climate was related to both individual-level unsafe behaviors and to the frequency of accidents at the group level, and their later research revealed that higher levels of safety climate were associated with increased tendencies to make internal attributions about the causes of accidents (Hofmann & Stetzer, 1998). Shortly thereafter, Zohar (2000) demonstrated the link between safety climate and objective measures of group-level injury rates, and Griffin and Neal (2000) showed that safety knowledge and motivation mediate the relationship between individual-level perceptions of safety climate and two types of safety behavior (safety compliance and safety participation). These studies provided a strong foundation for the future study of safety climate, and interest in the topic has increased considerably since that time.

In much the same way that the relationship between service climate and service-related outcomes has been consistently validated, the relationship between safety climate and safety outcomes (e.g., accidents, injuries) has received consistent support as well. For instance, in their recent meta-analysis, Christian, Bradley, Wallace, and Burke (2009) demonstrated that group-level safety climate had a mean corrected correlation of −0.39 with accidents and injuries. A subsequent meta-analysis by Beus and colleagues (2010) also showed support for the predictive relationship between safety climate and injuries and found that the strength of the relationship for injuries predicting safety climate was slightly stronger (a corrected correlation of −0.29 versus −0.24). Beus and colleagues concluded that this finding demonstrates the dynamic nature of safety climate, and how workers may recalibrate their perceptions of safety climate based on the occurrence of injuries. They observed that the stronger relationship for injuries predicting safety climate could be because of the direct link between the two, whereas the effects of safety climate on injuries are likely mediated by safety behaviors. One additional finding from these meta-analyses is worth noting. Both studies found that the relationship with accidents and injuries was much stronger for unit-level safety climate versus individual-level (or psychological) safety climate, despite the fact that both studies found many more studies of psychological climate than organizational climate (approximately twice as many in the Christian et al., 2009, meta-analysis). This finding is consistent with our emphasis throughout this book that climate is best conceptualized as a unit-level variable.

Beyond the relationship between safety climate and accidents/injuries, the construct has been studied in a variety of different ways and in relation to a variety of other safety-related variables over the years. For example, Probst, Brubaker, and Barsotti (2008) demonstrated that safety climate is also related to the reporting of accidents, with underreporting being much more likely in poor safety climates. Many different antecedents of safety climate have been identified, including general transformational leadership (Zohar, 2002; Zohar & Tenne-Gazit, 2008), safety-specific transformational leadership (Barling, Loughlin, & Kelloway, 2002), transactional leadership (Zohar, 2002), the safety climate of higher organizational levels (Zohar & Luria, 2005), and both management-employee relations and organizational support (Wallace, Popp, & Mondore, 2006). Safety climate has also been studied as a moderator on individual-level relationships, including Hofmann, Morgeson, and Gerras's (2003) research demonstrating that leader-member exchange (LMX) resulted in expanded safety citizenship role definitions when safety climate levels were high, and Probst's (2004) study showing that the negative effects of job insecurity on safety outcomes were attenuated by safety climate. In addition, the effects of safety climate at the unit level have been shown to be strengthened when the complexity of the work was high (Hofmann & Mark, 2006).

Methodologically, safety climate research has been extended beyond standard survey approaches to include the use of safety scripts (i.e., scenarios in which supervisors must report on their decisions at key points) as a proxy for supervisory practices (Zohar & Luria, 2004) and to include the role of communication and friendship networks in understanding safety climate level and strength (Zohar & Tenne-Gazit, 2008). Finally, from a theoretical perspective, the safety climate literature (and particularly Zohar's work) has had a substantial effect on the larger literature on organizational climate through the emphasis on the role of relative priorities in establishing an organizational climate, the differential role that policies, practices, and procedures play in climate research and practice, and in the interrelationships among climate and safety indicants across levels of the organization (Zohar & Hofmann, 2012; Zohar & Luria, 2005).

Justice climate. At the same time that the literatures on service climate and safety climate were experiencing sharp increases in attention in the late 1990s and early 2000s, the literature on justice climate began with research by Mossholder, Bennett, and Martin (1998) and Naumann and Bennett (2000). Although Mossholder and colleagues (1998) did not study climate per se, their research on procedural justice context formed the basis for the future development of the area. They were able to demonstrate that aggregated perceptions of the procedural justice context predicted job satisfaction beyond the effects of individuals' procedural justice perceptions. Naumann and Bennett (2000) built on that work and were the first to use the term "procedural justice climate," defining it as "a distinct group-level cognition about how a work group as a whole is treated" (p. 882). They were also among the first to study climate strength, although they referred to it as procedural justice climate agreement. They found that both work group cohesion and supervisor visibility in demonstrating procedural justice predicted increased agreement about procedural justice climate, and that the level of procedural justice climate predicted individual-level helping behaviors beyond the effects of individual procedural justice perceptions.

Since those initial studies, the literature on justice climate has expanded greatly. Perhaps most notably, it has expanded beyond a focus on procedural justice to include climates focused on distributive, interpersonal, and informational justice (e.g., Erdogan & Bauer, 2010; Liao & Rupp, 2005; Mayer, Nishii, Schneider, & Goldstein, 2007; Simons & Roberson, 2003). Research has revealed that the predictors of these various justice climates include team size and team collectivism (Colquitt et al., 2002), servant leadership (Ehrhart, 2004; Walumbwa, Hartnell, & Oke, 2010), and leader personality (Mayer et al., 2007). In terms of outcomes, justice climate has been shown to predict unit-level turnover and customer satisfaction (Simons & Roberson, 2003), team performance and absenteeism (Colquitt et al., 2002), and unit-level citizenship behavior (Ehrhart, 2004). At the individual level, justice climate has been shown to predict outcomes like job attitudes and individual citizenship behavior (Liao & Rupp, 2005; Naumann & Bennett, 2000; Walumbwa, Hartnell, & Oke, 2010), with some of those effects being moderated by both individual (justice orientation; Liao & Rupp, 2005) and structural attributes (group power distance; Yang, Mossholder, & Peng, 2007). Finally, the moderating effects of justice climate itself have been studied with regard to individual justice perceptions predicting job attitudes (e.g., job satisfaction and commitment; Mayer et al., 2007); individual work group identification and professional commitment predicting employee silence (i.e., withholding work-relevant information; Tangirala & Ramanujam, 2008); and LMX differentiation at the store level predicting individual-level attitudes and withdrawal behavior (Erdogan & Bauer, 2010).

Whitman and colleagues' (2012) meta-analysis of the justice climate literature provides a useful summary of the empirical findings on the topic. They showed overall justice climate (collapsing across dimensions) was significantly related to overall unit effectiveness as well as to each of its components (attitudes, processes, performance, and withdrawal). Furthermore, distributive justice climate had a stronger relationship with performance outcomes (like customer satisfaction or productivity) than either procedural or interactional justice climate, and that interactional justice climate had a stronger relationship with unit process outcomes (like cohesion and unit-level OCB) than either distributive justice climate or procedural justice climate. In terms of moderators, the relationships with effectiveness were stronger for units with greater climate strength, for units lower in the organizational hierarchy (teams versus branches or organizations), and when a unit-level referent was used for measuring justice climate.

Beyond empirical reviews of justice climate, a number of theoretical and review articles and chapters have appeared over the years, including those by Roberson and Colquitt (2005); Colquitt, Zapata-Phelan, and Roberson (2005); Rupp, Bashshur, and Liao (2007a, 2007b); Li and Cropanzano (2009); and Mayer and Kuenzi (2010). The level of interest in justice climate demonstrated by the rapid pace of research on the construct and the sizeable number of review articles (particularly relative to other focus climates) is likely due to the field of organizational justice being fairly large and relatively mature in its development, which has resulted in an influx of justice researchers interested in issues related to organizational climate. This development has been and will likely continue to be beneficial to the field of organizational climate, as the push to better understand justice climate will further refine and develop our understanding of organizational climate more generally. For instance, Roberson and Colquitt (2005) developed a model specifying social network characteristics that lead to justice climate, possible barriers that can prevent the convergence of justice perceptions within a team, and how different configurable patterns of justice can result as an alternative to a consistent, shared team climate. Such rich, theoretical insights not only are useful for research on justice climate, but also provide for thoughtful insights of issues of relevance to the entire field.

Diversity climate. Although it has not received the same attention as justice climate, research on diversity climate has received growing attention and will likely continue to do so in the years to come. The early influences on the development of the diversity climate construct were Cox's (1993) book in which he presented his interactional model of cultural diversity, and Kossek and Zonia's (1993) empirical research on perceptions of diversity climate among university faculty. Other highly cited early examples of diversity climate research include Mor Barak, Cherin, and Berkman's (1998) study of demographic differences in diversity climate perceptions of employees in an electronics company, and Hicks-Clark and Iles's (2000) study of the antecedents and outcomes of diversity climate perceptions in a UK sample.

Despite the progress of early research on the topic, there were some problems. One was that there was a tendency with the early scales to mix the referent of the items, such that some would ask about the individual's own views and experiences, and others would ask about management or the organization as a whole as the frame of reference. Furthermore, those individually referenced items often asked about the individual's beliefs and attitudes, and not about the organization's policies, practices, and procedures. For example, Mor Barak and colleagues' (1998) scale included a personal dimension (in addition to the organization dimension) with items like "I think diverse viewpoints add value" (personal diversity value factor) and "I feel at ease with people from backgrounds others than my own" (personal comfort factor). Another issue was the tendency for early research to focus on individual perceptions of diversity climate (or psychological diversity climate) with individual level correlates of those perceptions rather than to aggregate the data to higher levels of analysis. As a result, the research addressed how individuals perceived their organization and how their demographic attributes or their other job attitudes were related to those perceptions, but provided little insight into the organizational climate for diversity, including how units differed in diversity climate, how those shared perceptions came to develop, and what the implications of a diversity climate were for organizational or unit performance.

Some of the shortcomings of early diversity climate research have now been addressed, particularly with regard to investigating diversity climate at the unit level of analysis. For instance, McKay and colleagues (2008) showed that White-Black and White-Hispanic differences in sales performance were moderated by diversity climate. For Whites and Hispanics, the gap found in sales performance in less supportive diversity climates almost completely disappeared in more supportive diversity climates. In addition, the gap between Whites and Blacks not only vanished in supportive diversity climates relative to less supportive diversity climates, but Blacks had higher sales performance than Whites did when the diversity climate was more supportive. Another study by the same authors (McKay, Avery, & Morris, 2009) examined the interaction between aggregate employee perceptions of diversity climate and manager perceptions of diversity climate in predicting sales growth in retail stores. They demonstrated that the highest sales growth was found for stores in which both employees and managers reported that the diversity climate levels were high. In a final example, also with a retail sample, McKay, Avery, Liao, and Morris (2011) examined the effects of both diversity climate and service climate on customer satisfaction. They showed that diversity climate's relationship with customer satisfaction was strongest when both service climate levels and minority representation were high.

The research by McKay and colleagues has been important for the development of our understanding of diversity climate beyond individual-level perceptions. Of course, other researchers have also contributed to this topic. For example, Pugh and colleagues (2008) showed in a bank sample that the racial composition of the branch was related to the branch diversity climate (or in other words, that branch diversity served as a signal for the diversity climate) only when the diversity of the surrounding community was low. Another example is Herdman and McMilan-Capehart's (2010) study of the antecedents of diversity climate in a sample of hotels. They found that the presence of diversity programs predicted diversity climate, and that this relationship was moderated by both managerial racio-ethnic diversity and managerial relational values, such that diversity programs were more predictive of diversity climate when either of these moderators was high. A final example of research on diversity climate comes from Gonzalez and DeNisi (2009), who showed in a restaurant sample that racial/ethnic heterogeneity had a positive relationship with restaurant-level performance outcomes when diversity climate levels were high, but a negative relationship when diversity climate levels were low. For gender diversity, performance was found to be highest when diversity climate levels were high and gender heterogeneity was at moderate levels. What is most impressive about this research and that of McKay and colleagues (2009, 2011) is the relationships that have been revealed for diversity climate with unit-level customer satisfaction and financial performance indicators. We think these results are important not only for future research on diversity climate, but also for future work on all focused climates by demonstrating that organizations may benefit the most when they pay attention to both the critical strategic and process climates simultaneously.

Summary. The focused climate approach has become the dominant approach to studying climate in the organizational sciences. Moving from foundational work on service and safety climate, the focused climate construct has now been applied to countless areas as a way of demonstrating how the environment created by management can create a shared perception throughout the group or organization about what the imperative is of the unit and the processes that define it. As the use of the construct has grown and been applied in different areas, new insights have been gained about the various roles of climate in organizations and the various arenas in which the concept of organizational climate may be applied, such as justice and diversity. At the same time, increased interest in the climate construct has brought with it some applications that do not necessarily align with the most commonly accepted definitions of climate. For instance, there is a tendency in organizational research to use the term climate whenever an individual level variable is aggregated to the unit level of analysis without any effort to ensure that the construct aligns with accepted definitions of climate. Despite the need for more precision in the use of the climate label, we are excited about the future possibilities for research on focused climates and particularly for how multiple focused climates work simultaneously in organizations (cf. Kuenzi & Schminke, 2009).

CLIMATE STRENGTH

A more recent development in the study of organizational climate research has been to focus on variability in climate perceptions as a variable in its own right. Whereas focused climate research addresses the alignment of policies and practices around a specific process or outcome, climate strength research assesses the extent to which the perceptions of employees within a unit are aligned with each other. Although the empirical study of climate strength did not emerge until the late 1990s, the more general idea of studying variability in employee perceptions or behavior has roots that go back a half century or more. For example, Katz and Kahn (1966) discussed research on group cohesiveness by Seashore (1954) that showed that employees' reports on group cohusiveness correlated directly with observations of the variability of behavior within the group. Furthermore, Seashore found that highly cohesive groups were higher in performance when they accepted the organization's goals. In other words, when employees are aligned with each other within the unit (they are cohesive), and the unit as a whole is aligned with the organization (they accept the organization's goals), then productivity will be high. Research by Mischel (1968, 1973) also formed a foundation for the study of climate strength, particularly his idea that situations vary in the extent to which they are weak or strong (see Meyer & Dalal, 2009; and Meyer, Dalal, & Hermida, 2010, for recent extensions of Mischel's work; we will return to the idea of situational strength later in this chapter when we discuss research on climate as a moderator).

In the climate literature, some of the earliest thinking related to the concept of climate strength can be found in Evan (1968), who addressed two implications of variability in climate perceptions. He noted that when within-unit consensus about climate was lower, changing the climate should be easier. In addition, he suggested that in organizations where between-unit variability on climate perceptions was high that conflict levels are likely to be higher within that organization because its units share less in their perceptions—they have less in common. At the same time these early hints about the usefulness of focusing on variability within units existed, there were people (like Guion, 1973) who argued that a climate construct without very great agreement within units was not a viable construct. Although Payne and colleagues (1976) argued that means with less than 100% agreement could still be valid and that a lack of agreement could be meaningful, as we showed earlier climate researchers devoted their energies to the design of measures that could be defended in terms of aggregation. In other words, dispersion/variance should be fought against since it would deny the usefulness of aggregation, and aggregation had to be defended! It took agreement on how to defend aggregation before the study of dispersion/variability, in addition to the study of aggregate means, became possible in climate research.

Contemporary thinking on climate strength has been influenced by Chan's (1998) inclusion of dispersion models as one of several possible composition models in multilevel organizational research, which helped researchers consider aggregate level concepts not only in terms of means, but in terms of variability as well. Around that same time, empirical research on climate strength began to appear with studies by Bliese and Halverson (1998) on leadership climate consensus and by Naumann and Bennett (2000) on procedural justice climate agreement. Perhaps most influential was Lindell and Brandt's (2000) study of what they referred to as climate consensus in local emergency planning committees. Although they also hypothesized main effects for climate strength, the more influential aspect of their paper was the proposition that the effects of climate quality (or level) on outcomes would be moderated by climate strength, such that the relationship would be stronger when climate strength was stronger. The underlying idea for climate strength as a moderator is that high consensus (low variability within units) provides for a more reliable mean and with a more reliable mean, there should be greater validity in relationship with outcomes. Although this idea became foundational for subsequent climate strength research, Lindell and Brandt (2000) actually found little support for the moderating role of climate strength, especially when predicting organizational-level outcomes. Some possible reasons for failures to find such moderation effects for climate strength will be explored later.

Despite this lukewarm empirical support for the importance of climate strength, interest in the concept has grown. Research on climate strength has focused on molar climate, like Lindell and Brandt (2000; see also González-Romá, Peiró, & Tordera, 2002; and González-Romá, Fortes-Ferreira, & Peiró, 2009), as well as a number of focused climates, including procedural justice climate (e.g., Naumann & Bennett, 2000; Colquitt et al., 2002), service climate (e.g., Schneider, Salvaggio, & Subirats, 2002), and safety climate (e.g., Zohar & Luria, 2004, 2005). Below, we summarize some of the major research findings on the topic of climate strength.

Predictors of climate strength. One of the main goals of research on climate strength has been to clarify what factors contribute to the development of strong climates in work units; a summary of the findings is presented in Table 3.4. For example, Colquitt and colleagues (2002) found that team size and team diversity were negatively related to procedural justice climate strength, such that larger and more diverse teams had weaker climates. Climates have also been found to be stronger when within-unit social interaction was high (González-Romá et al., 2002), when the unit's social networks were more dense (Roberson & Williamson, 2012; Zohar & Tenne-Gazit, 2008), when unit members performed more sense-making activities (Roberson, 2006a), when units were more interdependent and had higher group identification (Roberson, 2006b), when units were more cohesive (Luria, 2008; Naumann & Bennett, 2000), and when average unit tenure was higher (Beus, Bergman, & Payne, 2010). Of all the issues that might influence climate strength, the most commonly studied has been leadership. Researchers have shown that units have stronger climates when leaders are described as higher on providing information (González-Romá et al., 2002), have more straightforward and less variable behavior patterns (Zohar & Luria, 2004), and are more transformational (Luria, 2008; Zohar & Luria, 2004; Zohar & Tenne-Gazit, 2008).

In summary, the take-home message from the research on the correlates/antecedents of climate strength is clear: When work units interact more, communicate more, and are more interdependent, and when leaders communicate more and share a clear strategic vision for the work, then the climate in those units will be stronger. These findings are consistent with the idea from Bowen and Ostroff (2004) that consistency in the message being sent is critical to how HR practices can have a positive effect in organizations and what they wish to achieve.

Outcomes of climate strength. Climate strength has been found to have both a direct effect on outcomes as well as a moderator effect on

TABLE 3.4 Research findings on the conditions that promote higher climate strength

Climates tend to be stronger when:
- work units are smaller
- work units are more cohesive
- there is high within-unit social interaction
- there is a dense social network
- unit members engage in higher levels of sense making
- units are more interdependent
- average tenure in the unit is high
- leadership provides high levels of information
- leaders are more consistent in their behavior
- leaders are more transformational

the relationship between climate level and outcomes. Despite Lindell and Brandt's (2000) initial findings casting some doubt on the moderating effect of climate strength, other research has supported such a relationship, at least in part. For instance, in a sample of automobile parts manufacturing teams, Colquitt and colleagues (2002) found that procedural justice climate strength moderated the relationship between procedural justice climate and both performance and absenteeism outcomes. In a sample of public health service work units, González-Romá and colleagues (2002) found evidence that climate strength acted as a moderator of the effects of climate level on unit average levels of satisfaction and average commitment in half of the interactions they tested. Similarly, Schneider et al. (2002) found significant moderator effects predicting customer satisfaction from service climate dimensions for a sample of bank branches, although only for their managerial practices subscale of service climate. As a final example, in a sample of bank branches González-Romá and colleagues (2009) found generally strong support for the moderating role of climate strength across employee-rated, supervisor-rated, and financial indicators of performance.

Thus, while these studies indicate a trend supporting the moderating role of climate strength in predicting outcomes, others have not found support for this relationship (Dawson, González-Romá, Davis, & West, 2008; Lindell & Brandt, 2000; Rafferty & Jimmieson, 2010; Sowinski, Fortmann, & Lezotte, 2008; Zohar & Luria, 2004). In three of these papers, significant main effects were found for climate strength. In Sowinski and colleagues (2008), a stronger service climate with regard to their customer orientation subscale was associated with higher store profitability, and a stronger service climate with regard to their means emphasis subscale was associated with lower turnover. In Rafferty and Jimmieson (2010), change information climate strength was significantly correlated with the team-level stress and well-being outcomes they studied. In addition, in Dawson and colleagues (2008), a nonlinear relationship was found between climate strength on the dimension of integration and overall hospital performance, such that both high and low climate strength resulted in lower performance relative to moderate climate strength.

Toward an understanding of the varying findings for climate strength. So what do we make of these varying findings? For one, we conclude that climate strength can matter. When management sends a consistent and clear message by its policies, practices, etc. about what it values, then it creates a strong situation in which behavioral variability will be relatively reduced (González-Romá et al., 2009). As a result, employees' expectations, reactions, and performance will be more consistent. In the service domain, the consistency of employee performance will result in less variability in the customer experience, which will then result in stronger relationships between service climate and customer outcomes (Schneider et al., 2002). In the domain of procedural justice climate, strength could mean that the treatment of employees is more consistent, strengthening the relationship between procedural justice climate and outcomes (Colquitt et al., 2002). It may also mean that process climates that describe virtuous effects for individuals within the group (i.e., fairness) lead to more frequent opportunities for the observation of those very processes within the team, reinforcing the perception of the climate.

However, we have to be tentative in what we conclude because this summary does not explain the lack of consistency in findings of moderator effects across studies for climate strength, studies that have varied according to the type of climate included, the industry studied, the type of outcomes studied, and more. Explaining differences in findings is likely tied to these differences in study design, but the explanation is not straightforward. One issue that is likely crucial is that there needs to be variability across units in their climate strength to find significant interaction effects. Several of the studies that did not find support for strength as a moderator seem to have had quite low variability in the level of agreement across units (e.g., Dawson et al., 2008; Sowinski et al., 2008; Zohar & Luria, 2004). As we noted earlier in this discussion, the focus has been so much on reducing variability within units to support aggregation that this is not surprising. The paradox of course is that by reducing within unit variability, one decreases the probability of finding a moderator effect for strength! This is because moderators can only be found when there is high variability in a variable across units—some units have to have high consensus and others low consensus, but if measures are all designed to produce high consensus then significant moderators will not be found.

There may be similar issues that explain why climate strength has direct effects in some circumstances but not in others. Lindell and Brandt (2000) demonstrated that the relationship between climate level and the maximum level of variability (i.e., the inverse of climate strength) is nonlinear and in the shape of an upside down U (see their graph on page 335). What this means is that at the highest and lowest levels of climate level, variability will be restrained—the only way to get a very high or very low level of climate is if everyone agrees. In contrast, at intermediate levels of climate level, the maximum variability is at its highest, for instance if half of the group reports very high levels of climate and the other half reports very low levels. (Note that one can have high agreement and moderate levels—it is possible for all employees to report that the climate is so-so in any given area). So when discussing the relationship between climate level and climate strength, it will likely vary across samples depending on the range of climate levels represented. If very low to moderate levels of climate are represented, then the relationship between climate level and climate strength will likely be negative (the lowest levels will be very strong and the moderate levels will likely be weaker on average). If moderate to very high levels of climate are represented, then the relationship will likely be positive (the moderate levels will be more likely to have weaker climate strength, with increasing strength as the level gets more extremely positive). If climate level is in the middle of the range, then the effects of level and strength are more likely to be independent and probably more likely to show independent effects on outcomes, in addition to increasing the potential for moderator effects. This conclusion indicates that climate measures should be designed as much as possible to eliminate very high and/or very low climate levels because such scores decrease our ability to distinguish the effects of climate level and climate strength.

Multilevel climate strength research. One interesting issue that we have not discussed to this point is the role of climate strength at multiple levels of analysis. In most of the studies of climate strength, the level of analysis is organizational subunits, such as work groups, bank branches, or store locations. There are a few examples of studies of climate strength at the organizational level, including Dickson, Resick, and Hanges's (2006) study of climate strength using data from organizations that participated in the GLOBE study of cross-cultural leadership (House, Hanges, Javidan, Dorfman, & Gupta, 2004), and Dawson and colleagues' (2008) study of climate strength in hospitals. However, research on climate strength does not typically cut across these levels (e.g., simultaneously examining the variability in branches and variability in banks).

One exception is research by Zohar and Luria (2005) on safety climate strength. They studied three types of climate strength: agreement across all individuals within the organization (organization climate strength), agreement across all individuals within groups (group climate strength), and agreement across groups within the organization (what they called climate variability). Thus, they captured the dispersion in safety climate perceptions at the organization level in two ways: one by looking at variability across individuals and one by looking at variability across groups. In a sample of almost 4,000 workers nested within just over 400 groups in 36 manufacturing plants, they found that organizational climate strength was positively related to group climate strength and climate variability, indicating that when the organization's top management communicates a clear message with regard to safety, then supervisors of individual work groups are able to pass along that message to their groups with clarity and coherence (group climate strength) in a consistent way throughout the organization (climate variability). Furthermore, they showed that routinization-formalization moderated these relationships, such that the effects of organizational climate strength were stronger when routinization-formalization was higher due to the decreased range of discretionary behaviors available to supervisors at lower levels in the organization, and the resultant consistency across groups within an organization. More research assessing climate strength across levels of analysis would make a substantial contribution to our understanding of how climate develops and has its effects in organizations. It may be, for example, that sometimes it is good to have variability across subunits in an organization (e.g., in the degree to which rules must be followed in an advertising agency) and sometimes not (as in the issue of subunits following safety practices). This is an issue in need of additional thinking and research.

Future research agenda on climate strength. In addition to developing our understanding of climate strength at multiple levels of analysis, there are a number of other areas for future research that might prove useful for the study of climate strength. One area of interest would be the potential negative effects of a strong climate. Studies of climate strength as a moderator have tended to show that when climate level is low, a strong climate is a bad thing for outcomes. That is, when climate is negative and strength is high, all employees agree that it is a negative environment and, for sure, bad things will follow. Recall that, at the same time, Dawson and colleagues (2008) have shown a nonlinear main effect of climate strength on overall performance in hospitals, and they suggested that in large organizations like hospitals, a strong climate may indicate that top management is overly controlling and heavy-handed, limiting the discretion and creativity lower-level employees have in performing their work. Furthermore, a climate that is too strong could indicate that employees are too homogeneous and therefore unable to respond to challenges in innovative ways, which could hurt organizational performance. More research exploring these issues is needed.

It is useful to note that research on strength, generically called research on dispersion models, has also begun to appear in other areas, most notably in leadership research on LMX (e.g., Henderson, Wayne, Shore, Bommer, & Tetrick, 2008; Nishii & Mayer, 2009) and transformational leadership (e.g., Cole & Bedeian, 2007; Spitzmuller & Ilies, 2010). Given the strong connections between leadership and climate, more research linking agreement about leadership and climate strength would be of interest. Finally, although researchers have started to focus more on the optimal approaches for measuring climate strength and other dispersion approaches (see Roberson, Sturman, & Simons, 2007), alternative approaches would be worth considering. For instance, Payne (2000) discussed using focus groups to determine the strength of consensus among employees about climate. A comparison of qualitative approaches along those lines with quantitative approaches that have become more typical in the literature might provide some insight about how employees perceive and experience climate strength in their organizations. As we said earlier, more research on these issues is warranted.

Summary. The study of climate strength has seen significant development over the past decade. After the 15–20 years of work on defending aggregation and striving to get dispersion low within units of analysis, climate researchers have looked back at the variance they tried to eliminate as a potential variable of interest. Some progress has been made in understanding some of the conditions under which variability will be high versus low (see Table 3.4), including in essence the consistency of the message sent within a unit about what is important there. However, there is a lack of good theory about when strength will behave as a moderator as it is frequently conceptualized to be. Perhaps the best explanation of failure for strength to be a moderator is that the variance in variability across units is too low when for a moderator to be significant, variability across the units being studied must be relatively high. Nevertheless, from a practical vantage point, it is clear that a positive and strong climate is usually superior to a weak climate—and definitely to a negative climate!

OTHER BOUNDARY CONDITIONS OF CLIMATE–OUTCOME RELATIONSHIPS

In addition to climate strength, researchers have also been interested in other potential moderators of the relationship between climate and outcomes. Although empirical research along these lines has not been common until the past 5–10 years, the idea that the effects of climate would vary depending on the situation is not new. Some of the clearest and most explicit early thinking along these lines was from Hellriegel and Slocum (1974), who described the issue this way:

> The evidence presented . . . suggests that most researchers have not specified the external environment impinging upon the subsystem, the type of technology, or the possible interactions of these variables on the individual's perceptions of his climate. Thus, one might expect the climate in subsystems with simple and static environments to be different from that in subsystems with dynamic and complex environments, and that the criteria for success operating in these two environments might be considerably different. An effective climate in a simple and static environment may prove to be dysfunctional in a dynamic and complex environment (p. 277).

In other words, the level of change and complexity in the organization's environment could act as a boundary condition or moderator for the effectiveness of climate, such that some climates will be more appropriate for certain environments than others.

Another example of thinking along these lines can be found in the service climate literature. Schneider (1994) suggested that the effectiveness of service climate vis-à-vis customer satisfaction will depend on the form of the service climate and its alignment with the organization's market segment. Thus, if the organization's service climate emphasizes fast and efficient service but customers expect high levels of personal warmth and customization and do not care about the speed of the service, then the climate will not be effective. Therefore, the market segment being served can act as a boundary condition on the effectiveness of a specific type of climate (e.g., a service climate) that has developed in the organization. Indeed, Schneider and Bowen (1995) suggested that the cafeteria style of service for restaurants would not be effective for all market segments—even though it is by far the most efficient way to feed many people in a short period.

In one of the first empirical studies of a climate's boundary conditions, Dietz, Pugh, and Wiley (2004) investigated whether the frequency of customer contact moderated the relationship between service climate and customer satisfaction. In a study of 160 bank branches, they showed that in branches where customers were more frequent visitors, the relationship between service climate and customer satisfaction was significantly more positive than in those branches where customers visited less frequently. In their research on grocery store departments, Mayer, Ehrhart, and Schneider (2009) found similar results to Dietz and colleagues (2004) by demonstrating that the level of direct customer contact across departments moderated the relationship between service climate and customer satisfaction. In addition, Mayer and colleagues (2009) investigated two other moderators: tangibility of the product and service employee interdependence. Their results revealed that service climate had a significantly stronger positive relationship with customer satisfaction when the product was less tangible (which increases the importance of the quality of the service provided and thus the service climate) and when the delivery of the service required more coordinated interaction among employees (which increases the importance for service climate to make sure all employees are on the same page and working together toward the same goal of delivering high quality service). Finally, in a sample of bank branches, Ehrhart, Witt, Schneider, and Perry (2011) examined internal service (provided to branch employees by corporate support units) as a moderator of the relationship between service climate and service quality, finding that branches with lower internal service showed weaker relationships between climate and service quality as compared to branches with higher internal service. They concluded that internal service "enables employees to provide service to external customers in the way they are motivated to deliver it by the service climate they experience" (p. 428).

In another example from research on strategic climates but in the domain of safety climate, Hofmann and Mark (2006) investigated the complexity of the patients' conditions as a moderator of the relationship between safety climate and safety outcomes in hospitals. They showed that safety climate was negatively related to nurses' back injuries and medication errors when patient complexity was high, but unrelated when complexity was low. There seems to be a link between the findings of this study and some of those on service climate described previously, in that services are more complex when there is more frequent customer contact, the product is less tangible, and more coordination is required. This emphasis on complexity fits well with what Gutek (1995, 2000) proposed happens in what she calls "service relationships." Service relationships are more complex because they are characterized by frequent contact, and frequent contact is associated with the purchase and delivery of less tangible services—and less tangible services may require a team to get it done well. Thus, one take-home message from this research is that strategic climates matter more when complexity is higher.

It is not only in the area of strategic climate that boundary conditions have been studied; there are several studies in the literature on process climates that have also investigated possible moderators of the effects of climate. For instance, we have already reviewed one study in the diversity climate literature earlier in this chapter along these lines; McKay and colleagues (2011) showed that there was a three-way interaction between diversity climate, service climate, and minority representation predicting customer satisfaction, such that the strongest effects for diversity climate were found when both service climate levels and minority representation were high. Several studies have also examined moderators of the effects of justice climate. Liao and Rupp's (2005) research on the cross-level relationship between justice climate and individual-level attitudes revealed that justice orientation (the extent to which individuals value justice and pay attention to fairness issues) was a moderator of the relationship between supervisor-focused procedural justice climate and supervisory commitment and satisfaction. In a similar cross-level study, Yang and colleagues (2007) demonstrated that work group power distance acted as a moderator of the relationship between procedural justice climate and individual level commitment and citizenship behavior, such that the effects of procedural justice climate were stronger when group power distance was low. In yet another cross-level study of justice climate, Spell and Arnold (2007) examined the relationship between two types of justice climate: procedural justice climate and distributive justice climate. In their conceptualization, procedural justice climate acted as a moderator of the relationship between distributive justice climate and individual-level depression and anxiety. Indeed, their results showed that a positive procedural justice climate buffered the potential negative effects of distributive justice climate. McKay and colleagues' (2011) and Spell and Arnold's (2007) studies are significant because they open the door to studying the interaction between various types of climate when predicting outcomes, an arena ripe for research because it is highly unusual for more than one kind of climate to be studied at any one time (Kuenzi & Schminke, 2009).

In summary, it is fair to say that the links between climate and outcomes, especially the links between focused climates and relevant outcomes, have reached a level of robustness such that the conditions under which those relationships are optimized have received increased conceptual and empirical attention. In addition, this attention has revealed that the direct relationships between climate and outcome have boundary conditions such that they are stronger under some conditions than under others. What is very interesting about these findings is that the conditions that maximize the relationship can be very useful to practitioners in (a) deciding when and when not to promote a specific climate of seeming interest, and (b) where to intervene to optimize the relationships of interest. In the former case, it becomes clear for example from the Dietz and colleagues' (2004) and the Mayer and colleagues' (2010) studies that when customer contact is high between servers and served, then a positive service climate is important for customer satisfaction. The practical advice follows: when customer contact is high and involves the close interaction of server and served to produce what Gutek (2000) would call a service relationship, then creating and maintaining a positive service climate makes sense. In contrast, when the product is very tangible and the interaction between the provider and customer is minimal, the return on investment on building a service climate may be low.

CLIMATE ITSELF AS A MODERATOR VARIABLE

Although research has begun to investigate various moderators of the relationship between climate and outcomes like customer satisfaction, early climate research was more likely to view climate itself as a moderator, usually of individual-level relationships. For instance, for Schneider and Bartlett (1968, 1970) individual performance was driven by both personal characteristics and the situation, but the emphasis amongst psychologists of all kinds including I/O psychologists at that time had been much more on the individual than on the situation. Therefore, they sought to test whether climate acted to facilitate (or inhibit) the expression of individual differences in work performance, the idea being that when climate facilitated the display of individual differences—i.e., when it was aligned with the individual characteristics necessary in a situation—then performance would be superior. Schneider (1975b) later referred to this possibility as a "climate for the display of individual differences" (p. 454) and suggested that some climates may allow the best employees to perform at their peak, thus increasing performance across the board. Subsequent empirical research by Schneider and his colleagues (Parkington & Schneider, 1979; Schneider & Bowen, 1985) could also be framed in a similar way, in that it was proposed that individual employees' service orientations would be related to role stress if those orientations were not aligned with perception of management's service orientation. This line of thinking is consistent with Mischel's (1968) concept of situational strength and his argument that personality would be most likely to predict behavior in situations that were relatively ambiguous or unstructured, or in other words, in what he called weak situations. Meyer, Dalal, and colleagues (Meyer & Dalal, 2009; Meyer, Dalal, & Hermida, 2010) have recently extended this research to the organizational research literature and have shown that conscientiousness is not as strongly related to performance when the situation (in terms of occupational norms) is strong (Meyer, Dalal, & Bonaccio, 2009).

Although empirical research on climate as a moderator of individual-level relationships is relatively rare, one recent example supporting this idea is a study of service climate by Grizzle, Zablah, Brown, Mowen, and Lee (2009) on a sample of employees in full-service restaurants. They found that the relationship between individual employees' customer orientation and their actual customer-oriented behaviors was moderated by service climate, such that they were significantly related when service climate was high but not when it was low. Grizzle and colleagues argued that when service climate levels are high, employees have the opportunity to act on their customer orientation when serving customers; in other words, the situation is strong for the display of those individual differences if they exist. When service climate levels are low, however, the environment limits the opportunities to act on one's customer orientation, weakening the relationship between customer orientation and behavior. The primary theme in studies taking this approach is that the context or environment plays a role in the degree to which individual characteristics have the opportunity to influence performance. When there is a fit (Parkington & Schneider, 1979; Schneider & Bowen, 1985) or synergy (Grizzle et al., 2009) between the individual and the environment, then the relationship between individual attributes and performance will be optimized.

Other researchers have examined climate as a moderator of the relationship between unit-level variables. Baer and Frese (2003) investigated the role that climate for initiative and climate for psychological safety played in the relationship between process innovation and firm effectiveness in 47 mid-sized German companies. They found strong support for their hypothesis that process innovation would be positively related to firm performance (in terms of goal achievement and return on assets) when climate for initiative and climate for psychological safety were high. In contrast, firms with high levels of process innovation but with low levels of climate for initiative or climate for psychological safety actually had worse performance than those firms who did not innovate at all. Two other studies we described in the diversity climate section are relevant here: McKay and colleagues' (2008) study of diversity climate as a moderator of racial-ethnic differences in sales performance, and McKay and colleagues' (2011) study of service climate and minority representation simultaneously moderating the relationship between diversity climate and customer satisfaction. As a final example, in a meta-analysis by Burke, Chan-Serafin, Salvador, Smith, and Sarpy (2008), safety climate was shown to moderate the relationship between safety training and injury and accidents such that safety training had a greater effect in reducing accidents in a positive safety climate.

Not frequently acknowledged in research on moderator (or interaction) effects is the notion that increased insights in the variables of interest (the predictors and the hypothesized moderators) may be obtained when reversing the role of these variables. That is, because the predictors and the hypothesized moderators are statistically equal in the quantitative analyses, the variables labeled as predictor and moderator can be switched, allowing for a different framing of the results. This notion can be applied to the studies just reviewed. For example, with regard to the findings by Baer and Frese (2003), reversing the predictor and moderator would lead to the conclusion that climate (for initiative or for psychological safety) has a strong positive relationship with firm performance when the level of innovation is high, but no relationship when innovation is low. Thus, similar to the studies described in the previous section on service climate, these particular climates appear to be more important for innovative companies than those that are not as innovative. The Burke and colleagues (2008) findings can also be re-interpreted in a similar way, such that safety climate has a stronger effect on safety outcomes when safety training is implemented in organizations. Thus, building a safety climate will make more of a difference in organizations that have the proper supports in place to ensure that employees have the knowledge and skills they need to actually put into practice the strategic goals being promoted by top management.

Thus, we have begun to think about research in which climate itself is studied as a moderator as no different from research in which moderators of the relationship between climate and outcomes are investigated. Therefore, in the previous section of the chapter, customer contact was studied as a moderator of the climate–customer satisfaction relationship with positive findings. It turns out, using our logic here, that those same findings also revealed that the relationship between customer contact and customer satisfaction is moderated by the service climate such that high customer contact yields customer satisfaction most when a positive service climate exists. That finding cautions organizations desiring more traffic to be very careful about what they wish for because increasing traffic will only pay off for them when they improve service climate!

ADDITIONAL APPROACHES TO STUDYING CLIMATE: ANTECEDENTS AND MEDIATORS

The last several sections have focused on moderated effects (either of climate's relationship with outcomes or with climate itself as the moderator), but before wrapping up this chapter we want to emphasize some of the other ways climate has typically been studied, specifically with regard to antecedents of climate and how climate mediates the effects of other variables on organizational effectiveness, as well as how other variables may mediate climate's effects on outcomes.

Leadership and climate. As we found when reviewing the history of the climate literature in the previous chapter, the earliest conceptualizations of climate by organizational scholars were focused on how climate influences organizational effectiveness. One theme that received a particularly heavy emphasis in those early years was that leaders are crucial to the development and maintenance of organizational climate. In effect, the proposal was that the effect leaders have through their behavior on unit effectiveness was mediated by the climates those behaviors created in their units. For Lewin and colleagues (1939), it was the democratic/participative style of the leader that created a social climate in the boys' groups, and this climate then led to the boys' behavior in terms of cooperation, smiling, and positive attitudes. For Fleishman (1953) it was the foreman's boss who created a leadership climate based on his expectations of the foreman; that climate then was the primary driver of the foreman's behavior and his unit's effectiveness. McGregor

(1960) viewed leaders as creating managerial climates for their relationships with subordinates based on their Theory X or Theory Y philosophy. These managerial climates then affected employees' goal accomplishment and satisfaction. Even though Likert (1961) did not use the term climate, he did discuss how leaders create an atmosphere within which all of the group's activities took place and which served as both a source of support and a basis for the group's goal accomplishment efforts. As a final example, in Litwin and Stringer's (1968) experimental study of leadership climate, leader behavior was manipulated to produce certain climates within the simulated work groups, which subsequently affected the group's satisfaction, innovation, and productivity.

Given this early emphasis on leadership in the climate literature, it is somewhat surprising to find that the role of leaders in creating climate has not received more research attention. Despite the fact that researchers like Kozlowski and Doherty (1989) were expressing the need for more theoretical and empirical attention to the linkages between leadership and climate in the late 1980s, almost 20 years later Zohar and Tenne-Gazit (2008) declared that "the notion of leadership as a climate antecedent has hardly changed over the past 50 years . . . although this has resulted in limited empirical work" (p. 745).

Nevertheless, there are several exceptions, and the literature on leadership and climate has developed in recent years from a number of different perspectives. Some examples include transformational leadership as an antecedent to safety climate (Zohar, 2002; Zohar & Tenne-Gazit, 2008), leader goal orientation as an antecedent to the goal-oriented climate in work groups (Dragoni, 2005), servant leadership as an antecedent to procedural justice climate and subsequently unit-level organizational citizenship behavior (Ehrhart, 2004), and management support as an antecedent of the climate for technology implementation (Klein, Conn, & Sorra, 2001). Although most studies tend to focus on leader behavior, some studies have also included the role of leader personality. Salvaggio, Schneider, Nishii, Mayer, Ramesh, and Lyon (2007) showed that the relationship between managers' core self-evaluations and the service climate in their units was fully mediated by the managers' service orientation. In addition, Mayer, Nishii, Schneider, and Goldstein (2007) investigated the influence of leaders' Big Five personality attributes on the procedural justice climates of their units, showing that leaders who are higher on Agreeableness and Conscientiousness and lower on Neuroticism would create more positive procedural justice climates. That such little research exists exploring the role of personality and climate is surprising given the findings by Holland (1997) on the role of personality and interests in creating unique environments across different occupational types.

One trend in the literature has been to adopt a focused leadership approach to couple with the focused climate of interest. In other words, if we want to best understand how a climate is created that sends a message to employees about the importance of a specific strategic imperative, then perhaps it is most useful to explore the behaviors performed by leaders that are also focused on communicating the importance of that specific strategic imperative. Research along these lines includes Schneider and colleagues' (2005) study of service leadership as a proximal antecedent to service climate, and Barling, Loughlin, and Kelloway's (2002) research on safety-specific transformational leadership as a proximal antecedent to safety climate. One possibility that emerges from research from this perspective is that perhaps focused leadership is needed for building a focused climate, whereas generic (or molar) leadership may be more influential in influencing the more general climate for well-being (or molar climate) experienced by employees. Including all of these issues simultaneously in one study would be an interesting extension of research on the relationship between leadership and climate.

The explanations given for why leadership has an effect on organizational climate also sheds some light on the distinction between the general and focused approaches to leadership and climate. When discussing general leadership, the focus is usually on such issues as the leader's concern for their subordinate's well-being, the prioritization of subordinate concerns, increased levels of communication, and consistency of behavior (e.g., Ehrhart, 2004; Zohar, 2002; Zohar & Tenne-Gazit, 2008). These issues are often characterized as increasing the social exchange relationship between leaders and subordinates and the motivation for subordinates to support the leader's values and priorities. However, leadership that is more specifically focused is then needed to communicate to subordinates where their increased motivation should be targeted. Leaders do this by explicitly stating their goals and priorities, role modeling the behaviors they expect subordinates to perform, and reinforcing the desired behaviors of subordinates through rewards and recognition (e.g., Barling et al., 2002; Dragoni, 2005; Schneider et al., 2005). Hong and colleagues' (2013) meta-analysis on service climate suggests that although both general and focused leadership are important predictors of climate, the effects of focused leadership are stronger, likely because of their immediate link to the content of the focused climate.

One issue that has not received much attention is how the role of leadership changes across levels of the organization. There is literature in several areas that points to the differences in leadership across organizational levels. For instance, research has shown that the types of skills required of leaders change as they move up the organizational hierarchy (Mumford, Marks, Connelly, Zaccaro, & Reiter-Palmon, 2000). Shamir (1995) has described how charismatic leadership differs depending on whether the leader is up close (e.g., an immediate supervisor) versus at a distance (e.g., the CEO). Furthermore, there is an entire literature on executive leadership that focuses specifically on leadership at the highest levels of the organization (e.g., Zaccaro, 2001). Researchers have discussed trickle-down or domino effects for leadership in organizations, such that the leadership styles of higher level leaders influences those of lower-level leaders (Bass, Waldman, Avolio, & Bebb, 1987; Mayer, Kuenzi, Greenbaum, Bardes, & Salvador, 2009). In the climate literature, the best example of research that addresses this issue of research across levels is Zohar and Luria (2005). They asserted that because direct supervisors provide frequent and immediate outcomes to subordinates, that they play a more proximal role in the development of climate at the work group level and have more of an effect on employee safety behavior than upper-level management. What they suggest is that the actions that affect employees' perceptions of an organization's overall climate are different in focus and immediacy from the issues that affect employees' perceptions of the climate of their more immediate work group. In turn, the behaviors performed by management to create climates at each of these levels likely differ, yet such differences have not been clarified well in the literature.

Additional antecedents of climate: Foundation issues. In addition to the research on the effects of leadership on climate and the mediated effects of leadership through climate on various organizational processes or outcomes, climate researchers have investigated other antecedents of climate and their potential effects on organizational effectiveness through their relationships with climate. As we described previously, a frequent approach of this sort combines the concept of molar climate with focused climates. In this approach, the generic (or molar) climate is conceptualized as a foundation on which the focused climate can be built and the focused climate is the proximal correlate of the focused outcome of interest and thus the mediator between the generic climate and the outcome. Schneider and colleagues (1998) called the generic climate "work facilitation" and proposed that work facilitation does not *cause* the service climate but provides a foundation on which such a climate can be built. Salanova, Agut, and Peiró (2005) used a similar approach to show that service climate fully mediated the effects of organizational resources and work engagement on employee performance and customer loyalty. With a focus on safety Wallace, Popp, and Mondore (2006) conceptualized and assessed two "foundation climates," managerial support and organizational rewards, and showed how they were only indirectly related to occupational accidents through their relationships with safety climate.

The theory and research surrounding generic, foundation, work facilitation, or worker well-being climates are important for a number of reasons. Theoretically, they provide one possible explanation for the inconsistency found in the validity of climate–outcome relationships before the more focused approach existed. That is, there exists variability in validity for molar climate approaches, but when combined with a focused climate perspective, the variability may be more easily understood by considering molar climate as a more distal predictor that has its effect on outcomes through the mediator of focused climate. Practically, this is important because it clearly suggests that just implementing a molar climate (e.g., for well-being) is not likely to have the intended effect unless the more focused strategic climate is also in place. The paradox is that the more strategically focused climate is not likely to be in place if the foundation issues associated with the molar climate are not there first!

We may conclude that both kinds of climate are needed as they support and focus each other.

Mediators of climate's effects on outcomes. Another way to discuss climate and mediated effects is to focus on what variables help explain the relationship between climate and outcomes. At the most basic level, the idea behind studying climate is that the psychological context employees experience sends the message for the kinds of behaviors required by the system to meet established goals and objectives. The problem is that there is scant research on the behavior! That is, even when validity evidence for climate is strong, it is validity for the climate predicting outcomes and not climate predicting behavior. In one exception, Schneider and colleagues (2005) proposed and found service-oriented organizational citizenship behavior (OCB) performed by employees mediates the relationship between service climate and customer satisfaction. Neal and Griffin (2006), in an even more sophisticated effort using a multiple mediator longitudinal design, showed that safety climate was positively related to safety motivation, safety motivation was positively related to safety behavior, and safety behavior was negatively related to accidents. As a final example, Klein and colleagues (2001) found that the relationship between implementation climate and innovation effectiveness was mediated by implementation effectiveness. In other words, the way that implementation climate influenced the overall effectiveness of the innovation being implemented was through employee implementation behaviors.

Ehrhart and Raver (in press) provide an in-depth discussion of how unit-level behavior plays a critical role in explaining how organizational climate (as well as culture) has its effects on organizational performance. Their review focuses not only on productive behaviors (like OCB), but also counterproductive behaviors, in addition to highlighting the role of motivation in explaining climate's effects and the importance of establishing behavioral norms to ensure that the behavior is institutionalized and thus more likely to continue to be performed in the future. More research is needed to clarify the role of motivation, behavior, and norms in mediating climate's effect on organizational effectiveness.

SUMMARY AND CONCLUSIONS

We have covered considerable territory in this chapter to bring readers up to date on where the field is at present. In addition, the current state of theory and research on organizational climate may certainly be classified as healthy. Some lingering issues have been resolved (aggregation and levels of analysis) to the extent that researchers are now looking at *lack* of consensus as a variable in its own right (via a focus on climate strength). We have a definition of organizational climate that integrates across the many themes that have characterized that work:

> *Organizational climate is the shared meaning organizational members attach to the events, policies, practices, and procedures they experience and the behaviors they see being rewarded, supported, and expected.*

This definition is reflected in the kinds of measures that have been developed for assessing climate in that the focus on things that happen in a setting (e.g., policies, rewards) has resulted in climate measures being more descriptive than evaluative or affective. In addition, from a levels of analysis perspective, it is clear from the definition that our focus is on shared meaning and not individual personal experiences (or psychological climate).

The primary approaches to studying organizational climate are the molar climate and focused climate approaches. The molar climate approach, which generically assesses a climate for well-being, is perhaps most useful when conceptualized as a foundation for the more strategically focused climates that have been shown to yield validity when studied against appropriately specific outcomes. Our detailed review of two examples of strategically focused outcome climates—service and safety—and two more process-oriented climates—justice and fairness—revealed that a climate conceptualization of important issues in organizations can be useful, providing insight into the numerous activities that occur in settings, the shared experience of those activities that people have, and the climate—the gestalt—they infer with regard to what those experiences mean.

There has been growing interest among climate researchers on the topic of climate strength. The paradox concerning research on climate strength is that researchers spent decades trying to eliminate variance within work units in climate perceptions and now we are going back to study the differences in variance across settings for the role such differences play. This role has been mostly conceptualized and studied as a moderator of climate level–outcome relationships, but it has also received some attention as a main effect. Some other boundary conditions of the climate–outcome relationship were also identified (e.g., customer contact as a moderator of the service climate–customer satisfaction link) but more research on such possible moderators is surely needed. Indeed more research on climate as a moderator of important other relationships is also needed.

We began this summary and conclusion with the thought that climate research is quite healthy, but we close with the thought that it is not time to be sanguine. All of the research we reviewed was done using surveys and, while such work is useful to be sure, there is little published climate literature using case/qualitative methods. We emphasize the word "published" because we know that case methods are very often used by practitioners and we wish/hope more of that would be published. Such methods would help link the climate approach to the culture approach and that would be a desirable outcome.

The arena most in need of attention in the future in our estimation is one identified so clearly by Kuenzi and Schminke (2009) in their extensive review: the need to study multiple climates simultaneously. We still do not know much about what happens when there is conflict between climates (Frederiksen et al., 1972; Schein, 1965; Zohar & Hofmann, 2012)—say a climate for safety and a climate for productivity—but we need to conceptualize the issue and study it, perhaps using qualitative methods as an introduction to what the issues are. Such methods will be discussed in more detail in the next section of the book on organizational culture.

CHAPTER

4

Foundations of Organizational Culture

In this chapter, we first present a brief review of the history of organizational culture research and then discuss: (1) various ways of conceptualizing and understanding organizational culture, (2) defining organizational culture, and (3) the methods used to study it. In the next chapter, we will continue with (1) how culture is thought to develop and is perpetuated, (2) how it is manifested, and (3) the degree to which assessments of culture are associated with organizational effectiveness. Before moving forward, it is important to provide some clarity on the scope of what we are trying to accomplish in these chapters. We decided to adopt a somewhat different approach for covering the literature on organizational culture than the one used for reviewing organizational climate. With climate, we heavily emphasized the history of the evolution and study of the construct and how that history has affected the way it is studied by researchers today. It was important to deal with the history of the climate construct because that history has not received the level of detailed attention that is necessary to fully understand where the research has taken us—and its continuing controversies and issues. In contrast, the history of the organizational culture construct has been much more thoroughly documented elsewhere (for example, see Alvesson & Berg, 1992; Ashkanasy, Wilderom, & Peterson, 2000b; Martin & Frost, 1996; Ouchi & Wilkins, 1985; Pettigrew, 1979; Smircich & Calas, 1987; Trice & Beyer, 1993). Therefore, we focus a bit less attention on the history of organizational culture and more on the various issues that characterize research in the area.

In what follows, we primarily focus on the literature in organizational behavior and industrial/organizational psychology, based on our own backgrounds in those areas, and do not attempt to provide the perspective from other disciplines, such as anthropology, sociology, or communication. In addition, given our emphasis on the relevance of the topics of organizational culture and climate for organizational effectiveness, we tend to focus on those issues that seem to have the most immediate practical import for organizations, which means we do not explore in depth some of the more philosophical debates on organizational culture (e.g., Martin, Frost, & O'Neill, 2006). Finally, the study of culture in organizations could be seen as a subset of the more general literature on culture, but that broader literature is outside the scope of this book; see the sources we cited above for more depth on the roots of the organizational culture literature. In short, although we acknowledge the depth and breadth of the literature on organizational culture, as we mentioned in Chapter One, our goal is not to provide an exhaustive review of that literature but rather provide a focused discussion of the relevant theory and research on the construct.

A BRIEF HISTORY OF RESEARCH ON ORGANIZATIONAL CULTURE

Pettigrew's (1979) article in *Administrative Science Quarterly* is the most commonly attributed starting point of contemporary organizational culture research because of the immediate effect it had at the time he presented it. Pettigrew, of course, was not the first to suggest that the concept of culture could be applied to organizations (Alvesson & Berg, 1992; Trice & Beyer, 1993). Prominent earlier examples of such application include research conducted as part of the Hawthorne studies on the influence of social relations on worker behavior (Roethlisberger & Dickson, 1939), Whyte's (1943, 1948) summaries of a Boston slum and the restaurant industry (respectively), Gardner's (1945) textbook applying a cultural perspective to organizations, the *Tavistock School* including Jaque's (1951) description of how social relations affected productivity at Glacier Metal Works, Selznick's (1957) concept of organizational character along with other work from the institutionalist school, Clark's (1970, 1972) research on the importance of organizational sagas in the historical development of a college, and Turner's (1971) book on organizations as microcultures.

There are three interlocking reasons why Pettigrew's (1979) article was so effective and stimulated so much interest in the topic of organizational culture. First, his presentation explicitly drew on anthropological concepts and methods, providing organizational researchers who for the most part were not already familiar with that field with an introduction to it and a demonstration of how it could be applied to the study of organizations. Second, the study of organizations was entering an unprecedented stage of growth and development in business schools in particular. Following the 1959 Carnegie Foundation's conclusion in their study of business schools that the failure to teach more about human behavior, especially leadership, was a disservice to students, there was a quick growth in such courses and research in these schools. As a result, by the late 1970s, the study of organizational behavior was not only commonly accepted, but also advancing rapidly. Third, management consultants had discovered the importance of studying whole organizations and the ways they were experienced by the people in them. Thus, a number of consulting firms were already well under way in their studies of these behavioral issues in organizations (e.g., Peters & Waterman, 1982) when Pettigrew's article appeared. In short, and tying these three reasons together, the article was an academically interesting cross-disciplinary application to a receptive emerging emphasis on people in business schools and to the world of business.

For the purposes of this book, it is imperative to highlight some of the overlap between the histories of organizational climate and culture in the I/O psychology and organizational behavior literatures as introduced in Chapter Two. Several critical early climate articles also discussed organizational culture. For instance, Fleishman (1953) used the term "culture" to refer to the broader environment or social situation and seemed to be primarily referring to the general norms for appropriate behavior that existed in the organization. Argyris (1957) also seemed to equate culture with behavioral norms, but rather than culture being the more general construct, he viewed climate as encompassing both the formal structures of the organization and what he called the "informal culture." Gilmer (1961, 1966) generally focused on climate, and when he did discuss culture, it was equated with climate. Unlike most climate literature, however, he included as part of climate artifacts such as the way managers dress and the cars they drive—artifacts that would now clearly be indicators of culture (Schein, 2010). When attempting to behaviorally define the concept of climate, Evan (1968) contrasted it with organizational culture, which he defined as "the set of beliefs, values, and norms that constitute blueprints for behavior" (p. 108)—not very different from the typical contemporary conceptualization of organizational culture, as we will see shortly. Evan concluded that culture was much broader relative to the concept of climate that was his focus. Finally, although they did not specifically mention culture, Litwin and Stringer (1968) referred to concepts usually associated with culture (history and tradition) or at least artifacts of culture (spatial arrangements) as having their influence on worker motivation and behavior through climate. In addition, they described climate as having nonrational components that may be out of the conscious awareness of workers, much like contemporary culture researchers (e.g., Schein, 2010) refer to the deepest layers of culture (e.g., underlying assumptions).

Other authors from the 1960s and 1970s that were more generally concerned with the role of the environment in organizations also suggested the importance of organizational culture (or related concepts). For example, in Gellerman's (1960) description of "company personality," the term could easily have been replaced with "organizational culture." He noted how management's attitudes "give the company a distinct atmosphere and philosophy of its own, making it a different kind of place to work in than any other company" (p. 73). He described the company personality as including traditions and assumptions that are rarely questioned or even put into words, as being unique, having a strong emotional element, and providing the unwritten guidelines for evaluating effectiveness. Furthermore, he discussed how executives who do not fit the company personality leave, how programs that do not fit with or that attempt to change the organization's personality are abandoned, and how outmoded or inefficient methods continued to be used because they are tied to the organization's personality.

Another example comes from Likert (1961); although he did not use the term "culture" specifically when discussing System 4 Management, he did discuss at the work group level the effect of the group's values, the stability of its values, and the effect of the group's behavioral norms on the behavior of group members. Schein's (1965) book on *Organizational Psychology* foreshadowed many concepts that would be central to his later (1985) model of organizational culture. For instance, he described how leaders must adapt to their group's norms, history, and tradition to be successful, how socialization practices vary across types of organizations, and how values and norms form the core of an organization's identity and must be effectively communicated by leadership. Finally, Katz and Kahn (1966, 1978) included many elements associated with organizational culture to describe the social situation in organizations, including norms, values, subcultures, taboos, folkways, and mores, and emphasized how the distinctive feeling of a group and its beliefs are passed on to new members (i.e., through socialization). They also described how the formal structures in organizations are reinterpreted by organizational members into informal structures—what we would refer to as culture—and how conflicts between these two (formal and informal structures) can be problematic for organizations. When discussing the role of the work group in organization change, they specifically focused on the idea that change is more effective when the group as a whole and its norms are addressed and not just individuals; in other words, the organization's culture must be accounted for when attempting change.

Against this backdrop, Pettigrew's (1979) article pushed the construct of organizational culture to the forefront, "legitimizing the very concept of organization culture for the first time" (Alvesson & Berg, 1992, p. 15) and showing how the concepts of beliefs, ideology, language, ritual, and myth could be applied to the study of organizations. His article, which described a longitudinal investigation of a British private boarding school, opened the way for the study of the symbolic in organizational research, viewing "man as a *creator* and *manager* of *meaning*" (p. 572, italics in original). He emphasized that beyond the rational and instrumental side of organizational life, an organization's culture is the "expressive social tissue around us that gives those tasks meaning. . . . Culture is the system of such publicly and collectively accepted meanings operating for a given group at a given time" (p. 574). This emphasis on the expressive and the symbolic had a great attraction for organizational researchers tired of the emphasis on rational, bureaucratic models (Trice & Beyer, 1993).

Pettigrew made several other important points that are worth highlighting. One is that he did not view culture as a unitary concept, but as a collection of concepts including "symbol, language, ideology, belief, ritual, and myth" (p. 574). This view has implications for any research conclusions on the entirety of an organization's culture, as opposed to more limited aspects of it. Another point is that Pettigrew viewed culture as evolving over time; as organizational members address the problems they face, the culture influences or constrains their actions, but the culture is also influenced by their actions. Thus, "man creates culture and culture creates man" (p. 577). A final point is that Pettigrew was concerned with the functional role of culture in terms of integration, control, and commitment, and particularly highlighted the role of the "entrepreneur" or founder in gaining commitment and creating behavioral norms through the communication of the leader's vision. Although it was not a focus in his 1979 article, Pettigrew later communicated his concern for the relationships among culture, strategy, and change in his edited book *The Management of Strategic Change* (1987b), noting in the introduction his interest in understanding the role of the "inner context" of organizations in strategic competitiveness (Pettigrew, 1987a). We will have more to say on the relationship between culture, strategy, and change later.

After the publication of Pettigrew's (1979) article, the literature on organizational culture greatly expanded among both academics and practitioners. Multiple causes have been identified for the rapid ascent and widespread popularity of the concept. Alvesson and Berg (1992) placed those causes into three general categories: the general societal and business context at the time, the effective marketing of organizational culture by both academics and consultants, and the dissatisfaction among some academics with more traditional perspectives on organizations. From an economic or business perspective, the US economy struggled throughout the 1970s, while at the same time Japan ascended as an economic force based on a very different model of business and management than the US. As a result, some of the most influential books about culture specifically addressed the challenge from Japan with such titles as *Theory Z: How American Business Can Meet the Japanese Challenge* (Ouchi, 1981) and *The Art of Japanese Management: Applications for American Executives* (Pascale & Athos, 1982). More generally, changes in technology resulted in increased rates of change and new organizational forms in organizations, and the shift in the US from a manufacturing economy to a service economy created a need to focus more on organizational culture both as a social glue to keep the organization focused on its core values and a control mechanism to ensure high levels of quality (Alvesson, 1993; Alvesson & Berg, 1992). As a society, the general cultural fragmentation and weakening of the nuclear family in the US moved individuals to look to their workplace as a source of meaning, identity, and community (Alvesson & Berg, 1992; Frost, Moore, Louis, Lundberg, & Martin, 1985a).

Against this backdrop, the timing for the message of "pop management" books on culture was perfect. There were four books (Deal & Kennedy, 1982; Ouchi, 1981; Pascale & Athos, 1982; Peters and Waterman, 1982) that were published in the US within just a couple of years that are most commonly cited as being particularly influential in marketing the concept of organizational culture and its implications for organizations (Alvesson & Berg, 1992; Trice & Beyer, 1993). Perhaps the most popular of them was Peters and Waterman's (1982) *In Search of Excellence: Lessons from American's Best-Run Companies*. Their book summarized research on the attributes that distinguished 62 "excellent" companies, which they defined as "continuously innovative big companies" (p. 13), from less excellent companies. Among other findings, they emphasized the need for a strong culture that was externally oriented to be adaptable to the organization's environment. Two of the other books, both of which were mentioned above, focused on how US companies could learn from Japanese management practices. Ouchi (1981) advocated for a specific, "clan" culture, characterized by trust, long-term employment, and close personal relationships, that he found evidence of in Japan. Pascale and Athos (1982) focused on the McKinsey 7-S framework (strategy, structure, systems, staff, style, skills, and superordinate goals) that they had developed with Peters and Waterman, and isolated four of those (the "soft" dimensions of skills, style, staff, and superordinate goals) for which the contrast between American and Japanese management was most clear and thus where the focus of American managers was most needed. The final book in this set of four was by Deal and Kennedy (1982). Interestingly it was the only one of them that was explicitly a book on organizational culture, with the title *Corporate Cultures: The Rites and Rituals of Corporate Life*. They made the case for strong culture as the critical factor for organizational success and outlined how managers can diagnose, manage, and change their company's culture.

One common thread among these books was their emphasis on the symbolic aspects of organizational life and the importance of creating shared values throughout all levels of the organization. Furthermore, they argued that if organizational leadership managed these elements effectively, then the organization's culture could be a source of competitive advantage, differentiating it from its competitors and resulting in improved organizational effectiveness and productivity. The effect was swift, and attention to and discussion of cultural issues became the norm both in organizational management and in the business media (Trice & Beyer, 1993).

The academic interest in organizational culture mirrored the interest among practitioners. Part of this interest was because it had become so popular among practitioners, and thus those academics who wanted to be relevant to business or who viewed themselves as serving the needs of management for knowledge and insight (who Alvesson & Berg, 1992, referred to as academic pragmatics) shifted their focus to the topic as well. For others, organizational culture garnered interest because it offered a way to bridge the micro and macro levels of organizational behavior and strategic management (Alvesson, 2002). For still others, the interest in culture grew out of dissatisfaction with the dominant positivist paradigm in organizational research (at least in the US and the UK) that emphasized the structural and objective aspects of organizational life, usually studied with quantitative methods summarized in "sterile" (Trice & Beyer, 1993, p. 31) research reports. Culture, in contrast, opened the door to the qualitative study of the expressive side of organizational life, the "drama, excitement, and high emotion that characterizes much of what happens daily in organizations" (Trice & Beyer, 1993, p. 31). Meyerson (1991b) described it this way: ". . . culture was the code word for the subjective side of organizational life . . . its study represented an ontological rebellion against the dominant functionalist or 'scientific' paradigm" (p. 256). Ashkanasy and colleagues (2000b) linked the rise of organizational culture with distaste for what some organizational scholars saw as an infatuation with technical minutiae in the climate literature, and the inability of climate to adequately represent the depth and richness of organizational life and its many manifestations and influences. Of course, part of what Ashkanasy and colleagues were referring to was that the climate literature of the late 1970s and through the middle 1980s was dominated by measurement-oriented psychologists, whereas the study of culture integrated the field of cultural anthropology with organizational studies, appealing to a broader audience across multiple fields (e.g., sociology, organizational theory, anthropology). As a result, the study of organizational culture was a dominant theme of the 1980s and much of the 1990s, whereas the construct of organizational climate received relatively less attention.

Examples of the extent of the interest in organizational culture throughout the 1980s have been well documented by Trice and Beyer (1993) and include five conferences on culture-related issues in a year and half across 1983 and 1984, three books based on the proceedings of those conferences (e.g., Frost, Moore, Louis, Lundberg, & Martin, 1985b), four special issues on culture in various journals (e.g., *Administrative Science Quarterly* and *Organizational Dynamics* in 1983), two organizational culture textbooks published in 1985 (Sathe, 1985; Schein, 1985), multiple other books and edited books in the years following (e.g., Frost, Moore, Louis, Lundberg, & Martin, 1991; Ott, 1989), the establishment of the Standing Committee on Organizational Symbolism in 1980, 19 doctoral dissertations on culture between 1980 and 1985, and the publication of more than 400 articles between 1979 and 1981 with the word "myth" in the title or abstract.

In addition to a focus on organizational culture itself, much of the discussion/debate during this time (and perhaps even to this day) was on how culture should be studied from both theoretical and methodological perspectives. Martin, Frost, and O'Neill (2006) summarized three primary debates: (1) between those advocating the study of culture as an over-arching, all-inclusive organizational construct versus those emphasizing the presence of multiple cultures/sub cultures in organizations (and later, versus those focusing on the ambiguity and inconsistency in culture); (2) between those using quantitative methods to study culture and those using qualitative methods; and (3) between those who studied organizational culture as a way to improve managerial and organizational effectiveness (managerialists) and those interested in advocating for workers at the bottom of the organizational hierarchy who they viewed as being controlled and manipulated by management (critical theorists). We explore many of these issues in detail in subsequent sections, but the point for now is that organizational culture was a hot topic during the 1980s and well into the 1990s, with many heated debates and strong stances taken on a variety of positions, creating a vibrant yet fragmented landscape. For some, like Miner (2002), these debates resulted in a "state of chaos" where "stridency of protestation becomes the major criterion for fleeting acceptance" (p. 613). Others, like Alvesson and Berg (1992), viewed this "chaos" in a more positive way, concluding that "the multitude of perspectives, definitions and theories existing in the field, and the loose coupling of these concepts to each other, is a strong theoretical advantage when it comes to research on cultural phenomena in organizations. In fact, culture is as rich as life itself, and simply reducing it to a rigid framework or precise and absolute definitions would seriously reduce its inborn complexity" (p. 48).

Somewhere around the late 1990s or early 2000s, a shift seems to have occurred in organizational culture research. It is not that organizational culture was suddenly viewed as inconsequential or uninteresting. Instead, as noted by Alvesson (2011), "Culture has become firmly anchored as one important aspect of, or element in, organizations and management. It is therefore viewed as a cornerstone in any broad understanding of organization and management" (p. 12). The problem, some asserted, was that it had perhaps become too mainstream and too routinized. As Martin and colleagues (2006) described it, "Culture has become a part of the hegemony within organizational theory and practice. This quixotic victory had the paradoxical effect of 'deaden-ing' culture's effect on open inquiry" (p. 744). Thus, although no one would say the concept of organizational culture was irrelevant, fewer academics were making it the primary focus of their research, perhaps because they had "run out of steam and fresh conversation topics or arguments around organizational culture" (Alvesson, 2011, p. 11). Relevant for this book, Alvesson (2011) compared the fall of interest in climate in the 1980s due to the popularity in culture with the more recent fall of interest in culture due to the popularity of the allied topics of identity (e.g., Whetten, 2006) and discourse analysis (e.g., Phillips & Hardy, 2002). As a side note, this shift away from a primary focus on organizational culture occurred at the same time that there was a considerable renewal of interest in the field of organizational climate, with more than three times as many articles on climate published in top management journals between 2000 and 2008 as there were in the 1990s (Kuenzi & Schminke, 2009).

APPROACHES TO UNDERSTANDING ORGANIZATIONAL CULTURE

Having briefly summarized from whence cometh the contemporary thinking and research on organizational culture, it is tempting to jump directly into how culture has been defined. However, the definitions do not make much sense without having a full understanding of the different ways researchers have conceptualized and understood the concept. In addition, obviously, how culture is understood will interact with how it is studied. Thus, we follow our overview of history in the last section with discussions of approaches to understanding organizational culture, definitions of organizational culture, and methods for studying organizational culture in this and the following sections.

At the most general level, perhaps the best way to distinguish approaches to understanding or conceptualizing culture is to contrast those that focus on culture as something organizations *have* versus those that describe culture as something organizations *are* (Smircich, 1983). From the "organizations have cultures" perspective (or the objectivist-functionalist view; Alvesson, 1993), researchers view culture as an organizational variable or attribute that is affected by and affects other organizational variables. The interest is usually functionalist, trying to understand how culture is linked to outcomes and effectiveness and thus how it can be changed to make the organization more efficient and more productive (Davey & Symon, 2001). Alvesson (1993) described this approach in terms of its technical interest, such that the goal is the development of understanding and knowledge of causal relationships to manipulate or control them to achieve desired outcomes (see also O'Reilly & Chatman, 1996). In this approach, organizational culture is often described in terms of its usefulness for achieving high levels of employee commitment and communicating the values of management so employees will be more likely to perform the behaviors that will be optimal for achieving organizational goals (Alvesson, 2002).

In contrast, from the "organizations are cultures" perspective (or the subjectivist-interpretive view; Alvesson, 1993), the researcher's goal is to understand, to "discover what being part of an organization means to people and the processes by which it is understood and enacted" (Davey & Symon, 2001, p. 124). Cameron and Ettington (1988) described the goal of this perspective as illuminating "nonrational, taken-for-granted, underlying assumptions that drive organizational behavior and the shared interpretive schemas of organizational members" (pp. 365–366). Culture, from this perspective, is a root metaphor (Smircich, 1983), such that "organizational culture is not just another piece of the puzzle, it is the puzzle" (Pacanowsky & O'Donnell-Trujillo, 1983, p. 146). The interest of researchers operating from this perspective is usually practical-hermeneutic (describing and understanding how meaning is created in organizations) or emancipatory (critically analyzing those aspects of organizations that limit personal autonomy; Alvesson, 2002). Symbolism often takes a central role in research from this perspective, as researchers attempt to understand the symbolic meaning organizational members draw from the rituals, myths, stories, and legends they encounter in organizational life (Alvesson, 2002; Frost et al., 1985a).

Another highly cited scheme for classifying different ways to understand culture is Martin's (1992, 2002) framework in which she distinguishes among the integration, differentiation, and fragmentation perspectives. In integration studies, researchers emphasize organization-wide consensus, clarity, and consistency among various cultural manifestations, and ignore conflict and ambiguity within the organization. Martin (2002) observed that integration studies tend to focus on managerial or professional employees and not lower-level employees, and tend to emphasize that even when conflict or ambiguity may appear at more superficial levels, consensus can be found at deeper levels (e.g., assumptions). According to Martin, when conflict or ambiguity are encountered or described in integration studies, they are viewed as a problem or shortfall that requires fixing to restore consistency. The second perspective on organizational culture identified by Martin is differentiation, in which inconsistent interpretations of cultural phenomena are emphasized because they represent the real world of organizations and are not just in need of fixing. Inconsistency across occupational, functional, and/or level subcultures is often the focus, but the subcultures are viewed as having consensus within themselves. Conflict among subcultures is often, but not necessarily, the focus of differentiation studies; however, subcultures can also be viewed as mutually reinforcing or independent. Martin's (2002) final perspective is the fragmentation perspective, in which ambiguity is the primary focus. Ambiguity is embraced and viewed as a normal part of organizational life. Fragmentation studies often focus on irony, paradox, and tension, and include multiple perspectives that can change across time and emerge in unknown ways and for unknown reasons. Although the differentiation perspective also allows for the possibility of conflict, ambiguity in that perspective is viewed as a byproduct of differences among subcultures.

Martin's framework is useful, although there appears to have been some confusion about whether these different perspectives represent different lenses to view an organization's culture or whether they are culture types, such that some organizational cultures are integrated, others are differentiated, and others are fragmented. Another issue and possible point of contention is that Martin wrote about the integration perspective in ways that often seem as though she is establishing a straw man to be shot down to extol the virtues of the other two perspectives. To be fair, Martin was transparent about how she found it "very difficult to present the integration view in an even-handed way" (p. 121). The most controversial aspect of Martin's framework, however, is the fragmentation perspective. Multiple authors (e.g., Alvesson, 1993; Alvesson, 2002; Payne, 2001; Schein, 1991; Trice, 1991) have questioned whether "the essence of any culture is pervasive ambiguity" (Martin et al., 2006, p. 732). Some, like Schein (1991), argued that "if there is no consensus or if there is conflict or if things are ambiguous, then, by definition, that group does not have a culture in regard to those things" (p. 248). Others, like Alvesson (2002), acknowledged that ambiguity is inherent in culture, but concluded that it is "not something about which most researchers are concerned on the level of the collective" (p. 163). Part of the confusion may be due to Martin's (2002) examples of the fragmentation perspective that seem to illustrate consensus among employees about the presence of ambiguity in the organization, thereby appearing to mix the integration and fragmentation perspectives.

As Trice (1991) observed, the paradoxes, contradictions, and inconsistencies that are central to the fragmentation perspective certainly exist in organizational life, but at the same time, individuals in organizations do tend to share some commonalities in their experiences, perceptions, and assumptions, without which organizations would be unable to function in the coordinated ways that are typically required. Thinking along these lines is represented in Martin's (2002) advocacy for a "three-perspective theory of culture" in which all three perspectives are used to analyze organizations simultaneously. We would characterize this approach as studying the macro general culture, the specific subcultures that might exist, and culture strength at the same time. We agree with Martin that such broad and multifaceted, multilevel thinking could lead to interesting advancements for the field, but we are unaware at this writing of studies taking all three approaches simultaneously to describing an organization, how organizations may differ in the way the three perspectives are manifested, and the subsequent implications for organizational effectiveness. We return to the ideas of subcultures and culture strength in later sections.

This high-level overview of approaches to understanding culture has certainly not been exhaustive, and thus we thought it might be helpful to pass along Alvesson's (2002) eight metaphors for how culture has been conceptualized, which we provide in Table 4.1 with a brief summary of each. This list gives a flavor for the variety of ways that culture has been conceptualized over the years. In addition, Alvesson (2002) provided five dimensions on which culture research consistent with these metaphors can be contrasted. The first, *functionalism versus nonfunctionalism*, distinguishes those approaches that view culture as promoting organizational effectiveness and the social good as opposed to those approaches in which culture serves no function or serves only the good of management to the harm of lower-level employees. The second, *objectivism versus subjectivism*, contrasts those who view culture as rooted in the objective systems and structures of organizations with those who view culture as being constructed in the minds and consciousness of employees.

In the third dimension, *cognition versus emotion,* culture researchers emphasize either employees' rational motives for goal-oriented behavior or the affective side of organizational life. The fourth dimension, *free will versus determinism,* addresses whether management can control culture, whether employees can also influence culture, or whether culture determines the behavior of all those who are part of it. The final dimension, *pro-management versus anti-management* (or managerial versus critical political interests in the language of Martin et al., 2006) contrasts researchers who uncritically adopt managers' problems as their own (Smircich, 1985) with those who reveal how the culture advocated by management limits the freedom and expression of those with less power. As a whole, Alvesson's (2002) metaphors and the five dimensions that distinguish them remind us of the variety of culture research that may not fit cleanly into a handful of categories.

Now that the reader has some sense for how researchers across various traditions have approached understanding organizational culture, we will wrap up this section with two final points. The first is to echo Louis's (1985) stance that the concept of culture is likely too large or comprehensive for any one lens to fully capture it. Her take is summarized quite well by this quote:

> Current efforts to understand organizational culture are analogous to the Sufi story of the blind men's effort to decipher the elephant. Many are interested; some pursue one end of the beast, others pursue another. For instance, some are concerned with the origins of workplace culture, others

TABLE 4.1 Metaphors for conceptualizing organizational culture based on Alvesson (2002)

1. *Culture as exchange-regulator:* Culture acts to indirectly control employee behavior through shared social knowledge of the exchange relationship between employees and the organization.
2. *Culture as compass:* Culture provides employees with a shared set of values that guides their goal-directed behavior toward effectiveness.
3. *Culture as social glue:* Culture as shared beliefs and norms that bring employees together in harmony and consensus.
4. *Culture as sacred cow:* Culture as core values that employees emotionally identify with, are committed to, and ultimately view as sacred.
5. *Culture as affect-regulator:* Culture as a means to communicate rules for appropriate emotional expressions as a means of management control of employees.
6. *Culture as disorder:* Culture as a jungle of ambiguity, characterized by uncertainty, contradiction, and confusion.
7. *Culture as blinders:* Culture is rooted in the unconscious with limited access by individuals and or understanding of its effects.
8. *Culture as world-closure:* Culture as a management-created social reality that restricts employees' freedom and runs counter to their interests.

Foundations of Organizational Culture 129

> with stories as evidence of that culture. Most proceed as if the single focus pursued were the sum total and the definitive focus. Almost no one has discussed the possibility that the beast is larger than any one focus. As a result, differing approaches are rejected rather than reconciled through appreciation of the differences among the issues they address . . . The issues are too vast, the subject too complex, and the territory too extensive for any one investigator or investigation to do it justice overall (pp. 82–83).

It seems that much of the discussion around how best to understand culture could be settled if researchers avoided making claims to understanding culture in its entirety and were more specific about the aspect of culture they were addressing. More progress could be made by attempting to learn from others' conceptualizations of culture and ways to study it at least by acknowledging that other approaches exist and no single approach will fully address all of the interesting issues and questions surrounding the topic of organizational culture.

The second and final point has to do with the practical value of these intense, sometimes heated, and often quite lengthy discussions of how culture should be understood and studied. As Alvesson and Berg (1992) stated, "there is little evidence today that anyone has had any real success in applying the culture concept at a practical level" (p. 182). Martin and Frost (1996) reached a similar conclusion:

> This academic battle about methodology and theory shows some considerable indifference to the fates of actual people in real organizations . . . even differentiation research, ostensibly so concerned about the fate of the disadvantaged and oppressed, contributes little so far to understanding how to make people's organizational lives better. Outside academia, in corporations the stakes are high. Managers do not generally care about the hair splitting disputes of academics, but they do care, deeply, about the considerable expense and unwanted consequences of ill-thought-out cultural change interventions. Many executives, consultants, and lower-level employees dismiss culture as 'yesterday's fad,' and predictably have turned elsewhere to find another 'quick fix' for corporate ills (p. 608).

It is not that the academic discussions about the nature of organizational culture and how it might best be conceptualized and studied have not yielded useful insights. The issue is whether the research on culture has also infiltrated the practical realm to make a real difference in people's day-to-day lives. The reasons are likely many—including our guess that the shallow embracing of an unspecified, loosely articulated "culture" early in the history of the application of culture to organizational performance caused many culture researchers to eschew the practical completely—but the answer seems pretty clear that the effect from a formal research perspective has been somewhat limited.

The best response to this concern that we have identified in the literature was offered by Denison (2001). He outlined five lessons (summarized in Table 4.2) for making culture more relevant to the change

TABLE 4.2 Denison's (2001) lessons learned for translating organizational culture research into practice

1. Take the "native's point of view" seriously by understanding their day-to-day concerns, even if they are instrumental- or results-focused.
2. Create a systems perspective by moving the primary focus away from the deepest levels of culture to how the different levels of culture are linked together, allowing practitioners to start with the outer levels of culture that may be easier to address initially.
3. Provide a benchmark or frame of reference for data while also acknowledging uniqueness. Comparing organizations' values or behavioral norms can provide some insights that can then be discussed in terms of a particular organization's unique context.
4. Focus on performance implications to better make the argument that culture issues are important; otherwise, it may be difficult to even get your foot in the door.
5. Highlight symbols and contradictions to better understand how the organization has dealt with problems of internal integration and external adaptation and how different groups in the organizations may view those issues differently.

process, although we would argue that his points could be applied broadly to making culture more relevant for all practitioners. Although these lessons represent a compromise position between many of the differences we have described in this section, some culture researchers will certainly cringe at some or all of these suggestions. Our argument above all else is that thinking along these lines is needed to come up with new and creative ideas to better translate the rich conceptual literature on organizational culture to practitioners who live in it and work with it on a daily basis. Perhaps a unifying definition of what culture is would help but that, like agreement on ways to understand it, has been elusive.

DEFINING ORGANIZATIONAL CULTURE

> Part of the problem with [defining] culture is that it is not just a concept but the source of a family of concepts (Pettigrew, 1979), and it is not just a family of concepts but also a frame of reference or root metaphor for organizational analysis (Pettigrew, 1979; Smircich, 1983; Morgan, 1986). However, some progress has been made, and most scholars now agree that organizational culture is a phenomenon that involves beliefs and behavior; exists at a variety of different levels in organizations; and manifests itself in a wide range of features of organizational life such as structures, control and reward systems, symbols, myths, and human resource practices (Pettigrew, 1990, pp. 414–415).

Given the vast array of approaches for conceptualizing and understanding culture just reviewed, it is not surprising that a wide variety of definitions of organizational culture have been introduced in the literature. Cameron and Ettington (1988) reported 18 different definitions from the literature between 1982 and 1986, and Verbeke, Volgering, and Hessels (1998) reported 54 different definitions from 1960 to 1993. Thus, it is easy to see why Van Maanen (1988) described culture as a "catchall idea ... stimulating, productive, yet fuzzy" (p. 3).

Despite this proliferation of definitions, commonalities have been identified. We doubt that any of these elements would find unanimous agreement by culture researchers; given the large variety of viewpoints and the disagreements that exist in the field, any expectation of consensus would be naïve. Below we attempt to capture what we see as the most commonly identified characteristics and functions of organizational culture (also summarized in Table 4.3), drawing from a variety of sources that have attempted a similar summary (e.g., Alvesson, 2002; Martin, 2002; Ott, 1989; Schein, 1991, 2010; Trice & Beyer, 1993). In addition, we identify contrary views or points of contention with regard to each.

- *Organizational culture is shared.* Most definitions of culture include the idea that it is shared. What is shared varies, and may include beliefs, values, perceptions, understandings, behaviors, norms, interpretations, ideologies, assumptions, and so forth. Whichever facet is highlighted by a particular commentator, what is common is that culture is something that characterizes the organization and reflects the organizational members' common experience. Those who disagree with the necessity of culture to be shared are those with a differentiation perspective, who emphasize differences among subcultures (although commonality within those subcultures), or those with a fragmentation perspective, who emphasize ambiguity and contradictions (Martin, 2002).
- *Organizational culture is stable.* Culture tends to be stable over time. Despite any number of changes that may occur in the organization's environment, certain elements continue. If the culture did not endure or provide continuity, then it would not have many of the functions scholars say it has—it would not form a central role in its members' identities, it would not have pervasive effects to the extent it does on the behavior

TABLE 4.3 The attributes of organizational culture

- Organizational culture is shared.
- Organizational culture is stable.
- Organizational culture has depth.
- Organizational culture is symbolic, expressive, and subjective.
- Organizational culture is grounded in history and tradition.
- Organizational culture is transmitted to new members.
- Organizational culture provides order and rules to organizational existence.
- Organizational culture has breadth.
- Organizational culture is a source of collective identity and commitment.
- Organizational culture is unique.

and functioning of individuals and groups, and so forth. At the same time, there is a recognition that culture can be always evolving due to changes in the organization's environment, its people, and the technology it uses, to name just a few. Can these both be true? Yes, depending on a variety of factors such as the period, the level of analysis (organization, department, or the individual), and the level/form of culture that is of interest. We return to this last issue in the next section and devote considerable space to the issue of organizational change in later chapters.

- *Organizational culture has depth.* Depth here refers to the relative tangibility and awareness of the cultural elements of interest. Many definitions of culture emphasize that culture often operates outside the consciousness of employees; that it is taken for granted by organizational members. Although members' thoughts and actions are affected by the organization's culture, they are not necessarily able to articulate why. The point of distinction in the culture literature seems to be whether only the deepest levels of culture (basic assumptions and values) are the "true" culture or whether culture encompasses all levels from the deepest to the most superficial or artifactual (e.g., paintings and posters on the walls of companies; Schein, 1991).
- *Organizational culture is symbolic, expressive, and subjective.* The central commonality among definitions that emphasize the symbolic aspect of culture concerns the meanings that are interpreted from various experiences and structures within the organization. As members share common experiences, personal and social sense-making processes result in a system of socially shared understandings. Researchers who emphasize these interpretive processes celebrate the idea that culture provides an avenue by which to include the expressive elements of organizational life that are seen as closer to the reality of members' everyday experiences (Martin, 2002). The emphasis here tends to be on the outer layers of culture, or artifacts that are then interpreted by members, rather than the values and assumptions that make up the deeper levels of culture (Alvesson, 2002).
- *Organizational culture is grounded in history and tradition.* The culture of an organization is the outcome of its past and the way the organization has effectively handled various challenges over time. The values and norms that are emphasized in the culture are heavily influenced by what has been reinforced in the past; in other words, those approaches, behaviors, and ways of thinking that are associated with past success tend to be repeated (Schein, 2010). Although not a particularly controversial point, some authors do argue that other factors external to the organization (e.g., practices characteristic of particular industries; Dickson, BeShears, & Gupta, 2004) have more of an influence on the organization's culture than is often recognized.
- *Organizational culture is transmitted to new members.* The literature on socialization focuses on how members learn the culture of their new organization. The transmission of cultural elements helps to explain how the culture remains stable and how newcomers come to share in the values and beliefs that currently exist in the organization. Although most discussions of socialization focus on how it functions to create shared values and beliefs, some scholars have varied from this theme to emphasize how new members can influence the organization's culture or

how there may be ambiguity or even contradictions for new members in the messages they receive when entering the organization. We devote considerable space to socialization processes in the next chapter.
- *Organizational culture provides order and rules to organizational existence.* Scholars have offered a variety of explanations for this attribute of culture, with some emphasizing the decreased cognitive load that results from employees having shared understandings of how things work and function (e.g., Krefting & Frost, 1985), and others emphasizing that order and rules help employees cope with their insecurities and uncertainties (e.g., Trice & Beyer, 1993). In either case, a function of culture is to clarify what is expected of employees and what is considered appropriate as employees go about their daily work lives (O'Reilly & Chatman, 1996). In fact, some culture researchers have made rules a primary focus of their definitions of culture, distinguishing between formal and informal rules, and describing how even though individuals create rules, they also come to be viewed as independent structures in the organization (Helms Mills & Mills, 2000).
- *Organizational culture has breadth.* As noted by Schein (2010), "Culture is pervasive and influences all aspects of how an organization deals with its primary task, its various environments, and its internal operations" (p. 17). This characteristic is particularly crucial for those who view organizations as cultures, as that perspective implies that all of organizational life can be included in cultural studies. Of course, the downside to being overly inclusive is that the concept can become an ambiguous catchall, lacking clarity in its definition. As described by Alvesson (2002), "Culture is . . . a tricky concept as it is easily used to cover everything and consequently nothing" (p. 3). Readers will recall a similar issue being raised in our discussion of macro-organizational climate. There we noted that prior to a focused climate approach ("climate for something"), generic or macro climate research contained dimensions of climate particular to each researcher's interpretation.
- *Organizational culture is a source of collective identity and commitment.* Due to the shared values, beliefs, and basic assumptions among most members of a culture (or subculture), members' individual identities become intertwined with the group's identity as a whole. Furthermore, that identity results in an emotional connection to the culture and a commitment to the group. The sense of identity contributes to the stability of the culture (Schein, 2010) and can help clarify the boundaries of the culture (Ott, 1989). Of course, some authors (e.g., Martin, 2002) have noted that viewing culture this way may not account for those groups who are marginalized within the organization or who simply do not identify as strongly with the culture.
- *Organizational culture is unique.* A final characteristic of culture that is often emphasized is its uniqueness. As described by Trice and Beyer (1993), "a particular culture will be based in the unique history of a particular group of people coping with a unique set of physical, social, political, and economic circumstances" (p. 6). In other words, no two cultures are alike because each has its own founding, people, challenges, successes, and so on that have created the culture as it stands today. This view by researchers is matched by individuals within the culture who take pride in the fact that their organization is not like any other

(Martin, 2002). Those who disagree with this view argue that certain cultural elements, stories, and rituals are held in common across similar organizations, a phenomenon labeled by Martin, Feldman, Hatch, and Sitkin (1983) as the "uniqueness paradox." A counterargument would be that despite overlap across cultures due to any number of factors (including similar competition, economic conditions, occupational cultures, industry, nation, and so forth), the particular *combination* of elements that makes up any one culture is not likely to be duplicated elsewhere.

In sum, the attributes attributed to organizational culture are many and varied so it is not surprising that definitions of organizational culture are similarly many and varied. As long lists of different definitions of organizational culture have been summarized elsewhere (e.g., Cameron & Ettington, 1988; Martin, 2002), we will not replicate them here. However, we thought it would be helpful for readers to see examples of definitions that have been provided over the years to get a sense for the variety of ways the construct has been defined and the ways in which the issues just reviewed are part of them. Here are a few:

- "A set of common understandings for organizing actions and language and other symbolic vehicles for expressing common understandings" (Louis, 1980, p. 227).
- "A pattern of beliefs and expectations shared by the organization's members" (Schwartz & Davis, 1981, p. 33).
- "A general constellation of beliefs, mores, value systems, behavioral norms and ways of doing business that are unique to each corporation" (Turnstall, 1983, p. 1).
- "The set of important understandings (often unstated) that members of a community share in common" (Sathe, 1983, p. 6).
- "A shared and learned world of experiences, meanings, values, and understandings which inform people and which are expressed, reproduced, and communicated partly in the symbolic form" (Alvesson, 1993, pp. 2–3).

Even in this short list of definitions, the authors vary in whether they emphasize culture as something that is shared, something that is symbolic, something that is unique, something that is assumed or unstated, or something that is behavioral. Recognizing this diversity in definitions and approaches to culture, we think it would be helpful to pick one definition to frame how we discuss culture in what follows. For that definition, we rely on one of the most highly cited authors on organizational culture, Edgar Schein, who defined culture as follows:

> Organizational culture is *"a pattern of shared basic assumptions learned by [an organization] as it solved its problems of external adaptation and internal integration, which has worked well enough to be considered valid and, therefore, to be taught to new members as the correct way to perceive, think, and feel in relation to those problems"* (Schein, 2010, p. 18).

LEVELS OF CULTURE AND CULTURAL FORMS

We now shift from discussing how organizational culture has been conceptualized and defined to consideration of the lenses through which organizational culture is studied. We frame this section in terms of two topics that are prevalent in the culture literature: (1) the level of the phenomenon—how deep culture resides in the psychology of an organization's members—and, relatedly, (2) the forms that organizational culture takes—how a culture manifests itself to its members.

Levels of Organizational Culture

A central issue for culture researchers is how deep in the psychology of members it is studied. When researchers discuss levels of culture, they are typically referring to the extent to which the cultural content studied is objectively viewable even by outsiders versus content not being consciously available even to insiders. Those things that can be accessed quite easily, perhaps just by looking around an organization, constitute the outermost levels of culture. Cultural information that requires more digging constitutes deeper layers or levels, until a core is reached that represents the very basic understandings of organizational members that may be so taken-for-granted and ingrained that they are outside of conscious awareness and cannot easily be articulated. These levels are linked, in that "more objective elements become vehicles for transmission of less tangible, more subjective facets of culture" (Rousseau, 1990a, pp. 157–158).

Numerous scholars have commented on the number of levels that exist for organizational culture, and the number of such generally ranges from two to five. Some examples of those who identify two levels include espoused values versus values-in-use (Ott, 1989), ideologies versus observable entities (Trice & Beyer, 1993; Beyer, Hannah, & Milton, 2000), observable manifestations versus underlying, interpreted meanings (Kopelman, Brief, & Guzzo, 1990), or espoused versus enacted content themes (Siehl & Martin, 1990). In these the obvious distinction is between what one can objectively identify (what is observable or espoused) and what is "really" going on at a deeper level.

The most commonly referred to framework on the levels of culture is the one proposed by Schein (1985, 1992, 2004, 2010) involving three levels of organizational culture: artifacts, espoused values and beliefs, and underlying assumptions. Artifacts are those elements that are readily accessible by outsiders but the meaning of which is not clear without further investigation. Examples may include how people dress, how the workspace is organized, the company's logo, stories, rituals, language, and architecture. Although many of these may objectively look the same across organizations, the meanings they have for people may be quite different. Therefore, a common approach to culture research is to start with artifacts and then investigate their symbolic meaning to employees. Many of the cultural forms we summarize later in this section would be at this level of culture.

The next level of culture identified by Schein is espoused values. These are the values stated by management that may or may not be consistent with the values that are actually communicated through the actions of those within the organization; the latter are the values in use. The reasons for this disconnect may be because they represent management's aspirations for what they want to become (Schein, 2010), because they are influenced by employees' impressions of management and social desirability biases (Siehl & Martin, 1990), or simply because employees are not aware that their behavior is inconsistent with the values management has espoused (Ott, 1989). Katz and Kahn (1966) had earlier captured this notion of espoused values versus values in use this way: "The stated purposes of an organization as given by its by-laws or in the reports of its leaders can be misleading. Such statements of objectives may idealize, rationalize, distort, omit, or even conceal some essential aspects of the functioning of the organization" (p. 15). This challenge of ascertaining what is really occurring in organizations is why qualitative researchers, and particularly ethnographers, discuss the importance of "penetrating the front" of the organization to get beyond the biases and facades that can be intertwined in the espoused values. The ultimate goal is to capture the underlying assumptions of the organization's culture, which is Schein's third level.

Underlying assumptions, the deepest level of culture, dictate how organizational members go about their day-to-day work lives, and they are so ingrained that they cannot necessarily be articulated. Once certain beliefs and values become reinforced enough through the organization's success, they become taken-for-granted assumptions that provide a common, perhaps subconscious, mental framework shared by organizational members that guides the way they think and how they behave. For Schein (2010) this is the real culture: "the essence of a culture lies in the pattern of basic underlying assumptions, and after you understand those, you can easily understand the other more surface levels and deal appropriately with them" (p. 32). Thus, to truly understand an organization's culture and the meaning of the artifacts and espoused values, one must gain insight into the organization's most basic assumptions. Whether culture researchers have adequately addressed these deeper levels of culture is of course a source of some debate (Barley, 1991).

Although Schein's three interconnected levels are the most commonly cited, other frameworks have been suggested, many of which build on Schein's work. For instance, Sathe (1985) also proposed three levels of culture: shared behavior patterns, shared rationalizations and justifications, and shared beliefs and values. Ott (1989) discussed four levels of culture: artifacts, patterns of behavior, beliefs and values, and basic underlying assumptions. In addition, Lundberg (1990) described the three levels: the manifest level, the strategic beliefs level, and the core level (values and assumptions).

Another conceptualization that we have found particularly helpful in understanding both the concept and the content of culture was presented by Rousseau (1990a). She proposed five layers of culture: artifacts, patterns of behavior, behavioral norms, values, and fundamental assumptions. Although the artifacts, values, and fundamental assumptions align with Schein's (2010) model, Rousseau's introduction of patterns of behavior (how members interact and coordinate to solve organizational problems) and behavioral norms (beliefs about acceptable and unacceptable behavior) is useful. Schein (2010) voiced skepticism about whether behavior should be considered a cultural manifestation, but Rousseau's (1990a) inclusion of these layers is important because so many measures of culture are largely focused on patterns of behavior and norms.

A third conceptualization we have found useful on the concept and content of culture is an extension of Schein's (1985) model proposed by Hatch (1993) in what she referred to as the cultural dynamics model. Hatch included cultural symbols as a fourth element beyond the three levels originally conceptualized in Schein's model to make a stronger connection with the symbolic-interpretive perspective on culture. More importantly, instead of focusing on Schein's levels independently, Hatch shifted the focus to the dynamic processes that occur in the relationships among the different levels. She proposed four processes: manifestation (linking assumptions and values), realization (linking values and artifacts), symbolization (linking artifacts and symbols), and interpretation (linking symbols and assumptions). Hatch emphasized that these processes were not unidirectional. That is, although assumptions can manifest to values, values are realized in artifacts, and artifacts are given symbolic meaning, the processes can also be reversed. In other words, management's espousal of new values can influence assumptions, or the introduction of new artifacts can result in a change in values to realign with the new artifacts. We highlight Hatch's model because although we find Schein's approach to be quite useful in understanding and communicating about the levels at which organizational culture exists, Hatch's processes provide insights into the interplay between and among the levels and particularly how the influence of one level on another can be bi-directional. This point will be relevant when we turn to the topic of organizational change later in the book.

Forms of Organizational Culture

As researchers consider the levels at which organizational culture exists, they face a choice between studying the whole organization (and the numerous levels of its culture) versus studying specific manifestations of the organization's culture in depth. Along these lines, Martin and Frost (1996) distinguished between generalist studies, which are more apt to provide a description of a culture as a whole including a variety of cultural manifestations, and specialist studies, which have a singular focus on a particular cultural manifestation. With regard to the latter approach, a number of cultural forms or foci for research have been identified in the organizational culture literature, most of which approach the study of culture at the artifact level.

And what are these so-called cultural manifestations? Although we will not attempt an exhaustive list, some include language, jargon, myths, stories, legends, folklore, jokes, slogans, rituals, rites, ceremonies, celebrations, traditions, heroes, behavioral norms, rules, taboos, dress, and physical arrangements. Trice and Beyer (1993) organized these various cultural forms into four general categories. *Symbols* are somewhat of an overarching category, in that the other cultural forms can be studied in terms of their symbolic meaning for organizational members. Trice and Beyer noted that research on symbols has generally focused on how objects, settings, and performers/functionaries can act as symbols of the deeper meanings for people. *Language* is a cultural form that encompasses jargon, slang, gestures, signals, signs, songs, humor, jokes, gossip, rumor, metaphors, proverbs, and slogans. The *narratives* category includes stories, legends, sagas, and myths. Finally, their fourth category was *practices*, which included rituals, taboos, ceremonials, and rites (including rites of passage, degradation, enhancement, renewal, conflict reduction, and integration). We will discuss the role these various cultural forms play in more detail as we move through our discussion of organizational culture and the ways it is studied.

Readers who perhaps wondered why we began the chapters on culture with conceptual and definitional issues instead of research on the topic should now understand that the study of organizational culture is a very complex issue. It is complex because of the variety of ways it has been conceptualized, the levels at which it exists, and the variety of manifestations that might characterize it. Indeed, the same manifestations or forms across organizations may take on different meanings and, as Hatch (1993) has so cogently noted, what seems to underlie culture in the way of basic assumptions may in fact be subject to alteration through changes in espoused and enacted values and/or the behavioral norms proposed by Rousseau (1990a). Given these complexities we can now move on to the methods used for the study of organizational culture that attempt to address these complexities in ways that make culture more tangible.

METHODS FOR STUDYING ORGANIZATIONAL CULTURE

The method used for studying culture is perhaps the most contentious issue in the field. We earlier showed, of course, that the way culture is understood is also very contentious, and it is clear that the two issues—understanding culture and studying it—are inextricably intertwined. Prior to getting into the sources of disagreement on this topic, we thought it would be useful to set the stage by discussing why culture is difficult to study and the conditions under which it may be most accessible. Pettigrew (1990) provided seven issues that capture why organizational culture is difficult to study (and change):

1. The *levels* issue (it is difficult to study deeply held beliefs and assumptions)
2. The *pervasiveness* issue (organizational culture encompasses a broad number of interlocking organizational elements)
3. The *implicitness* issue (organizational culture is taken for granted and rarely explicitly acknowledged and discussed)
4. The *imprinting* issue (culture has deep ties to the history of the organization)
5. The *political* issue (cultural issues are tied to differences in power or status in the organization)
6. The *plurality* issue (organizations rarely have a single culture, but instead have multiple subcultures)
7. The *interdependency* issue (culture is interconnected with a broad number of other issues both internal and external to the organization).

With all of these challenges facing culture researchers, it is not very surprising that there is debate over how best to approach the study of organizational culture, and as we will see, many of the tensions can be traced back to these challenges.

Differences in perspective about how culture should be studied are confounded with the epistemological approaches outlined previously. That is, in Smircich's (1983) terminology, researchers who view organizations *as* cultures tend to (almost exclusively) use qualitative methods, whereas researchers who view organizations as *having* cultures are more likely to use quantitative methods (although qualitative approaches are common as well). Several factors distinguish these two general approaches and contribute to the choice of method. Trice and Beyer (1993) emphasized that culture can be studied under the presumption that it has distinctive and unique elements or as having universal elements. Those who emphasize organizations as being cultures tend to highlight the distinctiveness of each individual organization's cultural manifestations and history, which typically results in the use of qualitative methods, whereas those who view organizations as *having* cultures emphasize those elements that can be studied and compared across multiple organizations, which typically results in the use of quantitative methods. A related issue is the emphasis on describing culture from the insider's perspective (i.e., an emic approach) versus applying a more general framework across multiple cultures (i.e., an etic approach). (Note that Trice and Beyer [1993] emphasized that both perspectives have value.) Because of the emphasis on taking the insider's perspective, those who view organizations *as* cultures tend to conduct inductive research, using qualitative methods to provide thick descriptions of what occurs in the organization (Sackmann, 2001). Those who view organizations as *having* cultures are more likely to use deductive approaches that require testing a previously devised conceptualization of the important cultural elements in an organization or across organizations; those who view organizations as cultures question whether such frameworks are actually valid in the settings to which they are being applied (Schein, 2010). Another issue is the level of culture that can be assessed with different methods. The goal of researchers who view organizations *as* cultures is to "penetrate the front" of organizations and better understand the deeper structures of the organization. They argue that quantitative research cannot access these deeper levels and question whether culture surveys are asking the right questions in the first place (Martin & Frost, 1996). We do not know of any claims by researchers from the organizations *have* cultures perspective that they are capturing the deeper layers of culture with quantitative methods, although they may not always be clear about what outer layer of culture (e.g., artifacts, behavioral norms, espoused values) they are measuring in their research.

One interesting aspect of this debate is that qualitative researchers seem to object much more strongly to quantitative research than quantitative researchers do to qualitative research. For instance, Ott (1989) stated, "The organizational culture perspective does not believe that quantitative, experimental-type, logical-positivist, scientific research is especially useful for studying organizations" (p. 2). Martin and Frost (1996) were also heavily critical of quantitative approaches, as demonstrated here: "Because such a superficial focus cannot 'penetrate the front' of people's desire to present themselves in a favourable light, it is far inferior to the depth made accessible by long-term participant-observation" (p. 607). Schein's (2000) critique of quantitative measures of culture was that they "force researchers to cast their theoretical nets too narrowly" (p. xxvii). He has also leveled more serious concerns about whether quantitative approaches to studying culture are even ethical (Schein, 1985, 2010).

Negative evaluations of and objections to qualitative research are much more difficult to find; quantitative researchers are more likely to simply not acknowledge qualitative research or to offer counterarguments to the objections of qualitative researchers by describing how quantitative research can have value as well (e.g., Denison, 2001). The primary explanation for this difference goes back to the roots of the contemporary study of organizational culture. For those academics who viewed organizations as cultures and performed qualitative research, the study of culture offered a way to rebel against the dominant positivist paradigm (Meyerson, 1991b), and thus the tensions over how best to study culture were embedded in a larger epistemological battle. For qualitative researchers, it seems the quantitative study of culture represents an infringement on turf that they had hoped could be a safe haven from an objectivist-functionalist perspective on methods. Quantitative researchers, in contrast, may be less likely to recognize this turf war and less likely to view the work of qualitative researchers as a threat to themselves.

Of course, the discussion thus far has been somewhat overly simplified, and there is more nuance than a simple dichotomy between qualitative and quantitative research. In particular, there is much more variability in qualitative culture research than is commonly recognized or acknowledged by quantitative culture researchers. Schein (1990) used five categories for characterizing research on organizational culture (note that all but the first are qualitative): survey research, analytical descriptive, ethnographic, historical, and clinical descriptive. Davey and Symon (2001) noted that qualitative research on organizational culture could generally (but not always) be divided into two categories: psychological perspectives that tend to be positivist and functionalist in their approach, and anthropological/sociological perspectives that tend to take a more subjective, interpretive approach. Louis (1985) described how qualitative methods might be used to compare across settings (an approach more commonly associated with quantitative researchers) if the goal of the research is knowledge of culture in general rather than knowledge of a specific setting. Ouchi and Wilkins (1985) divided empirical qualitative studies of culture into the categories of holistic studies (typically field observation studies that include all manifestations of culture) and semiotic studies (studies of communication via signs and symbols). And Martin and Frost (1996) described splits between those qualitative culture researchers who advocated pure ethnography (long-term with thick description) and those performing "smash and grab" ethnographs that use interviews or other short-term approaches. Therefore, although we tend to be a bit simplistic in much of our discussion to make some general points and comparisons, we want to at least acknowledge that there is considerable nuance that we are overlooking in thinking about this central issue as a simple dichotomy.

Moving beyond some of the splits and disagreements, some authors have noted the strengths and weaknesses of each method depending on the researcher's goal (e.g., Rousseau, 1990a), and that is the position we take on this issue. In Table 4.4 we provide a summary of what might be considered the pros and cons of each approach beginning with qualitative research.

One way to take advantage of the strengths of both approaches (and to avoid some of the weaknesses of using either approach exclusively) is to use multiple methods, and that is the point reached by many authors who have addressed this issue. For instance, Rousseau (1990a) distinguished between public and private research methods and data analysis, noting that richer insights can result when quantitative methods are coupled with qualitative analysis or when qualitative methods are coupled with quantitative analysis. Reichers and Schneider (1990) framed the issue in terms of capturing generic culture versus particularistic manifestations of culture. They advocated for conducting in-depth interviews prior to survey data collection, and using the information from those interviews to develop organization-specific questions to capture particularistic issues. Those questions could then be added to a survey with more generic questions that could be used across organizations for comparison purposes. Another approach, described by Sackmann (2001) would be to alternate between qualitative, inductive approaches and quantitative,

TABLE 4.4 The pros and cons of qualitative and quantitative research methods for studying organizational culture

Qualitative Research

Pros	Cons
• Provides a detailed description of an organization's culture	• Less likely to be theoretically driven
• Gives the "insider perspective" of what an organization's culture is like	• Less useful for comparing cultures because of emphasis on uniqueness of each individual culture and an absence of common issues studied
• More likely to study culture over time	• Difficult to obtain input from all members of an organization without long, intensive ethnographic approaches
• Can be used to study deeper layers of culture, getting past any misleading biases or fronts put up by organizational members	• Relies on subjective judgments of extent to which organization is characterized by a general culture versus subcultures and the extent to which there is agreement in the culture
• Allows for unexpected findings	

Quantitative Research

Pros	Cons
• Allows for comparisons of culture across settings	• Less likely to study culture over time; most studies are "snapshots" of the organization
• Better suited to show how culture is related to effectiveness outcomes	• Not as useful for studying deeper levels of culture (although some have argued this is possible if layers of culture are aligned; Ashkanasy, Broadfoot, & Falkus, 2000)
• Better suited to testing theory	• Difficult to judge if questions being asked are appropriate to and/or relevant for a particular culture
• Can survey all employees in the organization across levels and departments	• Difficult to evaluate influence of any presentational biases on employee responses
• Can statistically test for presence of subcultures and for level of agreement in culture	• Less likely to identify unexpected information about the culture that does not fit within the researcher's prior framework

deductive approaches. One suggested option would be to develop theoretical models earlier in the research project using qualitative methods and then to shift to quantitative methods to test those models in later stages of the research project (see Sackmann, 1991).

Yet another example of such an approach is Sutton and Rafaeli's (1988) study of the effects of employee emotional expression on customer behavior. Using data collected through the observation of employee-customer interactions, they first performed statistical analyses to test the hypotheses they had developed based on prior theory and research. When they encountered a surprising relationship counter to their initial predictions, they performed a follow-up qualitative, inductive study in which they spent a day as a clerk in the organization, interviewed management, conducted a workshop with customers, and visited different stores. The insights gained from this qualitative study were used to re-analyze the data from their quantitative study, which then clarified the initially unexpected finding. Unfortunately, this example of research blending quantitative and qualitative methods is much rarer than it should be. Nevertheless, we are hopeful that research along these lines may be more common moving forward than has been in the past, especially as the benefits of mixing qualitative and quantitative methods have been acknowledged by authors who have been some of the strongest critics of quantitative approaches.

For example, Martin (2002) has advocated for the use of hybrid research designs, noting how quantitative and qualitative approaches can reinforce (or triangulate) the findings of the other or reveal insights by looking at the same issue in different ways, which can then lead to a richer and more complex understanding of the research subject. Despite his strong words against culture surveys elsewhere (Schein, 1985, 2010), Schein (2000) presented a more balanced stance in his commentary for the first edition of the *Handbook of Organizational Culture and Climate*, describing the "ideal research design" as measuring present and desired norms using surveys and then following up with group interviews to discuss the discrepancies between the two, thus revealing the underlying assumptions present in the organization. Note that this approach is in the opposite order of that suggested by Reichers and Schneider (1990); our view is that the usefulness of starting with qualitative and moving to quantitative versus quantitative then qualitative is up for debate and is likely dictated by the goals of the research. Whichever path is taken, the outcome is likely to be stronger (i.e., yield a richer portrait) when multiple methods are used than when either approach is used alone.

In the rest of the book, we will revisit the issue of the method used for culture research at several points. In particular, in Chapter Five we describe in some detail quantitative research that has been done on the relationships between organizational culture and organizational effectiveness, as well as the responses to this line of research by those preferring qualitative methods in line with the organizations *are* cultures perspective. In addition, in Chapter Seven we return to practical issues surrounding the use of both qualitative and quantitative methods (including descriptions of specific quantitative instruments) as part of conducting a cultural inquiry.

SUMMARY: ON UNDERSTANDING AND STUDYING ORGANIZATIONAL CULTURE

At this point, readers will certainly be feeling that understanding, defining, and assessing organizational culture is complex indeed. The reason for this conclusion is that these are very complex issues with which researchers deal! There are different levels of culture, different possible methods for assessing these different levels, and the likely conclusion is that all of these are appropriate and relevant depending on the question of interest. Perhaps the best portrayal of this conclusion was proposed by Martin (2002), who argued that organizational culture in organizations is simultaneously integrated, differentiated, and fragmented—depending on at what levels and forms one is looking and for what reasons.

In short there is no one best way to understand and study organizational culture, and the focus for such study is not predetermined since it depends on the purpose for which a specific study of culture is being done. The organizational culture metaphor is vague with regard to what its elements might be but informative in identifying that the ways organizations are experienced by people in them will likely vary across both levels within an organization and between organizations. The ways in which those differences will be manifested is not known until the comparisons are made—and to what those differences may in turn be related is a question of interest, particularly to those who believe organizations *have* cultures (Smircich, 1983).

In the next chapter, we continue the discussion of organizational culture, switching to the ways in which organizational culture is thought to emerge and be transmitted over time and the consequences of such emergence for the strength of a culture and the relationship of culture with organizational effectiveness.

CHAPTER
5

The Emergence, Effectiveness, and Change of Organizational Cultures

In this chapter, we address the issues of how organizational culture develops and is transmitted in organizations and the role of organizational culture in organizational effectiveness. We then consider organizational culture change, which serves as a review of the materials that precede it because, as we will see, to change an organization's culture may require consideration of why and how it develops in the first place, how it is transmitted, and the effectiveness of organizations and their cultures. Although there are clear links between some of the material discussed in this chapter and the organizational climate literature discussed in Chapters Two and Three, we generally refrain from explicitly making those connections until Chapter Six, which is entirely focused on the integration of the concepts of organizational climate and culture.

THE EMERGENCE OF ORGANIZATIONAL CULTURE

There have been a variety of proposals for why cultures develop in organizations. Some authors (e.g., Krefting & Frost, 1985) have discussed organizational culture as functioning at the collective level in organizations in similar ways as individual level cognitive schemas. The emphasis is on how the shared understandings that are part of culture are useful because as collective schemas they reduce the complexity inherent in organizational life by reducing ambiguity and making life in an organization less complex. Such schemas emerge from and thus facilitate interactions among workers, as individuals can communicate more easily and better anticipate others' actions when the underlying assumptions that guide their thoughts and behaviors are shared. Other authors, like Trice and Beyer (1993), have taken this to another level by suggesting that culture is necessary to cope with the chaos that is always threatening. Their perspective is that the social order created by organizational culture allows members to avoid being overwhelmed by their fear of uncertainty and constant change, and thus be able to focus on functioning effectively in their day-to-day lives. Whether the basis for the development of culture is to reduce complexity or to cope with the fear of chaos, organizational cultures serve a very functional purpose in how individuals understand their organizations and work with their fellow workers within those organizations.

Whatever the reasons may be for why culture develops, the more interesting question in our opinion is how the specific content of any given organization's culture comes to be and the ways that content is manifested. Thus, in the rest of this section, we focus on the following issues: (1) the primary origins of the organization's culture in the founder of the organization; (2) the learnings and experiences of members as carriers of the culture; (3) the importance of context in an organization's culture, especially the national culture in which the organization exists and the industry in which the organization operates; and (4) the importance of the organization's people in creating and maintaining its culture, as articulated by the attraction-selection-attrition (ASA) model.

Founder Influences

Although others have emphasized the role of the founder (e.g., Ott, 1989; Trice & Beyer, 1993), Schein has perhaps written most persuasively and specifically about the critical influence the founder has on the formation of organizational culture. In fact, one of Schein's earliest articles on the topic was entitled "The role of the founder in creating organizational culture," which was published as part of a special issue on organizational culture in *Organizational Dynamics* in 1983. In the article, Schein summarized the primary foundations of organizational culture in this way: "The ultimate organizational culture will always reflect the complex interaction between (1) the assumptions and theories that founders bring to the group initially and (2) what the group learns subsequently from its own experiences" (p. 14).[1] We will address the second issue shortly, but as for founders, Schein argued that they play a unique role as they are the ones who have the idea that forms the basis for the new company, and they also have strong, usually implicit, assumptions about how best to bring that idea to fruition based on their own characteristics and past experiences. The founder then goes about communicating those assumptions or beliefs through various actions he or she takes, actions Schein referred to as embedding mechanisms. Although Schein initially listed them in one block and described some as playing a more important role than others play, he later formalized the distinction between primary and secondary embedding mechanisms, such that the primary mechanisms create the culture and the secondary mechanisms reinforce the messages sent by the primary mechanisms (Schein, 2010).

Schein's (2010) culture embedding mechanisms are summarized in Table 5.1. We will focus more on these mechanisms as we discuss the role of leadership in organizational culture/climate change and as we address the integration of the climate and culture literatures in Chapter Six. The main point here is that founders communicate their values and beliefs through these mechanisms—what they pay attention to, how they react to crises, to what they allocate scarce resources, how they personally behave and serve as role models, the behaviors they reward, and with whom they surround themselves. Because of founders' unique role in establishing the organization, they will have a particularly strong impact on the formation of the organization's culture at its earliest stages. And although their impact on the culture may diminish over time as they retire and/or give up direct control of the organization to others, founders will tend to bring others into the organization, and specifically onto the management team, that are like themselves in terms of beliefs, values, outlook, background, personality, and even theories on how to succeed (Ott, 1989). As a result, the culture that founders initially create is likely to persist even though they are not present as the new leaders use the embedding mechanisms in consistent ways to communicate similar values and beliefs.

TABLE 5.1   Culture embedding mechanisms (Schein, 2010, p. 236; used by permission)

Primary embedding mechanisms
- What leaders pay attention to, measure, and control on a regular basis
- How leaders react to critical incidents and organizational crises
- How leaders allocate resources
- Deliberate role modeling, teaching, and coaching
- How leaders allocate rewards and status
- How leaders recruit, select, promote, and excommunicate

Secondary articulation and reinforcement mechanisms
- Organizational design and structure
- Organizational systems and procedures
- Rites and rituals of the organization
- Design of physical space, facades, and buildings
- Stories about important events and people
- Formal statements of organizational philosophy, creeds, and charters

Although there is a consensus about the importance of the founder across the literature on organizational culture, there is some disagreement about the role of the founder relative to other factors that influence culture. For example, Martin, Sitkin, and Boehm (1985) argued that the cognitive biases of salience and attribution result in the founder being credited with more influence than is deserved, and that other factors, like the organization's stage in its life cycle, likely have as much of an impact on the development of the organization's culture as the founder. Others have voiced similar objections, with Trice and Beyer (1993) noting that "organizations do not automatically build their cultures around the ideologies and values of the founders" (p. 269), and Alvesson (1993) pointing out that "the influence of founders on organizational culture cannot be assumed" (p. 87). We agree that the role of founders and leaders in general may be over-romanticized (in line with the work of Meindl and his colleagues with regard to leadership; Meindl, 1990, 1993, 1995; Meindl & Ehrlich, 1987; Meindl, Ehrlich, & Dukerich, 1985), but the opposite perspective—that organizational culture would develop in the same way regardless of the founder—is untenable. It seems to us that the founder plays a critical and prominent role in the development of organizational culture, which is not to say the process is always intentional or that there is a perfect correspondence between the founder's values and the values that develop in the organization (Martin & Siehl, 1983). Rather, there are multiple influences simultaneously at work, including the founder and other factors that are highlighted next, none of which is THE single driver of organization culture. Instead, it is the unique blend of all of them and how they evolve over time that make an organization's culture what it is (Aldrich & Ruef, 2006).

Member Experiences and Learnings

Although founders influence culture by offering solutions to problems that are infused with their own values and beliefs, those solutions are not accepted blindly by followers as important; the proposed solutions must work prior to followers assuming their importance as a foundation for what the organization becomes as a culture. As described by Schein (1983), the leader's influence gets the group moving in a certain direction, but it is only when the solutions offered by the leader are useful that the elements become implicitly and perhaps explicitly accepted by the group and ultimately part of the group's culture. Thus, the second source of an organization's culture is the collective learning and reinforcement process that takes place over time.

Schein (1983, 2010) divided the learning process into aspects that address problems of external adaptation and aspects that address problems related to internal integration. Problems of external adaptation essentially address why the organization exists, what its goals are, and what it must do to continue to exist. Schein (2010) argued that organizations primarily rely on positive problem solving to address external adaptation;

they try different solutions to problems, discard those that do not work, and continue those that do work. As certain approaches continue to have success, they become more and more ingrained in the organization as the "right" way to do things, to the point that they become unquestioned assumptions that implicitly guide life in the organization. As long as those approaches continue to work, organizational members will continue to approach problem solving in a similar way.

Schein's (1983, 2010) second category of learning processes addresses internal integration, or how the group interacts and functions as it goes about solving the problems of external adaptation. Internal integration is driven by anxiety avoidance, in that members need to feel some level of security and comfort to focus on external adaptation and survival. Thus, the group develops such characteristics as a shared language, common understandings of power and status issues, norms for peer relationships, and consensus on what rewards versus punishments accrue to effective and ineffective behavior. Whether it be problems of external adaptation or internal integration, individuals will continue to behave in ways that have resulted in success in the past, such that "culture ultimately reflects the group's effort to cope and learn; it is the residue of that learning process" (Schein, 2010, p. 91). These early experiences and learnings will likely differ from one organization to another as they form the foundations for an organization's early culture.

We do not want to give the impression that this is a perfectly efficient system, such that individuals adapt as soon as solutions no longer work, leaving old norms behind and developing new ones. Unfortunately, that is not how it works; individuals typically persist in the ways that have been effective long after they may have stopped being effective precisely because they were rewarded in the past for such assumptions, beliefs, and behaviors. That is the effect of culture. Behaviors that were highly functional at one point, and likely for a long time, now may be performed "for reasons that are incomprehensible to outsiders and in ways that are incongruent with formal decree" (Van Maanen & Barley, 1985, p. 37). Alternatively, as Miller (1990, p. 3) put it:

> Many outstanding organizations have followed such paths of deadly momentum—time-bomb trajectories of attitudes, policies, and events that lead to falling sales, plummeting profits, even bankruptcy. These companies extend and amplify the strategies to which they credit their success [leading to their decline].

How cultures might change to avoid such inefficiencies is the focus of a later section of this chapter.

The Larger Environment of the Organization

The third category of origins of organizational culture is the organization's environment, and we specifically highlight the culture of the broader society and the industry within which the organization functions as two of the primary environmental influences. The general argument here is that each organization's culture is influenced by its environment, and the society and industry are two of the strongest environmental influences on an organization. Although we focus on these two, we acknowledge other extra-organizational influences on organizational culture such as these highlighted by Trice and Beyer (1993): transnational cultures (ideologies that transcend national boundaries like science, capitalism, or Protestantism), regional cultures (within-country variability; see Ott's, 1989, example of two small towns in Pennsylvania that were 15 miles apart but whose stories differed markedly when they attempted to attract garment firms to their area), and other organizations' cultures (when organizations are so heavily dependent on each other or work together so closely that their cultures influence each other; Aldrich & Ruef, 2006).

National culture. With regard to societal culture, an organization is not independent from the society in which it operates, and the assumptions that are shared throughout a society will inevitably influence the organization's culture, although the organizational culture should not be considered a subculture of the national culture (Hofstede & Peterson, 2000; Ott, 1989). That being said, the relationships between national culture and organizational culture are not necessarily simple ones; as Kwantes and Dickson (2011) concluded at the end of their chapter on the topic, "The premise of a societal culture–organizational culture effect appears simple; understanding the what, when, and how much of that effect is anything but" (p. 509).

Some of the earliest focus on national culture was in comparing organizations in the US and Japan, with the understanding that differences in how organizations operated were tied to differences in national cultures (Ouchi, 1981; Pascale & Athos, 1982; see analysis by Brannen & Kleinberg, 2000, for more detail). Hofstede's (1980) work was highly influential in this regard, as he demonstrated that organizations operating in multiple countries developed both a common organizational culture and unique subcultures in each country that aligned with that country's national culture (see the summary of these issues in Hofstede & Peterson, 2000). More recent research as part of the GLOBE study of culture and leadership across 62 national cultures indicated that national culture explained between 21% and 47% of the variance in the organizational culture practice dimensions (Brodbeck, Hanges, Dickson, Gupta, & Dorfman, 2004), although others have noted that the relationships between national culture and organizational practices are generally weaker than the relationships with organizational values because practices are more constrained by other environmental factors (Dickson, Aditya, & Chhokar, 2000). Furthermore, some authors, like Gerhart (2009), have argued that the constraining role of national culture may be less than has been suggested in the literature, allowing for more opportunities for differentiation among organizations within a single society. Adding yet another twist, the effect of national culture on organizational culture may actually vary across national cultures, such that there is more of a range of organizational cultures in loose cultures (e.g., the US) relative to more constrained variability in tight cultures (e.g., Japan; Gelfand, Nishii, & Raver, 2006; Kwantes & Dickson, 2011).

Obviously, the issues surrounding the relationship between national and organizational culture present a forest and trees paradox. That is, when looked at from a high level, a forest contains seemingly undifferentiated trees but on the ground, the differences among trees are clear. Research clearly shows a main effect for national culture on organizational culture, but within national cultures, there is also a main effect for organizational culture (Hofstede & Peterson, 2000; House, Hanges, Javidan, Dorfman, & Gupta, 2004).

Industry effects. In addition to societal culture, individual organizational cultures are shaped by the industry in which they operate (Gordon, 1991). Deal and Kennedy (1982) described the industry or business environment as "the single greatest influence in shaping a corporate culture" (p. 13). Ott (1989) described three reasons why the nature of the organization's business has an effect on its culture, and thus why organizations within certain industries will tend to have similar cultures. First, industry dictates the dominant professions of those working in the organizations, and thus organizations in industries dominated by certain professions will share numerous attributes. For example, research on occupations (e.g., Holland, 1997) tells us that the people who make up different occupations have distinct personalities and values, and thus the primary occupations in an industry and the unique characteristics of those occupational members will influence the culture that develops in those organizations. Note that the role of occupational cultures is typically discussed in terms of their effect on the development of organizational subcultures, a topic we discuss in more depth later in this chapter.

Ott's (1989) second reason for the effects of industry on organizational culture was that the organization's business drives the external stakeholders with whom the organization must interact (e.g., customers, regulators). The characteristics of customers and their demands will shape what makes the organization successful, and thus they define the reinforcements the organization is likely to receive for its external adaptation accomplishments discussed earlier. For instance, Gordon (1991) described how customer demands for reliability versus novelty would shape the culture that forms within the organization. Thus, whether an organization primarily works with artists, farmers, psychotherapists, or the military will have an effect on what behaviors and practices are successful in the organization, and thus the culture that develops over time.

Third, Ott (1989) highlighted two marketplace factors (taken from Deal & Kennedy, 1982) that influence how organizational culture develops: risk and speed of feedback. Monopolies develop different cultures than organizations with many competitors (risk), and online retail companies develop different cultures than companies in the oil or aerospace industries (speed of feedback). Other factors related to industry may include the historical development of the industry, its dominant technologies, the rate of environmental change, or its societal expectations (Gordon, 1991; Trice & Beyer, 1993).

Somewhat surprisingly, when Brodbeck and colleagues (2004) analyzed the GLOBE study data to compare the effects of national culture and industry on organizational culture, they found that industry had relatively small effects (0%–11% of variance explained across the organizational practices) relative to the larger effects described previously for national culture. Nevertheless, what they did find was that industry interacted with national culture for four of the nine organizational practices they studied. Specifically, there were stronger relationships between national culture and organizational culture for the telecommunications and food industries than for firms in the financial sector. Brodbeck and colleagues (2004) attributed this difference to industry differences in the sensitivity to global market norms, with the financial industry being most sensitive to those norms and thus the least likely to develop industry-specific cultural practices. These findings should not be taken to mean that industry does not matter; the GLOBE study was designed to focus on those areas where there were differences across societies and not necessarily the variance that might exist in the critical factors that differentiate industries. What it does tell us is that the external influences on organizational culture are multiple and often interacting; complexity cannot be ignored.

The ASA Model

In stark contrast to models for understanding the emergence of organizational culture based on primarily contextual influences is a framework developed by Schneider (1987) that rests on the personal characteristics of those in an organization. Thus, unlike most models of organizational culture that have emphasized the influence of the situation on individuals, the ASA model placed individuals in the central role of influence, and argued that situations are created by the nature of the people within them. Specifically, Schneider contended that individuals within organizations become more homogeneous in terms of their values and personality through the processes of attraction, selection, and attrition. In other words, those individuals who are attracted to certain organizations (and their cultures) will be more homogeneous than the applicant pool in general; those individuals who are selected will be more similar to the current employees and fit better with the current culture than those employees who are not selected; and finally, those employees who stay with the organization and who do not voluntarily or involuntarily leave the organization will be more similar to each other and the typical employee than those who leave.

The ASA framework (Schneider, 1987) proposed that these processes start with the founder, who is likely to surround him or herself with similar individuals who agree with his/her vision for the company. The personality and values of the founder and those individuals form the foundation of the organization's culture. Over time, the culture is perpetuated because the employees who remain throughout the ASA processes will be those that tend to share the organization's core values and will tend to have homogeneous personalities. Those individuals will tend to share the same assumptions and will agree with and be likely to continue the various cultural forms that exist in the organization. So rather than treating culture as something that exists separately from the people within it, the ASA model emphasized that the culture exists because of the people within it, and as long as nothing prevents the ASA cycle from continuing, the organization will continue to be homogeneous (if not increasingly so), and the culture will stay relatively the same. Schneider is not the only individual to place such an emphasis on the influence individuals have on organizational culture; Alvesson (1993) made a similar argument as illustrated by this quote: "People are thus culture creators and are not simply transferring and adapting meaning mechanistically. But they are also cultural products (Löfgren, 1982); they are formed by culture, as well as by reproducing and forming it" (p. 81).

Summary

After reading this section, it becomes clear to readers that what is blithely called "the culture" of an organization emerges out of numerous interrelated and multilevel interacting streams. From the emphasis on a single individual (the founder) to consideration of broader environmental effects (e.g., national culture and industry), it is apparent that culture emergence can vary dramatically across organizations because of all of these interacting elements. Organizational culture is not simple because if it was then everyone would get it right—whatever "right" means. Clearly the sense one has of an organization merely by wandering around in it and making observations makes it clear that organizations can vary greatly in the beliefs and values and basic assumptions by which they operate and that these, in turn, are manifest in a great number of ways. This complexity in what an organizational culture is and its corresponding causes makes trying to change an organization a daunting task, as we will see when we discuss culture change later in this chapter. For now, it is sufficient to appreciate the many layers and ways in which culture emerges and understand that like all living systems the drama is in the details that underlie what we think we see.

SOCIALIZATION AND THE PERPETUATION OF ORGANIZATIONAL CULTURE

No matter the sources of an organization's culture, it must be passed on to new employees to ensure its usefulness and existence over time. Van Maanen (1976) defined socialization as "the processes by which members learn the cultural values, norms, beliefs, assumptions, and required behaviors that permit them to participate as effective members of an organization" (p. 89). This process is so critical to the construct of organizational culture that it is at times included as part of its definition. For instance, Van Maanen and Barley (1985) described culture in terms of strategies developed by members to solve problems that are "remembered and passed on to new members" (p. 33). Beres and Portwood (1979) also made the perpetuation of organization culture central to their definition of culture: "A cognitive frame of reference and a pattern of behavior transmitted to members of a group from the previous generations of the group" (p. 171). Finally, Schein (2010), as one of the most well-known and highly cited authors on organizational culture, included the passing of culture to new members in his definition, noting how culture is "taught to new members as the correct way to perceive, think, and feel" (p. 18).

Some of the earliest organizational culture research focused on the issue of socialization. The Hawthorne studies, which have had a tremendous effect on the development of the fields of organizational behavior and industrial/organizational psychology, have provided some of the earliest documentation of newcomer socialization processes. As part of the famous bank wiring room observations (Roethlisberger & Dickson, 1939), employees were described as "binging" (punching in the shoulders) newcomers who were thought to be rate-busters as they wired the boards for use by operators in companies. Thus, the existing employees sent a clear message about the group's shared values and what were the acceptable behavioral norms.

Other early discussions of employee socialization include Parsons (1951), who discussed the importance for the newcomer to learn the necessary knowledge to perform well in his/her new role. Note that this information was not narrowly defined in terms of task knowledge, but instead included information in the social and political arenas that is typically also the domain of organizational culture. Another early example comes from Etzioni (1961), who focused on the need for new employees to understand the sources of power required to take action in their organization for them to function effectively. Finally, in describing their open system theory of organizations, Katz and Kahn (1966) observed the following: "Just as a society has a cultural heritage, so social organizations possess distinctive patterns of collective feeling and beliefs passed along to new group members" (p. 66).

One reason why socialization was the focus of early culture research and continues to be included in the very definition of culture itself is that socialization is central to our understanding of why culture remains stable over time and has such strong effects on organizational members. Van Maanen and Barley (1985) perhaps summarized the issue best when they observed, "Cultures endure only to the degree that their content is transmitted from one generation to the next" (p. 35). As we observe cultures being carried on over the successive generations in organizations even as members come and go, we cannot help but wonder about the processes that explain how that transmission—and the stability that follows—occurs. Another perspective for why there is such interest in socialization processes is that they are anything but simple and straightforward. As described by Louis (1990), "Cultural knowledge is tacit, contextual, informal, unofficial, shared, emergent. Together these characteristics make teaching or otherwise transmitting local cultures to newcomers problematic" (p. 89). Being socialized into a culture is more than being able to recite its history; it entails participation in deeply held assumptions about work and relationships that both existing and new members may not be able to articulate. Thus, it is both the importance of the issue and its complexity that has made socialization such a critical topic for organizational culture researchers.

It is one thing to discuss the academic vantage point on the interesting topic of socialization but it is also important to understand the meaning of socialization and the purpose it serves from the vantage point of the newcomer. The primary mechanism most often discussed as underlying the process of socialization is uncertainty reduction. In their model of socialization, Saks and Ashforth (1997) placed uncertainty reduction at the center, arguing that the information that comes from various organizational, group, and individual factors and actors serves to both reduce the uncertainty experienced by newcomers and increase their learning across the various content domains covered by socialization. As uncertainty and anxiety decrease and learning increases, there are proximal outcomes such as higher role clarity, higher perceptions of fit, and increased social integration, which then lead to more distal outcomes such as a stronger culture, higher cohesion, and improved effectiveness at the individual, group, and organizational levels. As we discussed earlier, one reason why organizational culture itself exists is its role of reducing complexity, streamlining cognitive processing, and providing shared understandings of language and acceptable behavior (Krefting & Frost, 1985; Trice & Beyer, 1993). These benefits of organizational culture can be seen as newcomers enter the organization and try to understand it. At first, the amount of information is overwhelming, whether it is about their job, their peers, or the organization as a whole, and the assumptions that guide the language and behavior of current organizational members are not readily apparent. However, as newcomers go through the socialization process, they learn the information they need from a variety of sources, which helps them to develop mental models for how to function in their job, role, group, and organization. Their status as full members of the organization can be identified by when the very assumptions of their coworkers that were so foreign to the newcomers initially are so fully accepted that they become the newcomers' own assumptions, operating outside of conscious awareness.

At this point, it is important to clarify that the literature on organizational socialization has developed in such a way that it is distinct from the literature on organizational culture. In fact, some discussions of the topic of socialization do not directly mention organizational culture at all (e.g., Bauer, Bodner, Erdogan, Truxillo, & Tucker, 2007). With that in mind, it would be beyond the scope of this book to try to provide a thorough review of the socialization literature. Instead, we will highlight some of the primary topics that have been addressed in this literature with an emphasis on those that are most relevant for our discussion of organizational culture.

Stages of Socialization

The idea that newcomers proceed through stages of socialization has its roots in the anthropological work on rites of passage. Of all the forms of organizational culture discussed in the last chapter (e.g., language, stories, jokes, traditions, heroes, behavioral norms, rules, taboos, dress), rites of passage are the most relevant for the socialization process in that they mark the newcomer's progression from outsider to full member of the organization. Trice and Beyer (1993) based their summary of the rites of passage on the work of Van Gennep (1908/1960), who discussed rites of separation, rites of transition, and rites of incorporation. The goal of rites of separation is to provide a clear break from the old and entry into the new. The most commonly cited example of this rite is the entry of a new recruit into the military. The recruit's old clothes are replaced by the standard, military-issued uniform, the recruit's hair is cut short to conform to military regulations, and the recruit is subject to severe consequences if his/her behavior does not fall in line with the group. The next rites of passage are rites of transition. In most organizations, this phase involves going through a training or orientation process to learn how the organization and their job work, which may include bonding experiences to bring together the group of new hires or "up-ending experiences" to demonstrate to new employees the problems with their previous ways of thinking and what they still have to learn. Once again, military boot camp provides a very vivid example of this phase, but any organization's training or orientation for new employees (e.g., Van Maanen's, 1991, discussion of the University of Disneyland, now called Disney University) would fit as well. The final rites of passage are the rites of incorporation. These rites typically involve the new employees beginning work in their new roles, perhaps with some sort of graduation ceremony or party (or even something as small as being issued permanent identification badges; McDonald, 1991) to mark their shift from trainees to regular employees. This phase is also marked by learning "the way things really are" in contrast to how they might have been described in orientation. Although not all of these rites may be fully incorporated in all organizations, they are likely to be found in some form or fashion in most socialization processes (perhaps in abbreviated or informal forms in many cases; Trice & Beyer, 1993).

In contemporary research on organizational socialization, various models have been proposed for the stages of socialization. Ashforth,

Sluss, and Harrison (2007) asserted that there are four stages that are generally agreed upon across models. The first stage is *anticipation*. This stage occurs prior to organizational entry and includes the expectations that the individual develops about the organization as well as the information the organization communicates about itself (whether accurate or not). The second stage is *encounter*, which addresses the individual's entry into the organization and the comparison of his or her actual experiences with the expectations developed during the anticipation stage. Louis (1980) highlighted the surprises that occur at this point, and the importance of the individual's affective reactions to the met and unmet expectations the individual encounters. Next is the third stage, *adjustment*, in which the individual overcomes the surprise or shock of the initial encounter and goes through the process of making sense of their experiences (Louis, 1980) and becoming integrated into the organization. This phase includes the individual's own efforts to learn about the organization as well as the organization's efforts (training, mentoring, etc.) designed to aid in the socialization process. The final stage, *stabilization*, is when the individual becomes a full member of the organization, including all the indicators that the shift from outsider to insider is complete.

The experiences newcomers have are, of course, of the levels and forms of organizational culture described earlier—the values, beliefs, norms, and behaviors that characterize an organization. In addition, those experiences may happen due to explicit interventions (classroom training, formal meetings with a supervisor or mentor) or implicitly (participating in discussions at lunch with new colleagues). It is to the tactics of socialization that we turn next.

Socialization Tactics

Building on the above, one area of particular interest among socialization researchers has been the tactics the organization uses to socialize its employees. Van Maanen and Schein (1979) presented a model of six tactics, each operating on a bipolar continuum. These tactics were collective versus individual (whether newcomers are socialized as a group or separately as individuals), formal versus informal (whether the activities for newcomers occur separately from current employees, e.g., in classes, or on the job in the presence of current employees), sequential versus random (whether or not there is a clear, step-by-step progression through the phases of the socialization process), fixed versus variable (whether the timetable for the socialization process is set or open), serial versus disjunctive (whether or not the newcomer has assistance during socialization from current employees or a mentor), and investiture versus divestiture (whether the organization is accepting of the employee and his/her characteristics or desires to have the employee separate from his/her pre-entry identity).

Jones (1986) proposed these socialization tactics might be clustered into two main domains: individualized socialization (individual, informal, random, variable, disjunctive, and divesture) and institutionalized socialization (collective, formal, sequential, fixed, serial, and investiture). In general, institutionalized practices have been found to be positively associated with higher job satisfaction, self-efficacy, intentions to remain, role clarity, social acceptance, job performance, organizational commitment, and lower rates of turnover (Bauer et al., 2007). There is some evidence, however, that individualized tactics may be more related to the levels of innovation displayed by new employees (e.g., Allen & Meyer, 1990; Jones, 1986).

Precisely how organizations communicate and perpetuate their culture during the stages of socialization and/or using these tactics has not been a primary focus of research in this area, but some insights have emerged. During the anticipation stage, organizations can use institutionalized forms of communication about their culture through their marketing, website, or news releases (Cable, Aiman-Smith, Mulvey, & Edwards, 2000). This information allows employees to make a preliminary judgment about whether they might be a good fit with the organization and its culture. Once individuals enter the organization, management can attempt to perpetuate its culture by explicitly reinforcing behaviors that are consistent with the organization's beliefs and values, or by influencing those beliefs and values directly through the individualized justifications that are provided for why things are done the way they are done (Sathe, 1985). Culture-relevant information is also communicated explicitly and implicitly through rites of passage, stories and sagas, organizational jargon and language, and any of the other symbolic cultural forms discussed previously (Ott, 1989; Trice & Beyer, 1993). Finally, the organization can perpetuate its culture by removing those individuals who deviate from the organization's norms and values. As noted by Ott (1989), "The departure of people who do not buy into the organizational culture transmits important symbolic messages about cultural expectations and the price of 'deviance' to all who remain" (p. 93).

Individual Proactive Socialization

The above literature primarily focuses on what the *organization* does to foster socialization, but the individual can also take a proactive role during this process. As Bell and Staw (1989) described it, much of the early socialization literature had treated newcomers using a sculpture metaphor rather than a sculptor metaphor. In other words, newcomers were treated as malleable subjects of the organization's socialization efforts to be sculpted to its culture, rather than as active, independently thinking participants creating their own sculpture. As literature on proactive socialization behavior has increased in recent years (see Bindl & Parker,

2010, for a review), there has been a rise in research specifically focusing on the role of proactivity during the socialization process.

The basic notion of this research is that as newcomers face the novelty of their new organizational context, they play a proactive role in trying to overcome their anxiety, stress, perceived lack of control, and perceived lack of information or knowledge (Ashford & Black, 1996; Crant, 2000; Griffin, Colella, & Goparaju, 2000; Miller & Jablin, 1991; Morrison, 1993). Miller and Jablin (1991) described the types of newcomer proactive behaviors as overt/covert questions, direct/indirect questions, third parties, testing limits, disguising conversation, observation, and surveillance. In a similar vein, Ashford and Black (1996) discussed them in terms of information-seeking, feedback-seeking, relationship-building, general socializing, networking, job-change negotiating, and positive framing. Through such proactive tactics, a newcomer learns more about his/her job, role, and most importantly for this book, the culture of his/her new organization.

What Is Learned and from Whom?

It is obviously one thing to discuss the stages of socialization and the tactics, both personal and organizational, by which socialization happens, but it is another thing to explore who does the socialization besides the newcomer and what constitutes the learnings associated with the new role. Drawing on the work of Feldman (1981) and Fisher (1986), Ostroff and Kozlowski (1992) studied four content areas of learning during socialization: task (how to perform the assigned job), role (clarifying the individual's authority, responsibility, and expectations), group (how the group interacts and what its norms are), and organization (the culture, including politics, values, mission, and leadership). Subsequent research by Chao, O'Leary-Kelly, Wolf, Klein, and Gardner (1994) focused on more specific areas of learning during socialization; of their six dimensions, one could be considered in the task domain (performance proficiency) and one in the group domain (social), but the other four would be considered in the organizational domain (politics, language, organizational goals/values, and history). These latter four dimensions shed light on the specific areas of organizational culture that are the particular focus for learning during socialization. One interesting finding by Ostroff and Kozlowski (1992) was that learning about the organization was actually less important than learning about the task, role, and group in the earliest stages of socialization. What this indicates is that the newcomer is likely to be more focused on those issues that immediately affect him/her (those that are more closely associated with the job itself) before issues involving the more macro organizational culture become more salient.

In addition to the content of what is learned, the sources of that information are also relevant. Although researchers have presented a variety of sources of information during socialization, Cooper-Thomas and Anderson (2006) proposed five general categories. Three can be grouped as organizational colleagues, including coworkers, supervisor, and mentor. The other two sources are organizationally sanctioned information sources: formal socialization programs (including training) and organizational literature. In their model, Cooper-Thomas and Anderson (2006) placed these sources on the following continuum ranging from most control to least control: organizational literature, formal socialization programs, mentor, supervisor, and coworkers. Those sources that are less controlled by the organization and more "natural" are likely to be more useful, which is consistent with research evidence (Louis, Posner, & Powell, 1983; Nelson & Quick, 1991; Ostroff & Kozlowski, 1992). These distinctions have particular relevance for the organizational culture literature. The level of control the organization has over each source is going to be related to the types of messages that are communicated about the organization's culture, and whether they are consistent with management's desired portrayal of the culture versus the "true" culture that exists in the organization. Furthermore, if there are significant subcultures in the organization (which we discuss in more depth in the next section), the portrayal of "the" organization's culture may vary significantly across these sources depending on the subculture with which the target of socialization is most familiar.

Summary

From the newcomer's vantage point, socialization is all about coping with the new environment—absorbing, learning, and exploring. He or she does this to reduce ambiguity and stress, and to learn to become a part of their new world. At the same time, organizations both implicitly and explicitly define for newcomers what it is they will learn and from whom they will learn it. In addition, this learning occurs in stages with first issues surrounding the task and the local job environment and later issues surrounding the larger organization and its history. From an organizational culture vantage point, it is the transmission of the existing culture to newcomers that yields stability of the culture over time, and consistency in how the organization is experienced and the behavioral norms that characterize it.

ORGANIZATIONAL CULTURE AND ORGANIZATIONAL EFFECTIVENESS

Much of the interest in the construct of organizational culture in the early 1980s by US researchers and practitioners concerned its potential effect on the bottom line. As US companies struggled to keep up with the quality products emerging from Japanese manufacturing, copying the Japanese quality-oriented culture seemed to offer promise for reducing the gap in quality and ultimately organizational effectiveness (Ouchi, 1981; Pascale & Athos, 1982). Early practitioner-focused publications (e.g., Deal & Kennedy, 1982; Peters & Waterman, 1982) were popular because of the potential they offered for leveraging culture as a way to improve organizational effectiveness. However, the results of practitioners' efforts to change organizational culture were largely disappointing with thinking on the topic shifting to recognition that culture change is not easy and certainly not a quick fix (Burke, 2011). This led some to wonder if culture change to improve organizational effectiveness was even possible at all (Siehl & Martin, 1990). Obviously, proponents of the link between organizational culture and organizational effectiveness fall into Smircich's (1983) organizations *have* cultures school of thought. That is, the reason to study organizations and their cultures is to understand differences among them and to establish a link to organizational effectiveness and not just to study organizational culture in the abstract (like the organizations *are* cultures school). The logic behind this supposed linkage is worth exploring.

Drawing on the writings of Kotter and Heskett (1992) and Denison and Mishra (1995), we highlight three reasons why this relationship between organizational culture and organizational effectiveness is thought to exist. The first is goal alignment, meaning that the organization's culture can be a vehicle for communicating and accomplishing organizational goals. When there is a strong culture, there is clarity for employees in where and how they should prioritize their energy and effort; everyone is on the same page. More broadly speaking, all the systems in the organization should also be aligned because they emerge from and are infused with the organization's core values. That is, following Schein (2010), only those processes that are initially effective and later consistent with the organization's culture will become part of the organization's cultural fabric.

Second, organizational culture can be a tool for management to informally influence or even control employee behavior without introducing the more negative consequences that typically accompany numerous formal rules and bureaucracy. Denison and Mishra (1995) referred to this informal influence on employees as consistency or normative integration. In other words, employees know how they are supposed to behave and handle certain situations based on the core values of the organization that have been communicated to them since they were newcomers, rather than a set of formal procedures that has been laid out in numbing detail.

The third reason why culture is thought to affect performance is the increased effort and motivation that a strong human-oriented culture elicits from employees. That is, as described by Kotter and Heskett (1992), much of the early work on organizational culture focused on the humanistic values that are part of the culture with writers such as Ouchi (1981), Pascale and Athos (1982), and Peters and Waterman (1982), emphasizing issues such as participation in decision making, recognition of employee contributions, or support for employee well-being. Denison and Mishra (1995) described how increased involvement increases employee ownership and responsibility, which subsequently results in higher levels of commitment and autonomy as well as higher quality decisions. In addition, part of the effect of an organization's culture is that it clarifies the organization's mission or direction (Denison & Mishra, 1995). By clarifying the importance of their work, employees experience increased levels of personal meaning, which yields higher levels of commitment and loyalty.

Recent reviews of research attempting to link organizational culture and effectiveness have been modestly encouraging. For example, in Wilderom, Glunk, and Maslowski's (2000) review, they identified ten studies that best represented the empirical literature on the relationship between organizational culture and organizational performance. Although the studies did show some support for a culture-performance relationship, a number of concerns about the operationalizations of both culture and performance, as well as various study design issues, led the authors to conclude that the ambiguous and less than convincing findings had resulted in little progress being made on the topic. In a follow-up review of the decade after the Wilderom and colleagues (2000) review, Sackmann (2011) identified 55 studies that examined the direct link between culture and performance. She was much more optimistic about the support for this relationship, concluding that it "seems to exist across industries and nations with somewhat similar trends regarding culture dimensions and culture types" (p. 212) and that cultures that are more "open-, adaptive-, outside-, customer-, mission- or goal-, achievement-, competitive-, people-, innovative-, and quality-oriented" (p. 217) will have higher performance.

More support for the relationship between organizational culture and performance can be found in Hartnell, Ou, and Kinicki's (2011) meta-analysis of this relationship based on the competing values framework (CVF; Quinn & Rohrbaugh, 1983). As we introduced in Chapter Two, the CVF is captured by a 2X2 framework created by crossing two bipolar dimensions: flexibility versus stability in structure, and an internal versus an external focus. The four resulting culture types are labeled clan (internal and flexible), adhocracy (external and flexible), market (external and stable), and hierarchy (internal and stable). Clan cultures tend to focus on affiliation and trust, adhocracy cultures on growth and innovation, market cultures on competition and achievement, and hierarchy cultures on structure and control. A summary description of each of these culture types in terms of levels of culture (e.g., assumptions, beliefs, values, and artifacts) is shown in Table 5.2 (from Hartnell et al., 2011; and based on Quinn & Kimberly, 1984). Hartnell and colleagues coded studies using a variety of measures of culture according to the CVF and then analyzed the relationships between the CVF and three criteria of organizational effectiveness (employee attitudes, operational performance, and financial performance). In addition to finding that clan cultures had the strongest

TABLE 5.2 A summary of the competing values framework from Hartnell et al. (2011)

Culture Type	Assumptions	Beliefs	Values	Artifacts (behaviors)	Effectiveness Criteria
Clan	Human affiliation	People behave appropriately when they have trust in, loyalty to, and membership in the organization.	Attachment, affiliation, collaboration, trust, and support	Teamwork, participation, employee involvement, and open communication	Employee satisfaction and commitment
Adhocracy	Change	People behave appropriately when they understand the importance and impact of the task.	Growth, stimulation, variety, autonomy, and attention to detail	Risk-taking, creativity, and adaptability	Innovation
Market	Achievement	People behave appropriately when they have clear objectives and are rewarded based on their achievements.	Communication, competition, competence, and achievement	Gathering customer and competitor information, goal-setting, planning, task focus, competitiveness, and aggressiveness	Increased market share, profit, product quality, and productivity
Hierarchy	Stability	People behave appropriately when they have clear roles and procedures are formally defined by rules and regulations.	Communication, routinization, formalization, and consistency	Conformity and predictability	Efficiency, timeliness, and smooth functioning

From Hartnell, C.A., Ou, A.Y., & Kinicki, A. (2011). Organizational culture and organizational effectiveness: A meta-analytic investigation of the competing values framework's theoretical suppositions. *Journal of Applied Psychology, 96,* 677–694, Figure 2, p. 679. Copyright © 2011 by the American Psychological Association and reprinted with permission.

relationships with employee attitudes and quality of products and services and market cultures had the strongest relationships with innovation and financial effectiveness, they showed that all four culture types were moderately positively correlated with each other and suggested that the four culture types may be complementary rather than competing. In other words, it may be best to be strong across multiple areas to take advantage of the synergistic effects of the culture types across multiple outcomes.

Despite the generally optimistic conclusions described previously, there is still much resistance to the idea that there should be a direct relationship between organizational culture and organizational performance. One concern is that the evidence is based on quantitative measures of culture, which as we have already described, tend to focus on the outer layers of culture (e.g., behavioral norms, espoused values) but may be less useful in penetrating culture's deeper layers (Alvesson & Berg, 1992). Thus, researchers like Saffold (1988), Siehl and Martin (1990), and Alvesson (2002) have bemoaned the simplicity of this research and how it ignores the complexity of the variety of forms and levels by which culture may be manifested in an organization's performance—as well as the very definition of organizational performance. Included in this lack of complexity is that an overall integrated strong culture is assumed and the presence of multiple subcultures is ignored. In other words, the literature on the link between organizational culture and organizational performance has essentially proposed a direct relationship between the two when there may be numerous boundary conditions on that relationship.

Two possible boundary conditions on the link between culture and effectiveness are the presence of organizational subcultures and the strength of the culture. The literature on these topics is extensive, and we cover each in subsequent sections of this chapter. At this point, we simply note that the two issues are closely related in that fewer subcultures should result in a stronger organizational culture, and similar to the climate literature, we would expect stronger relationships between organizational culture and organizational effectiveness when organizational culture is stronger. Another possible boundary condition concerns the fact that it is more than likely the case that the impact of certain elements of culture on performance will vary across contexts. Drawing a parallel to the findings on leadership in the GLOBE research (House et al., 2004), even if certain elements of culture are universally effective, it is likely that there are just as many or more that vary in their effectiveness across national cultures or industries (see Sørensen, 2002, for evidence of industry characteristics as a moderator). Recent literature has suggested that another possible boundary condition for the effects of specific culture dimensions (e.g., consistency) is the presence of high levels of other culture dimensions (e.g., involvement, adaptability, and mission; Kotrba, Gillespie, Schmidt, Smerek, Ritchie, & Denison, 2012); in other words, having a consistent culture may only be beneficial when the rest of the culture's content is positive.

Relevant for the discussion of the boundary conditions of the relationship between organizational culture and performance is Cooke and Szumal's (2000) discussion of why organizations with "negative" cultures can still be effective. They provide two reasons for this occurrence: the defensive misattribution of success and the culture bypass. The defensive misattribution of success captures the idea that "organizations that enjoy strong franchises, munificent environments, extensive patents and copyrights, and/or massive financial resources are likely to perform quite adequately, at least in the short term" (Cooke & Szumal, 2000, p. 160). The presence of these conditions makes it possible for organizations to implement ineffective systems and structures that lead to a negative culture without negative consequences, and in fact, they may attribute their success to their negative culture without realizing their success occurred *in spite of* their culture. The second explanation, the culture bypass, captures those organizations that essentially create systems and technologies that minimize the effect of culture on outcomes, allowing for the possibility that negative cultures can develop without the organization suffering the deleterious consequences typically associated with them. One example of this could be fast-food restaurants, in which "highly efficient technologies for operations at the store . . . level have been developed to maintain control, promote consistency, and reduce the need for a highly skilled or expensive workforce" (Cooke & Szumal, 2000, p. 161). In both of these cases, Cooke and Szumal (2000) argued (and we agree) that more positive cultures would still be beneficial for organizational effectiveness.

On the topic of effectiveness, a wide variety of performance measures have been used in this linkage research. Our review of the literature on this relationship since 2000 revealed some of this variety with outcomes including objective financial measures of performance (e.g., Denison, Nieminen, & Kotrba, 2012; Gregory, Harris, Armenakis, & Shook, 2009; Kotrba et al., 2012; Lee & Yu, 2004), customer satisfaction (e.g., Gillespie, Denison, Haaland, Smerek, & Neale, 2008), goal achievement (e.g., Xenikou & Simosi, 2006), and top management reports (e.g., Chan, Shaffer, & Snape, 2004; Glisson, Schoenwald, Kelleher, Landsverk, Hoagwood, Mayberg, & Green, 2008), as well as less traditional outcomes like the percentage of women in management (Bajdo & Dickson, 2001) and the odds of children receiving mental health care (Glisson & Green, 2006). Such diversity is encouraging in terms of demonstrating the effects of organizational culture on a variety of organizational performance and functioning indicators. At the same time, some concerns have been voiced in the literature with regard to the lack of theoretical justification for why the particular measures chosen should be the ones that culture is linked to or impacts the most (Wilderom et al., 2000), as well as the lack of acknowledgement that certain aspects of culture can have positive effects on some outcomes and negative effects on others (Saffold, 1988). In our view, the preferred approach would be to identify those elements of culture that are most relevant for specific outcomes in the same way that the climate literature has taken on a more strategic focus (we build on this point when we discuss the integration of these perspectives in Chapter Six). Along the same lines, it seems imperative to show *how* culture has its effects; in other words, identifying the possible mediating mechanisms for culture's relationship with performance is critical. For example, Gregory and colleagues (2009) demonstrated in a hospital setting that employee attitudes and physician attitudes mediated the relationship between organizational culture and the outcomes of controllable expenses and patient satisfaction. Other potential examples that we will come back to later include climate or specific employee behavior.

Arguments along these lines led Pettigrew (1990) to conclude that "culture does not provide a direct explanation of performance; it is only one component of a much more complex set of relationships that the process of competition contains" (p. 430). In light of the compelling arguments for approaching the climate-performance relationship in more complex ways than a simple direct relationship, what are some of the alternative perspectives that could add more insight into how culture has its effects? In Table 5.3, we provide a list of alternative perspectives that have been offered in the literature that address at least some of the criticisms described above. In her review, Sackmann (2011) provided

TABLE 5.3 Alternative perspectives on the relationship between culture and effectiveness

- *Mediated relationships:* What are the mechanisms that explain how culture has its influence on organizational performance?
- *Moderated relationships:* What are the environmental variables (national culture, industry, etc.) that explain when culture will have more or less of an effect?
- *Configurational perspectives:* What is the right mix of cultural dimensions to produce the desired outcomes?
- *Nonlinear relationships:* Is there such a thing as too much of certain cultural traits or dimensions?
- *Reciprocal relationships:* What is the effect of culture on organizational performance versus the effect of organizational performance on culture?
- *Fit or alignment perspectives:* What other aspects of the organization (structure, strategy, HR practices, and climate) must culture be aligned with to maximize performance outcomes?
- *Culture strength perspective:* Does the strength of the culture have direct or interactive effects on performance? Does the extent to which the culture is shared across individuals or subcultures affect the culture-performance relationship?
- *Negative cultures:* What cultural manifestations are the most detrimental to performance?
- *Adaptive cultures:* Is it possible to have a culture that is flexible enough to adapt to changing environmental conditions while also maintaining a set of constant core values—perhaps, indeed, the core value of change itself?

examples of culture-performance studies that examined the link in terms of indirect or mediated effects, nonlinear effects, moderated or interactive effects, and reciprocal effects. Although some of these studies focused on individual performance and others had design limitations, we are encouraged that researchers have begun to take a more complex perspective on how culture is related to organizational performance in line with Saffold's (1988) admonition that "a more sophisticated understanding of the tie between culture and organizational outcomes must be developed" (p. 546).

Before closing this section, we want to return to the point that some authors, particularly those from the organizations *are* cultures perspective, question the nature of this research on organizational effectiveness as a whole. For instance, Siehl and Martin (1990) voiced their concern that not only does a focus on the relationship between organizational culture and performance distract researchers away from other more innovative or more in-depth investigations of culture, but it may also have pernicious effects for employees, particularly women and minorities, by taking a managerialist perspective that promotes the control of employees' thoughts and emotions. Others, like Alvesson and Berg (1992), have voiced a perhaps more moderate perspective that although culture is "clearly relevant for the functioning of organizations and is of crucial importance in understanding corporate management, influences on people, etc." (p. 186), quantitative studies like those reviewed by Wilderom et al. (2000) and Sackmann (2011) reduce culture to just another organizational variable. In a similar way, Alvesson (1993) concluded that ". . . the goal of promoting effectiveness tends to rule out complicated research designs and 'deep' thinking" (p. 6). At the same time, research ignoring culture's link to effectiveness (largely from the organizations *are* cultures perspective), has had little practical effect on organizations (Alvesson & Berg, 1992; Martin & Frost, 1996), as noted earlier. So what are researchers to do?

We propose that there are some key steps researchers could take that would balance the concerns for lack of depth and lack of practicality. For researchers from the organizations *have* cultures perspective, and specifically those that use quantitative measures of culture, it would be useful to more regularly acknowledge that their measures do not capture the full organizational culture in all of its levels, depth, and complexity, but only specific facets or layers of that culture. Accordingly, conclusions from research on organizational culture and effectiveness should be explicit about what can and cannot be concluded based on the research designs used. Furthermore, arguments made about changing organizational culture based on a quantitative survey research project are specious at best. Performing research that supplements quantitative methods with qualitative research would be the ideal extension, allowing researchers to not only draw conclusions about broad relationships that exist but also to clarify those findings with more specific details and perhaps contradictions. See Denison and Mishra (1995) for an excellent example of the insights that can be gained from mixing quantitative and qualitative methods.

For researchers from the organizations that *are* cultures perspective, tough decisions must be made about standing by principles and maintaining a critical, anti-managerialist perspective versus acknowledging managers' concerns and integrating culture's connection to effectiveness in their research. Furthermore, collaborating with culture researchers who tend to use quantitative methods could result in mutual enlightenment and potentially much more effective research than either could perform alone. Martin (2002) calls such studies "hybrid" because they use both qualitative and quantitative methods. In her description of the ways in which such hybrid studies can be conducted and the results that can emerge, she reports on a study by Martin, Su, and Beckman (1997). The results of this study of a small publishing company were informative because both the survey data used and the qualitative information gathered revealed evidence for all three of Martin's (2002) perspectives in different though related ways. Martin (2002) provided an extensive discussion of qualitative, quantitative, and hybrid research paradigms and a very instructive evaluation of each, along with the possibilities and learnings that might emerge from those who use the hybrid approach (see her Chapter Seven: "To Count or Not to Count"). She was particularly emphatic about the use of the hybrid approach for exploring "empty spaces" in the research on organizational culture, a topic we return to in our later attempt to integrate the climate and culture literatures and approaches. Especially for researchers interested in the linkage between organizational culture and organizational effectiveness it would seem to be true that the hybrid model is potentially the most useful. This is because not only might such a link be established, but also the underlying cultural manifestations that yield the link will be identified and thus be useful in proposed actions to actually enhance effectiveness.

ORGANIZATIONAL SUBCULTURES

As we noted in the previous section, one issue that might prevent or inhibit the establishment of a link between culture and effectiveness is the presence of subcultures in organizations. That is, if there is no "culture" but many subcultures, what is the independent variable in the hoped-for link? Van Maanen and Barley (1985) defined an organizational subculture as "a subset of an organization's members who interact regularly with one another, identify themselves as a distinct group within the organization, share a set of problems commonly defined to be the problems of all [in the group], and routinely take action on the basis of collective understandings unique to the group" (p. 38). That is, as has been highlighted by Martin (2002) in her description of the differentiation perspective, all aspects of organizational culture are not necessarily shared throughout an organization. Instead, subsets of organizational members may share perceptions and values that differ from other groups or the organization as a whole. Martin and colleagues (2006) portrayed differentiation studies as sharing three characteristics: "(1) interpretations of manifestations are inconsistent; (2) consensus occurs only within subcultural boundaries; and (3) clarity exists only within subcultures" (p. 730).

Martin and Siehl (1983) identified three types of subcultures that may be found in organizations. The first, an enhancing subculture, exists when a certain subgroup within the organization identifies more strongly and is "more fervent" about the organization's core values than is found elsewhere in the organization. The second type of subculture is an orthogonal subculture. In this case, the subculture both accepts the organization's core values and identifies with a separate set of values that does not conflict with those of the organization (such as those of an occupational group). The third example is a countercultural subculture. In this case, the subculture shares a set of values that is directly contradictory to the values of the core or dominant culture.

There are many examples of subcultures in the literature, mostly based on qualitative research. For instance, Gregory (1983) investigated subcultures within Silicon Valley from a "native" perspective, finding a variety of distinctions among workers such as by department (engineering versus marketing versus sales), by the type of product being worked on (hardware versus software), and by the broader occupational community (engineers versus scientists), all of which may also share some values and perspectives with each other. In a fascinating example, Martin and Siehl (1983) described the countercultural subculture created within a division of GM headed by John DeLorean. They first identified three core values at GM (respecting authority, fitting in, and being loyal) and then analyzed how DeLorean both ridiculed these values and articulated an alternative set of values in contradiction to the core values of the general GM culture. DeLorean successfully violated these cultural norms by developing a series of cars in the 1960s for the Pontiac division of GM (the GTO muscle car, the Firebird, and the Grand Prix) that were completely different from anything else GM had.

Van Maanen (1991), who conducted some of the most significant early work on cultural socialization reviewed earlier, discussed the insider culture of Disneyland, where he identified both a general subculture difference between supervisors and line staff, as well as a hierarchy among employees based on specialized, differentiated skills. At the top of the hierarchy were the ambassadors and tour guides, followed by "skilled" ride operators, all other ride operators, "sweepers," and food and concessions workers. These levels shared macro-cultural experiences and perspectives but differed significantly on some others. In a similar vein, Bartunek and Moch (1991) related their findings of organizational subcultures in a commercial bakery. They found differences between top management (who tended to emphasize control), plant managers (who emphasized their responsibility for all plant-level decision making), line employees (who passively expected others to make change and improve conditions), and machinists (who had a primarily competitive view of other employees driven by differences in union membership).

A final example of these subcultural differences in organizations is of interest because of its use of the hybrid research model described earlier (see Martin, 2002). In their study of an urban police department, Jermier, Slocum, Fry, and Gaines (1991) performed cluster analysis on survey data and discovered five subcultures. Using information from their qualitative observational work, they illustrated the differences among these subcultures across a number of variables such as commitment, rank, assignment, shift, tenure, and work performance. Their findings revealed that only one of the subcultures was closely aligned with the "official" culture of the police department, whereas the other four shared some aspects of the official culture but contradicted it in other ways.

These examples indicate how subcultures may be a result of a vertical "slice" of the organization, such as a department, division, geographic location, or a horizontal "slice" that cuts across units, such as by job or level in the organization (Louis, 1985). They also demonstrate some of the factors that drive subculture development. Van Maanen and Barley (1985) described several such possible factors including "physical proximity, the sharing of common tasks or status, dependencies in the workflow, demands made by some members on others, and even accidents of history" (p. 37). Based on these factors, individuals interact more regularly, share similar problems, develop collective understandings, and create a shared interpretive or sense-making system that drives the normative behavior in the subculture. Trice and Beyer (1993) identified similar factors (differential interactions, shared experiences) as well as personal characteristics (such as similarity in age, ethnicity, or education) that help to create social cohesion among individuals that forms a foundation for the development of a subculture. Subcultures can also develop based on a number of other issues, such as a merger or acquisition or shared mistreatment that brings various groups together (Trice & Beyer, 1993).

One important distinction that has been made in terms of the types of subcultures is between those that exist within the boundaries of the organization versus those that cut across or transcend organizations (Louis, 1985; Trice & Beyer, 1993). With regard to the latter, Louis (1985) has discussed how organizational subcultures may exist due to broader differences that exist outside the organization that then act as "feeder cultures" (Louis, 1985) to the organization's subcultures. Abrahamson and Fombrun's (1994) concept of macrocultures captures a similar line of thinking. Schein (1996) described three transcendent organizational subcultures, or subcultures to be expected across all or most organizations: the operator subculture (comprised of line employees who must use specific technology to perform the work collaboratively with other operators), the engineering subculture (comprised of employees who design the technology and focus on creating elegant and precise solutions to problems), and the executive subculture (comprised of top management whose primary focus is on the financial issues that are of interest to shareholders, boards, and the markets). He depicted the operator culture as developing locally based on the technologies and processes used to perform the work, and thus could be considered organization-specific, whereas the engineering and executive cultures cut across organizations due to the similar nature of the problems faced and the educational background of the employees, resulting in cross-organization occupational communities or subcultures.

The presence of occupational subcultures has perhaps received the most attention in the literature on subcultures. In many ways, how occupational subcultures develop and persist is a duplication of the processes that contribute to macro-culture (Trice & Beyer, 1993; Van Maanen & Barley, 1984). For instance, occupational members experience socialization processes, including various rites and rituals, to mark the transition from an outsider to a member of the occupation. Occupational members may have to meet certain educational requirements and/or demonstrate required knowledge through licensing examinations. Much like organization cultures, occupational cultures are also manifested in a variety of similar forms, such as language, jargon, myths, stories, traditions, and rules, which can be perpetuated through professional associations or unions that act as the gatekeepers for the occupational group. One key difference from organizational cultures is that occupational subcultures form more based on the commonality of experiences of the members and less so based on specific leader or founder behaviors. The "embedding mechanism" of occupational subcultures is commonality of experiences; the experiences are common, and it is not a question of what works or fails to work to produce effectiveness, as we have described occurring with the overall organizational culture.

In much the same way that organizational cultures exist as a function of the individuals that make them up, occupational cultures reflect the individuals within them. For example, as a precursor to the organizational attraction processes in the initial stages of the ASA model (Schneider, 1987), individuals are attracted to certain occupations. Holland's (1997) work on career environments provides the clearest evidence of how certain types of individuals tend to be attracted to certain occupations, and it is the common values and characteristics of those individuals that create the occupation's culture. By way of example, consider two of Holland's (1997) six career environments, the Artistic Career Environment (e.g., advertising agencies, ballet companies) and the Realistic Career Environment (e.g., accounting firms, manufacturing organizations), and the kinds of people one would expect to find in them. Holland has documented that certain traits (shown in Table 5.4) characterize people in these two kinds of career environments. Along these lines, one can easily imagine the differences that would exist in the two different occupational subcultures. The occupational cultures represented in an organization and the relative influence and status that different occupations have within the organization will have a strong influence on the general organizational culture that emerges.

TABLE 5.4 Personality types in artistic and realistic careers (based on Holland, 1997)

Realistic Types	Artistic Types
Conforming	Complicated
Dogmatic	Disorderly
Hardheaded	Expressive
Inflexible	Imaginative
Natural	Intellectual
Normal	Introspective
Practical	Precise
Realistic	Intuitive
Robust	Open
Self-effacing	Original

At this point, we have discussed a number of different subcultures that may exist in organizations. How these different subcultures function in organizations is complex because they can intersect, overlap, and coexist simultaneously. For instance, certain individuals may share a particular job in the organization, come from a similar occupational background, have similar education or training, and be of a similar demographic (e.g., gender and/or ethnic group). One can see how these confluences of characteristics and attributes may naturally emerge in organizations especially when viewed through the lens of the ASA model (Schneider, 1987). In addition, such discussions highlight the overlap between the literatures on organizational culture and organizational identity (for more on this overlap, see Fiol, Hatch, & Golden-Biddle, 1998; Hatch & Schultz, 1997, 2000; Kreiner, 2011; and Ravasi & Schultz, 2006).

Before moving forward, it is important to note that there is a tension in the organizational culture literature as to whether it is more appropriate to study organizations as having a singular general culture or as many unique subcultures. The nature of this tension and which of these perspectives is dominant is unclear. Some have characterized these as warring perspectives, with the dominant (or integrated) culture perspective as the standard that was being challenged by the disenfranchised and marginalized researchers who preferred to focus on subcultures (Martin & Frost, 1996). Others viewed the landscape much differently, noting, "few scholars doubt the presence of subcultures in organizations, but some doubt that organizations have organization wide umbrella cultures" (Trice & Beyer, 1993, p. 13). As these perspectives have evolved, the answer seems to be much less of an either/or but a both/and (Martin, 2002; Trice & Beyer, 1993). In other words, the answer to the question of whether organizations have a general culture or subcultures is in most cases "yes." There are certainly cases when an organization can have a single general culture and no identifiable subcultures, and perhaps also cases when there are such distinct separate subcultures that no clear general, shared culture can be identified (e.g., a conglomerate with distinct, independent business units). However, in most cases, especially in larger organizations, there are likely to be cultural elements shared across all employees while simultaneously cultural elements that are distinct in individual subcultures.

In our view, Van Maanen and Barley (1985) offered the most useful way to think about the simultaneous existence of a general organizational culture and its subcultures. They described the subcultures of an organization as circles in a Venn diagram. The area of overlap among all of the circles can be viewed as *the* organizational culture. When there are high levels of overlap among the circles and very little areas that are not shared, then the organization is best characterized as having a general integrated culture with little differentiation within it. However, if the area of overlap among the circles is relatively small compared to the space that is not within overlapping circles, then a subculture lens will be appropriate, with perhaps only a few elements that could truly be viewed as shared across the entire organization. Where most organizations likely exist is somewhere in between, with some elements that are relatively homogeneous across subcultures and other elements in which there is much differentiation.

Van Maanen and Barley (1985) identified some of the conditions that may directly result in an organization's placement on that general continuum. For instance, an organization may be more likely to have a unitary culture when it is small with dense social ties, when it faces a crisis, or when organizational members all come from a strong occupational culture. We are reminded here of the point we made earlier with regard to national culture and industry influences on organizational culture. In that case, we recalled the forest and trees metaphor suggesting that one may view the forest from on high and find little differentiation but when one gets closer to the trees then there is obviously differentiation in the kinds of trees in the forest. We see a similar metaphor being appropriate in the case of subcultures in organizations. That is, depending on the issue being studied and the comparative frame of reference, the presence of subcultures may be more or less apparent.

CULTURE STRENGTH

The idea of culture strength is closely related to discussions about organizational culture and organizational effectiveness as well as about organizational subcultures. When distinguishing between culture content and culture strength, there is a shift from describing the assumptions, values, beliefs, and norms in the organization to describing how much agreement, acceptance, or penetration those assumptions, values, beliefs, and norms have in the organization. The idea of culture strength is related to both the differentiation perspective and the fragmentation perspective in Martin's (2002) framework. The differentiation perspective emphasizes the existence of subcultures in the organization. When an organization has sharply distinct subcultures with few common elements shared among them, then the overall culture strength for the organization will be low (although it may be high in each individual subculture). When the subcultures have more shared elements and fewer elements in isolation and/or direct conflict, then the overall culture strength for the organization will be high.

In the fragmentation perspective, the focus on ambiguity in the culture seems to align well with the idea that individuals in the organization may not agree about the content of the culture (i.e., low culture strength). However, there are aspects of the fragmentation perspective that are distinct from the idea of culture strength. Although there can be ambiguity in the extent to which people view the organization's culture (resulting in low culture strength), there can also be shared perceptions about the ambiguity that is part of employees' daily organizational experiences (resulting in high culture strength on the issue of ambiguity). For instance, the loose structure among hospital social workers studied by Meyerson (1991a) created a great deal of "structural ambiguity," but there seemed to be a clear consensus among the social workers about the nature of the structure and the presence of that ambiguity. As another example, Feldman (1991) described the lack of clarity about the organizational goals within the Department of Energy, but at the same time, the workers were "clear . . . that the organization was not doing a very good job at whatever it was supposed to be doing" (p. 149). Thus, we would consider the employee perceptions of ambiguity to be an issue of the content of the culture, whereas variability (or consensus) about the presence of ambiguity (or any other content) would be an issue of culture strength.

Researchers have acknowledged since at least the mid-1980s that there are a variety of ways to think about culture strength. Louis (1985) and Saffold (1988) used the term "cultural penetration" to capture what is often referred to as culture strength. They described the following four types of cultural penetration or strength (the first three from Louis, 1985, and the last one from Saffold, 1988):

- *Sociological penetration* is probably the most commonly implied meaning of culture strength; it refers to the extent to which the culture is shared across the members of the organization as a whole, including across various groups or subcultures in the organization (horizontal penetration) and across layers of the organizational hierarchy (vertical integration). This type of strength has also been described in terms of cultural consensus (versus dissensus; Trice & Beyer, 1993), strength of consensus (Payne, 2000, 2001), crystallization (Mannix, Thatcher, & Jehn, 2001), and value congruence (Meglino, Ravlin, & Adkins, 1989, 1991).
- *Psychological penetration* involves how deeply individuals in the organization hold the assumptions, values, and beliefs that make up their organization's culture. This type of strength has also been described in terms of psychological intensity (Mannix et al., 2001; Payne, 2000, 2001).

- *Historical penetration* introduces the element of time and involves how long the culture has consistently existed within the organization. Implied in this type of strength is the effectiveness of socialization efforts in passing along the culture to new members.
- *Artifactual penetration* captures the extent to which the more deeply held assumptions values are manifested in the outer layers of the organization's culture (i.e., in its artifacts). In this case, the stronger the culture, the more likely it will be to have penetrated throughout all aspects of the organization including those most observable in the form of pictures, displays of various awards and honors, and so forth.

Other, related conceptualizations of strength focus more on the breadth of assumptions or values that are impacted by the culture. For instance, Sathe (1985) discussed strength in terms of how many assumptions there are (Sathe, 1985), and Payne (2000, 2001) included the dimension of pervasiveness in his model of culture to capture the "range of beliefs and behaviors that the culture attempts to define and control" (Payne, 2000, p. 167). Despite the variety of ways culture strength has been conceptualized, our take is that the most commonly implied meaning of culture strength is in terms of the "sharedness" of culture perceptions, and thus most of our discussion will focus on strength from that perspective.

Before moving forward with that discussion, we wanted to highlight another closely related idea to culture strength: cultural alignment, which is sometimes referred to as cultural congruence (Cameron & Ettington, 1988) or fit (Kotter & Heskett, 1992). There are at least two types of alignment that can be discussed with regard to organizational culture: the alignment among internal elements within the organization and the alignment between the internal elements and the external environment. In Schein's (2010) writings, this distinction was discussed in terms of internal integration and external adaptation; Saffold (1988) framed these as elemental coherence and strategic fit. Our purpose in mentioning the issue of alignment here is to clarify that it is a related but separate issue from culture strength. Although some authors treat the two as almost interchangeable (especially with regard to internal alignment; see Deal & Kennedy, 1982), the two are distinct in important ways. Most notably, internal cultural alignment is likely a precursor to a strong culture, such that the more aligned the various structures, processes, and communications within the organization are, the more likely that members will agree about the nature of the organization's culture (e.g., what is valued in the organization). It is likely best to think of external alignment as a separate issue; an organization can have high internal alignment and a strong culture, but it may or may not be a good fit with the external environment and the demands of the marketplace.

Having clarified at least some of the conceptual issues regarding culture strength, we now turn to some of the key findings on the topic and the implications of culture strength for organizational effectiveness and change. A starting point is the relationship between culture strength and organizational performance. Although it is difficult to make broad generalizations about research in this area because of the variety of operationalizations of culture strength that have been used (Wilderom et al., 2000), there is some evidence that culture strength is related to organizational effectiveness. Some of the strongest evidence comes from research by Denison (1990) and Gordon and DiTomaso (1992). They both used measures of variability (variance and standard deviation, respectively) in employee responses to survey items to operationalize culture strength and found that stronger cultures were significantly associated with better organizational performance (based on objective indicators of performance like return on investment [ROI] and growth in assets), at least in the short term (roughly the next 2–4 years after measuring culture strength).

Kotter and Heskett (1992) used a direct measurement of perceived organizational culture strength in their research by collecting reports of organizations' culture strength from officers of other organizations in the same industry. They found a positive relationship between this perceived culture strength and performance as measured by ROI, although the correlation was relatively weak ($r = 0.31$). Sørensen (2002) used the culture strength data from Kotter and Heskett (1992) with the additional outcome of operating cash flow, and found a significant zero-order correlation of similar magnitude ($r = 0.29$). We suspect that some of the relationship found in these studies is due to a bias in the respondents who provided the data used for assessing culture strength. In the Kotter and Heskett data, respondents were reporting on the culture strength of their known competitors. The financial accomplishments of known competitors are also of course known. Implicitly people may be likely to believe that a financially successful company must have a strong culture so they report that company A (successful) has a strong culture while company B (less successful) is said to have a weak culture.

Even if this measurement issue did not influence the positive findings for culture strength from Kotter and Heskett (1992) and Sørensen (2002), there are some reasons that a direct relationship between culture strength and performance is likely an oversimplification of the effects culture strength can have for organizations (much in the same way that a direct relationship for the content of culture is likely oversimplified). One issue is that it is obviously possible to have a strong culture that leads to ineffectiveness. However, as Kotter and Heskett (1992) have argued, this case would be rare because such organizations would be unlikely to survive for very long. A more likely issue is that the simple presence of a strong culture does not mean it is the optimal culture for organizational success. This argument was made by Kotter and Heskett (1992) and was the reason they went beyond a simple "strong culture" argument to explore "strategically appropriate" cultures, or those that fit the environmental demands the organization faces. Along similar lines, Sørensen (2002) argued that a strong culture will not be universally beneficial, and specifically that industry volatility will moderate the effects of culture strength on organizational performance. In support of this line of thinking, he found that a strong culture was beneficial under stable environmental conditions, but the benefits decreased as industry volatility increased. Thus, he concluded that strong cultures will not be as able to perform the exploratory learning (discovering new ways of doing things) or benefit when such learning does occur, preventing the occurrence of the broader-based organizational change that is required in a volatile environment. In line with these findings, Lee and Yu (2004) found that culture strength was related to organizational performance in manufacturing and insurance firms, but not hospitals, suggesting that industry characteristics might moderate the effects of culture strength.

The literature described above has implications for the role of culture strength in organizational change, a topic that has been of much interest to culture researchers over the years (as we discuss in the next section). In line with Sørensen's (2002) findings, some authors have argued that a strong culture can be problematic for change, and that ambiguity in a culture can make change easier. Sathe (1985) suggested that organizational change involves replacing old assumptions with new ones, which will be harder to do for organizations with stronger cultures, especially if a large-scale change effort is contemplated. Thus, organizations with weaker cultures are actually better targets for change as they will encounter less resistance to change from their employees. Other authors like Kotter and Heskett (1992) and Flynn and Chatman (2001) have offered an alternative perspective. Kotter and Heskett (1992) proposed the idea of adaptive cultures, which are cultures with a strong "core" but are flexible otherwise. Specifically, they argued that an organization would maximize its likelihood for sustained success when it is willing to adapt all aspects of its functioning to achieve its core *goal* of simultaneously satisfying the interests of customers, employees, and shareholders. When adaptability and flexibility are the primary cultural values, a strong culture is not necessarily detrimental to change. Similarly, in an insightful article on the relationship between strong cultures and innovation, Flynn and Chatman (2001) argued that a strong culture does not necessarily impede innovation, but instead it depends on the content of the culture that is strong. Specifically, they distinguished between conformity, in terms of forces that encourage agreement and harmony, and uniformity, which translates into exact consistency of the attitudes and behaviors of organizational members. Thus, a strong culture can emphasize cultural content such as creativity and risk-taking that form the foundation for innovation without resulting in uniformity.

Although there has been progress in theory and research on culture strength, the literature on the topic is still limited. Going back to Schein's (1991, p. 248) quote that "if things are ambiguous, then, by definition, that group does not have a culture," it is not clear how much consensus around a certain element is necessary for it to be "culture." Alvesson (2002) has criticized the concept of culture strength, noting that "to suggest that cultures can be measured on the single dimension of 'strength' deprives the concept of analytic and interpretive capacity: culture is a complex web of meanings, not a bundle of muscles" (p. 49). His point is well taken, and it is certainly possible for a culture to be strong with regard to certain content and weak with regard to others. Much in the same way that we emphasized the need for specificity in the dimensions of culture that might predict organizational effectiveness, there is a need for focus on specific areas of culture and their strength rather than attempting to make general conclusions that may or may not apply across the culture as a whole. In fact, it may be a certain configuration of culture strength, strong in some areas but weak in others, that is optimal for organizational effectiveness.

Finally, the focus in the literature on culture strength has primarily been on the consensus or agreement about culture. Not only are there different types of consensus (e.g., agreement within subcultures but lack of consensus across subcultures versus a more general lack of consensus across all organizational members), there are also a number of other conceptualizations of culture strength, as outlined above, that have not received much attention in the literature. More work is needed on these other types of strength and how they may integrate together to influence organizational functioning and outcomes.

ORGANIZATIONAL CULTURE CHANGE

Organizational change, broadly conceptualized, has been of long-term interest to industrial/organizational psychologists, organizational development specialists, and management consultants. For example, by 1961 there was sufficient material on organizational change for what has since become an iconic edited book of readings, *The Planning of Change: Readings in the Applied Behavioral Sciences* (Bennis, Benne, & Chin, 1961; the very same Warren Bennis of more contemporary leadership fame). The book outlined the learnings to that time from such efforts as the Training Group Movement (T-Groups) that emerged first in the field of education and then expanded to business and industry. T-Groups were based initially on the writings of Kurt Lewin (1951) and the work he did during World War II to change people's attitudes using the vehicle of groups. The authors in the edited volume read like a who's who in the history of the study of organizational change: Robert Merton, Alvin Gouldner, Ronald Lippitt, Talcott Parson, Dorwin Cartwright, Herbert Kelman, Herbert Shephard, and Douglas McGregor. The *Journal of Applied Behavioral Science*, devoted to reporting on research concerning organizational change, published its first issue in March 1965 and is still going strong today.

Our point is not to review the literature on organizational change (see Burke, 2011, for an excellent review) but to make the reader aware of the fact that change in organizations has been a long-term concern in general and that the approaches to change based on thinking about organizational culture may make a significant contribution to ways of conceptualizing it. Morgan (2006, p. 138) put the usefulness of a culture framework for understanding organizations and their change this way:

> There can be little doubt that the culture metaphor offers a fresh way of thinking about organizations. It shows that the challenge of creating new forms of organization and management is very much a challenge of cultural change. It is a challenge of transforming the mind-sets, visions, paradigms, images, metaphors, beliefs and shared meanings that sustain existing business realities and of creating a detailed language and code of behavior through which the desired new reality can be lived on a daily basis.

We agree. Our perspective is that consideration of the ways organizational culture emerges in organizations and is maintained over time and the central role of leadership in that emergence and maintenance are the keys to understanding organizational change as well.

The extent to which organizational culture can and does change has been a pervasive issue in the culture literature. As we noted in Chapter Four, a recurring theme in the definition of culture is that it is relatively consistent, stable, and even static over time, thereby suggesting that it is difficult to change. For example, when describing their attempts to change culture, Deal and Kennedy (1982) noted, "In time, we came to recognize that culture is *the* barrier to change. The stronger the culture, the harder it is to change. Culture causes organizational inertia; it's the brake that resists change because this is precisely what culture should do—protect the organization from willy-nilly responses to fads and short-term fluctuations" (p. 159). In fact if a major reason for people to have a sense of the culture in which they work (or live) is to reduce ambiguity about the rules and their roles, then it is clear what change will lead to—ambiguity! Perhaps most importantly we typically enter existing organizations to study their cultures after those cultures have already developed—with the emphasis on the word *developed*. When we get to work in and study and try to change organizational culture we always must remember that it is the way it is because of the process of trying alternatives and keeping the ones that succeeded; in other words, it worked. Organizational culture can appear rigid, static, consistent, and stable to consultants and managers who underestimate the changes that got the organization to where it is and, because of its successes, found that culture useful. It is wise to have this developmental framework in mind so that the difficulties associated with planned culture change will be expected.

Most of the literature has recognized that cultures do change in some form or fashion since they evolved to get where they are. All cultures change, but after the initial burst of evolution the changes are usually slower; cultures look like they are rigid and static precisely when someone wants them to change. That is, under "normal" circumstances stability is good because it provides the consistency in rules and roles people need to be aware of what is expected of them and to what they should direct their energies and competencies. When someone wants engagement and competencies to be directed in new ways—they want people to have an altered set of what is expected of them—then the issue of culture change emerges. Until the question of change emerges, no one thinks people are resisting change because they are doing precisely what is expected of them.

To our way of thinking, issues of culture change are no different from the issues we have previously discussed with regard to the growth and development of cultures, their maintenance over time, and the import of leaders in making these happen. So, what results in change are the same actions on the part of leaders that embed culture in the first place. In what follows, we first illuminate the stages of culture emergence in organizations through the typical organizational life cycle and then address the specific issue of leadership and culture change.

Organizational Culture: Stability and Natural Evolution

We have already highlighted that it is common for researchers to describe culture as generally stable such that it can provide decreased cognitive load (Krefting & Frost, 1985) and reduced uncertainty (Trice & Beyer, 1993) for organizational members. Along those lines, Schein (2010) emphasized, "Culture is something that survives even when some members of the organization depart. Culture is hard to change because group members value stability in that it provides meaning and predictability" (p. 16). Similarly, Ott (1989) emphasized the stability of culture while recognizing that it does evolve over time, albeit slowly.

Others place a heavier emphasis on the dynamic nature of culture. For instance, Hatch (2000) argued that culture changes continuously as new artifacts are introduced and given meaning, and as fundamental assumptions become manifest in new artifacts. She concluded that "culture never stops changing; rather, it is in continuous dynamic flux" (p. 259). Markus (2000) described a similar perspective: "Rather than approaching OC [organizational culture] as a naturally inert structure in which change requires explanation, however, I approach OC as a dynamic system in a natural state of flux such that stability requires explanation" (p. 297). From his view, culture is "day in and day out being shaped and reshaped through dynamic processes" (p. 300). Thus, there is a tension in the literature between the emphases on culture stability versus change. That tension is captured by this quote from Trice and Beyer (1993): "While cultures create continuity and persist across generations of members, they are not static, but dynamic. Cultures continually change" (p. 7).

One middle ground position on stability and change in organizations involves consideration of the life cycles of organizations. From this perspective, an organization's culture will naturally evolve as it goes through the various life stages organizations tend to experience and its members cope with the issues that they confront at each stage. Examples in the culture literature integrating the ideas of organizational life cycles and culture include Payne's (2001) description of the four stages of organizational culture development (conception, conversion, consolidation, and collapse), and Cameron and Quinn's (2011) connection of their work on the competing values framework to organizational life cycles by suggesting that organizations typically move through the types in the framework in a certain order (starting with adhocracy and then moving through the clan, hierarchy, and market types).

Schein (2010) dedicated considerable space to the discussion of how organizational cultures are affected by their stage in the life cycle. He described three general stages that organizations experience: founding and early growth, midlife, and maturity and decline. As we have previously discussed with regard to the sources of culture, Schein (2010) noted that in the earliest stages of the organization the culture is largely driven by the founder's values that he/she infuses into the culture through the various embedding mechanisms he or she enacts. At the same time, the culture must adapt to the various environmental challenges it faces as well as the growth it experiences. It is in this very early stage that the core values of the corporation become more fixed as it copes with the variety of challenges such new companies encounter. In the absence of a major crisis, the core organizational values begin to be fixed relatively quickly and are unlikely to change drastically during this stage. However, those values may take on different forms or manifestations in different parts of the organization depending on what has worked best to deal effectively with the challenges members have faced and the kinds of people recruited to deal with those challenges. For instance, the more functionally/occupationally oriented new people are, the more likely there is to be differentiation and the formation of subcultures within an organization.

Schein (2010) marked entry into midlife by the shift from the original founders to the next generation of management of the organization. At this point, the culture is much more likely to be taken for granted by members, such that what were once the founder's values have become the organization's values. At the same time, the values may be weakened due to the founder no longer being as active as early in the organization's life cycle. Indeed he or she may no longer even be present, possibly resulting in some disorientation and conflict within the organization as new executives come aboard and try to have an impact. Although Schein (2010) explicitly did not associate the midlife stage with size or time (see Flamholtz & Randle, 2011, for a size/sales/revenue perspective on organizational life cycles), he did acknowledge that it is likely that organizations in midlife will begin to see the formation of subcultures associated with such size-related factors as functional differentiation, geographical decentralization, and/or divisionalization. Thus, there are increased challenges related to keeping the different subcultures on the same page and working toward the organization's common goals in a coordinated way, while perhaps at the same time allowing for some variation in cultural elements across subcultures.

In Schein's (2010) last stage, organizational maturity and potential decline, the organization's culture is at its strongest and the basic assumptions are the most deeply embedded. Schein (2010) noted that at this stage, there could be a marked distinction between the assumptions that guide how the organization really operates and the espoused values the organization's management says guide the organization. That is, management perhaps becomes aware of where it needs to be going into the future and espouses certain perspectives, but those of course lag well behind where the organization's functional operating basic assumptions and values are. Unfortunately, the challenges associated with such strong cultures and disconnects between levels of manifest and operational values and culture often make planned culture change nearly impossible. If the organization cannot change but the environment does, then the organization will likely decline until a crisis motivates change or the organization dies.

In a related example, Martin (2002) reported two qualitative studies on the evolution of culture in organizations applying her three frameworks as a vehicle. In brief, very early in an organization she viewed fragmented cultures as being most common because everything is new and the processes involved in embedding culture have not yet begun to have an effect. Then, she noted, as the organization grows and develops and experiences success, there will be a shared sense of who the organization is and how it functions, yielding a more integrated vantage point on the culture. She noted that in her case studies, the integration perspective could sometimes emerge in the face of a crisis such that the necessity for people to work together intensely and for long hours to overcome the crisis helps form a more integrated view of the culture. Success in coping with problems can lead to further success requiring differentiation as connected to functional/occupational differentiation. Then, as new leaders are introduced and try to implement (or embed) new goals and strategies, there can be a return to fragmentation with those accompanying the new leadership approaching things from different vantage points than those who have been in the company for a while. Martin (2002) did caution that her view is not a stage model of cultural evolution over time but that all three perspectives can be simultaneously active at any stage, and it is the presence of relatively momentary events that determine increased activation/presence of one of the perspectives. She put it this way (p. 148): "The three perspectives view of cultural change is based on the premise that at any one point in time, all three perspectives are relevant. This approach then is not the same as views of cultural change that assume that a culture passes from one perspective to another, one at a time."

So are cultures stable or dynamic? The answer is probably both. Katz and Kahn (1966) and more recently Leana and Barry (2000) have noted how the most effective organizations balance the need for stability with the need for change and adaptability. In many cases, it likely depends on the lens and level through which one examines culture. Change will be more apparent at the outer layers of culture, as artifacts may come and go over time. However, the deeper assumptions of the organization's culture are less likely to change. In addition, there are likely some cultural values that change over time, especially as the organization grows and differentiates itself, while at the same time there are values that are almost perfectly consistent over time. It may be the case that the subset of general values that is common across subcultures of the organization remains relatively constant and identifiable, while those features unique to individual subcultures are more dynamic. Change may be more apparent in smaller subunits of the organization; because they have fewer members, their subcultures will be more influenced when some members leave and new members introduce new values based on their national culture, occupational culture, experiences in other organizations, and so forth. Units focused more externally will likely be more dynamic as they will be more vulnerable to various environmental influences than those units primarily focused internally. However, even for those aspects of organizations that do appear to be relatively constant, that consistency requires refreshing and reinforcement, which is the crux of what Hatch (2000) and Markus (2000) suggested.

What we like about the life cycle model of cultural evolution and Martin's (2002) perspective is that they raise several cautions about organizational change that have not been central to that literature. The most important caution is that change will require different approaches as a function of where in the life cycle an organization is. It is useful to invoke Martin's three perspectives view and understand that changing an integrated culture will be different from changing one in which there is great differentiation and/or fragmentation. Aldrich and Ruef (2006) in their book on organizational evolution considered this issue when they looked at different theories of how organizations change over time. They put it this way: "Institutional and ecological theories [of organization change] have generally taken an integrative perspective . . . The theories have treated organizational forms and their surrounding environments as unitary objects, containing a single view of what is legitimate. In this respect, the fragmentation and differentiation views, carried to their extreme, contain a major challenge to the ecological and institutional [organization change] perspectives, for how can organizations be institutions if they have multiple or ambiguous cultures?" (p. 130). The answer is that they certainly can be when it is acknowledged that multiple subcultures can overlap in ways that produce an "institution," keeping in mind that both the subcultures and their overlap can change over time across different stages of the organizational life cycle.

The Persistence of Organizational Culture

Paradoxically, perhaps the most important point to make about understanding culture change is that cultures are maintained and persist over time. Although strong cultures can have positive consequences for organizations, the stronger the culture, the more difficult it will be to change. Moreover, although we suggested above that subcultures might be easier to change than the overall organizational culture, it is the case that organizational change in an organization with multiple strong subcultures will require change efforts targeted toward each of those subcultures. Consider the issue of two companies involved in a merger/acquisition. The two organizations may be seen as subcultures of the future organization and truly integrating the two cultures, perhaps in the hopes of producing a new and unique integrated culture, would be a massive undertaking.

Reger (2006), for example, reported that GE has done numerous successful acquisitions, each of which was accompanied by a culture diagnosis of the firm under consideration. In one case, GE Capital was intending to acquire a British company, and the two met to clarify GE's expectations of how this would proceed. "The discussion surfaced some key differences [in culture], which prompted GE to look more closely at the target's culture. Its conclusion: Walk away despite the favorable financials" (Reger, 2006, p. 124). Reger's book (2006) is one of the more comprehensive treatments of the issues and processes in mergers and acquisitions, and it details the approaches used successfully by IBM to produce the integration with PriceWaterhouseCoopers Consulting that was a significant part of the final change at IBM from a products to a service company. We are especially appreciative of their effort to display in detail many if not all of the cultural issues that, taken together, require attention when change is contemplated. See Table 5.5 for a reproduction of their table and note how many issues (called "business practices" in the table) require attention when considering organizational culture change.

We believe that the organizational change literature in general has proceeded without a full appreciation of the ways by which cultures are perpetuated in organizations and thus take a surface/simplistic approach to change. Morgan (2006, p. 145) put it this way: "Traditionally the change process has been conceptualized as a problem of changing technologies, structures, and the abilities and motivations of employees. Although this is in part correct, effective change also depends on changes in the images and values that guide action." In short, if we are going to change an organization's culture, it is imperative to understand the many levels and forms that culture takes in organizations and the fact that the most mundane of everyday activities that occur have symbolic meaning for those who experience them and participate in them. It is the last item in Reger's (2006) list of "business practices," leadership, to which we turn next for ways to understand culture change

Leadership and Organizational Culture Change

One continuing question within the literature on organizational culture change has been the extent to which leaders can move their cultures in

TABLE 5.5 Issues that constitute organizational culture and require attention when change is contemplated (from Reger, 2006)

Decision processes/ governance	• Who are the decision makers and for what specific types of decisions? What is the role of staff functions in decision making? • Is consensus preferred, and if so, among whom? Do people expect to "vote" on certain decisions? • What decisions are made centrally? Locally? • Once made, who ensures the decisions are fulfilled? • What drives governance (for example, regulations, organization's history)? Are some topics more sensitive; if so, which ones and why?
Financial/investments	• How are funding decisions made? • Is information shared openly, or held closely among a few leaders? • Who is involved in budgeting and other financial plans? • What happens when results exceed, or fall short, of expectations? • What is the relative importance of financial results to other areas such as customer satisfaction, brand image, and employee satisfaction?
Problem solving	• How are exceptions handled? How are they perceived? • When determining solution alternatives, is it better to identify and discuss all options, or only the best ones? • Who needs to be involved in what types of problems? • How much planning is needed before action should be taken? • How are people expected to handle conflicts?
Processes	• To what degree are employees expected to follow processes versus exercise their own judgment? Are some roles allowed more latitude, and if so, under what circumstances? • Are some processes and circumstances handled differently, and if so, who decides? • Who needs to get involved with what aspects of processes as they are being executed?
Accountability, monitoring	• How are measures used throughout the organization? • How should people respond to measures? • What rewards and recognition are given to people who meet or exceed specific objectives? Which objectives? • What happens when people fail to meet objectives?

(Continued)

TABLE 5.5 *(Continued)*

Priorities	• How are employees expected to view customers? The market? The organization's mission? • When handling global issues, do local or global answers rule? • How are priorities identified and reinforced? • Is it best to focus on the long term or short term?
Nature of the relationship	• How important are interpersonal relationships, and how should they be nurtured? • How important are titles, and how should people interact across different organizational levels? • How should teamwork and individual work be applied? • When working outside the company—such as with customers, vendors, alliance partners, and so on, what is the orientation and expected relationship?
People decisions	• How is work assigned? Who makes the decisions? • What is the hiring strategy (for example, promote from within, "best and brightest," diversity)? • What is the preference for tenure vs. "new eyes"? • How are employees developed (for example, training, mentoring, apprenticeship)?
Policies	• To what degree are employees expected to follow policies versus exercise their judgments? • Who can exercise judgment and when? • Do the policies apply differently in various circumstances, and if so, who decides?
Leadership process, approach, and style	• Are leaders primarily people managers, or are they also involved in the hands-on work of their groups? • How should they interact with subordinates, peers, and superiors? • How are leaders expected to communicate? How often and through what processes and communication media? • How much openness is expected, and on what topics? • What power is invested, and in what leadership positions?

Reger, Sara J. Moulton. Can Two Rights Make a Wrong? 1st Edition, © 2006, p. 98–100. Reprinted by permission of Pearson Education, Inc., Upper Saddle River, NJ

a certain direction within the context of attempts to improve organizational effectiveness. Often framed in terms of whether a culture can be "managed," this question is more specific than whether culture changes at all; even though cultures may change due to a variety of reasons (as we discussed above), the role of leadership in initiating and guiding those changes is a topic of much dispute. In this section, we present some of the main issues that are disputed and summarize the primary points of view.

It may be easiest to think of this issue as a continuum with more extreme views at either end and more contingencies discussed in the middle. The two extreme views are, on the one hand, that leaders cannot influence culture and, on the other hand, that leaders can easily change culture. As an example of the perspective that leaders have no or very little effect on culture, Meek (1988) put it quite simply, "leaders do not create culture, it emerges from the collective social interaction of groups and communities" (p. 459). Alvesson and Berg (1992) asserted that from a symbolic management perspective, leaders cannot change culture. As they stated, "a corporate culture cannot be forced upon a collective, nor can it be controlled or manipulated at will. A true strategic change programme does not impose anything, but makes people aware of and illuminates certain aspects of the culture in which they exist" (p. 168). As another example, Martin and Siehl (1983) questioned whether managers could have any influence on culture, and if they did, characterized the level of influence as very limited: "It may be that cultures cannot be straightforwardly created or managed by individuals. Instead, cultures may simply exist and managers may capitalize on cultural effects they perceive as positive or minimize those perceived as negative. Perhaps the most that can be expected is that a manager can slightly modify the trajectory of a culture, rather than exert major control over the direction of its development" (p. 53).

On the other end of the continuum are those authors who perhaps oversimplify the ease with which culture can be changed. For example, Tichy (1982) described culture as a strategic variable that can be manipulated by managers through "role modeling, jargon, myths, rituals as well as the use of the human resource systems of selection, development, assessment, and rewards to shape and mold corporate culture" (p. 12). Other authors have reduced culture change to a series of straightforward steps (e.g., Turnstall, 1983), although many of these do include warnings about the difficulty of culture change and the time required to achieve successful change (e.g., Cameron & Quinn, 2011; Deal & Kennedy, 1982).

Some have suggested that the differences along this continuum are an issue of the definition of culture that is used. For instance, Martin (1985) stated, "If they choose a relatively superficial definition of culture, or if they focus on a relatively limited scope of change, then they are more likely to echo the pragmatists' conclusion that culture can indeed be managed. The authors who define culture in unusually deep or broad terms, and who contemplate massive cultural changes, are less sanguine about attempts to control the trajectory of a culture's evolution" (p. 96). In many ways, this issue reduces to the organizations *are* cultures perspective versus the organizations *have* cultures perspective that we discussed previously (Smircich, 1983). If culture is treated as a variable along the lines of other organizational variables that researchers study and leaders attempt to influence, then culture change may seem like an easily attainable goal. Such a goal would particularly be the case when culture is defined in terms of its outer layers, such that norms or espoused values are the target for management's change efforts, rather than deeper level of beliefs and basic assumptions. Alternatively, if cultures are viewed as subsuming everything that occurs internally in the organization (i.e., organizations are cultures), then any attempt by organizational leaders to change the whole culture in a meaningful way would seem to have a small likelihood of success. Furthermore, many from this perspective approach culture with a concern for the treatment of individuals with less power within the organization, and thus view culture change as an unethical attempt by management to impose their values and will on employees (Alvesson & Berg, 1992; Smircich, 1985).

As a middle ground, the ability of leaders to change culture could be viewed from a contingency perspective, with the level of influence varying depending upon a variety of issues (Alvesson & Sveningsson, 2008). For instance, Louis (1985) suggested that managers' ability to change culture will depend on the stage in the organization's life cycle (young versus mature), the level of the organization (subunit versus whole organization), the presence of a clear need for change (crisis), and the leader's ability to communicate a clear need for change and vision for the future. Lundberg (1985) took a similar perspective, outlining four major conditions that provide an appropriate time for leaders to try to make change (we show these in Table 5.6). The presence of these conditions will predict both whether change will be attempted by leaders and whether it will be successful. The gist of this perspective is that culture change can

TABLE 5.6 Conditions suggesting that leaders pursue culture change (based on Lundberg, 1985)

1. **External enabling conditions.** This issue concerns both the presence of threats in the external environment and the extent to which the organization fits with its external environment, with a moderate level of fit to be optimally motivating for a leader to initiate culture change.
2. **Internal permitting conditions.** This captures whether the organization has the internal resources, readiness, and coordination that permit capable leadership to make a culture change effort successful.
3. **Precipitating pressures.** These may come from performance demands or stakeholders and can originate in changes in organizational size (growth or decrement) or in a crisis (real or perceived) that causes uncertainty for the organization; crises and ambiguity are good conditions for leaders to initiate change efforts because people are attuned to alleviating both crises and ambiguity.
4. **Triggering events.** These are the most proximal condition for culture change. These may include major changes in the organization's environment, technological breakthroughs, or unexpected departures in the top management team.

occur, but the conditions have to be right, where right means the organization is ready for change. If the situation is not right, then the culture change effort will fail because the parties required to get involved will not see the import of participating to make the change happen.

One of the contingencies suggested by Louis (1985) that has received particular attention in the organizational culture literature is the organization's stage in its life cycle. Previously, we discussed the topic of life cycles at length with regard to the evolution of organizational culture over time, acknowledging that organizational cultures do tend to change across their life span. The question here is at what points in their life cycle are cultures more susceptible to management's change efforts. Siehl (1985) argued that the best condition for changing culture may be during the transition from the entrepreneurial stage to the formalization and growth stage (which would parallel the transition from the founding and early growth stage to the midlife stage using Schein's, 2010, terminology). This is an opportune time because the requirements for continuing the growth and development of the organization will require different skill sets on the part of leadership. Of course, this need may not be generally seen by everyone, so once again the importance of communication to all employees about where the organization is and where it needs to be becomes clear. Siehl (1985) noted that if the organization has been relatively successful, change might be more difficult and limited to the outer layers of culture. Alternatively, if the organization has been struggling or there exists widespread dissatisfaction with the organization and its culture, deeper change may be possible.

Similar to Siehl (1985), Schein (2010) provided an in-depth discussion of the effect of the organization's stage in its life cycle on leadership's attempts at culture change, and specifically how organizations can overcome the difficulties of culture change at the midlife stage. One option he highlighted was that the promotion of "hybrids" into key leadership positions could increase the likelihood for culture change. He defined hybrids as "insiders whose own assumptions are better adapted to the new external realities" (p. 279). Such individuals have lived in and know the current culture and therefore are palatable as leaders to current employees. Although they have lived with the existing culture, there are aspects of their background or experience sufficient to also somewhat differentiate them from the current culture, providing them with insights on how the organization will need to change to continue to be successful. Another option described by Schein (2010) for leading culture change at the midlife stage is through management's decisions about new employees. The opportunity for change will increase as more employees enter the organization whose values are consistent with the desired culture, especially if they displace those employees who most strongly identify with the old culture (consistent with the ASA model; Schneider, 1987). Yet another option for organizations in the midlife stage is for management to encourage change through the support or facilitation of a particular subculture. In this approach, the leadership of the organization attempts to exploit the inevitable development of subcultures and the diversity that they bring to guide the organization's overall culture. Change can be facilitated by pushing the development of the organization's culture to be more like that of a particular subculture by, for example, promoting individuals from that subculture to higher levels of management. As the organization moves from midlife to the later stages of its life cycle, its culture becomes more and more deeply ingrained; as a result, the alternative tactics available to leaders to make change become more extreme. Schein (2010) suggested several, including turnarounds, mergers/acquisitions, or destruction and rebirth (i.e., through bankruptcy proceedings).

Related to the contingency perspective is the idea that there are many influences on culture, and leaders are just one (Alvesson & Svenings-son, 2008). In this view, many of the issues mentioned as contingencies above could also be thought of as competing influences on culture. As examples, Louis (1983) cited changes to the setting or new technologies, and Dyer (1985) mentioned unanticipated crises and leadership changes. The point is that there are other factors that have the potential to yield culture change, and the presence of those other factors competes with top management's goals and the direction it may want to take the culture. Thus, as suggested by Martin and Siehl (1983), top management may be more inclined to try to influence the effects of these other influences rather than to attempt a complete overhaul of the culture. Along the same lines, Krefting and Frost (1985) suggested that because top management's ability to control culture (and all of the other factors that constitute and influence culture) is limited in the short term, the culture change attempts might actually result in outcomes that are undesirable. Thus, they highlight the risk in even attempting culture change, suggesting that the downside is not simply the status quo, but instead is actually an even worse situation than the organization originally faced. This is because change can yield great ambiguity for people, resulting in a loss of sense of place, the very thing culture is thought to provide. As another alternative, change can be adopted at different paces in different places in an organization depending on the focus of such change, again yielding ambiguity. Schneider and Macey were personally involved in a very interesting culture change process wherein the outcome of the diagnosis preceding change itself was to note the features of the culture that people said should NOT be changed. People explicitly said they wished to retain the history of the firm that gave it uniqueness in its business. Leaders, understanding the importance of retaining such anchors for the culture, were able to think about portraying the change as adding to the history rather than a replacement for it.

When leaders understand that the changes they envision must be considered for their meaningfulness and symbolism, then they understand what culture is and they can diagnose beforehand with some accuracy the symbolic as well as practical consequences of what they do. To use Morgan's (2006) idea, culture is a holographic not a mechanistic construct. As such, it has hundreds of components, each interacting with another across forms and levels, and it is when leaders understand this level of interaction and systems-wide interrelationship that the possibility exists that they can proceed with the initiatives that can eventuate in change. They can initiate change and watch it happen, always understanding that they can never control all facets of it.

The source material for most if not all of this section on leadership and organizational change has been primarily theoretical. Although leadership has regularly been linked with organizational culture, especially in the literatures on transformational and charismatic leadership (Bass & Bass, 2008; Hartnell & Walumbwa, 2011), empirical research on the topic has been relatively paltry relative to the theoretical literature. Nevertheless, there has been some empirical research suggesting that leaders' values and behaviors are related to their organizations' cultures, implying that leaders can and do change culture. For example, in a sample of 26 Israeli companies, Berson, Oreg, and Dvir (2008) found that chief executive officer (CEO) values were related to relevant aspects of organizational culture, so that the value of self-direction was related to an innovative culture, the value of security was related to a bureaucratic culture, and the value of benevolence was related to a supportive culture. In another example, Tsui, Zhang, Wang, Xin, and Wu (2006) used a mix of quantitative and qualitative methodologies to explore the relationship between the strength of CEO leadership behavior and the strength of the organizational culture in China. In addition to finding that strong leadership was generally coupled with a strong culture, their data revealed a number of environmental variables that restrained the influence of leaders on culture, including degree of control by the parent company, the age of the organization, and the size of the organization, so that leadership was more closely linked with culture when the organizational had more autonomy, was younger, and was smaller. In combination, these two studies show that CEOs can influence culture, but consistent with the contingency perspective, the extent of their effect may be limited by a number of other factors. In addition, it may be possible that the culture is influencing the leader and his/her values and behavior; as Alvesson (1993) has observed with regard to leaders that "it is possible to be at the same time a product of a culture, to be constrained by it, and to some degree to be able to change or at least modify it" (p. 90). Thus, although empirical work along these lines has provided interesting insights into the relationship between leadership and organizational culture, such research is limited; there is still much to be done.

To wrap up this overview of the literature on the relationship between leadership and culture change, our view is that culture change is extraordinarily difficult, and leaders must be prepared for challenges should they attempt it. We see two almost opposite perspectives that perhaps represent the best alternatives for leaders intent on achieving organizational culture change. One is the idea of an adaptive culture from Kotter and Heskett (1992). As described previously, they argued that organizations can maintain consistent, core values of serving the needs of their stakeholders (i.e., customers, employees, and shareholders) while being flexible in how those ideals are manifested. Of course, saying this and doing this are two different things. However, the idea that leaders can build a culture that will adapt to changing circumstances without losing its core values is an attractive one. On the opposite end of the spectrum is Schein's (2000) admonition that "management should seek not to change culture, but to change effectiveness" (p. xxix). Given the time and difficulty associated with culture change, leaders who understand that organizations can naturally evolve and change, and who understand that what they do in the way of embedding mechanisms always has symbolic meaning, can approach change with a long time horizon. Using Schein's more limited emphasis on effectiveness, the organization can focus on the aspects of its culture that are the most aligned with effectiveness and try to build on those in hopes that even small changes can yield eventually large consequences in terms of culture.

SUMMARY: THE EMERGENCE, EFFECTIVENESS, AND CHANGE OF ORGANIZATIONAL CULTURES

Organizational cultures, as is true also of all cultures, serve the purpose of reducing ambiguity for the members of the culture. Especially when cultures are strong, people's roles and the rules by which they operate are taken for granted and may not even be available to consciousness. As such, cultures are implicit unquestioned guidelines for organizational life. However, cultures do not usually exist in their full-blown form when we get to study them or work in them. Cultures emerge from a process that is, in our estimation, best described by Schein's (2010) explication of the culture embedding mechanisms under the control of founders. In brief, Schein argued that to what the founder devotes scarce resources determines the values and beliefs taken on by those with whom he or she works early on, and that this is especially true for the actions taken that are shown to be useful for organizational growth and development. These early actions result in various learnings and experiences that become embedded in the way decisions are made and problems are solved to further reinforce the culture begun by founder behavior.

The organization's culture then is transmitted to newcomers through formal and informal socialization practices in organizations, and the result of such socialization practices is further deepening and strengthening of the culture of the organization. Because the cultural manifestations that are experienced and passed on to future generations of employees are those that have been proven effective, organizational culture should hypothetically be related to organizational effectiveness. There is some evidence that this is true, but it is not clear whether studying the direct link between organizational culture and effectiveness is a viable approach to understanding this complex relationship. Such a direct link is unlikely if the specific facets of organizational culture that might be important for effectiveness vary from setting to setting. Furthermore, weak organizational cultures—cultures in which there is not shared understanding—might also moderate the relationship between culture and effectiveness. One explanation for weak cultures is that organizations may frequently contain subcultures resulting from occupational differences and other possible differences (organizational level, demographic composition, and so forth) across people in an organization. It is important to take into account these and other potential contingencies in exploring the relationship between culture and effectiveness.

Whether or not there is a simple, direct link between organizational culture and effectiveness, there is no doubt that organizational culture has important implications for the effectiveness of organizations and thus needs to be taken into account in any change program. Many of the issues involved in changing culture are the same as when culture is created, implying that those who fail to appreciate why cultures exist and how they form will fail at organizational culture change. They will fail because they will not grasp the holographic (Morgan, 2006) nature of organizational culture and will rather focus on artifacts and immediately tangible issues as if changing them will change an organization's culture. Even when organizations understand the conditions most likely to result in effective culture change and the role of leadership at various stages of an organization's life cycle in effecting change, culture change will never be quick, straightforward, or easy.

NOTE

1. Schein later added "new beliefs, values, and assumptions brought in by new members and leaders" (2004, p. 225).

CHAPTER
6

Integrating Organizational Climate and Organizational Culture

This chapter is about integrating the climate and culture approaches to understanding the organizational context in which people work. The previous chapters have dealt in detail with the history of research on climate and culture, the various conceptualizations of the two constructs, and the validity of the constructs with regard to being correlates of various indices of organizational effectiveness. Occasionally we noted how one of the constructs was similar to or different from the other, but by and large we avoided such comparisons preferring to present each in their more or less pure form—the way they have tended to exist in the literature. Now that readers have the prior chapters as background information, in this chapter we switch to discussing the two constructs simultaneously. We do this to better understand their shared attributes and the potential for the combination of the two to make additional contributions to organizational theory, research, and practice. In what follows we assume the reader has the details of the prior chapters, so to speak, so we do not include as many of the citations to the work of others as we included earlier.

The chapter unfolds by first noting how infrequently connections are made between these two constructs. Then we explicitly identify a series of similarities and differences between the constructs. Next, we develop the idea that climate researchers might profit from culture research approaches, then we reverse the issue by identifying how culture researchers might benefit from climate approaches. We then consider ways the two constructs have been and might be integrated into a common research paradigm, and we conclude the chapter by discussing how an integrated framework sheds light on the always perplexing issue of organizational change.

ON THE RELATIVE ABSENCE OF THE INTEGRATION OF CLIMATE AND CULTURE

In the earliest years of the study of organizational context and environmental variation, simultaneous discussions of climate and culture were relatively rare and largely inconsistent. Some authors viewed culture as a broader construct than climate (e.g., Evan, 1968; Fleishman, 1953), some viewed climate as broader than culture (Argyris, 1958), and some used the terms interchangeably (Katz & Kahn, 1966). As the literatures on both topics developed, commentaries on the relationship between climate and culture remained relatively uncommon, leading multiple researchers to observe how the fields have existed on parallel tracks with little explicit conceptual overlap (e.g., Ashkanasy, Wilderom, & Peterson, 2000b; Reichers & Schneider, 1990). Of course, there have been exceptions, perhaps most notably by Denison (1996), and such exceptions have seemingly become more common in recent years, including handbook chapters by Ostroff, Kinicki, and Muhammad (2012) and Zohar and Hofmann (2012), and a number of publications in the mental health services literature (e.g., Aarons & Sawitzky, 2006a, 2006b; Glisson & Green, 2006; Glisson, Schoenwald, Kelleher, Landsverk, Hoagwood, Mayberg, & Green, 2008). However, given the now considerable accumulation of research on each construct over the last three to four decades, the little progress that has been made on their integration is quite disappointing. Even in the very popular recent editions of the *Handbook of Organizational Culture and Climate* (Ashkanasy, Wilderom, & Peterson, 2000a, 2011), it is difficult to find examples of bridges being built between the two research areas. Instead, there are chapters on culture and, to a lesser degree, chapters on climate, but very few examples that could truly be labeled as chapters on culture *and* climate.

Over the years, there has been at least some degree of tension between researchers on these topics, largely due to their differing approaches to studying and understanding organizations, and perhaps also due to differences in their popularity. We observed earlier that climate researchers have been much more willing to acknowledge the value of culture research than the other way around. For instance, Trice and Beyer (1993) dismissed climate as only reflective of individuals' experiences of their organizations and lacking unique indicators. Others have seemed to similarly downplay the role of climate, labeling it as "transient" (Ott, 1989), "idiosyncratic" (Rousseau, 1990a), "superficial" (Alvesson & Berg, 1992), or aligning it with the physical layout or appearance of the organization (Schein, 2000, 2010). We disagree with all of these characterizations of climate research, and it is easy to see in our coverage of the climate construct in previous chapters that these descriptions are not in alignment with the definitions and validity of contemporary climate research. Our position is that both constructs and their histories bring unique perspectives to essentially the same table and not only are both useful independently, but the two literatures can grow and develop by examining the contributions of each to the other. As Schein (2000) put it, "[T]o understand what goes on in organizations and *why it happens in the way it does*, one needs *several* concepts. Climate and culture, if each is carefully defined, then become two crucial building blocks for organizational description and analysis" (pp. xxiv–xxv, italics in original).

Before moving forward with our discussion of the similarities and differences between the two constructs, it is important to emphasize what has hopefully been clear from our discussions to this point. That is, there are inconsistencies in definitions and modes of study within the work in each arena depending on who is doing the research. Sometimes researchers discuss and study culture and climate in ways that are very similar and other times in ways that are quite different. Thus, we will attempt to capture the various perspectives that are used to study both constructs and to be specific in our discussion about to which approach we are referring so that the proposed integration can become clear. Our goal is to illuminate what Pettigrew (1990) said over two decades ago as he summarized the edited volume by Schneider: "The clear message from this book is that climate and culture are complex, multidimensional, and multilevel constructs. They are systemic constructs that come alive when they are studied in a holistic fashion and when they are linked to key themes or problems of organizational functioning" (p. 421). We attempt in what follows to display the similarities and the differences in approaches and to lay the foundation for the ways each may benefit from knowledge of the other.

SIMILARITIES BETWEEN ORGANIZATIONAL CLIMATE AND CULTURE

There are many similarities between the constructs of organizational climate and organizational culture. This overlap has resulted in some researchers treating the two terms as interchangeable (e.g., Markus, 2000) or so similar that "it is possible to claim that climate is a way of measuring culture" (Payne, 2000). Although we think there are important distinctions between the two, we want to first acknowledge some of the key similarities in the thinking about and research perspectives on organizational climate and culture: (1) the focus on a macro view of the organizational context and attempts to understand how that context emerges for the participants there; (2) the focus on context rather than the individuals in the context; (3) the focus on sharedness of experiences; (4) the role of meaning; (5) the role of leadership; (6) the issues of strength and alignment; and (7) the relationship with organizational effectiveness. These are displayed in Table 6.1 and elaborated on in what follows.

The Focus on a Macro View of the Organizational Context

Climate and culture attempt to grapple with the total effects of the context on people and their behavior. In contrast to much of the thinking and research in industrial/organizational psychology and organizational behavior, climate and culture approaches work with the bundle of attributes people experience rather than those attributes one at a time. Climate and culture approaches do not focus on pay for performance, or performance management systems, or job attributes, or co-worker support, or management fairness; instead, they focus on all of these simultaneously and explore from whence they cometh and their consequences. Both constructs are seen to emerge for people through many different channels of information and experiences, with such information directly or indirectly reflecting and suggesting the implications of the larger context for people.

The Focus on Context and Not on Individuals

Similarly, a common thread that runs through the constructs of organizational climate and culture is that they both focus on the organizational environment or context (Denison, 1996). Although the idea of measuring and understanding the organizational environment may seem like old hat these days, with multilevel theorizing and analysis becoming the rule

TABLE 6.1 Similarities in climate and culture theory and research

- The focus on a *macro view* of the organizational context and attempts to understand how that context emerges as it is for the participants there
- The focus on the *context* in which people work rather than on the individual attributes of people there
- The focus on *sharedness* of experiences of people rather than the individual differences among them
- The centrality of the *meaning* of the context for people and their subsequent behavior
- The role of *leaders and leadership* in creating the context and the meaning attached to it
- The issues of *strength and alignment* as important in understanding climate and culture effects
- The relationship of climate and culture to *organizational effectiveness*

rather than the exception, the role of the environment in understanding individual behavior was the major issue that gave rise to the literatures on organizational climate and culture (Schneider, 1985). Climate and culture researchers have taken very different approaches (for the most part) in studying these environments, but at the core, the issue both groups are trying to understand is very similar.

The Focus on Sharedness in Experiences

Another key similarity between organizational climate and culture is that they tend to be shared, and as such, they tend to operate at the unit level of analysis rather than the individual level. Almost all definitions of climate and culture, either explicitly or implicitly, include the idea that they capture elements of the organization about which there are shared perceptions, meanings, and/or understandings. Of course, as we have already highlighted in the chapters on culture, not all researchers embrace the idea that culture is shared, especially across the organization as a whole (Martin, 2002). Along similar lines in the climate literature, there is the idea that climates can be low in strength, indicating there is not a consensus and suggesting, in fact, the presence of subclimates and/or fragmented climates (though one does not see those terms used). Even in these cases, it is conceptually difficult to move away from the "sharedness" of climate and culture among employees as an essential attribute of these constructs. For culture, when there are elements for which there is not a shared culture across the entire organization, there are likely subcultures within which there are shared perceptions or understandings. With regard to the ambiguity in cultures that yields the fragmentation perspective, many of the examples Martin (2002) tended to cite are situations in which there is likely, and somewhat paradoxically, consensus about the fact that there is ambiguity in the workplace. As for climate, researchers have not done a good job of clarifying when, why, and under what circumstances climates may be low or high in strength (for an exception see Bowen & Ostroff, 2004). In particular, lack of climate strength may be a function of temporary issues (e.g., a new supervisor, a new chief executive officer, or a merger), the implementation of new work processes (e.g., via new information technology), or ambiguity in what the future is likely to bring. We acknowledge that there may be situations when elements of climate and culture are not shared, but overall, the perceptions and understandings that make up climate and culture require that there be "sharedness" as a fundamental attribute for the constructs to have meaning beyond an individual's own experiences.

The Centrality of the Meaning of the Context

For both organizational climate and culture researchers, meaning plays a central role in how the constructs are defined and the ways by which they affect employees. This emphasis has been more explicit in the culture literature, as researchers have commonly discussed the processes through which the outer layers (or artifacts) in the organization are interpreted and come to have socially shared meanings by the organization's members. In the culture literature, this is discussed in terms of the values, beliefs, and basic assumptions by which the organization exists. Indeed, this meaning is revealed in myths and stories and transmitted to newcomers through socialization practices.

In the climate literature, discussions of meaning are not as common, and the link to meaning has not always been made explicit. Nevertheless, from the early stages in the development of the climate construct, meaning has taken on an important role. For instance, Schneider (1975b) placed climate as an intervening variable between the policies and practices of the organization and the resulting employee behavior. Climate was critical to understanding employee behavior because it captured the meaning the various policies and practices held for employees. From a Gestalt psychology perspective, Schneider outlined how workers organize and assign meaning to patterns or bundles of individual cues in their organization, and how the organization's climate develops out of the shared experiences and sense-making processes among employees. Thus, conceptually climate is not the policies, practices, and procedures themselves, but the shared meaning that is assigned to them by the organization's employees. Paradoxically, the measurement of climate has focused on the policies, practices, and procedures far more than the more macro meaning assigned to them. Schneider, Ehrhart, and Macey (2011a) showed how the typical measure of such policies, practices, and procedures could also include the more macro meaning of the work environment for employees.

Zohar and Hofmann (2012) built on this logic to argue that the basis for organizational climate is organizational employees' identification of "the overall pattern and signals sent by this complex web of rules and policies across competing domains" (p. 7). In fact, they portray climate as an intermediate layer of culture that captures the perceptions of the enacted values and priorities of management. They described it this way: "Once the implicit priorities and enacted values associated with each climate domain are combined or integrated, their joint meaning can be considered as forming an interim layer of culture whose specification should make it easier to map observable artifacts with basic assumptions and core values" (pp. 29–30). Thus, the meaning-making process takes on a central role in their perspective on climate.

The Role of Leaders and Leadership

For the most part, leaders are viewed as playing a critical role in both organizational climate and culture. In organizational climate research, the importance of leaders has been taken for granted to the point that researchers have only recently begun to directly study their influence on climate. In the organizational culture literature, the importance of the founder has taken center stage, with some controversy about the extent to which leaders influence culture once the organization has developed and the culture has been firmly established. Although the role that leaders play and the nature of the discussion about leadership may differ some between the two fields, it is clear from both literatures that leadership is closely intertwined with both. Perhaps the best illustration of this overlap is from Schein's writings on culture embedding mechanisms. For many years, he has discussed embedding mechanisms as the way leaders "reinforce the adoption of their own beliefs, values" (Schein, 2010, p. 235) and "teach their organizations how to perceive, think, feel, and behave based on their own conscious and unconscious convictions" (Schein, 2010, p. 236). Although in his earlier work those mechanisms were described as the "mechanisms for culture embedding and reinforcement" (Schein, 1985, p. 224), in the more recent editions of his book, Schein described them as creating "what would typically be called the 'climate' of the organization" (Schein, 2010, p. 236). Thus, not only is leadership a critical component of both climate and culture, but leaders influence both climate and culture through similar mechanisms—what they do, to what they assign valued resources, and so forth. Later in the chapter, we discuss the implications this has for integrating research on climate and culture and specifically for understanding how climate and culture influence each other.

The Issues of Strength and Alignment

Both organizational climate and culture researchers have been concerned with the related ideas of strength and alignment. In the climate literature, strength is discussed primarily in terms of the extent to which there is consensus about the climate, which is assessed with an index of variability such as the standard deviation. Culture researchers have proposed a number of additional ways to think about culture strength, such as the different types of penetration described by Louis (1985) and Saffold (1988) or the idea of pervasiveness described by Payne (2000). Denison and Neale (2000) have taken the approach of directly asking employees about strength issues rather than calculating some index of agreement or consensus. For example, survey respondents are asked about the extent to which the internal organization is integrated towards goal achievement (coordination/integration), employees agree with each other and are able to resolve differences (agreement), and there is a shared set of values that employees can identify with (core values). Whatever the approach, there is a common idea in both literatures that organizations (or units within them) may vary in the extent to which people agree about the climate or culture.

On a related front, both literatures also discuss the idea of internal alignment. Climate researchers frame this in terms of the gestalt that is created through the implied messages sent through the organization's policies, practices, procedures, and reward systems (Schneider, 1975b). For instance, employees get the message that service is a priority for the organization when management creates alignment in the ways it communicates the importance of service, rewards service quality, hires individuals based on their ability to provide quality service, provides support systems that are needed to deliver quality service, and so on. When these are aligned, a climate for service will result. In the culture literature, there are similar discussions of alignment across various organizational structures and processes or across the layers of culture (Schein, 2010). As described by Schein (2010), it is when the outer layers of culture are experienced as not being in alignment that the deeper underlying assumptions are most revealed. That is, when what management says and what employees actually do are not aligned, this gives insight into the deeper-level assumptions that explain how these contradictions have come to exist.

The Relationship with Organizational Effectiveness

A final general similarity we highlight is that both organizational climate and culture are presumed to be related to organizational effectiveness. Such a link is certainly controversial in the culture literature, as we have discussed in the preceding chapters. What seems to be controversial is not the general idea that the culture of an organization will have implications for its effectiveness, but rather treating culture as yet another predictor of organizational performance and attempting to empirically demonstrate that link. Thus, even those who take the perspective that organizations *are* cultures would likely agree that the underlying assumptions and the unique history that undergird the various cultural manifestations in an organization have implications for how employees behave and subsequently how the organization as a whole performs. Whether that should be a primary topic of research or whether such a focus favors the goals of management over employees with relatively less power are separate issues about which there is more disagreement. With regard to climate, the relationship with effectiveness has been more common, perhaps because of the tendency for I/O psychologists to take a more functionalist perspective. The controversy in the climate literature has been more about whether general (i.e., molar) measures or specific (i.e., focused) measures of climate best predict effectiveness.

Summary

Over time, the literatures on climate and culture have come to have more in common than was true earlier in their histories. The early differences were likely due to the disciplinary influences from which they emerged and the resultant similarities are likely due to their common interest in the implications of the macro organizational context for the people within them. For climate, a focus on effectiveness was there from the beginning but so was a focus on individual experiences—now both climate research and culture research focus on effectiveness and on the context rather than the individual. Reichers and Schneider (1990) claimed that climate and culture were two ways of approaching the influence of context on behavior but that they were traveling down parallel, nonoverlapping tracks. The more recent literatures we have summarized suggest that there is now much more overlap, especially when focusing on specific segments of either literature. For instance, recent research using surveys to study the outer layers of organizational culture (like behavioral norms) has a considerable overlap with climate research focusing on employees' general perceptions of the molar climate of their organization. However, culture approaches that do not use surveys and/or that focus on the deeper assumptions of culture have less in common with climate approaches that are focused on specific organizational strategies or processes. We focus more on these areas of distinction in the next section.

DIFFERENCES BETWEEN ORGANIZATIONAL CLIMATE AND CULTURE

Despite the commonality between the constructs of organizational climate and culture, there are important distinctions between them as well. Our intention here is not to review all differences between them but rather, based partially on Denison (1996), to highlight what we consider to be the critical differences: (1) their theoretical roots and research methodology, (2) the breadth of their operationalizations, (3) the awareness of climate and culture by organizational members, (4) their malleability or receptiveness to change attempts, and (5) their strategic focus. These points of distinction are summarized in Table 6.2 and detailed below. Furthermore, this material provides the foundation for our later section on what the two fields can learn from each other and how research on the two can be integrated.

Theoretical Roots and Methodology

As has been clear in our discussion of the climate and culture literatures, researchers in these areas have historically approached the study of the organizational environment from different theoretical traditions. Organizational climate research was begun by industrial psychologists, who approached organizations with an emphasis on individuals and how best to predict individuals' performance in their jobs. Thus, they struggled early on with how to study an organizational-level variable using individual-level perception data. In addition, their psychological tradition led them to use survey methods to assign numbers to the various dimensions of

TABLE 6.2 Differences in climate and culture theory and research

- *Theoretical roots and methodology*, with climate emerging from psychology and its focus on attitude surveys and culture from anthropology with its focus on case/qualitative studies
- *Breadth with which the constructs are operationalized*, with culture including more levels of inferred and observable variables and climate focusing on the observables almost exclusively
- *Awareness* of the culture/climate by employees in the organization; culture has different levels with the deepest levels below consciousness, whereas for climate, the variables are observables
- *Malleability*, or the relative ease with which climate might be changeable compared to the difficulties inherent in changing the many levels of culture
- The *strategic focus* of climate research, with much less evidence for such a focus in the culture literature

climate and subject those scores to statistical analyses so that comparisons could be made across people or units. In contrast, organizational culture research was rooted in anthropological traditions where the emphasis was on providing in-depth understanding of social groups from an insider's perspective. Qualitative methods, preferably along the lines of ethnography, were needed to provide the desired depth and insight into comprehensively describing single cultures. In addition, part of the early organizational culture tradition was a clear disapproval of and distancing from the dominant logical positivist tradition as well as what was seen as a management bias for corporate success at the expense of people.

Breadth

There are clear differences between organizational climate and culture thinking and research in the range of organizational variables included. Organizational culture is most definitely the broader of the two, particularly when the organizations *are* cultures perspective is considered. Because in this view the culture of an organization as a whole is studied, everything that occurs within the organization is on the table to be the subject of cultural analysis, and the focus is on how organizational members experience the various facets of their organization and assign meaning to them. In terms of Schein's (2010) levels of culture, the deepest layers of culture (the basic assumptions) will be manifested in everything that occurs in the organization in some form or fashion, from the pictures on the wall to the color of those walls and from the furnishings of the executive suite to the behavior of its occupant. Of course, fully capturing the breadth of the manifestations of culture is a large task, and thus the focus tends to be on single organizations, making between-organization comparisons difficult.

Organizational climate research tends to be narrower in its focus, although there is some variability within the field in this regard. Molar climate researchers are interested in dimensions of the overall environment as perceived by employees, and thus they tend to include all aspects of the organizational environment that are considered most relevant to employees. Focused climate researchers are more narrowly interested in the environment as it relates to a specific process or strategic outcome. Thus, for something like diversity climate, the interest may be only in those processes and procedures that directly relate to what management does to support diversity. Some strategic climates may be broader in their approach because so many aspects of the organization send messages about management's strategic priorities; nevertheless, the focus on policies, practices, procedures, and reward systems that is typical in climate research is still much more focused on strategic- and process-relevant observables than the typical breadth of culture research.

Awareness

Organizational culture, at its deepest levels, functions outside the conscious awareness of organizational members. Additionally, what members report as being the espoused values of their organization may differ from the values in use that they experience. Accordingly, Schein (2010) advocated for a clinical approach for understanding a culture that involves an outsider conducting focus groups with employees to try to identify what the "true" culture of the organization is beyond what employees may immediately experience. Alternatively, climate has been viewed as something that is based in employees' shared perceptions of what happens to them and around them. As employees experience the various policies, practices, and procedures of the organization and as they interact with other employees, working together and communicating about their experiences at work, they (typically) come to agree about what the organization's priorities are and what it is like to work for that organization. Because it operates within the conscious awareness of employees, climate can be viewed as "both the manifestation of culture . . . and the data on which culture comes to be inferred and understood" (Reichers & Schneider, 1990, p. 24). Thus, we agree with Alvesson and Berg (1992) that "climate is comparatively close to experience . . . and readily accessible," although we disagree that it is therefore "superficial" (p. 88). Organizational climate captures the meaning employees infer from the policies, practices, and procedures of the organization, including assessments of the alignment between espoused values and enacted values that provide important insights to the organization's underlying values and beliefs (Zohar & Hofmann, 2012). Although climate does not directly address employees' deeply held assumptions, it is anything but superficial.

Malleability

As described in the last chapter, it is fairly well established that organizational culture is difficult to change (e.g., Alvesson & Berg, 1992; Deal & Kennedy, 1982; Martin & Siehl, 1983; Schein, 2010). In contrast, in the climate literature, it is taken for granted that the climate of an organization can be changed, but there are not many explicit discussions of how easily it can be changed or how to go about doing so. Somewhat surprisingly, culture researchers have been more likely to address the issue of changing organizational climate, although their conclusion has often been to treat climate as so malleable (or transient; Ott, 1989) that it can be easily dismissed. Along these lines, Cameron and Ettington (1988) described how climate's focus on attitudes and perceptions explains why it "may change more quickly than organizational culture" (p. 362). Although contemporary conceptualizations of climate do not include job attitudes, we do agree that climate is likely more malleable than culture. The question is just how malleable is it.

We would object to any characterization of climate as being easily manipulated by management or quickly changed. Such a view simply does not align with any of our experiences in working with organizations and trying to influence the shared perceptions and meanings employees hold about the strategic focus of their organization, the process climate in which they work, and/or the molar climate for well-being in which they work. If climate was simply the policies, practices, and procedures of the organization, then perhaps it could be viewed as relatively easily changed (although even then there would be a number of challenges). However, climate is not simply those things; climate is the meaning those carry as a gestalt for the organization's employees. Even if the organization could swiftly implement drastic changes to its operating procedures and day-to-day practices, it would take time for employees to recognize and accept the new priorities of management. Given that it is much more likely for management to take a piecemeal approach, changing a policy here and a reward system there, getting employees to buy in to the new climate that management is trying to create would be difficult and take time. Work on information processing tells us that once humans establish an image of what something is, it takes a great deal of counter-information to bring about change (Lord & Hanges, 1987). Thus, while we agree that climate is more malleable than culture, such an acknowledgement by no means should be interpreted as implying that climate is easy to change. Paradoxically, management seeks "culture change" by contracting with consultants when it is more likely that "climate change" is needed as a stepping-stone to embarking on the more difficult culture change (Burke, 2011).

Strategic Focus

Since Schneider (1975b) advocated that climate research should have a particular focus—that it should be a climate "for something"—research in the field has more and more shifted in that direction, to the point that most research on climate in top management and organizational psychology journals uses a focused climate approach. Schneider's point was that if one wants to predict particular organizational outcomes, one should identify those aspects of the organizational environment that will be most relevant for predicting those outcomes. Therefore, for instance, if the goal were to improve service quality and customer satisfaction one would study the service climate, including all aspects of the organization's practices and procedures that relate to the delivery of service.

Organizational culture researchers, in contrast, have largely avoided studying culture in such a focused way. One reason is that the focus of culture is typically quite broad and inclusive, and issues related to a specific strategy are viewed as only one small piece of a larger puzzle. For instance, there are discussions of fit with environment (Kotter & Heskett, 1992) or external alignment (Schein, 2010), but those are usually addressed in broad terms and may include a number of specific strategic imperatives. Another reason for the lack of a specific strategic focus in culture research is the view that having such a focus is taking on a managerial perspective for how to lead the organization to achieve its strategic goals, which is often equated with management attempting to control and limit the autonomy of their employees for their personal gain (Siehl & Martin, 1990). Whether this has actually been the case in climate research is questionable. For example, Denison (1996), a consultant on issues of both organizational climate and culture, has described climate researchers' ability to balance both sides of this issue, noting that "they seldom contest the managerial creation of organizational contexts, but they often represent the interests and perspectives of the non-managerial employees who operate within that context" (p. 639).

In any case, there are some exceptions within the culture literature on the issue of strategic focus that should be noted. Among qualitative studies of culture, research by Ogbonna and his colleagues (Ogbonna & Harris, 1998, 2002; Ogbonna & Wilkinson, 1990) has focused on the implementation of change programs within the grocery industry in the UK. Among other issues, one focus of those change programs was creating a more customer-friendly environment in the stores, and they outlined some of the challenges that were faced in attempting to change some of the organization's values with regard to customer service. Other examples can be found within the quantitative research on organizational culture, especially when the culture survey has a dimension that suggests a strategic focus. For instance, O'Reilly and colleagues' (1991) Organizational Culture Profile (OCP) includes the dimension of innovation, and the Denison Organizational Culture Survey (Denison & Neale, 2000) includes a dimension of customer focus within the cultural trait of adaptability. Although the primary focus of these instruments is not innovation or service, respectively, their inclusion does represent some common ground with the literature on strategic climates.

Summary

Although the concepts of organizational climate and culture have grown in similarity over time, the two are not synonymous, nor can climate be dismissed as just another artifact of culture. In our view, there are still key differences when it comes to their historical roots and research methodology, breadth, awareness by organizational members, malleability, and strategic focus. These five areas do not represent all possible differences between organizational climate and culture, but we believe they do capture some of the fundamental differences between the two, in addition to suggesting some areas where each field could learn from the other. We explore this idea in more detail in the next two sections.

WHAT ORGANIZATIONAL CLIMATE RESEARCHERS COULD LEARN FROM ORGANIZATIONAL CULTURE RESEARCH

We first tackle the question of what organizational climate researchers could learn from thinking and research on organizational culture. This discussion is particularly relevant to the topic of focused climates, and especially strategic climates, which have the least amount of overlap with culture research. We highlight seven areas in Table 6.3 that have typically been within the domain of organizational culture research that would enhance the conceptual underpinnings of climate research and practice: (1) the deeper psychology of organizations, (2) breadth, (3) socialization, (4) the external environment, (5) development and change, (6) qualitative methods, and (7) passion and richness.

TABLE 6.3 What climate researchers could learn from culture research

- A focus on the *deeper psychology* of organizations rather than only focus on immediately observable policies, practices, and behavior
- A focus on the *breadth* of variables of potential influence on climate, including myths, stories, architectural design, and so forth
- A focus on *socialization* to the organization and how new employees learn about the organization's climate
- A focus on the larger *external environment* in which the organization functions, including national culture, technology segment, and the nature of the larger economy
- A focus on *development and change*, both of which are almost nonexistent in the climate literature
- A focus on more *qualitative methods* that would capture an increased range of important variables for understanding organizational climate
- A focus on *passion and richness* rather than just observable behaviors because certain process and strategic climates create not only appropriate behaviors, but also meaningful feelings of engagement

The Deeper Psychology of Organizations

Organizational climate researchers have done an excellent job of showing how climate, especially strategically focused climates, are reliably, significantly, and practically related to a variety of indices of organizational effectiveness. In addition, because such measures have focused on observable policies, practices, procedures, and behavior the research has also demonstrated likely antecedents to these focused climates. Thus, from the leadership practices focused on creating a safety climate (Zohar & Luria, 2005) to the internal service quality needed to support those who work with customers and subsequent customer satisfaction (Schneider, White, & Paul, 1998), likely sets of drivers of strategic climates have been identified. These efforts, however, have perhaps only scratched the surface of the range of levels and factors that yield the foundation for organizational climates, particularly strategic climates.

Incorporating issues that have typically been the domain of culture researchers, such as beliefs and values, would provide additional insights for climate researchers. Along these lines, Ehrhart and Raver (in press) have suggested that Schein's (2010) category of assumptions about external adaptation (e.g., mission and strategy, goals, means, measurement, and correction) might be most relevant for understand the foundation for strategic climates, whereas assumptions about internal integration (e.g., language, group boundaries, the distribution of power and status, and relationship norms) might be most relevant for process and molar climates. Along similar lines, it would be useful for climate researchers to study the assumptions that underlie the particular climate of interest, possibly disentangling those that support the climate, those that detract from it, and those that may have relatively little effect or are neutral. Perhaps most relevant to this issue is the work of Zohar and Hofmann (2012). Their model provides a step in the right direction by rethinking climate as shared perceptions of enacted values and arguing that the contrast of those perceptions with espoused values creates insights into the values and beliefs that underlie the organization's climate and culture. We discuss their model in more depth later in this chapter, but the motto for this approach to climate would be "deeper is better."

Breadth

Organizational climate has typically focused on the policies, practices, procedures, and reward systems in organizations, but climate research does not need to be limited to those areas or facets of organizational behavior. Climate research could expand to investigate the interplay between these facets of climate and issues that have typically been the domain of culture research, such as myths, stories, rituals, and history. Other artifacts of the organization, such as employee dress, arrangement of space, geographic dispersion of the organization, and the posters on the walls, are likely correlates of the presence of focused climates within organizations. Much like Schein (2010) differentiated between the primary and secondary embedding mechanisms through which leaders influence culture/climate, perhaps climate researchers need to differentiate between the primary sources of climate information (the traditional policies, practices, procedures, and reward and expectations systems) and secondary sources (more indirect indicators such as stories, posters, and the arrangement of space).

As we write this, it becomes clear that climate researchers who accept the definition of climate to include "behaviors that get rewarded, supported, and expected" have focused on reward systems but less so on the support or expectations. We have long been aware of the literature on positive organizational support (Eisenberger, Huntington, Hutchison, & Sowa, 1986), and that research would clearly be helpful to include in future climate studies. And Eden's (2003) work on expectations would seem to be a natural for inclusion in climate research. For example, we are unaware of any climate surveys that ask employees about what they are expected to do. Such questions could rest on the same foundation of values and basic assumptions we are suggesting should be incorporated into climate research, laying a rich foundation for future thinking and research.

Socialization

How organizational members learn about the organization's culture and pass it on to future generations of employees through socialization processes has received extensive attention in the culture literature, but little is known about how these processes occur with regard to climate and how new employees learn about the strategic goals toward which they should be focusing their energy. For instance, how do new employees come to learn about their organization's safety climate, and how long does it take before they become adequately familiar with the safety climate prior to it actually affecting their job behavior? How much of the organization's climate is communicated through formal versus informal socialization mechanisms? Such research might investigate the role that the organization's climate plays in the employment brand of the organization, how and on what bases the organization selects its new employees, and whether employees decide to stay with the organization over time (i.e., based on their fit with the strategic climate).

The External Environment

Organization culture researchers have generally been much more concerned with the role of the organization's external context than have climate researchers. For instance, culture researchers are more likely to discuss the effect of issues like national culture, occupational culture, the state of the economy, industry, and so on as correlates of internal organizational culture. Furthermore, they have focused on how the organization's culture fits with the demands placed on the organization by its environment (e.g., Kotter & Heskett, 1992; Schein, 2010). Although research on strategic climate has investigated the extent to which a certain strategic imperative is communicated and established throughout the organization, climate researchers typically do not discuss whether this is actually the right strategic focus for the organization. Perhaps these issues have been too macro for researchers who have typically come from a more psychological background. Regardless of the cause, an increased attention to these features of the external environment would be beneficial for climate research and might yield important connections with the literature on strategic management (we explore this issue in more depth later in this chapter; see also Schneider, Ehrhart, & Macey, 2012).

Development and Change

Organizational culture researchers have expended much energy into understanding how culture develops and how (or if) it changes, but these topics have received very little attention in the climate literature (Ostroff et al., 2012; Schneider, Ehrhart, & Macey, 2013). There are many perspectives on how climates emerge and become shared phenomena, including structuralist explanations, ASA processes, social interaction, sense-making, and leadership (Ostroff et al., 2012; Zohar & Hofmann, 2012), but longitudinal research examining these mechanisms with a specific focus on climate emergence and durability of climate are rare. A likely reason is that the preferred methodology for climate researchers has been survey research, and the type of access and data required for extensive longitudinal investigations of climate development and change are hard to come by. The issue of methodology will be explored in more detail next, but the critical issue for now is that little is known about the factors that are critical in the development of particular focused climate.

Of course, a central issue in the development of culture emerged with Schein's (1985) explication of what he called culture embedding mechanisms. The implicit suggestion in his more recent writing (Schein, 2010) in which he has suggested these are perhaps best thought of as climate-embedding mechanisms is that we need to begin studying the development—and perhaps change—of process and outcome climates. Such studies, grounded in the "embedding" logic would provide a firm conceptual foundation for climate research as well as suggest potentially fruitful approaches to organizational climate change.

Qualitative Methods

The integration of qualitative methods would likely be necessary for climate researchers to address at least some of the issues raised above. Doing so would also bring climate researchers closer to the organizational phenomena they study. As described by Denison (1996), "Climate researchers often have seemed inextricably (and inexplicably?) wedded to a limited form of contact with the organizations that they study: the collection of questionnaire data, the sine qua non of climate research (Trice & Beyer, 1993). This approach may require some contact with a research site (at least by mail), but it seldom requires direct contact with the social psychological phenomena that are the primary objects of study" (p. 643). Although we would not expect or want climate researchers to completely abandon their quantitative survey mindset, we do think that openness to mixed methods would be beneficial for the field. Small steps could include conducting interviews prior to surveys to better understand the issues within an organization and perhaps to tailor the surveys appropriately. A good example of such work is the development of the service climate measure by Schneider and his colleagues (Schneider, Wheeler, & Cox, 1992) that has subsequently been used in many studies of service climate (Hong et al., 2013). Schneider and colleagues had notes from 100 focus groups they had conducted with branch bank employees across several banks questioning participants about the kinds of experiences they had with regard to their branch's focus on service to customers. They content-analyzed those notes and produced a set of contextual descriptions that suggested a strong "passion for service" in those describing their experiences. The issues that emerged formed the foundation for the later service climate measure (e.g., Schneider et al., 1998).

Alternatively, qualitative methods could be used after survey data are analyzed to help explain the results and raise questions for future research. One area that could benefit from this approach is research on climate strength. Although much progress has been made in integrating the idea of dispersion in climate research, we do not know much about why certain units are low in strength; a follow-up study using qualitative methods could help address those questions.

Passion and Richness

One of the issues that made the concept of organization culture so attractive, particularly for those from the organizations *are* cultures mold, was that it offered a way to add richness to our understanding of organizations and to capture the passion and emotion experienced by workers. Although such "touchy-feely" issues may sound to some climate researchers as being outside the bounds of serious scientific research, the fact of the matter is that employees do feel a passion (or what some may refer to as engagement; Salanova, Agut, & Peiró, 2005) about service or safety or innovation when they are in climates reflecting those strategies. Nevertheless, climate research does not do a good job of capturing or understanding that passion. This may be because of the issue raised by Denison (1996) that climate researchers tend to be too disconnected from the organizations they study to understand the full range of the experiences of employees. Perhaps by taking on some of the recommendations above, such as including a broader range of organizational variables or a mix of quantitative and qualitative methods, climate research can begin to better understand the passion that is central to the climates they study.

WHAT ORGANIZATIONAL CULTURE RESEARCHERS COULD LEARN FROM ORGANIZATIONAL CLIMATE RESEARCH

We now turn the tables and address what organizational culture researchers could learn from research on organizational climate. This section is a little more challenging because there is such variability in culture research, particularly with regard to the qualitative versus quantitative methods used to study culture. Therefore, we have attempted to identify those issues that apply to research on organizational culture in general, and when they apply to only portions of the culture literature, to be clear about those distinctions. As summarized in Table 6.4, we propose six areas that have typically been the domain of organizational climate research that could be useful to culture research: (1) focus on effectiveness, (2) strategic focus, (3) mediators and moderators, (4) mixed methods, (5) levels of analysis, and (6) relevancy.

Focus on Effectiveness

A focus on organizational effectiveness has been a central idea in climate research from the very beginning. For example, work on service

TABLE 6.4 What culture researchers could learn from climate research

- An increased *focus on effectiveness*, however it may be defined, to demonstrate the practical value of culture for organizations
- The development of a *strategic focus* for culture to demonstrate how specific elements of culture contribute to the achievement of the organization's strategic goals
- The inclusion of *mediators and moderators* in the relationship of culture with organizational effectiveness to better capture the complexity of how culture has its effect in organizations and on organizational effectiveness
- The increased use of *mixed methods* to better capitalize on the strengths of both quantitative and qualitative approaches
- The demonstration of appropriate *levels of analysis* by using statistical tests to show which levels are important for outcomes at different levels of analysis, keeping in mind that it could be multiple levels that have an influence
- An increased attention to *relevancy* so that culture research can have more effect by paying more attention to the issues that organizational leaders care most about

climate was stimulated by the idea that internal reports by employees of what happens in their organizations would predict customer reports of the quality of service they received (Schneider, Bowen, Ehrhart, & Holcombe, 2000). Although some culture researchers, particularly those who use surveys to study culture, have investigated the relationship between culture and organizational effectiveness (see reviews by Sackmann, 2011; and Wilderom et al., 2000), there continues to be an apparent general distaste for studying the relationship between culture and performance, especially financial performance. Some researchers are concerned about reducing culture to "just another predictor" of performance, and others note that by focusing on effectiveness, researchers adopt manager's priorities as their own, ignoring the plight of those with less power in organizations. However, one result of this hesitancy to focus on effectiveness is that culture research overall (though, of course, not the *idea* of culture) has had limited practical effect on organizations (Alvesson & Berg, 1992; Denison, 1996; Martin & Frost, 1996). An increased focus on the validity of culture assessments for effectiveness would increase the effect that culture research could have. And for those researchers who may object to pure financial outcomes, a broader view of effectiveness to include issues related to diversity/inclusion or employee well-being may offer a middle ground that would still have practical value for organizations; research on the competing values framework (CVF) discussed earlier (e.g., Hartnell et al., 2011) is a good example of this possibility.

Strategic Focus

Building on the previous point, part of climate's success in understanding organizational effectiveness has come from its focus on those aspects of the organization related to specific strategic imperatives. As we reviewed earlier, a large variety of strategic climates have been studied, providing insight into the internal issues that organizations face when attempting to achieve their strategic goals. Integrating such a strategic focus into culture research would help to show how culture links to effectiveness (even if not in very straightforward ways), and would aid in increasing the practical effect of culture research. Organizational culture is such a broad construct that it is already necessary for researchers to specify a particular piece or manifestation of culture that will be their focus. Including strategic issues as one of those areas of focus would seem to have the potential to add a number of practical and theoretical insights. Several examples of possible strategic cultures were described in the second edition of Ashkanasy et al.'s (2011) *Handbook of Organizational Culture and Climate*, including work-family culture (Duxbury & Grover, 2011), error management culture (Keith & Frese, 2011), and the cultures of sustainable organizations (Russell & McIntosh, 2011), and there has also been some empirical literature on the topic of ethical culture (Schaubroeck, Hannah, Avolio, Kozlowski, Lord, Treviño, Dimotakis, & Peng, 2012). The challenge is to differentiate clearly what is unique about these focused cultures relative to their climate counterparts, rather than measuring climate but using a culture label. For instance, in Chapter Seven, we discuss the work of an independent review panel done at BP after the 2005 disaster in the Gulf of Mexico, which employed a safety climate measure relabeled as a safety culture measure. In contrast, Hudson (2007) provided an excellent example of safety culture thinking that builds on the frameworks of both organizational culture and organizational climate to produce a rich portrait of safety in the gas and oil industry. We encourage additional research along these integrative lines.

Mediators and Moderators

Climate researchers have established strong relationships between climate (especially strategic climates) and organizational outcomes and, more recently, researchers have moved to better understand the complex nature of those relationships. For instance, researchers have examined the conditions under which climate is more strongly (or weakly) related to outcomes, as well as the specific employee behaviors that mediate climate's relationship with outcomes (see summaries by Kuenzi & Schminke, 2009; and Schneider et al., 2011b). The culture literature that does focus on organizational effectiveness, typically involving culture surveys, is not as well developed in this regard. There are some exceptions, of course, including Sørensen's (2002) work on industry volatility as a moderator of the effects of culture strength and Kotrba et al.'s (2012) study of cultural consistency as a moderator of the effects of other culture dimensions, as well as Gregory et al.'s (2009) research on employee attitudes as a mediator of culture's effects on outcomes. Nevertheless, the general lack of studies on the moderators or mediators of culture's effects on outcomes is somewhat surprising given that culture is likely a more distal predictor of organizational effectiveness than climate. In other words, there are likely numerous mechanisms through which organizational culture ultimately has its effects on organizational performance that have not been addressed. Then again, the empirical study of climate's relationship with organizational effectiveness has been in existence longer and thus has had a bit of a head start on culture research in that regard. More thinking about culture's relationship with organizational effectiveness in terms of moderators and mediators consistent with the complexity of culture and its various manifestations is needed.

Mixed Methods

Survey research has clearly dominated climate research, but there is a divide among culture researchers as to whether surveys are an appropriate method to study culture. In the same way that we advocated for climate researchers to integrate more qualitative methods in their studies, we would advocate for qualitative culture researchers to be more open to the quantitative methods that characterize climate research and some culture research. Doing so would allow for empirical tests of some of the assumptions that are made in qualitative research and would provide tests of the existence of relationships suggested in case studies or ethnographies. One example of such research is that by Siehl and Martin (1988), who used information from interviews and observation to create survey measures of typical culture concepts like company jargon, organizational stories, and tacit knowledge. They then showed that familiarity with these manifestations of an organization's culture was significantly related to tenure in the organization. Other examples of the application of mixed methods include Jermier et al. (1991), who subjected quantitative data to cluster analysis to identify subcultures in a police organization and supplemented these results with qualitative data from interviews with police officers. In a similar vein, Denison and Mishra (1995) used case studies to form the bases for a series of hypotheses that they then tested using survey data. This type of integration of the survey methods championed by climate researchers (and some culture researchers) with more typical qualitative culture research can provide additional insights beyond what would be found with either alone.

Levels of Analysis

Climate researchers have dedicated much energy to clarifying levels of analysis issues and developing statistical techniques to judge the appropriateness of using a specific level of analysis in a given piece of research. The extent to which culture is shared seems to be more of an assumption in much of the culture literature. Even in alternative perspectives such as differentiation or fragmentation (Martin, 2002), the existence of subcultures or the ambiguity of cultural elements is rarely put to any sort of formal test. Culture researchers from these perspectives have been accused of only highlighting the cultural elements that best fit the story they want to tell (Martin et al., 2006); it would seem that employing quantitative methods and applying statistical tests to ensure that data analyses are conducted at the appropriate level(s) of analysis would help clarify some of these issues. Researchers could then judge the extent to which there is agreement across the organization as a whole, whether and where there are subcultures within the organization, and the extent to which there is confusion or disagreement on the constructs of interest to the researcher.

For example, in the same vein as Jermier et al. (1991), it would be interesting to have data from a more comprehensive culture survey (e.g., the Denison measure) and submit those data to cluster analysis (Aldenderfer & Blashfield, 1984; Everitt, Landau, Leese, & Stahl, 2011) or better yet, latent class modeling (Nylund, Asparouhov, & Muthén, 2007), asking the question: at what levels and in what ways do groupings of similar responses occur? Such analyses would be useful because they deal with profiles of attributes rather than one attribute one at a time, which fits the idea that the whole organization in its many manifestations is of interest. Groupings of employees might emerge in terms of occupation, racial/ethnic identity, level in the organization, and so forth. The researcher can examine the groupings to determine if they make sense conceptually and can also make comparisons between different numbers of groupings to determine what fits the data the best (including the possibility that only one grouping—the entire organization—exists). We will have more to say about this potential in Chapter Seven.

Relevancy

We would be hesitant to bring up the issue of relevancy if it had not already been raised by top researchers in the field of organizational culture (Alvesson & Berg, 1992; Denison, 1996; Martin & Frost, 1996). There is considerable discussion about what organizational culture should and should not include and how it should and should not be studied, but relatively little attention on how the literature on organizational culture can be used to affect how organizations function and the decision making of leadership (see Schein, 2010, for a notable exception). There is such a strong sentiment among some culture researchers to avoid making culture just another tool for management that research is in danger of not being of use at all to employees at any level. A middle ground is needed. Understanding management's priorities and attempting to find common ground with their goals may provide a foot in the door to allow for more effect. Demonstrating a relationship with effectiveness, which as previously noted has been a strength of climate research, is one example of a way to get the attention of organizational management (Denison, 2001). Such efforts do not have to result in a complete rejection of the core values that have dominated some lines of culture research. Take the literature on diversity climate as an example, which has empirically demonstrated the benefits of a diversity climate not only for the employees themselves, but also for the organization as a whole (McKay et al., 2009). In other words, instead of an "either-or" issue, it has become a "both-and" proposition. More creative thinking on how to demonstrate the importance of the critical issues of interest to culture researchers across multiple stakeholder groups in organizations is needed.

TOWARD INTEGRATING ORGANIZATIONAL CLIMATE AND CULTURE

Having discussed how climate and culture are similar and different and what researchers in the two fields can learn from each other, the next step is to discuss how the two can be integrated into our thinking and research on organizations. The earliest example we could identify in which climate and culture were discussed in an integrative fashion is found in Litwin and Stringer (1968). Although they did not explicitly use the term "culture," they did describe how "certain factors such as history and tradition, leadership style, spatial arrangements, etc. do influence, through climate, the motivation and behavior of individuals" (p. 39). These relationships were not developed in depth, but they do indicate a view that the deeper layers of culture (history and tradition) and its manifestations (spatial arrangements) influence workers through climate. More recent discussions of how climate and culture may work together as part of organizational life have framed the relationship between the two in various ways. For instance, Kopelman et al. (1990) depicted culture as providing an organizational context, such that organizational culture influenced the HRM practices that formed the foundation for climate, which subsequently was related to employee cognitive and affective states, behavior, and ultimately productivity. In another example, Moran and Volkwein (1992) drew from Schneider and Reichers (1983) in describing climate as the result of a process by which interacting individuals respond to various situational contingencies in their environment. As part of that process, organizational culture, operating primarily at the deeper level of basic assumptions, manifests its influence on the internal environment and informs and enhances or constrains the climate formation process.

Denison (1996) has provided one of the more in-depth discussions of the relationship between climate and culture. Although he comprehensively described several areas of contrast between the two literatures in terms of epistemology, point of view, methodology, level of analysis, temporal orientation, theoretical foundations, and discipline, his main point was to highlight the areas of convergence across the two literatures:

> Both perspectives . . . could be regarded as examining the internal social psychological environment of organizations and the relationship of that environment to individual meaning and organizational adaptation. Both perspectives entertain the possibility of a shared, holistic, collectively defined social context that emerges over time as organizations struggle with the joint problems of adaptation, individual meaning, and social integration (p. 625).

Thus, he concluded that the two constructs address the same phenomenon, and it is only the differences in the research traditions that separate the two.

Although we do agree that at a broad level the two constructs are addressing the same issue (the organizational environment or context), our view is not entirely overlapping with that of Denison. Historically, the roots of both constructs are in the idea that the environment experienced by workers will have substantial influence on their collective attitudes and behaviors, in addition to the effects on the organization's overall performance. Denison's view seems to be that, by focusing on the differences between climate and culture, we have been distracted from the more fundamental goal of deepening our understanding of the organizational context. Our view is that the two constructs are more different than is acknowledged by Denison, and that the differences have been critical in providing distinctive insights into the organizational environment. At the same time, we share the common goal of seeing more integration between the two areas as being very useful, although little progress has been made toward that goal. By acknowledging the differences between the two constructs and how they are studied, our hope is that we can better understand how each area can learn from the other and move forward with renewed energy and insight.

Three recent frameworks that have been proposed in the literature in fact do help move toward the goal of the integration of the climate and culture literatures. Below we provide a brief overview of each, noting the specific qualities that distinguish it from the others and thus how each adds to both our understanding and potential integration of both culture and climate.

Schneider, Ehrhart, and Macey (2011b)

In one of our own recent handbook chapters, we proposed the "climcult framework" as one way to integrate the literatures of organizational climate and culture (see Figure 6.1). Noting the general lack of a strategic emphasis in the culture literature, we focused on the extent to which the organization's culture communicates the priority of employee well-being. As such, we viewed culture as taking on two roles. The first is to provide a foundation for strategic climates. A positive culture that values employees will not automatically result in the strategic climate or foci needed for success in the marketplace. At the same time, however, it is a necessary precursor for the successful implementation of strategic imperatives. That is, logically we believe that if employees do not view their organization as caring about them and attempting to fulfill their needs, then, following the social exchange model (Blau, 1964; Cropanzano & Mitchell, 2005) they will be unlikely to put forth maximum energy in attaining the organization's strategic goals. The second role for a culture of well-being is to create a positive environment that is attractive for both future and current employees. When the organization supports its employees, it will be able to retain talent and become an employer of choice through the positive reputation or employer image the organization develops.

In our model, we positioned leadership as critical for both culture and climate, such that culture is driven by the positive values about people that are espoused and enacted by organizational leaders, and climate is

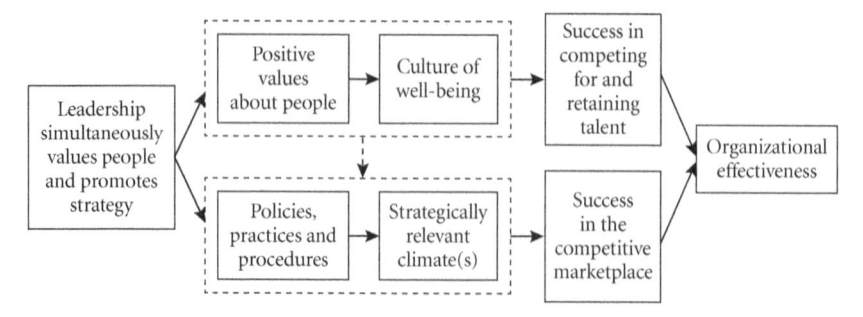

Figure 6.1 Schneider, Ehrhart, and Macey's (2011b) "climcult" model

From Schneider, B., Ehrhart, M.G., & Macey, W.A. (2011b). Perspectives on organizational climate and culture. In S. Zedeck (Ed.), *APA handbook of industrial and organizational psychology: Vol. 1. Building and developing the organization* (pp. 373–414). Washington, DC: American Psychological Association. Figure 12.1, p. 405. Copyright © 2011 by the American Psychological Association and reprinted with permission.

driven by the policies, practices, and procedures leaders create in embedding simultaneously their climate, their culture, and by clear implication, their strategic foci. For simplicity's sake we did not include the mechanisms by which climate and culture lead to success or feedback loops in the model, although we have shown in our own research that unit-level behavior is a mediator of the relationship between climate and outcomes (Schneider, Ehrhart, Mayer, Saltz, & Niles-Jolly, 2005) and that outcomes have a reciprocal relationship with climate (Schneider et al., 1998).

The focus in the climcult model is on strategic climates because they have the immediate effect on the organization's ability to implement effective strategies for competing in the marketplace. But it has become conceptually clear to us that the kind of well-being we see as a necessary foundation for strategic climates includes a focus on process climates (e.g., justice) as well. So, although these were not a focus of the "climcult" model, in our other writings (Schneider et al., 2011a) we have discussed how those climates can contribute to a foundation for strategic climates as well, and thus we would position them between the culture of well-being and strategic climate.

Ostroff, Kinicki, and Muhammad (2012)

This handbook chapter was an updated version of Ostroff, Kinicki, and Tamkins (2003) in which the authors provided an overview of both the climate and culture constructs as well as a model that integrates both. They viewed climate and culture as both focusing on the shared meanings of the organizational context, with climate focusing on perceptions of *what* happens in organizations (behaviors, support, and expectations) and culture focusing on *why* those things happen (basic assumptions

Figure 6.2 Ostroff, Kinicki, & Muhammad's (2012) multilevel model of organizational culture and climate. Used by permission.

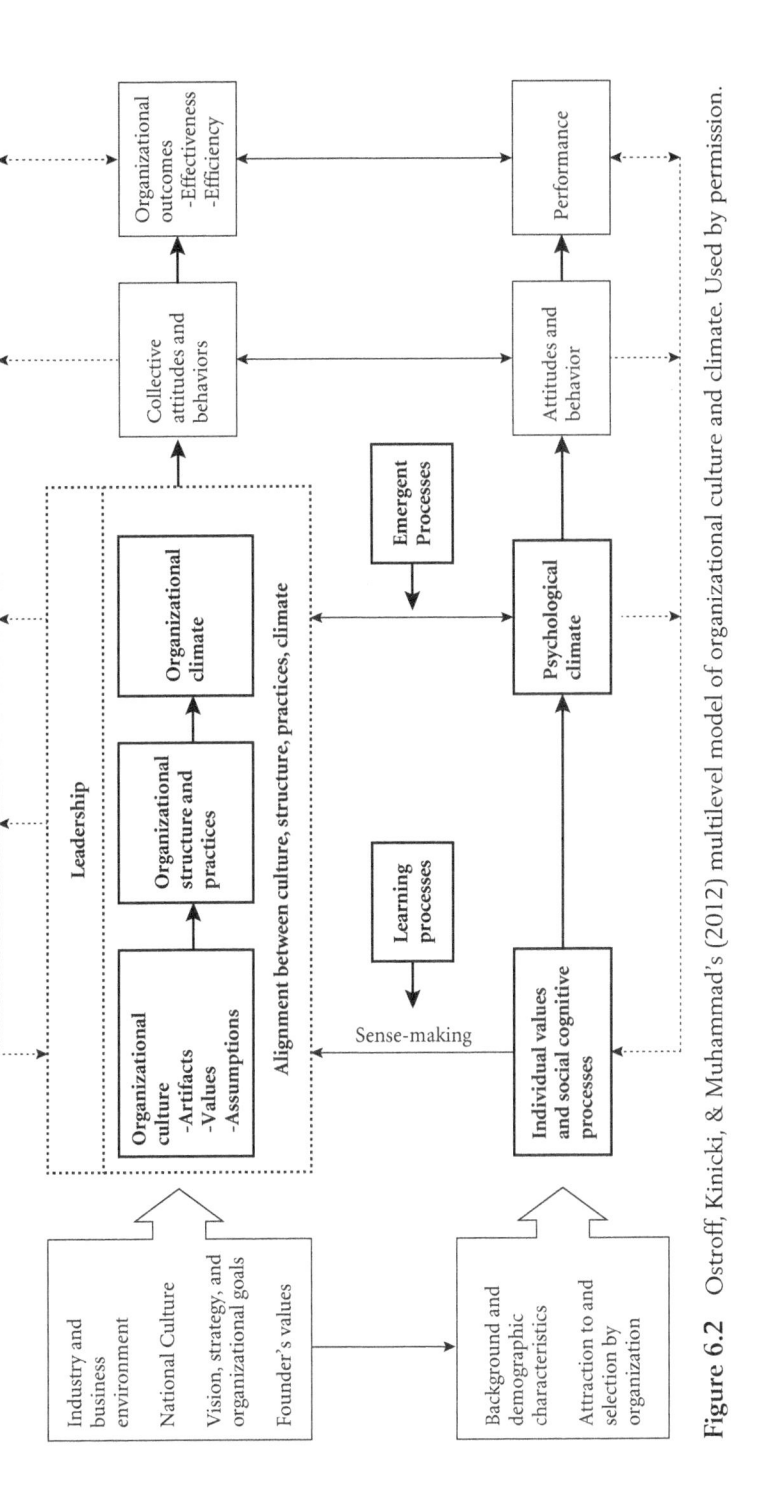

values, and beliefs). In an interesting conceptual move, they emphasized that policies, practices, and procedures (practices, for short) are neither climate nor culture, but instead the linking mechanism between the two. These practices are manifestations of the deeper assumptions and values of culture and form the basis for climate as organizational members perceive, interpret, and assign meaning to them.

The framework of Ostroff and colleagues (2012) is shown in Figure 6.2; there are several aspects of it worth noting. The first is that the relationship between culture and climate is mediated by organizational structures and practices, neither of which is thus viewed as within the realms of culture or climate. Leadership is depicted as influencing each of these facets of the context, and the alignment among them is specifically mentioned within the model. The outcome of organizational climate is the collective attitudes and behaviors of workers and, ultimately, organizational effectiveness and efficiency. The model thus focuses on what we have called the molar climate and does not depict either process or outcome strategic climates. A noteworthy part of the model is its multilevel portrayal of both the individual and organizational levels of analyses and how the two influence each other. Feedback loops are also included, indicating how climate or outcomes can also influence organizational culture.

Zohar and Hofmann (2012)

In Zohar and Hofmann's (2012) climate and culture handbook chapter, there is considerable emphasis placed on the deepest layers of organizational culture and the difference between core values, representing the organization's moral criteria for the right way to act, and basic assumptions, emerging out of the organization's history of successes and failures. These deeper layers of culture are manifested in the outer layers of culture that include the organization's priorities, policies, practices, norms, and artifacts. Climate, in contrast, is viewed as a shared, global assessment of the relative priorities of management. Employees are seen as coping with a complex organizational context, perceiving and integrating across the various policies and practices to decipher what behaviors are most likely to be rewarded. Three complex assessments are required by employees: (1) the relative priorities management places on strategic goals, (2) the relative alignment between management's espousals and enactments (i.e., their words and their deeds), and (3) the internal consistency among the various policies, practices, and procedures experienced across levels of the organization. In their framework (shown in Figure 6.3), climate perceptions summarize the meaning of the artifacts of culture into pattern-level information on the enacted values and priorities of management and provide insight into the deeper level core values and assumptions that underlie multiple process and outcome climates. What we like about this model is the explicit acknowledgement of the

Integrating Organizational Climate and Organizational Culture 223

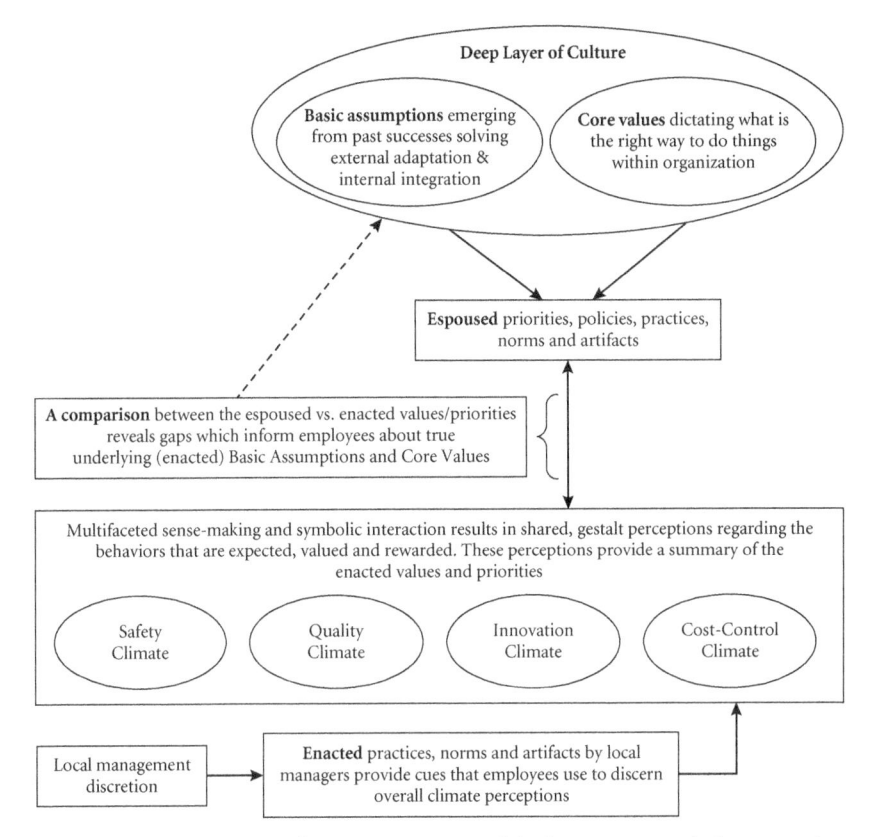

Figure 6.3 Zohar & Hofmann's (2012) model of organizational climate and culture, Fig. 20.1 Graphic Description of the Theoretical Model, p. 662.

From Zohar, D., & Hofmann, D. H. (2012). Organizational culture and climate. In S.W.J. Kozlowski (Ed.), *The Oxford Handbook of Industrial and Organizational Psychology* (pp. 643–666). © Copyright Oxford University Press; by permission of Oxford University Press.

challenges employees face in deciphering the context in which they are immersed and the simultaneous vision it provides for management of the wide variety of issues to which it must attend to create and maintain specific strategic climates.

There are several other areas to highlight in Zohar and Hofmann's model. One is that the model explicitly takes into account the layers of culture and their different roles in relation to climate. Another is that the model focuses specifically on strategic climates; other types of climate are not included, which is consistent with Zohar and Hofmann's definition of climate as a shared perception of the relative priority among competing strategic imperatives. Their framework also places a heavy emphasis on the distinction between what is enacted and what is espoused. In fact, they specifically contrasted their model of culture, which has enacted values as the intermediate layer, with Schein's (2010) layers of culture, which have espoused values as the intermediate layer. Thus they described their model as a bottom-up model based on employee's perceptions of what actually happens (or what is enacted) versus Schein's top-down model based on management's stated philosophies or priorities (or what is espoused). Finally, Zohar and Hofmann presented a multilevel model of the organization by contrasting local and work unit enactment of values with top management's espousals. By doing this, they introduced a kind of gaps model that has not received much attention in either climate or culture thinking and research and which offers a fresh and exciting potential for future research.

General Conclusions

Each of these models provides a unique contribution to understanding how climate and culture relate to each other and how together they may influence organizational outcomes. We were tempted to try to integrate the models but quickly realized that such a massive, overly complicated model would do little to move the fields forward. Given the complexity of the issues, it is likely more effective to develop models that address specific issues and areas for integration, rather than searching for THE singular model of climate and culture. Looking across the three models, we reach the following conclusions:

- Climate and culture are related to each other but, at the same time, they are conceptually distinct and play unique roles in understanding employees' experiences of the organization and the organization's strategic priorities and overall effectiveness.
- Organizational culture is a deeper-level construct, particularly with regard to the basic assumptions and values at its core, that forms the foundation for the climate of the organization.
- There are a number of reciprocal relationships between climate and culture and between organizational outcomes and climate and culture. For instance, although culture is more typically thought of as influencing climate, climate can influence the deeper layers of culture. In addition, climate and culture are typically thought of as affecting key organizational outcomes, but those outcomes can influence both climate and culture.
- There are likely multiple paths through which culture and climate influence organizational effectiveness. Two such paths are through a general support for employee well-being and through specific strategies related to desired outcomes.
- Climate and culture have implications that span multiple levels of analysis, including the individual, the unit (group, department, etc.), and the organization as a whole.
- We gain new insights into how organizations influence employees' experiences and meanings when we separate the layers or elements of

organizational culture rather than portraying culture as an overall undifferentiated entity.
- Alignment issues are core to discussions of the relationship between climate and culture and between climate and culture and organizational effectiveness. These may include the general alignment among culture, climate, leadership, and the organization's practices, or between the organization's espoused and enacted values and priorities.

It is encouraging to see such clear steps toward the integration of climate and culture in understanding the organizational environment, and we look forward to the research that is stimulated by these and future related models. We explore some of the issues in these models in more depth in the next sections on competitive advantage and organizational change.

CLIMATE, CULTURE, AND COMPETITIVE ADVANTAGE

It is probably obvious by now that our approach to climate and culture is oriented towards helping organizations be more effective than they have been in the past. Perhaps more importantly we see climate and culture as potential keys to competitive advantage—not only being better than in the past, but also being more effective than the competition. Achieving this kind of effectiveness requires attention both to the people issues (molar climate and a culture supporting well-being) and to the process and strategic foci (focused climates) that give employees clues about the true priorities of management. In this section, we delve into the literature on the resource-based theory of organizational effectiveness to provide more detail on how organizational climate and culture are related to competitive advantage.

The resource-based theory of organizations is concerned with how the various resources controlled by organizations are linked to sustained competitive advantage (Barney, 1991). Barney defined resources to include "all assets, capabilities, organizational processes, firm attributes, information, knowledge, etc. controlled by a firm that enable the firm to conceive of and implement strategies that improve its efficiency and effectiveness" (p. 101). Thus, resources are described very broadly and the exact bundle of resources that are relevant will depend on the organization's specific marketplace. Resources can be more tangible, such as financial or physical capital, or intangible, such as human or organizational capital (Barney & Arikan, 2001). In our discussion, the focus is on the intangible resources of organizational climate and culture and how they can be utilized for competitive advantage.

According to Barney (1991), a resource will result in competitive advantage when it has four attributes. The first is that it must be valuable. In other words, it must in some way contribute to increased efficiency or effectiveness for the organization. If the resource fails to add value, then it will not create competitive advantage. Second, it must be rare, such that it is not common among competing companies. If everyone has access to the resource, then it will be unlikely to create competitive advantage. Third, it must be inimitable or at a minimum very difficult to imitate. If other organizations can easily imitate the resource and its use, then any competitive advantage will at best be short-term and not sustainable. The fourth attribute Barney described is that the resource must be nonsubstitutable. In other words, if a competitor can introduce a substitute for the resource that has the same value, then having the resource will not create a competitive advantage.

In 1986, Barney made the argument that organizational culture can provide a competitive advantage for some organizations based on the first three criteria above. With regard to value, he suggested that some firms' cultures allow them to perform in ways that result in levels of economic performance that would not be possible without their culture. For instance, an organization's level of innovation, the competencies of its employees, and its focus on the customer are all issues tied to its culture that have important economic consequences for the organization. At the same time, Barney emphasized that not all organizations' cultures will have a positive economic effect, and in fact, some cultures can have negative consequences for the productivity of the firm.

Barney then noted how some cultures are likely rare based on the unique circumstances of their founding and events in their history, as well as in the unique set of personalities that make up the employees and management there. Once again, Barney pointed out that not all cultures will be rare, and there are factors that could result in high levels of similarity among the cultures of some organizations. For example, the nature of the industry in which organizations operate and even the national culture in which they function could limit the variability in the assumptions and values of those organizational cultures.

With regard to the third factor, inimitability, Barney described how path dependency, causal ambiguity, and social complexity lead to cultures being difficult to imitate. Path dependency refers to the development of the resource and the perhaps unique historical conditions that contributed to the organization's ability to obtain and effectively use the resource. Applied to culture, the same history that can make a culture rare can also make it difficult to imitate; as Barney put it, "history defies easy imitation" (p. 661). Causal ambiguity refers to the difficulty other firms have imitating a resource if it is unclear exactly which resources the firm controls and how they are intertwined and collectively contribute to the firm's competitive advantage. For many of the same reasons that individuals within the organization may find it difficult to describe the deep-level assumptions that drive their culture, other organizations will likely also find it difficult to determine exactly what aspects of an organization's culture and in what combinations are most relevant for creating value. Finally, social complexity refers to the difficulty in imitating resources derived from complex social interactions as well as physical resources that require complex social relations for the resource to be fully exploited. To imitate a culture, managers must be able to effectively lead culture change; however, the complexity of organizational culture described in the last chapter suggests that it is very difficult to manage and change. Based on these factors, Barney concluded that organizational culture had the potential to provide sustained competitive advantage for at least some organizations.

We should note that Barney's perspective on competitive advantage through organizational culture was actually quite deterministic, in that he proposed that cultures that did not provide a competitive advantage would likely never do so. That is, if a firm's culture did not provide for competitive advantage, then attempting to change it would be unlikely to result in competitive advantage. If the organization could change its culture to be like another organization's culture, then it would not necessarily provide an advantage, but would just make that culture less rare and thus not tied to competitive advantage. In addition, if culture were so easily changed, then other organizations would likely do the same, once again removing the competitive advantage. Successful change would require a culture primed for change and management with the skills to do so, a combination that Barney argued to be valuable, rare, and inimitable in and of itself. Thus for most organizations without a rare, inimitable culture that is currently providing value, or without a culture that would allow for change to create value and competitive advantage, management must rely on other means to differentiate themselves from competitors and gain sustained competitive advantage.

Although the concept of organizational culture has been discussed with regard to resource-based theory and competitive advantage, there has not been any discussion of which we are aware on these topics with regard to organizational climate. We propose that the concept of strategic organizational climate, working hand-in-hand with organizational culture, may offer organizations a useful perspective for the creation of competitive advantage. A strategic climate can be thought of as a bundle of resources, a resource itself, or a strategy for managing resources. However it is conceptualized, strategic organizational climate fits well with the four attributes of competitive advantage from Barney (1991). In terms of value, there is the large literature we earlier reviewed showing that various strategic climates have robust relationships with their respective strategic outcomes. With regard to rarity, what is rare in the case of strategic climate is the combination of the various policies, practices, and procedures that create the overall gestalt for employees that signals to them that there exists a particular management priority. It is easy for organizations to institute a single policy or practice, but what is rare is to bundle them together in a coordinated mutually reinforcing way.

Strategic climates are also difficult to imitate. Each of the three reasons for inimitability applies to strategic climates. With regard to path dependency, the particular practices and procedures that make up a strategic climate are likely shaped by the organization's unique history and culture. So, as we noted earlier, strategic climates can only exist when they rest on firm foundations to support them, and this is where the role of the larger organization's molar culture comes into play. That is, service policies and practices cannot exist in an organization if they are not aligned with the deeper culture of the organization or if management espouses one set of values but enacts another. The second element, causal ambiguity, is relevant because the tactics for the creation of a strategic climate are ambiguous and difficult to identify precisely because they are bundles of reinforcing practices, not one or a few individual practices. In much of human resource management and I/O psychology research and practice, unfortunately, the focus is on individual practices—the much-sought-after "silver bullet"—and the silver bullet approach to competitive advantage is not causally ambiguous. Moreover, the practices must be aligned with the larger organizational culture to be effective, making the causal nature of the climate even more difficult to discern. With regard to social complexity, part of the value of a strategic climate is that it yields a common perspective for employees and acts as a kind of glue by coordinating the common focus of their behavior towards shared strategic priorities. So it is not just the presence of the policies and practices, but rather it is the shared interpretation and perceptions and thus the coordinated behaviors that ultimately constitute the climate (which, of course, are supported by the social complexity implied by the culture construct).

Finally, a strategic climate is not easily substitutable to achieve the same long-term advantages. Short-term approaches may provide some immediate results, but those approaches will probably not match what climate and culture provide in the long term. The extensive literatures on both climate and culture (that require an entire book just as an introduction to them!) would not exist if there were easily available substitutes for them. These are complex issues; seeking simple replacements is a fool's errand.

Based on this analysis, we conclude that strategic climates developed in cultures that support and are aligned with them fit the criteria for providing a basis for competitive advantage to organizations. Although both organizational climate and culture have potential for sustained competitive advantage, we argue that strategic climates may offer the more useful starting point for organizations. As we asserted in the last section, climate addresses the issues (policies, practices, procedures, and rewards) over which managers have more direct control, and strategic climate is likely more malleable and more proximally linked to the organization's strategic goals than culture. Enacting such a climate should, through repetition and success, reinforce the basic assumptions and values for a sustainable organizational culture. Thus, the challenge is one of determining where competitive advantage looks to be possible in the marketplace, assessing the likelihood that the elements necessary for the creation of a strategic climate exist, and then evaluating the degree to which the existing culture will be supportive of and serve as a firm foundation for the strategic climate. We delve deeper into the issue of organizational change and the practical steps that build from this discussion in the next section and in the final chapter.

CLIMATE, CULTURE, AND ORGANIZATIONAL CHANGE

Building on our discussion of competitive advantage and as we begin to transition towards the more practical implications of organizational climate and culture, it is important to consider the role of climate and culture in organizational change, and specifically, whether climate or culture should be the focus of organizational change efforts. The foundation of any discussion of this topic is the idea that culture and climate are reciprocally related. For instance, Reichers and Schneider (1990) viewed culture and climate as "reciprocal processes, the one causing the other in an endless cycle over time. In this manner, climate . . . is both the manifestation of culture . . . and the data on which culture comes to be inferred and understood" (p. 24). In this way of thinking, climate can be viewed as an outcome of culture, and specifically an outcome of the values and assumptions of the deeper layers of culture. The policies, practices, and procedures that form the basis for climate are initiated by leaders who are both influenced by those values and assumptions and who potentially at its inception embedded those values and assumptions in the organization's culture. This direction of causation is the most common one found in the literature that discusses how climate and culture relate to each other.

The reverse direction of causality—climate as a cause of culture—is less commonly discussed, likely because culture is viewed as deeper and more stable, and thus it is easier to think of culture as influencing the more observable aspects of the organization than how it is influenced by them. It is our view that culture does change, albeit slowly, and the influence of climate on culture can be found in the creation of culture and the evolutionary changes in culture that occur over time. From the beginning of the organization, the leader's values are communicated to employees through the policies, practices, procedures, and reward systems that he or she enacts as the organization copes with the problems it confronts. This process of enactment occurs through Schein's (2010) primary and secondary embedding mechanisms. Schein's acknowledgement that these mechanisms would best be thought of as creating climate opens the notion that the climate suggests by inference what the basic assumptions and values of the organization are. In other words, how organizations cope with the ongoing issues and challenges (and thus the climate that is created in the organization) serves as a signal as to what is valued by management. Furthermore, those practices that are successful are reinforced by repetition over time, yielding a subconscious connection to effectiveness, which in turn yields basic assumptions about how organizational members should behave to be successful in the future.

A helpful parallel to thinking about climate and culture change may be to think about the individual level relationship between behaviors and beliefs or values (Sathe & Davidson, 2000; Schneider, 2000). Like culture, beliefs exist at a deeper level and are more stable than behavior, which is analogous to climate. Although it is possible to change beliefs, it is quite difficult. What is more effective, as was shown in the very early attitude change studies at Yale University (Hovland, Janis, & Kelly, 1953), is to change behavior, which then triggers a rethinking of one's deeply held attitudes and beliefs. Along these lines but in the context of discussing culture change, Sathe and Davidson 2000) suggested that the "shock" of a positive reinforcement might help to unfreeze the norms of the organization and cause individuals to bring their beliefs and values to a conscious level for possible reconsideration. The example they give is a "Mistake of the Month" award to reinforce risk-taking and innovation. Essentially, what they were arguing is to focus first on the climate of the organization to create behavioral change, with the idea that over time through repetition the culture will be affected as well.

A similar approach was advocated by Michela and Burke (2000; see also Burke, 2011) in discussing how to create a culture for quality and innovation. They borrowed from the quality management literature to discuss the importance of three areas for producing culture change: training, measurement, and rewards. Although they did not discuss climate, clear connections can be made between the three areas they mentioned and Schein's (2010) embedding mechanisms (that create climate) and the policies and practices that form the bases of climate perceptions. They noted that if behavior can be changed and employees experience it as beneficial, then value change will follow, and then one can conclude that culture has changed. Thus, in essence they advocated for changing climate first to change behavior and then to ultimately change values and culture.

From our perspective, it seems that the most fruitful approach to change would be to start with climate rather than culture. As we argued earlier, much of what organizational leaders want to do when they discuss culture change is to change the climate of the organization rather than the culture. Leaders typically are interested in reaching a goal or increasing effectiveness, and they want to implement tactics in their organizations to help them achieve their strategic objectives. Culture change in and of itself would be rather nonsensical because it would require direct attention to basic assumptions and values, upending all of what the organization stands for and is. By metaphor, it would be like deciding to destroy the house and its foundation when one is unhappy with the way the living room looks and feels! Moran and Volkwein (1992) stated it this way: ". . . since climate operates at a more accessible level than culture, it is the more malleable and, hence, the more appropriate level at which to target short-term interventions aimed at producing positive organizational change" (p. 16).

At the same time, that does not mean that culture issues can be ignored. The success of attempting to change or build a new climate is directly tied to the alignment of the change with the underlying assumptions of the culture. As Schein (2000) put it, "Climate can be changed only to the degree that the desired climate is congruent with the underlying assumptions" (p. xxix). Along similar lines, Hatch's (1993, 2000) cultural dynamics model included the idea that how artifacts are interpreted is affected by the underlying assumptions of the current culture, and the tendency is to confirm the current assumptions. Based on this logic, attempts to change climate first may be complicated by how that climate is interpreted through the lens of the current assumptions of the culture. For instance, trying to build a service climate can be interpreted as just a temporary effort that should not be taken seriously if past efforts at change, especially change to a service climate, have been short-lived or not properly administered (see Ogbonna & Harris, 2002, for a case study illustrating this point). Or in a culture with poor labor-management relations, such efforts could be taken as a means to make more money for management that will not be passed on to line employees (and thus will be less likely to be implemented).

Therefore, what leaders must do is evaluate the extent to which the culture either supports or inhibits the desired changes in climate (Schein, 2000). If certain cultural assumptions will be obstacles for building the desired climate and thus for achieving the organization's strategic priorities, then leaders must make the hard decision of whether pursuing culture change is a worthwhile endeavor given the time and energy it would require. In brief, without alignment between the desired climate and the underlying culture, the potential for successful change will be limited.

One last point: the Zohar and Hofmann (2012) model of the complexities and challenges employees face in an organization as they attempt to decipher its priorities is a useful model to have in mind when thinking about change. The model makes it obvious that organizational change requires clear and focused reasons and approaches so that employees can decipher how the proposed changes fit with their existing conceptualizations of the priorities. This means that the new practices put in place must be thought through very carefully for both the intended and unintended consequences they will imply especially with regard to the issue of espoused values versus enacted values.

CONCLUSION

As we noted at the beginning of the chapter, there are a number of similarities and differences between organizational climate and culture. As a result, there are numerous ways that supporters of each might learn from one another to enrich their understanding of the larger organizational context. Some recent thinking reveals how climate and culture might be integrated by emphasizing the potential reciprocal relationships between the two constructs. In light of resource-based theory, a combined strategic climate/organizational culture approach to the achievement of organizational goals might just yield competitive advantage for firms that try it. Thus, there are a number of actions that organizations can take when pursuing organizational change to benefit from a strategically focused and culturally aligned climate. Thinking along these lines raises a number of practical issues for the application of climate and culture in organizations, some of which we pursue in more depth in the next chapter.

CHAPTER

7

Thoughts for Practitioners on Organizational Cultural Inquiry

This chapter is about the critical issue of cultural inquiry—ways to diagnose and understand where an organization is and what it stands for. Although we see inquiries into the organization's culture as the necessary first step when thinking about organizational change, the chapter is not about change per se (see Chapters Five and Six for more explicit discussions of organizational change). We discuss here the different conceptual and methodological vantage points from which to approach cultural inquiry and detail the issues that require consideration along with their implications. Although our primary focus is on issues relevant to practitioners, we believe that these issues are relevant to researchers as well.

In the preceding chapters, we have discussed the distinctions between organizational culture and climate as well as related constructs such as alignment and strategy. We depart in this chapter from these important but more academic distinctions and focus instead on how practitioners address issues of culture and climate in their organizations or in those with whom they consult. Our goal here is to emphasize both the practical context in which culture and climate are investigated in organizations and how they are used—i.e., leveraged or changed—within a management framework to achieve particular organizational ends. We discuss culture from the perspectives of the key stakeholder (typically the executive) and the practitioner whose role is to diagnose and potentially support the organization in any cultural inquiry and/or change effort. Because the term "culture" is most commonly used in the world of practice, we primarily use that terminology when discussing issues related to organizational culture and climate in a broad sense. When the distinction between culture and climate is important, we are more explicit.

The chapter begins by reviewing what culture means to key organizational stakeholders. We follow with a presentation of the critical issues that surface when the practitioner pursues cultural inquiry and then an elaboration of a basic framework for evaluating alternative methods to fulfill that purpose. Throughout, we emphasize how the choice among the inquiry methods presented can determine the practitioner's success in communicating with and having an influence on major stakeholders. To aid practitioners in making the choice of inquiry method, we present in considerable detail a variety of issues or questions that should be considered so that a thoughtful decision can be made.

WHY EXECUTIVES CARE: STRATEGY, LEADERSHIP, AND ORGANIZATIONAL CULTURE

In Chapter Five, we highlighted the implications of organizational culture for organizational performance, and then in Chapter Six, we further argued that competitive advantage follows from a focus on strategic climate and culture. This is not new information to executives even though it may provide a new perspective on research for some academics. Contemporary executives strongly believe that culture is an essential condition that determines their likelihood of success. Lou Gerstner (2002) devoted one-fifth of his memoir as chief executive of IBM to organizational culture, and has been often quoted as saying "Culture is everything." In context, what Gerstner was writing about in his description of the transformation he led at IBM was that, even with all the assets he would otherwise need in place to achieve his goals—and in fact to survive—he would need to lead several hundred thousand employees through "wrenching" culture change. In light of our discussion in the last chapter about the relative lack of a strategic emphasis in the literature on organizational culture, it is noteworthy that Gerstner's entire positioning of culture is in the context of strategy, which in his way of thinking is a direct consequence of what he calls personal leadership.

Through what they read, their conversations with other executives, and confirmed by their own observations and experience, executives believe that their strategies can only be achieved to the extent that there is *alignment* around how to achieve that strategy. Their perspective is that the implementation of strategy requires all employees to both accept and commit to a common course of action. Culture, in this view, is what emerges from the aligned purpose of individual and team actions, with both in turn aligned with the organization's strategic goals (e.g., Kaplan & Norton, 2001). Strategically focused cultures are characterized by institutionalized systems (particularly including measurement systems) that implicitly (culture) and explicitly (climate) direct the intentions and efforts of all involved. The concept of culture in everyday executive use includes all of these concepts—strategy, leadership, climate, and what we have been calling "culture"—and they are not distinguishable. We recall here the remarks of Weick (1985) who argued that it is difficult to distinguish strategy from culture in successful organizations. He proposed that strategy is what the organization wants to do, culture is the process by which it can happen, and when they are aligned, they are indistinguishable.

This way of thinking is very well positioned by Kaplan and Norton (2001) in their description of the practical steps needed to create what they call a "strategy-focused organization." In their view, strategic focus follows from the following principles:

- Articulating the strategy into operational terms
- Aligning what people do to the strategy
- Creating a "mindset" where everyone sees strategy as part of their job
- Continually reinforcing strategy
- Making change the responsibility of executive leadership.

From this perspective, culture emerges as a concept of interest simply because of the assumption that *something* needs to be changed, perhaps especially in people's mindsets that would otherwise hinder achievement of the strategy.[1] What is clear is that this change in mindset will only happen when executive leadership does the things necessary to articulate the strategy, align people with it, and continuously reinforce it. The somewhat hidden message in what Kaplan and Norton (2001) described is that even though we often focus on the fact that what needs to be changed is resistant, embedded, and implicit, once a change has been made for the better, we very much want the new norms to become resistant, embedded, and implicit for them to be preserved. Thus, not often stated is the idea that culture is a concept of interest with regard to not only resistance to change, but also when the discussion turns to preserving that which is good or "great" about the institution. In any case, Kaplan and Norton (2001) clearly assumed that the desired culture follows when leaders directly or indirectly initiate and/or sustain the conditions and activities that align individuals to implement a particular plan of action, with the plan itself reflecting a particular strategy.

It is out of the actions required to pursue a strategy that culture emerges. As Schein (2010) suggested, culture represents the "accumulated learning" that allows both adaptation to the external environment and the opportunity for internal efficiency, such that successful lessons need not be continually relearned. Macey, Schneider, Barbera, and Young (2009) proposed that culture effectively provides a substitute for leadership (Kerr & Jermier, 1978) in the sense that what is known and transmitted within the group reinforces leadership messages and can substitute in the short term for leader time and effort. Similarly, we have stated that what leaders want is to create a self-sustaining culture, one in which individuals model and reinforce the behaviors that have driven success (Schneider et al., 2011b). Almost twenty years earlier, Kotter and Heskett (1992) implied as much in their description of firms where employees' productive efforts could be channeled in a unified direction because of the unwritten rules and common understanding about what is important, and in particular, where team members encourage those new to the team to follow the practices of others in the group. We note later that although there is an allure to substituting a focus on leadership for attention to culture or climate, there are challenges and risks in doing so.

When organizations sense that the existing culture is no longer serving them effectively, the issue of the necessity for change emerges. So a culture that was once appropriate to the leader's purpose can outlive its usefulness and require change. In this chapter, we confront the issues involved in diagnosing where an organization is and where it might require change.

THE BASES FOR CULTURAL DIAGNOSIS AND CHANGE

In Chapter Five, we presented Lundberg's (1985) conditions for when leaders are likely to initiate culture change. Here, we build on his suggestions to consider what might lead an executive (i.e., a sponsor) to pursue "cultural inquiry," with such inquiry serving to provide the evidence and foundation to use as a basis for actual change. In what follows, we consider the three conditions under which cultural inquiry is required: precipitating events, changes in strategic goals, and a need to know where one is before initiating actual change. Before doing so, however, it is important to acknowledge that the first stage of the diagnostic process is to determine the reasons behind the need for a cultural inquiry. The initial meeting with the organization sponsor is a critical event in framing the cultural inquiry, particularly as it frames the later discussions as to the outcomes expected from the inquiry effort. Invariably, that initial conversation includes a discussion of what the sponsor sees as the present state of the firm and the reasons behind the need for change. From the very first exploratory conversation, regardless of its level of formality or its context, the initial discussions with the organization are intended to gather sufficient information to understand the motivation and expectations of management and to establish a framework for subsequent conversations and methods of inquiry.

Precipitating Events Lead to Inquiry

The interests of executives in organizational culture often follow from some precipitating event, specific problem, or concern. These occurrences draw executives' attention to culture and represent the drama around which efforts to change emerge. "Culture" is often the explanation for poor performance, whether expressed in poor financials or in specific events embarrassing to the firm. Such events are detailed daily in the popular press: Profit shortfalls at J.C. Penney are explained as a cultural issue ("It is all because of the legacy of Mr. Penney's ways"), legal difficulties regarding women at Wal-Mart are described as a result of the culture ("Wal-Mart is a male-dominated culture"), and ethical lapses at any number of firms that hit the pages of *The Wall Street Journal* and *The New York Times* are explained as a consequence of culture ("The winner-take-all culture is what led to these lapses"). Indeed, later we highlight how a cultural inquiry was the centerpiece of an investigation in response to personal injuries and death in the 2005 disaster at the BP Texas City refinery. Thus, cultural inquiry can follow these kinds of incidents because of the very serious need to investigate why such events have occurred and to provide a foundation on which to establish a course of action that will ameliorate additional possible negative consequences and ensure they will not happen again.

Cultural inquiry is particularly relevant in mergers and acquisitions out of concern for opposing value systems and the anticipation of conflict and displaced energy to deal with gaps between the parties involved in the proposed integration (Weber, 1996). Indeed, hopefully there has been at least a brief reflection on organizational culture issues in the due-diligence process as the buyer considers the risks inherent in a merger or acquisition strategy. As Schein (2010) suggested, if left on their own the different cultures that are parties to a merger or acquisition will evolve in some way, most likely with one culture—usually the acquirer—dominating the other. Forced executive change creates significant disruption as well, which points to the importance of leadership both in driving culture transformation and in preserving what is good in the culture and what is likely to be important to success in the future.

Changes in Goals Lead to Identifying Gaps and the Readiness for Change

Regardless of whether there are specific precipitating events, organizations in their everyday lives continually confront the setting or revising of strategic goals in response to the marketplace, customer input, and so forth, which invites if not requires change. In such circumstances, organizational development practitioners typically collaborate with those who have a central stakeholder interest to consider the range of possible issues that must be addressed to identify and possibly close the gaps between current and future desired states. Culture frameworks provide a useful starting point in these efforts because leaders willingly accept the premise that the existing culture—which arguably would be resistant to change—must be a focus of the change effort and that envisioning the future organizational culture is one way to identify the gaps that should be the focus of change efforts.

Cultural inquiry can also be used to diagnose the very readiness of the organization to embark upon change (see the recent review on change readiness by Rafferty, Jimmieson, & Armenakis, 2013). So, not only can diagnosis yield where the gaps are between the present and the required future states but the degree to which the organization is ready to fill those gaps. Are people aware of the need for change? Are people flexible enough to change? Are people so committed to the present state that change is viewed as unnecessary and possibly even harmful? Answers to these kinds of questions can prove very useful when the actual change effort is begun.

Leveraging Culture for Success Requires Knowing Where You Are

Our focus here on cultural inquiry rests on a fundamental assumption: It is wise to know where you are before beginning to change. The point is that if culture change will be seen as a lever for success, as it usually is, then knowing where you are is the best way to identify the changes necessary. So, for example, in the culture assessment process that Schein (2010) described, the artifacts, espoused values, and assumptions of the culture are identified, and that information forms the foundation for understanding how the culture will serve as an aid or a hindrance to the organization accomplishing its strategic goals.

A recent pre-IPO filing with the Securities and Exchange Commission (Workday, 2012) spoke directly to the importance of culture in achieving success:

> *Leverage our Unique Culture.* We believe that building and maintaining a remarkable culture benefits our customers and employees, who together form the Workday Community. Engaged and loyal employees provide high levels of customer satisfaction, leading to greater adoption of our applications and recommendations to potential customers. We believe that this culture is the foundation for the successful execution of our strategy and, as a result, is a critical requirement for our growth agenda.

Culture is thus regarded as a prized possession, and as such something to be both cherished and preserved. It is an *asset*. Like other assets, it can be a source of competitive advantage, as we have detailed in Chapter Six. But like any other asset, its value is not in its potential but in its use, and that value is continually subject to risk. It is this way of thinking that leads the organization to seek methods for identifying and preserving what is unique and important. And it is under these conditions that a practitioner can lead a client into a conversation about the various means by which a company can ensure fit (or alignment) between the culture and the organization's long-term strategy.

The leveraging of culture for organizational success extends beyond the walls of the organization. Management consulting firms specializing in corporate branding and communication rely heavily on their understanding of culture to guide their analysis and recommendations. Moreover, brand specialists emphasize the view that the brand image supports management efforts to establish and maintain organizational culture and that the two act in reciprocity. As part of their work, it is not atypical for consultants in this field to use cultural inquiry methods to identify issues that might prevent success in building a brand or to identify what can be leveraged to facilitate a brand's success. As they market their services, brand consultants emphasize the importance of brand image on employee recruitment, engagement, and commitment as well as the importance of the brand in the marketplace.

Summary

There are many reasons why executives may decide to undertake a cultural inquiry. Inquiry may be beneficial when precipitating events occur that make executives aware of the role of culture in organizational performance, as well as when shifts in strategic goals make it necessary to identify readiness for change and/or gaps between where an organization is and where it strategically needs to be in the future. In the same way, attempts to leverage the culture for its potential benefits require a foundational knowledge of the current state of the organization's culture. With such knowledge in hand, executive leadership can construct tactics to promote the strategically oriented growth of the organization going forward.

TALENT MANAGEMENT AND CULTURAL INQUIRY

Before moving forward with the specifics of conducting a cultural inquiry, we first want to emphasize the important relationship between cultural inquiry and talent management. Practitioners who work with climate and culture issues, especially the issues of climate and culture change, are sensitive to many features of life in organizations: structure, reporting relationships, conflicts between sales and production, customer focus, and so forth. Executives, too, are sensitive to the variety of parameters and issues that cumulate to characterize an organization and its style or ways—or its culture. But practitioners of a more humane orientation have an additional—and to our mind's eye, important—focus on the human resources practices of the organization. The alignment or fit of the talent management practices with where the organization needs to be in the future must be a focus of thought and inquiry.

Human resource executives are chartered with the responsibility of implementing talent management practices that sustain and build the culture to support organizational strategy and to fill gaps in the talent required to move forward. For example, through recruitment practices, the organization seeks to define a value proposition that will attract the kinds of talent that are necessary for its success. Through selection practices, it chooses those who will work best in the planned strategic environment. At the more senior executive ranks, the match between the person and the environment is generally regarded as an absolute must, and executive failure is often blamed on the simple lack of fit between individuals and the organizational culture or the subculture they join within the organization. Similarly, socialization practices are explicitly intended to protect the vital elements of the culture so unintended change does not occur.

Although unintended changes occur frequently, sometimes due to inadvertent cultural slippage and sometimes as a result of some perturbations in the larger marketplace, we focus here on a potential major cause of cultural slippage: the talent recruited by, selected, socialized, and managed in an organization. For example, even elements of the US financial collapse of 2007–2008 are blamed on deviations from the previously successful organizational cultures in those organizations by new talent in the financial world. That new talent brought personal predilections and a different mindset, resulting in the violation of long-standing guidelines and principles and ultimately to the collapse of the entire sector. Flamholtz and Randle (2011) detailed how AIG's management made missteps and displayed a failure to adhere to core cultural elements that led to the near collapse of the firm. Specifically, AIG brought into the company new kinds of risk-takers that did not adhere to the core values of AIG that had produced the effectiveness that made it so important in the world of finance, and the consequences were far-reaching.

Of course, it is possible to attract and retain people with too much similarity to the culture as revealed by the fact that American car companies retained their core values by continuously hiring people with similar predilections and were thus unable to adapt to changes in the marketplace (Miller, 1990). These seemingly conflicting concerns—the need for change and the need to preserve—heighten management sensitivity to organizational culture, but this sensitivity must include the nature of the talent in the organization. Thus, while culture is viewed as an asset and in need of preservation, in times requiring change, culture and existing talent can also be an anchor to movement. This idea is similar to what we discussed in Chapter Five in terms of bringing in hybrids (i.e., those who are familiar with at least part of the culture but who also have an outsider perspective) or facilitating the rise of certain subcultures that carry cultural characteristics in line with the overall organization's desired culture. Transformation is critical when the issue of culture change becomes salient, as does the need for an inquiry into talent management and other HR processes as a basis for changes that may be required—and practices that might be retained.

THE MEASUREMENT FRAMEWORK FOR CULTURAL INQUIRY AND DIAGNOSIS

Change initiated without cultural inquiry as a foundation can be a wasted effort, for it might be directed at incorrect or even irrelevant issues and/or in inappropriate hierarchies of importance. Cultural inquiry is therefore an essential part of a transformational process because it provides both descriptive and evaluative information about existing corporate assets and this information serves as the very foundation for change. The practitioner faces the choice of how to best approach the task of cultural inquiry given not only the diagnostic purpose but also in anticipation of how the results of the inquiry will be communicated and used in the organization change context. We hasten to add that because the final work product of the inquiry will reflect the observational or measurement framework suggested and/or imposed by the practitioner, we devote considerable space to precisely that issue: the measurement framework for describing and differentiating cultures.

Across methods for cultural inquiry, when a scale of measurement (whether nominal, ordinal, or interval) is imposed on the data gathered, it becomes possible to both cumulate the observations and to differentiate cultures. The choice of measurement scale(s) used to capture judgments or ratings is distinct from the content being measured (although some measurement scales may be better suited for some content than others). For example, employees may respond to survey items regarding leadership using a five-point Likert scale, but that scale might be one of agreement (strongly disagree to strongly agree), effectiveness (highly ineffective to highly effective), or importance (unimportant to highly important), among many other options. In a quantitative study, the leadership dimension "score" may be the simple arithmetic average of scale values for the relevant items, whereas in a qualitative study the metric may be a simple count of the number of times the theme of leadership emerges in a series of interview transcripts. In addition, the nature of the question asked and measurement scale used will also affect whether the respondent is guided to supply a description of their experiences in the organization or an evaluation of how they think the organization is performing with regard to certain criteria (an issue that has been addressed in much depth in the climate literature; see Chapter Two). Of course, the two are not completely independent because describing an organization as bureaucratic would typically imply a negative evaluation and describing it as innovative would typically imply a positive evaluation. The critical point we want to make is that the interpretation of the data depends on the way the data are measured.

The validity of the interpretation of the data also depends on the knowledge and perspective of the sources used to provide the data. Simply put, there is a different level of expertise, knowledge, and/or experience needed to supply data with reference to some very specific criteria than to report general observations or experiences as an organizational member. For example, not all employees may be in a position to rate the efficiency of a business operation or the degree of innovation in products or services. However, employees with less tenure or who have less knowledge of the organization's history may be an excellent source of information about the organization's culture because its unique aspects have not become as "taken for granted" as they have with more experienced employees. In the end, the quality of the data about the organization's culture will depend upon both the nature of the data and its source.

The description of organizational culture invariably leads to some form of summarization and/or reduction of the data. One common approach is to classify the data into categories or themes. This classification basis may be chosen *a priori* or determined inductively in a way that is indigenous to a specific organizational environment. Dimensions of culture can represent themes such as leadership, structure, communication, HR practices, and so on (Ashkanasy, Broadfoot, & Falkus, 2000). These dimensions or constructs along which the culture is described serve the same purpose as a set of factors or dimensions used to describe personality in that a common set of dimensions can be applicable across organizations and settings. For example, a given culture can be described as being more or less bureaucratic than another or more or less service-oriented or innovative, and so forth. The basis for differentiation of organizations on these cultural dimensions is variable-centric in that the comparison is with reference to particular constructs or dimensions, each of which is considered separately, although the dimensions may or may not be correlated.

Another approach for summarizing cultural data is to describe a profile across dimensions considered simultaneously (Jung, Scott, Davies, Bower, Whalley, McNally, & Mannion, 2009). Presentation of results by profile is common among many of the quantitative measures we will describe later (although it is much more common in the culture literature than the climate literature; see Schulte, Ostroff, Shmulyian, and Kinicki, 2009, for an exception using a profile approach when studying climate). Profile shapes are often labeled as organization "types" and interpreted metaphorically with attributes descriptive of how one might describe people, particularly in terms of dysfunctional syndromes. Flamholtz and Randle (2011), for example, described various profiles such as The Arrogant Company, The Gambler, The Paranoid Corporation, and so on, each of which had a different profile of culture dimensions. The scale values on each dimension provide the basis for profile shape, and it is the shape of the profile rather than single dimension scores one at a time that is of interest. We will have more to say about profiles or types versus the presentation of data by dimension later.

Another way cultures can be compared is based on strength. One legacy of the popular management press in the 1980s and 1990s is the notion that organizational performance follows from strong cultures (e.g., Deal & Kennedy, 1982; Kotter & Heskett, 1992). In Chapters Three and Five, we discussed at length what climate and culture strength, respectively, are and how they differ from other related concepts such as fit and alignment. We also indicated that the challenge with a strong culture is that it is difficult to change precisely because there is good agreement on "who we are and what we stand for." Of course, strength may vary across different areas of the organization or across different dimensions, and it is possible to have a strong culture *for change* (or as Kotter & Heskett, 1992, called it, an *adaptive* culture) that must receive continuous attention, be reinforced, and have the assets and scarce resources required for periodic realignments and disjunctures (Burke, 2011). Thus, properly documenting the areas of relative strength and weakness across the organization's culture can be an important outcome of cultural inquiry. One particular challenge for doing so is that the method used to describe the culture places limitations on how culture strength can be defined. When using quantitative measures, statistical procedures can be used to assess relative strength by examining variability (see Chapter Three), in contrast to qualitative data inferences of strength that are more judgmental but that may provide more flexibility in how strength is conceptualized (see Chapter Five).

Although the approaches addressed thus far are the most common ways of understanding and comparing cultures, there are other approaches as well. One less utilized approach is to discuss cultures in terms of their dynamic properties or their trajectories over time. As Yammarino and Dansereau (2011) described, process approaches and the grounded theory method can lead to an understanding of how culture processes unfold over time. While we regard culture as relatively stable and enduring (consistent with Schein, 2010, and others), they can also evolve over time, perhaps quickly in some areas while in other areas not at all. Longitudinal frameworks allow cultures to not only be compared with the change trajectories in other organizations, but also internally to the organization's own culture in the past. Another approach is to have organizational members describe the dimensions or attributes of a culture in terms of salience or personal importance, as when employees evaluate a particular characteristic such as "informal" as more or less desirable or important for them to consider when evaluating a potential employment opportunity. We will later describe one such approach in our discussion of quantitative methods of cultural inquiry.

Of course, as we have alluded to, one of the major aspects of the measurement framework is the method to be used, and whether the cultural inquiry will follow a qualitative, quantitative, or a blended approach. This choice reflects the need to balance depth with practicality and the bases for differentiation from other companies as we have just described. Most importantly, the practitioner who chooses to rely on either or both approaches needs to recognize the assumptions that guide the inquiry approach chosen. For example, qualitative methods are most appropriate for description in language of the organization, or in other words, to create an indigenous typology. On the other hand, there are numerous commercial products, services, and frameworks for diagnosing culture using quantitative surveys, although not surprisingly, some may be better for certain purposes and contexts than others. A combination of qualitative and quantitative approaches perhaps deployed in an iterative fashion may be ideal; we return to this idea at the end of the chapter. Importantly, the practitioner will need to determine that mix based on certain practical constraints, which include not only time and resources, but also personal expertise in qualitative research and exposure to subject matter experts (SMEs).

In the sections that follow, we provide an in-depth discussion of a number of qualitative and quantitative approaches that might be used for cultural inquiry. We begin with qualitative approaches because the choice of quantitative technique may be informed by qualitative research outcomes.

QUALITATIVE APPROACHES TO CULTURAL DIAGNOSIS

We have deliberately chosen to limit our discussion of qualitative approaches to those that can be implemented as part of a diagnostic strategy within a relatively short time frame and that do not require total immersion in the work environment. Thus, we do not consider here ethnographic approaches, which are characterized by both extensive time commitments and personal presence, nor do we consider the role of the practitioner as an active change agent because our focus is entirely on the nature of qualitative inquiry itself and the outcomes/reports from it rather than any resulting change per se. The techniques common to action research strategies provide a convenient starting point for how qualitative data can be gathered and evaluated. Three examples of such approaches will be briefly highlighted here: Appreciative Inquiry, Cooperative Inquiry, and Narrative Inquiry. Our goal is to share the key features and commonalities across these approaches as an introduction to possible methods for conducting qualitative cultural inquiry. We supply citations to key sources on each of these approaches so that interested readers can find more detailed information about them if they are interested.

As the label suggests, Appreciative Inquiry focuses on what works and should be emphasized as strength in the culture rather than what is broken or needs to be fixed. Such an approach has the benefit of overcoming resistance from participants and helping to build trust (Schall, Ospina,

Godsoe, & Dodge, 2004). The technique used typically is one of asking questions in a group setting about positive experiences with respect to a specific theme or topic, such as experiencing the feeling of dignity and respect, having a project run efficiently, and so on. The product of these sessions is a list of "provocative propositions" (Hammond, 1996) that are derived from shared experiences or stories that are both inspirational and grounded in the history and traditions of the firm.

As outlined by Heron and Reason (2006), Cooperative Inquiry emphasizes the dual role of researcher and observer. Participants work through a multiphased approach that involves (1) deciding on what is important to explore and how to best record their experiences, (2) exploring new ways of doing things and reporting their experiences doing so at increasing levels of immersion, and (3) sharing their experiences and reconsidering their initial ideas and thoughts through the lens of their experiences. One critical distinction between Cooperative Inquiry and other qualitative approaches is its unique placement of the researcher as a participant in the process both with respect to what is studied and how.

In Narrative Inquiry (Clandinin & Connelly, 2000), the emphasis is on constructing stories that place the participant (and inquirer) within boundaries of time, social context, and place. Critical to this approach is the notion that the observer or inquirer enters into a process not at the beginning of participant's experiences but at some other point in time. The narrative or story is something that can be told retrospectively through an interview but can also reflect what is experienced as it unfolds during the course of the research effort. The product of the inquiry is a conversion of the experiences and stories to text that can then be analyzed according to different frames of reference.

What is common to these approaches is the emphasis on (1) the reporting of experiences that people (employees or other observers) share, and (2) a relatively balanced perspective on those experiences that avoids a singular focus on the negative or what needs to be changed and includes an exploration of future possibilities. The value of these approaches is that they fulfill the practical goal of developing a story line or narrative that describes the culture with sufficient fidelity that stakeholders and researchers can reliably agree. Thus, the qualitative techniques that are most appropriate for cultural inquiry are those that elicit narratives that capture the richness inherent in employees' or other stakeholders' experiences. These narratives can be collected in a variety of ways, including structured or semistructured interviews or structured written descriptions with appropriate instructions provided.

It should be obvious that as the inquiry unfolds the practitioner makes choices about what fits or does not fit the eventual storyline. Some information is discarded or ignored, and other information and perspectives are highlighted. The choice of what to ignore or classify as irrelevant is obviously critical, and this is a challenge with qualitative approaches, regardless of who might be involved in making those choices. Fortunately, this dilemma can be resolved at least in part by ensuring that the narratives that are captured or reported meet several criteria. Borrowing from the logic of the three approaches to inquiry above, these criteria might include (1) completeness (the narrative must have social and physical context), (2) an explicit reference in time (the narratives must be anchored at a relative point in time in the narrator's personal history with the organization), and (3) an evaluative frame of reference (the narrative should have an explicit link to what made the experience positively or negatively salient to the narrator).

Gundry and Rousseau (1994) described a particularly insightful use of a qualitative approach for cultural inquiry in which they asked organization newcomers to relate formative events that were meaningful to them in understanding "what it is like to work here." They followed a modified critical-incident approach (Flanagan, 1954) by asking newcomers to describe what made an impression on them when they first joined the company, who was involved, when it occurred, and the message that they understood from the event. This general approach can be easily modified to extend beyond the early stages of the employment period; we have found in our own work that individuals remember these events long into their careers, which is obviously telling of the effect such events have on organizational newcomers.

We next discuss three particular challenges to collecting qualitative culture data. The first is the question of data sufficiency. It is particularly difficult to know when the body of narratives or observations has adequately covered the cultural domain. In large part, the question is who to involve as participants in the inquiry. The second challenge concerns the way in which interviews are conducted, including whether the focus is on individuals or groups. The third significant issue is how the data points are categorized and analyzed to make the most effective use of the information.

Who to Involve

A critical decision in qualitative approaches to cultural inquiry is who to involve as active participants or storytellers. The practitioner will face resource and time trade-offs as well as the practical implications of internal politics when requesting access to subject matter experts. It is often very difficult—even with the highest form of organizational sponsorship—to gain ready access to executive time. Moreover, the sequencing of individual interviews with firms is itself a practical issue. For example, it may be necessary to interview a given senior executive before contacting or interviewing his or her direct reports. Of course, such constraints are themselves indicators of culture as well.

Most importantly, the practitioner should recognize that subcultures often form at different levels of the organization, and that access at some levels of the organization may require more complete sampling and representation. That is, the culture as experienced by senior leaders may be very different from that experienced by middle managers, professionals, support staff, or other groups. There are a number of other possible issues that differentiate subcultures (as we reviewed in Chapter Five), many of which may not be readily apparent. The challenge is to determine the criteria to be used in identifying which subcultures are of the most relative importance and then to ensure that members of those subcultures are adequately represented in the inquiry.

Determining the Format to Be Used

From a practical standpoint, the choice of individual or group interview format is largely driven by timing, accessibility, and costs. There are considerable benefits to conducting focus groups, as it is often the case that the act of participating—hearing others' stories—in a group setting stimulates both participation and recall. In addition, it can be argued that diagnostic interviews should be conducted in group settings as culture is something that is shared (Schein, 2010). However, we have found in practice that at the executive level within the organization, individual interviews may be necessary to obtain the desired breadth and depth of information.

Assuming that at least part of the cultural inquiry takes place in groups, additional decisions must be made concerning how those groups should be composed. The consultant will have to decide whether the groups should be segmented by levels of management or by subcultures, or should be mixed. Unfortunately, there is no one right way to compose focus groups; the approach will depend on the exact situation in the specific organization. If the only goal is to identify the shared cultural aspects that cut across all employees, and especially if there are already norms for open communication across layers of the organization, then mixing groups by including individuals across levels and subcultures may not be problematic. However, such an approach may not uncover in-depth information about individual subcultures and it may result in only hearing the dominant voices of management (thus providing an idealized view of the culture rather than its true character), especially when open communication is not the norm. The main point here is to thoroughly think through the goals of the inquiry and the nature of the organization when making decisions about these issues.

Analyzing Qualitative Data

Analyzing qualitative data implies the imposition of a structure on the information gathered, which can be narratives (i.e., the text recorded) and/or the evaluation of narratives by the stakeholders and/or researcher. The structure ideally follows inductively from the data, although it is certainly the case that the process can be an iterative one that evolves over multiple phases of data collection and from multiple sources. The work of Schneider, Wheeler, and Cox (1992) in which focus group data were content analyzed as a basis for later service climate measures (as discussed in Chapter Six) fits this iterative paradigm. The inductive model builds upon the choices of words used by participants rather than a structure imposed by the researcher. It should be apparent that one significant benefit of inductive approaches is that the expression of culture is in the language of the people and, thus, the firm.

Generally, two forms of analysis can be applied to narrative data. The first is simple categorization of the topics discussed. Frequency of topic area suggests what is salient and most relevant to the description of culture. Also, narratives can be coded for valence. Gundry and Rousseau (1994), for example, classified narratives collected in the form of critical incidents as positive, neutral, or negative in valence. Sentiment scoring—the equivalent of valence coding—is a key feature of text analytics software that allows narratives to be coded at various levels, including an entire narrative or even at the within-sentence phrase level.

One particular challenge of qualitative approaches arises when the volume of data (or narratives) is larger than can economically and/or practically be managed and analyzed. Computerized software techniques of narrative analysis are becoming broadly available and reflect advancements in text analytics, which were developed mostly within the field of computational linguistics but have been more broadly applied, for instance, in studies of customer satisfaction (see Shanahan, Qu, & Wiebe, 2006). These techniques presume the ability to develop a linguistic structure to be analyzed, or in other words, the key words, terms, or expressions that can be categorized and interpreted for sentiment. What may be most valuable is the ability to rapidly and iteratively update the categories to which text can be assigned, counted, and evaluated. The field of computational linguistics is evolving quickly, and the methods in this field open new possibilities for streamlined analysis of qualitative data. Such techniques can be used to "score" transcripts from focus groups or individual interviews, narratives that research participants are asked to write, or responses to open-ended questions that are frequently part of quantitative survey approaches. They can also be used to analyze organizational documents; for example, many organizations maintain active blogs that can be rich information sources for qualitative analysis.

Summary

Qualitative approaches to inquiry can provide richly detailed insights into organizational culture. They are best considered as the reporting of stories or narratives which describe experiences of people within a given period and which provide information on the specific messages or meanings attached to those experiences. The challenges facing the practitioner include who should participate as the storytellers in the research effort and the collection, management, and analysis of the qualitative inquiry data.

QUANTITATIVE APPROACHES TO CULTURAL DIAGNOSIS

We now turn to the use of quantitative approaches for cultural diagnosis and inquiry. In Chapter Four we detailed some of the pros and cons of qualitative vs. quantitative approaches to data gathering, including how quantitative surveys may be more cost effective and allow for a broader sampling of the organization while sacrificing some of the richness and depth of information that qualitative approaches provide. With those distinctions in mind, we begin by providing several examples of survey instruments used to assess culture or climate, which reveal subtle and not so subtle differences among them. We then evaluate their strengths and weaknesses on a number of different dimensions, along with a consideration of the specific issues and implications around the choice of approach.

Examples of Quantitative Measures of Culture and Climate

Our choice of which measures to include here was based on a number of factors. We wanted to highlight those surveys that were generally better known and commonly used but that also represented a range of forms of the genre as well as different measurement and conceptual frameworks that may have differential value to the practitioner depending on the particular problem, issue, or outcome of salience to a company. We follow our description of four quantitatively based culture surveys with one example of a very specific implementation of a strategic climate survey.

Organizational Culture Assessment Instrument (OCAI). The OCAI is based on the competing values framework (CVF; Quinn & Rohrbaugh, 1983) as introduced in previous chapters and described in considerable detail by Cameron and Quinn (2011). The data collection approach for the OCAI is unique. Respondents are given six questions, which are labeled dominant characteristics, organizational leadership, management of employees, organization glue, strategic emphases, and the criteria for success (Cameron & Quinn, 2011). The items seem to capture a mix of behavioral norms and values of both employees and management. For each question, there are four alternatives that represent one of the four different overall organizational values or styles of the CVF: clan, adhocracy, hierarchy, and market. As described previously, these styles represent different quadrants formed by the crossing of two dimensions: (1) flexibility and discretion vs. stability and control, and (2) internal focus and integration vs. external focus and differentiation. The resulting 2 × 2 matrix is represented in Figure 7.1.

FLEXIBILITY and DISCRETION

	CLAN	ADHOCRACY	
INTERNAL FOCUS and INTEGRATION	• Family-type organizations • Commitment to employees • Participation and teamwork	• Dynamic and enterpreneur organizations • Cutting-edge output • Innovation	EXTERNAL FOCUS and DIFFERENTIATION
	HIERARCHY	MARKET	
	• Formalized and structured organizations • Smooth functioning • Stability	• Competitive organizations • Increasing market share • Productivity	

STABILITY and CONTROL

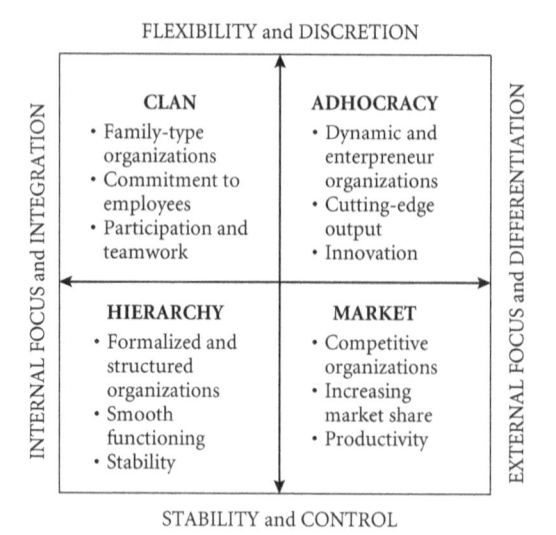

Figure 7.1 The competing values framework (source: Cameron & Quinn, 1999)

As an example of an item from the OCAI, here is one of the four alternatives within the set describing dominant characteristics that is aligned with the clan culture: *"This organization is a very personal place. It is like an extended family. People seem to share a lot of personal information and features"* (Cameron, 2008, p. 442). Within each of the six sets of questions, respondents must assign a total of 100 points to the four alternatives presented, and the accumulation of points across the six sets provides evidence for which of the four styles predominates in an organization. Users can plot the organization's profile to show the overall scores across the four dimensions. According to Cameron and Quinn (2011), the average scores across all respondents in an organization can be analyzed in six different ways: (1) a comparison across the dimensions to see which is the current dominant type of the organization, (2) a comparison of the current and preferred scores, (3) the strength of the culture based on how high the score was for the dominant type, (4) the alignment of scores across different subgroups within the organization, (5) a comparison of the scores relative to the benchmark data that have been found with other organizations and industries, and (6) a comparison of the scores with the trends that have been identified using the instrument.

The measurement model for the OCAI is significantly different from the approaches we will review shortly. The basis for comparison is the organization itself; scores are based on the total points allocated to each type, not on any comparison with other organizations with an absolute response scale.[2] In other words, the scores tell us how dominant a certain type is within an organization, but not how the organization's scores compare with other organizations. In addition, the measurement does not yield dimension scores, but rather a characterization of how similar the focal organization is to the ideal types of the four styles. At the most simplistic level, the style with the highest score is interpreted as that organization's cultural type; interpretations that are more complicated take into account the overall pattern of scores across the four types (Cameron & Quinn, 2011). Although we describe later variations on this approach that effectively treat the four styles as dimensions or themes with raw scores for each, the scoring described above represents the original scoring of the OCAI.

With regard to research evidence for this measure, Cameron and Quinn (2011) have suggested that the four types are associated with different outcome effectiveness criteria: clan with employee satisfaction and commitment, adhocracy with innovation, market with product quality, productivity, and market share, and hierarchy with efficiency and timeliness. Thus, the typology translates to effectiveness with respect to specific criteria of organizational success. Also important is that organizational effectiveness is conceptualized as a broad, multidimensional construct, such that the "ideal" profile for an organization will vary depending on the criteria of interest. The number of published studies using the OCAI is fairly limited, but for a sample of studies providing validity evidence for the CVF and different versions of the OCAI, see Cameron and Freeman (1991), Quinn and Spreitzer (1991), and more recently, Gregory et al. (2009). For a broader test of the CVF, see the meta-analysis by Hartnell et al. (2011). In addition to meta-analytically testing the relationships between the different dimensions of the CVF with various effectiveness criteria (which we reviewed in Chapter Five), Hartnell and colleagues (2011) also examined the internal structure of the framework. Their results showed the four dimensions of the model were generally positively related to each other (average correlation of 0.54), raising questions about the extent to which the culture types are independent or competing.

Denison Organizational Culture Survey (DOCS). The cultural framework represented in the DOCS (Denison, 1990; Denison & Neale, 2000) uses the same underlying dimensions as the CVF, in that it combines the ideas of flexibility versus stability and internal orientation versus external orientation. The four resulting dimensions are the following (based on Denison, 1990; Denison Nieminen, & Kotrba, 2012; Gillespie, Denison, Haaland, Smerek, & Neale, 2008; Kotrba, Gillespie, Schmidt, Smerek, Ritchie, & Denison, 2012): involvement (the extent to which employees have input in decision-making, a team orientation, and a sense of ownership in the organization), consistency (the extent to which beliefs and values are aligned with policies and practices and the system is coordinated and integrated), adaptability (the extent to which the organization's internal structures are flexible meeting the demands of the external environment, and particularly to customers), and mission (the extent to which the organization has a shared sense of purpose and management communicates a clear vision and direction). Each of these broad dimensions is further segmented into three subdimensions (see Figure 7.2), including capability development, team orientation, and empowerment (for involvement); coordination/integration, agreement, and core values (for consistency); creating change, customer focus, and organizational learning (for adaptability); and strategic direction, goals and objectives, and vision (for mission). One feature that distinguishes the DOCS from the CVF is that the dimensions are not portrayed as competing. Denison (1990) described it this way: "Instead of arguing, however, that the classification of an organization's culture must be an either/or type of decision, this framework assumes that an effective culture must provide all of these elements . . . the reconciliation of conflicting demands is the essence of an effective organizational culture" (p. 14).

The DOCS is a 60-item survey where respondents provide ratings on a five-point Likert scale (strongly disagree to strongly agree). The survey measures the series of four dimensions mentioned earlier based on the management practices incumbents report they experience. Some sample items include the following: (1) for capability development, "There is

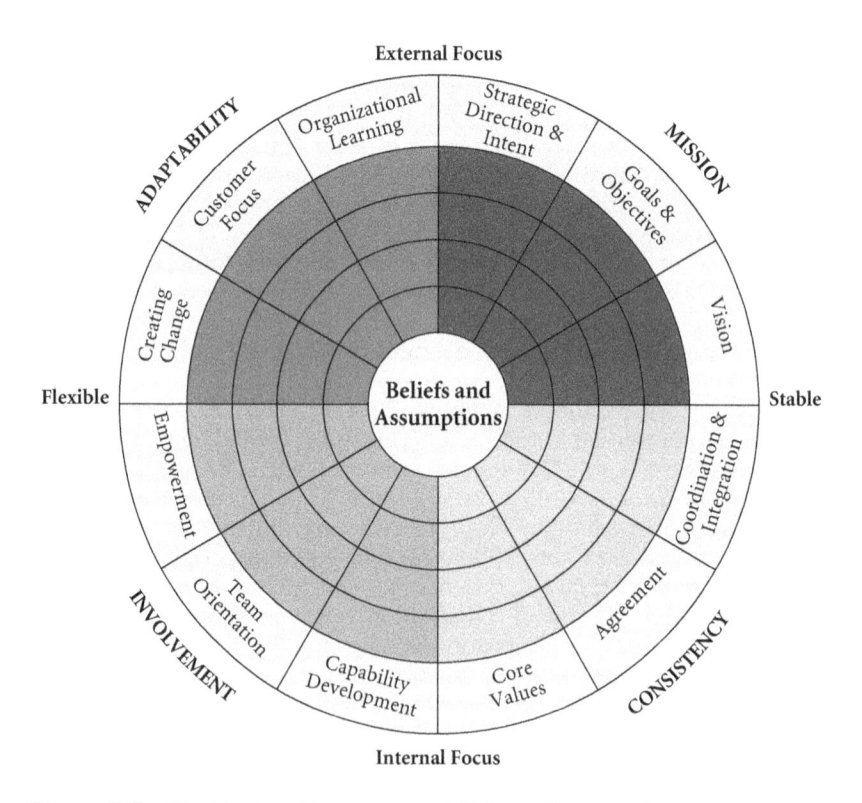

Figure 7.2 The Denison Organizational Culture Framework

© Denison Consulting. All Rights Reserved. Used by permission.

continuous investment in the skills of employees"; (2) for team orientation, "Cooperation across different parts of the organization is actively encouraged"; and (3) for empowerment, "Decisions are usually made where the best information is available." Items such as these are quite similar to items found in traditional employee surveys, particularly regarding content related to leadership and strategy. For example, one item on the DOCS is "Our strategy leads other organizations to change the way they compete in the industry." A similar item in the Mayflower Group[3] employee opinion survey Core Item set (Johnson, 1996) is: "My company is making the changes necessary to compete effectively."

Despite such similarities between the DOCS and other employee opinion surveys, there are significant differences in how team and organizational scores are presented in reports provided to management. In particular, DOCS scores are presented in percentile form by comparing organizational responses to selected benchmarks (e.g., by industry). The more conventional form of reporting employee survey results is in terms of percentages (in particular, the percentage responding favorably, neutral, or unfavorably) or by presenting raw scores side-by-side with various possible benchmarks ("Best Companies to Work For," "Fortune 500 Most Admired Companies," etc.). In brief, then, the data reported for the DOCS emphasize relative scores that are benchmarked, rather than raw scores. For reporting purposes, these scores are plotted on a circumplex (see Figure 7.2), such that the placement of the subdimensions reflects their nesting within each dimension, and the organization of the dimensions and subdimensions reflects their relationship to the opposing themes of flexibility versus stability and internal orientation versus external orientation.

Although the instrument has primarily been used outside of academia, Denison and his colleagues have been rigorous in documenting the psychometrics and validity of their approach, much of which has been published in the organizational research literature or is easily accessible from their website (www.DenisonConsulting.com). For example, Denison et al. (2012) summarized the research they have done in 160 companies on the reliability and validity of the measure. The scales all have internal consistency reliability estimates of 0.70 and higher, the subscales are intercorrelated (about 0.60 on average across companies), and the subscales also reveal statistically significant validity coefficients against employees' ratings of outcomes like sales growth (average r of 0.26), profits (average r of 0.25), and quality (average r of 0.36). They also reported support for the nested structure of the instrument via confirmatory factor analysis and evidence for the aggregation of the scale to the organizational level of analysis. Other support for the validity of the DOCS (which we also briefly addressed in Chapter Five) can be found in Gillespie and colleagues (2008) and Kotrba and colleagues (2012), with additional evidence for the cross-cultural generalizability of the instrument presented in Denison, Haaland, and Goelzer (2003) and Fey and Denison (2003).

Organizational Culture Inventory® (OCI®). The OCI is offered by Human Synergistics, Inc., a consulting firm offering multiple solutions for individual and organizational assessment purposes. The survey consists of 120 items representing 12 different behavioral patterns or norms. The survey originated in the authors' earlier research with an individually focused assessment instrument, the Life Styles Inventory™ (Cooke & Szumal, 1993). The 12 norms of the OCI reflect two fundamental dimensions of organizational life: a concern for people and/or a concern for tasks. In addition, the norms are differentiated by whether they fulfill higher-order satisfaction needs versus lower-order security needs. A circumplex model is used to depict how the twelve norms cluster within three broader organizational culture styles or types (see Figure 7.3): Constructive (a focus on both people and tasks with a goal to fulfill higher-order needs), Passive/Defensive (a focus on people with the goal of maintaining security), and Aggressive/Defensive (a focus on tasks with the goal of maintaining security). Each of the three general styles captures four behavioral norms: (1) Constructive cultures include Achievement, Self-Actualizing, Humanistic-Encouraging, and Affiliative norms; (2) Passive/Defensive cultures include Approval, Conventional, Dependent, and Avoidance norms; and (3) Aggressive/Defensive cultures include Oppositional, Power, Competitive, and Perfectionistic norms. The norms separated by 180 degrees on the circumplex appear to represent opposites (e.g., Achievement vs. Dependent).

Sample items for the OCI reported in Balthazard, Cooke, and Potter (2006) included the following: "help others grow and develop" (Humanistic-Encouraging norm); "work on self-set goals" (Achievement norm); "rules more important than ideas" (Conventional norm); "do what is expected" (Dependent norm); "look for mistakes" (Oppositional norm); and "never make a mistake" (Perfectionistic norm). Respondents rate each item using a five-point scale based on the extent to which it is expected or required in their organizations (1 = not at all and 5 = to a very great extent). The fundamental dimensions of the OCI are quite similar in orientation to widely used measures of leadership, an issue we return to later. Like the DOCS, the scores for each style are reported in percentile terms and are associated theoretically with organizational, team, and personal effectiveness.

Some evidence for the reliability, within-unit agreement, test-retest reliability, and validity of the OCI can be found in such sources as Cooke and Rousseau (1988) and Cooke and Szumal (1993). In addition, Rousseau (1990b) found in a sample of fund-raising organizations that the passive/defensive behavioral norms were significantly, negatively related to dollar amounts of funds raised, but the positive relationships between the constructive norms and funds raised were not significant. Cooke and Szumal (2000) summarized the research that has been accomplished with the OCI predicting group and organizational outcomes. They showed that constructive norms related consistently positively to teamwork, quality of work relations, product/service quality, and customer

Thoughts for Practitioners on Organizational Cultural Inquiry 255

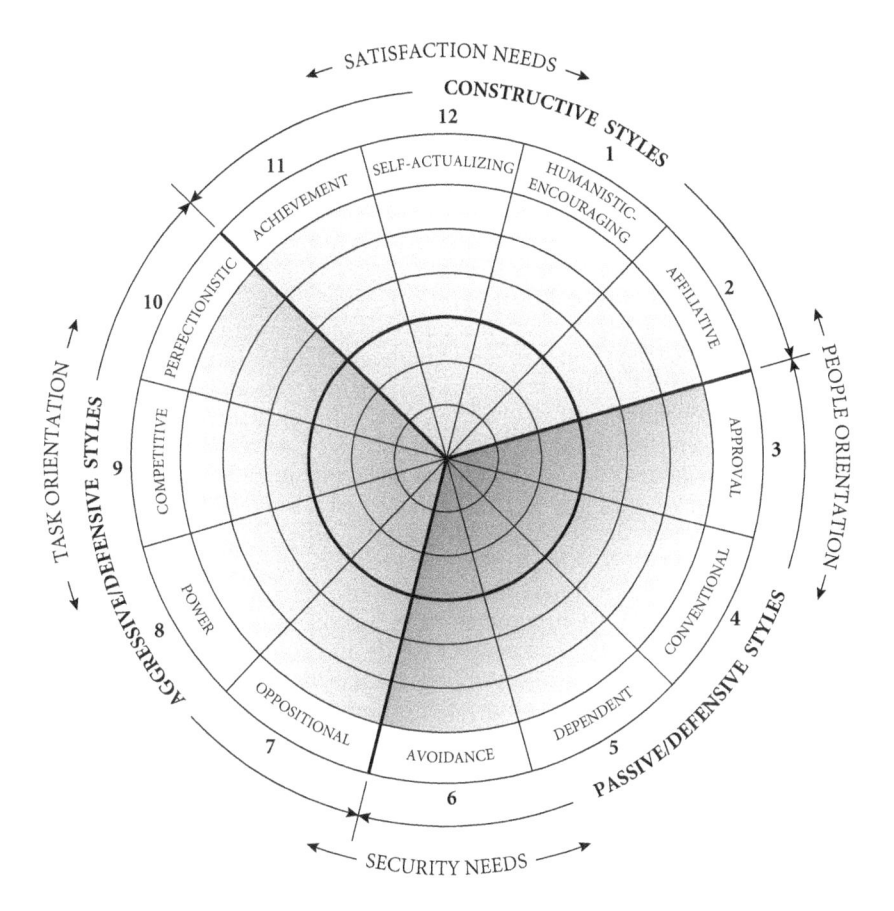

Figure 7.3 The OCI circumplex

Note: The OCI measures culture along the 12 circumplex styles in terms of shared behavioral norms (i.e., the extent to which each style is expected or implicitly required of members); the Ideal version of the OCI measures culture in terms of values and beliefs (i.e., the extent to which members believe the styles will lead to goal attainment and effectiveness).

Source: The OCI style names, survey items, and Circumplex are reproduced with permission from the Organizational Culture Inventory by R.A. Cooke and J.C. Lafferty. Copyright © 1987 by Human Synergistics International.

satisfaction; passive/defensive norms related negatively but weakly to the same outcomes; and aggressive/defensive norms related negatively but weakly to teamwork and quality of work relations but not to the other dimensions. Balthazard and colleagues (2006) also summarized OCI data from a sample of over 60,000 respondents collected over 3.5 years at Human Synergistics. They reported correlations between the OCI and what they called performance drivers (including fit, satisfaction, quality, and turnover intentions, among others). Although most correlations were statistically significant, the drivers were from the same source as the culture measures, and analyses were conducted at the individual level. Additional work on the OCI includes research by Xenikou and Simosi (2006) investigating the relationship between the achievement and humanistic norms and organizational performance, as well as research by Glisson and colleagues in the mental health field on a variation of the OCI (Glisson & James, 2002; Glisson & Green, 2006).

Organization Culture Profile (OCP). One of the most commonly referenced cultural assessment tools in the academic literature was developed by O'Reilly, Chatman, and Caldwell (1991). In their paradigm, participants sort 54 values or attributes (reproduced in Table 7.1) from most to least characteristic of their organization (or "fully" to "not at all") according to the following Q-sort distribution: 2-4-6-9-12-9-6-4-2. Examples of the values assessed by the measure include adaptability, stability, and informality. Some of the characteristics represent attributes of employment, including working long hours, high pay for good performance, and security of employment. It seems common in the literature for an individual study to conduct exploratory factor analysis to create dimensions, and thus there appears to be no set number of dimensions captured by the OCP. For example, O'Reilly and colleagues (1991) found seven dimensions (innovation, stability, respect for people, outcome orientation, attention to detail, team orientation, and aggressiveness), Chatman and Jehn (1994) found a similar factor structure but used the label "easy-going" instead of "aggressiveness," and Lee and Yu (2004) found five factors, labeled as innovation, supportive, team, humanistic orientation, and task orientation.

TABLE 7.1 Items in the organizational culture profile (OCP; O'Reilly et al., 1991)

1. Flexibility
2. Adaptability
3. Stability
4. Predictability
5. Being innovative
6. Being quick to take advantage of opportunities
7. A willingness to experiment
8. Risk taking
9. Being careful
10. Autonomy
11. Being rule oriented

(Continued)

TABLE 7.1 (Continued)

12. Being analytical
13. Paying attention to detail
14. Being precise
15. Being team oriented
16. Sharing information freely
17. Emphasizing a single culture throughout the organization
18. Being people oriented
19. Fairness
20. Respect for the individual's right
21. Tolerance
22. Informality
23. Being easy going
24. Being calm
25. Being supportive
26. Being aggressive
27. Decisiveness
28. Action orientation
29. Taking initiative
30. Being reflective
31. Achievement orientation
32. Being demanding
33. Taking individual responsibility
34. Having high expectations for performance
35. Opportunities for professional growth
36. High pay for good performance
37. Security of employment
38. Offers praise for good performance
39. Low level of conflict
40. Confronting conflict directly
41. Developing friends at work
42. Fitting in
43. Working in collaboration with others
44. Enthusiasm for the job
45. Working long hours
46. Not being constrained by many rules
47. An emphasis on quality
48. Being distinctive-different from others
49. Having a good reputation
50. Being socially responsible
51. Being results oriented
52. Having a clear guiding philosophy
53. Being competitive
54. Being highly organized

Reproduced with permission of the ACADEMY OF MANAGEMENT.

The value statements in the original research were drawn from extant culture research and were selected as relevant for describing organizational culture as well as personal values. This reflected O'Reilly and colleagues' (1991) purpose of measuring person-organization fit. For example, in the original validation research (Chatman, 1991), incumbents reported on their accounting firms, and applicants to those firms reported their preferences. Data from following those applicants longitudinally revealed that the better the fit between an applicant and the firm they join, the more likely they were to be satisfied, to stay with the firm, and to perform at high levels.

When used as designed in the forced distribution Q-sort format, the OCP also yields values scores that are reflective of a within-organization comparison, similar to the results from the classic form of the OCAI described earlier (i.e., ipsative measurement). That is, scores that suggest that the organization is characterized by stronger values on one dimension than on other dimensions do not have a frame of reference outside the organization being studied. Consequently some researchers have used the 54 value orientations from the original instrument to create conventional Likert-scale questionnaires (Sarros, Gray, Dentsten, & Cooper, 2005), so that it is easier to compare one organization's scores to another (because each organization has a score for each dimension on the same response scale).

The values that are sorted or rated in these efforts by incumbents can also be labeled as employment attributes as they clearly define the employment proposition that characterizes a firm. As such it is possible, as in the original OCP, to ask *potential* employees to rate these employment attributes (or values) as to their desirability in a possible employing firm. Lundby, Lee, and Macey (2012) found that rankings of similar attributes by incumbents and by potential employees can be used as a basis for identifying different patterns or segments of potential employees. This form of analysis lends itself particularly well to identifying the messages that the company is perceived to deliver and what potential employees are seeking. Those areas where matches exist suggest the levers that can be used for attracting talent that is a good match for the organizational culture. Furthermore, the approach lends itself well to identifying areas where improper messaging is likely to be deleterious to the employment brand.

With regard to research evidence for the OCP, the strongest evidence has been for the implications of the fit between individual preferences and the organization's culture, with results from O'Reilly and colleagues (1991) and Chatman (1991) showing that fit was a significant predictor of newcomer adjustment, commitment, and turnover. In addition, the test-retest reliability correlation with a 10–12 month gap between administrations was found to be 0.78 (Chatman, 1991). Although the majority of studies using the OCP have tended to focus on individual outcomes, one example of an organization-level study is Lee and Yu (2004). They found that culture strength—measured by the extent to which organization respondents fit a common cultural model—was correlated with return on assets in manufacturing firms and growth in annual premiums in insurance firms. Nevertheless, the overall pattern of results for predicting organizational performance was mixed.

Anatomy of a strategically focused culture/climate survey. In contrast to the four measures described above that capture an organization's general culture, in this section we address how a customized survey can be developed for an organization that wants to address a targeted strategic area. Although we continue with the use of the "culture" term due to its accepted use in organizational settings, the type of survey we discuss here is more in line with climate surveys that ask about employee perceptions of strategically focused policies, practices, and procedures. In addition to providing an illustration of a customized culture/climate survey, the example illustrates several important principles that can inform practice as to the critical issues in framing and assessing a cultural diagnostic effort.

As we discussed earlier in this chapter, there is often a precipitating event that leads to a cultural inquiry; in this case, the impetus of the study was the March 23, 2005, explosion at the Texas City Refinery owned and operated by BP, which resulted in 15 deaths and more than 170 injuries. In response to the urging of the US Chemical and Safety Board, BP commissioned an independent review panel, chaired by former Secretary of State James Baker, to investigate the effectiveness of BP's safety practices and safety culture. Following their detailed and lengthy investigation, the panel prepared a report that is publicly available and is rich in the detail of the methodology and findings (Baker, 2007). As such, it is a useful resource for identifying how culture measures can be used to guide decision-making and likewise points to issues that create challenges for interpretation.

As part of its investigation, the panel conducted a comprehensive "culture" survey. The content of the survey was quite similar to the safety climate surveys we described in Chapter Three (e.g., the work by Zohar & Luria, 2005). The survey questions tapped themes such as "process safety reporting," "safety values/commitment to process safety," "procedures and equipment," "empowerment," "safety training," and "supervisory involvement and support." Employees responded using a five-point Likert scale ranging from "strongly disagree" to "strongly agree." Example items included "Operational pressures do not lead to cutting corners where process safety is concerned," and "Refinery management puts a high priority on process safety through actions and not just empty slogans."

In drawing their conclusions, the writers of the report highlighted overall trends as well as differences by employment category and facility. The data were presented in terms of the percentages of people who responded "strongly disagree" or "disagree" to the individual items. The report described the panel's approach to interpreting the data:

> The Panel believes, however, that response rates to a survey related to process safety, which involves potentially catastrophic accidents, should be

viewed differently from workforce surveys generally. To some extent *this is intuitive* . . . the Panel believes that it should use more stringent criteria, or effectively "raise the bar," in its evaluation of the process safety culture survey data . . . The Panel generally viewed positive response rates greater than 80 percent and negative response rates less than 20 percent as indicating an overall positive perception of the process safety culture . . . However, the Panel tended to view negative response rates approaching or exceeding 20 percent as deserving of increased attention and focus from BP management. (Baker, 2007, p. 10, italics added)

Noteworthy here is that the standards by which the safety culture at BP was judged were seemingly arbitrarily drawn though they may have been supported by good judgment. This highlights the fact inherent in all diagnostics: some conclusions must be drawn from the observations, records, and findings, and those inferences are thus open to interpretation. One significant challenge facing the practitioner then is how to advise stakeholders about the meaning or interpretation of survey results.

Another important observation of the Baker investigation is the emphasis on accountability for the survey findings. Specifically, despite the finding that "BP has not provided effective leadership on or established appropriate operational expectations regarding process safety performance" (p. xii), the writers were specific in noting that senior executives, while not directly and personally responsible for what happened at the local operating management level, were certainly responsible for a failure to affect BP safety culture through establishing safety as a core value. The critical point here is that culture assessments should lead to actionable outcomes—as in the Baker report. To re-emphasize the point, cultural diagnosis is done for a purpose. The practitioner's choice of method greatly determines how well that purpose will be satisfied.

Summary and comparison. The OCAI, DOCS, and OCI represent broader approaches to describing fundamental organizational culture and are therefore less suited for assessing strategic culture or climate. The framework upon which each measurement model is built links in a different way to organizational effectiveness. The OCAI is unique in that each of the "types" underlying the competing values framework is tied to specific organizational success criteria (e.g., the clan type is specifically linked to employee commitment and motivation, and the adhocracy type is specifically linked to innovation). The DOCS references key dimensions that are not evaluative, but reflect dimensions or themes on which better performing organizations tend to score higher. The OCI prescriptively connects behavior patterns to styles that are more evaluative than descriptive in context (e.g., proactive vs. inactive) and therefore is tied to organizational effectiveness, albeit indirectly.

The OCP uniquely describes organizational culture in terms of the attributes that differentiate organizations based on preferred work environments. These attributes or characteristics are useful descriptions even if their measurement is relative. Beyond scholarly interests in measuring P-O fit, the approach is a useful one for identifying how organizational culture plays out in the employee value proposition and thus has unique practical value for both employee image and branding purposes.

All four of these approaches differ considerably from the survey described in the Baker report, which does not address general issues but is focused on a specifically focused strategic culture/climate. Although the information provided cannot definitively speak to the drivers or foundations of climate (in this case, safety climate), for its intended purpose it represents a very unique and insightful example of how a precise characterization of a strategic climate can yield findings specific to the issue of interest. We propose that the combination of a more general culture measure (or molar climate measure, such as the OCM; Patterson et al., 2005) with a focused climate measure may provide practitioners with the information they need on the environmental elements most relevant for a specific strategic outcome of interest as well as the more general cultural issues that define the general tone of the organization and that underlie the strategic culture/climate (in line with our recommendations for more work integrating culture and climate). We return to this idea shortly.

Criteria for Selecting a Quantitative Approach to Cultural Inquiry

We reviewed these specific examples of quantitative measures because of the differences they reflect in approach, content, and measurement. The differences represented by these measures give rise to a number of issues and concerns that the practitioner must resolve in choosing a model or framework for cultural inquiry. We consider seven such issues in this section: (1) the clarity and sufficiency of the approach chosen, (2) a focus on the dimensions assessed by the approach versus the degree to which the data are presented in profile form and/or as typologies, (3) the stakeholders who participate as respondents to the surveys used, (4) the scoring and benchmarking of the inquiry method(s) used, (5) whether ideal states of the firm as well as the firm's current state are assessed, (6) the degree to which subcultures are identified through inquiry, and (7) inquiry vis-à-vis leadership versus inquiry vis-à-vis culture. Note that we could have also presented these issues as a series of questions the practitioner must ask and answer so that the choices made address as many concerns as possible. While at first glance it may seem a bit overwhelming to consider all of the issues we present, it will serve the practitioner well to have a position on each one of these issues so that later application of the inquiry process will rest on a carefully thought out choice process rather than an off-hand decision without consideration of these issues. Based on our experience, each of these decisions matters a great deal with regard to the confidence one can place in the results of assessment, and they provide a firm foundation on which future use of the evidence generated can rest.

Clarity and sufficiency of the assessment method chosen. Within the world of practice, the "language" of organizational culture generally falls within one of three categories. In the first, culture is described in terms of the goal or target that is deemed the strategic end state to be achieved. So, stakeholders speak of a culture for innovation, efficiency, etc. Second, discussions of culture are at times focused on processes or styles, for example, a culture of collaboration or teamwork, that are thought to enable the attainment of more strategically focused outcomes. Third, cultures are described by what employees or other stakeholders value (e.g., autonomy, empowerment). Each of these three orientations takes the practitioner along a different path in terms of the problems, issues, or concerns that can be addressed or identified.

The soft edges in the stakeholder's interpretation or understanding of organizational culture result in part from a lack of precision in the words used to describe culture as well as the lack of a clear specification of what they are trying to achieve. "Innovation" is a term that exemplifies the potential for confusion. To Ashkanasy, Broadfoot, and Falkus (2000), the cultural dimensions of innovation represented the organization's preference for risk and the extent to which the organization supports innovative or creative efforts. Similarly, Flamholtz and Randle (2011, p. 33) described the dimension of "commitment to change and innovation" as "how a company views, embraces, and reacts to change and innovation." The conceptual challenge here is that the same nomenclature is used to describe the culture itself and the criterion by which organizational effectiveness is evaluated. That is, in some cases the taxonomic categories used for classification connote positive or negative valence, thus confounding cultural description and evaluation. Fortunately, this problem can be resolved if the focus of the culture measurement is on what can be observed as process or behavior. We believe this is important because the cultural characterizations provided through the approach to inquiry are the basis for stakeholders to both understand and frame their plans. Labels that focus on process are more actionable than those that focus on outcomes; process leads to and is not at all isomorphic with outcomes. The practitioner also cares about the labels simply because careful messaging avoids communication and interpretation difficulties.

The implication here is that there are certain key dimensions or factors that are essential to creating a climate or culture for particular strategic purposes. In past chapters, we described this in terms of culture or molar climate forming the foundation for strategic climate; however, for practitioners, the issue is framed differently. Their concern is whether the inquiry leads to the identification of the support mechanisms required for employees to engage in the behaviors associated with the achievement of a particular strategy as well as the identification of the barriers preventing those behaviors. This raises the question of whether a cultural diagnosis can be complete without measurement of the foundational issues that must also be addressed before a strategic culture or climate can be realized. In other words, and returning to the Baker (2007) report on safety climate, it is one thing to encourage new policies and practices and processes to promote safety, but it is another thing to address whether a foundation exists of a more basic cultural nature regarding, for example, worker trust in management, worker sense of personal support from local leadership, the appropriate equipment and technology being available to do the job, and so forth. Our clear impression is that neither the foundation nor the strategic focus alone can do the job; it is in the combination of the two that both process and strategic goals can be accomplished.

A focus on cultural dimensions versus profiles/typologies. In this section, we focus on the issues the practitioner must consider when deciding whether to take a "dimensions" approach to culture versus a "type" approach to culture. Before moving forward, it is worth restating that cultures are distinctive only to the extent that they are different from others. Without that distinction, organizational culture cannot be useful as an explanatory concept for differences in organizational performance nor can it be leveraged for competitive advantage. And this point is very important: In the simplest terms, doing what others are doing, no matter how good they are doing it, will not differentiate an organization from others and thus will not yield competitive advantage. To understand these differences between organizations and their cultures, the practitioner can focus either on individual dimensions of culture or on cultural profiles or types.

Dimensions. Generally, the labels used for culture dimensions vary considerably across the models used by practitioners and reflect the dissimilarities in what is of interest to the practitioner. In some frameworks, the labels represent areas of possible strategic focus (e.g., the "customer focus" dimension in the DOCS), and for others the labels are descriptive of broad organizational styles such as "perfectionistic" or "competitive" (e.g., Boglarsky & Kwantes, 2004), or specific organization ("trust") or job ("challenge") characteristics. Whatever the case may be, the tendency when dimension-level data is available is to emphasize the individual components of culture rather than the overall pattern of dimensions or variables across the organization, which is why the former could be considered a variable-centric approach and the latter could be considered an organization-centric approach.

In any given culture measure, the dimensions have typically been derived through some form of statistical analysis of culture survey data or through qualitative data collection and analysis. Each dimension score is usually represented by a series of items shown to be statistically linked to each other, and the name of the dimension is based on the similarity the researcher finds in the items that define it. For example, the factor "strategic direction and intent" in the DOCS represents items such as "There is a clear mission that gives meaning and direction to work." Other dimensions in this and similar frameworks include themes such as goal setting, customer focus, empowerment, and so forth. Importantly, standardized approaches such as represented in the DOCS and OCAI reflect a set of assumptions about how cultures can be described and how different organizations can be compared or contrasted.

The interpretation of dimension scores often focuses on those dimensions with the lowest scores, with the assumption that those are the areas that need the most attention from management. Such an approach makes little sense, however, in the absence of a clear relationship to external criteria. We have experienced numerous instances in which the evidence indicates that a company that scores relatively high on a dimension should invest even more time, effort, and money to make improvements in that domain because that dimension is the key driver of the outcome of interest. Thus, an examination of how the dimensions relate to key outcomes should be a central part of the interpretation of quantitative culture dimension data.

The organization-as-individual metaphor as in the OCP (Chatman, 1991) is relevant to this discussion of dimensions, as a dimension seems both more easily interpretable and suggestive of the types of people needed to achieve alignment and promote strategically salient achievements. For instance, if the company is seen as "innovative" and people who seek employment there desire a company that is innovative, then the alignment issue is seemingly more straightforward. But the use of a single dimension in communicating with stakeholders runs the risk of misunderstanding the emergent characteristics of the organizational culture. In other words, culture is a function of many personal and contextual variables in interaction over time and emerges out of the mix of people and context in interaction. What is critical for the practitioner (and stakeholder) to recognize is the overall set of dimensional differences in the cultural description that differentiates where the organization is today versus what is deemed necessary for success in the future.

Typologies/Profiles. Typologies address the limitations to treating dimensions independently by considering a number of dimensions of culture simultaneously—think a profile of dimension scores. For example, the "Arrogant Company" described by Flamholtz and Randle (2011) is characterized by a certain pattern of attributes: lack of customer orientation, the inappropriate acceptance of untested assumptions, and a reluctance to change. Along these lines, a type represents a specific combination of distinguishing dimensions. If the profile or type is dominated by a single characteristic or dimension, then the dominant underlying dimension becomes isomorphic with the organizational description. So, for example, if the dominant characteristic of the organization is a concern for people, then the label "humanistic orientation" seemingly applies. As we described earlier, this is the approach used with the OCAI (Cameron & Quinn, 2011). But it can be more difficult to provide an accurate or even reasonable characterization of a profile that is characterized by high scores on many key dimensions, or a profile consisting of low, medium, and high values across several different areas, especially as the number of dimensions under consideration increases.

Nevertheless, despite such difficulties, typologies tend to resonate with stakeholders because they seem relatively easy to grasp. Profiles fit corporate lore or well-known published anecdotes. That is why popular management self-help books invariably mention many different dimensions of organizational functioning implying a profile of attributes or dimensions. Profiles represent specific combinations or patterns of characteristics, and it is those patterns in shape and level that link differentially to organizational effectiveness. And that is the key point. If competitive advantage follows from the unique blend of cultural elements, then that mix is represented by a recipe captured in the typology. The difficult part is knowing just which parts of that recipe can or should be changed and which are less critical. So when comparing any two cultures, the similarity of shape in cultural profile may not be a sufficient indicator of predicting equivalent success (or failure). It is very possible that the pinch of whatever spice your grandmother used in her secret recipe but never told you about may not be captured at all.

That organizations can be profiled along multiple dimensions suggests why studies of dimensional correlates of organizational performance can show inconsistent patterns across research investigations. That is, the focus on the correlates of single cultural dimensions, one at a time, against various performance criteria does not capture the likelihood that it is unique composite profiles of numerous cultural dimensions studied simultaneously that may represent the source of superior organizational performance (or, in the opposite, represent dysfunctional "syndromes"). Thus, we believe that empirically derived typologies have value in understanding the existing patterns of relevant cultural attributes and are particularly valuable in identifying the critical issues requiring further attention. In addition, profiles of attributes (and their labels) can be used for commercial purposes regarding general brand image as well as the image of the company as an employer. Finally, profiles of attributes can be compared to other organizations' profiles, but rather than trying to make the cultures more similar, approaches to change can be identified that might maximally differentiate a client organization from competitors to increase competitive advantage.

To illustrate the point that it is the configuration of cultural elements that leads to cultural interpretation, consider the hypothetical profile of a firm represented in Figure 7.4. The dimensions used in this example are taken from Ashkanasy, Broadfoot, and Falkus (2000), although we have made minor edits to the description to facilitate interpretation. The profile describes an organization led by a visible and influential founder (high on leadership) that provides extreme flexibility to its employees (low on structure) in responding to the marketplace (high on market facing). Risk is encouraged (high on innovation and risk preference), and good bets are reinforced through fair and generous reward systems tied transparently to performance measures (high on job performance). There is also a high degree of concern and care for employees (high on respect for people). We could describe this organization as an innovative,

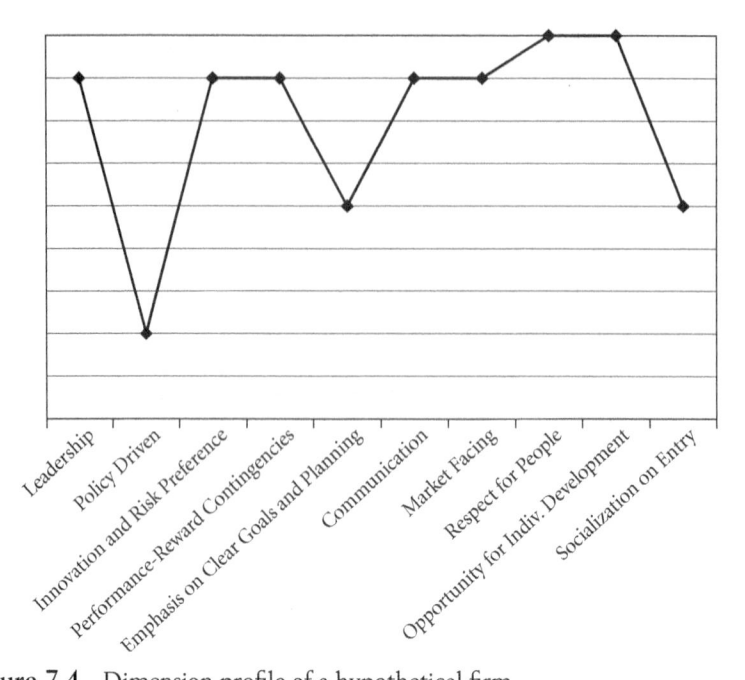

Figure 7.4 Dimension profile of a hypothetical firm

responsive, and market-facing company that depends on the innovative contributions of its people for success, and we would conclude that what makes this firm successful is the configuration or pattern of the cultural elements. What would our impression of the culture be though, if score on the job performance dimension was very low? Our entire interpretation of the culture would change! Now, we would be describing an organization where people run freely to do what they want, taking risks that go unchecked—a fun place to work where there are no consequences for taking risk. Thus our point: As with individual personalities, organization cultures are complex, and the meaning we give to the interpretation of one characteristic or attribute is necessarily within the framework of everything else we know about the organization.

Mixed approaches. The CVF represents one of the more distinctive foundations for typing organizational cultures. Hartnell and colleagues (2011) cleverly applied a dimension approach to the archetypes represented in the CVF. They reviewed the research literature on organizational culture and mapped the measures used in that literature to the CVF dimensions. That is, they carefully reviewed studies of culture that also had outcome effectiveness data and made judgments about how the dimensions of those measured mapped onto the CVF typology. For example, dimensions corresponding to the clan type included "Constructive Culture" from the OCI, and "team orientation" from the OCP. So, an organization with high scores on "team orientation" would have high scores on a clan culture *dimension score*. Note that in doing this, a measurement variable or dimensional construct (team orientation) was used to characterize a type (in this case, clan). Thus, unlike the OCAI approach in which the organization's foci are apportioned across the four CVF types, Hartnell and colleagues created dimension scores for those variables they determined to best fit the four types. In essence, they departed from the within-organization base for comparison on dimension scores (as noted earlier, technically an ipsative approach) implied by the CVF and were therefore able to compare organizations across studies on the four types now characterized by dimension scores.

Although these studies show that it is possible to move from an organization-centric approach to a variable-centric approach, the question arises as to whether such an effort is appropriate and meaningful. That is, in efforts to capture an archetype (i.e., a pure rather than mixed type in terms of salient characteristics), it is assumed that there is a psychometric and conceptual equivalence of the construct to that type. Nonetheless, typologies represent blends of characteristics, and efforts to dimensionalize them represent a seemingly useful way of separating the component parts in ways that lend the data useful to efforts for assessing relative importance and relationships among the component parts. Along these lines, Hartnell and colleagues (2011) found evidence across many studies that the facets of the CVF have some distinctiveness in predicting outcome effectiveness as they proposed (e.g., clan predicts job satisfaction and commitment consistently better than does adhocracy). Of perhaps more interest, they revealed that the dimensions of the CVF do not compete even though they were derived as such (yielding the label the "competing" values framework). What they showed is that organizations that are superior on one dimension of the CVF also tend to be simultaneously superior on another, and the more superior they are the more likely they are to also be effective on the set of multiple effectiveness outcomes studied. In brief, it appears to be true that the good are good on many features of organizational culture, and being good on many things, complex as it is to achieve, gets reflected in success on many outcome indices of effectiveness. Once again, competitive advantage seems to be achievable by having a bundle of many good things happening simultaneously in a company.

Challenges in isolating types of cultures. It is critically important to note that typologies such as those described in the management press are abstractions and at best generic characterizations of particular cultures. Because they are unique, the profiles cannot be parsed in some elemental way to simplify the relative contributions of the component parts, because it is the mix or bundle of issues that produces the uniqueness of the culture and the cause for success. We would suspect that pure forms of a cultural archetype are unlikely to be found and that most organizations represent a blend of more than one type. We think this is true because effectiveness requires a certain level of accomplishment on numerous dimensions of organizational behavior, and thus companies that survive and prosper will be those that do multiple things well.

Given this conclusion, three challenges emerge. The first is whether it is possible to identify a reasonably finite set of types that can be meaningfully distinguished. The "meaningfully" part is important, because if organizations tend to be blends of types, as suggested above, then it may be the case that the differences between types is much fuzzier than theory suggests. We find it curious that little work has been done to empirically identify types based on profile shape (for exceptions see Ketchen, Thomas, & Snow, 1993; Schulte et al., 2009; and Tsui, Wang, & Xin, 2006), particularly given the advances in latent class (mixture) modeling of the last decade (e.g., Nylund et al., 2007). On a related and second point, the issue surfaces of assessing how similar one cultural profile might be to another. Organizations may want to determine the extent to which new profiles fit existing profiles—for example, to understand the fit between new employees and the existing culture or the similarity between the cultures of two organizations undergoing a merger. Third, the question arises as to whether mixed types of cultural profiles can be differentiated in terms of organizational performance. Again, if most organizations are blends of types, then they may differ in the specific blend and the implications for organizational performance are important to understand.

As an example of empirical research addressing some of these issues, Lee and Yu (2004) used Q-type factor analysis to identify four similar cultural profiles using the OCP. While the authors did not label the resulting profiles, our review of their results suggests profiles based on (1) performance orientation, (2) reputation and risk prevention, (3) flexibility and people orientation, and (4) clarity of roles and responsibilities. Lee and Yu found that while organizations did possess different profiles, variation was more across industries than within industry, which reflects the context effects we discussed in Chapter Five. While their results do not speak to links between organizational effectiveness and profile shape, such a comparison would seem a natural extension of their work.

Because the goal of the practitioner is ultimately to solve some important problem or address some particular issue, it is useful to illustrate the challenge in understanding how dimensional and typology frameworks inform management planning and decision-making. For example, continuing with our focus on innovation, what is it about the culture of an organization that might result in more innovative outcomes? Within the competing values framework, the adhocracy culture is characterized by the behaviors that people would describe as risk-taking, such as trying out new ideas that are fundamentally distinctive of a culture of innovation (Cameron & Quinn, 2011). The organizational dimensions relevant to that type include flexibility, experimentation, decisiveness, adaptability, and so on. Presumably then, the relevant metrics for assessing whether the culture supports innovation would be variables measuring such dimensions, and organizational leaders interested in achieving higher levels of innovation would focus on improving those metrics. In short, from the practitioner's perspective, as we noted in discussing the BP safety climate report (Baker, 2007), it may seem most appropriate to directly measure the attributes that are critical to the outcome variable of interest rather than focusing on a more abstract cultural type (in this case, adhocracy). The danger, as we described above, is that other variables critical to the profile could be overlooked, as could the way in which the different dimensions combine within the type. Thus, it may be most useful to simultaneously employ both a more abstract (molar) type approach and a more specific, strategy-based dimension approach.

Summary. In sum, the practitioner faces a critical choice in how to both measure and describe organizational culture. Culture can be described in terms of individual dimensions and/or in terms of types/profiles. Before initiating a cultural inquiry, the practitioner should carefully consider the choice of assessment model and how the results of any inquiry will be communicated and subsequently used. As we emphasized at the beginning of this chapter, these considerations will be influenced by the original charter derived from the first conversation(s) with the organizational sponsors. The practitioner may find it helpful to play out in advance the conversations that he or she will have with stakeholders and anticipate the challenges stakeholders will have when interpreting equivocal results (e.g., dimension scores that are generally middle-of-the-road for the organization or at similar levels across organizational units, or profiles that point to a mixture of different styles or types). The practitioner may also find that different examples of the same underlying framework may be available that allow concepts to be framed in a more stakeholder-friendly manner. For example, in one commercial adaptation of the CVF (see competingvalues.com), the types clan, adhocracy, market, and hierarchy are recast as collaborate, create, compete, and control. Of course, the content and profiles of data being reported were collected from certain stakeholders, which is our next issue for consideration.

Which stakeholders are the most appropriate respondents? The question of who provides input into the description of culture is often overlooked until it is too late. That is, once the data are collected they represent whoever was chosen to respond. To some extent, the consulting approach chosen dictates this choice. Cameron (2008), for example, detailed how the OCAI can be used as part of a change initiative by asking stakeholders to provide their views on both the current and the future states (what the culture should look like at some future point in time such as five years out). In Cameron's recommended approach, the stakeholders do not complete the survey instrument as individuals, but collectively by consensus. This approach is consistent with Schein's (2010) recommendation that stakeholder observations be collected in group settings as culture reflects shared assumptions.[4] Similar to our earlier discussion of how groups should be formed for performing qualitative focus group research, this approach calls for very careful choice of who should comprise the groups that are responding. Cameron (2008) suggested that the relevant stakeholders are those who have a broad perspective of the organization's culture, will be part of the change process, and who are thus key to successful buy-in to change efforts that might follow. Although the sample is clearly limited to a select subset of the organization, the process should meet the criterion that all relevant stakeholders see the participants as representative of the salient constituencies. Therefore, management and all of the various functions should participate, both back room and frontline people should be represented, and there should be salient demographic representation.

Other organizations deploy survey administration more broadly. Denison Consulting (www.DenisonConsulting.com) suggests that all employees who will be part of any action taken based on survey results should be given the opportunity to complete surveys. They suggest surveying employees from all levels within the organization, based on the observation that broad representation within the organization is likely to increase acceptance and commitment, and that including all employees conveys the view that all employees are valued. From a measurement perspective, employees are often in the best position to describe the current state of the organization where the rubber meets the road, so to speak.

That being said, it is not uncommon in practice to administer an organizational assessment instrument to a subset of the population. In fact, such an approach can serve as an introduction to the process and can be useful in evaluating the subculture of a particular part or level within the organization. Ray and Sanders (2008) administered the OCI to the entire leadership team, from team supervisors to directors, of a healthcare organization, but focused their change efforts on the director level under the premise that organizational change would be stimulated by the senior leadership team's efforts to initiate activity, thus serving as a model for the transformation the team wished the rest of the organization to make. The practitioners then segregated the data by level to identify differences in perceptions that might exist as a guide for further discussion.

The I/O or organizational development (OD) practitioner can also be considered a useful source of information. In our own work, we have assembled diagnostic teams who produce organizational profiles of dimension scores that portray the organization's culture by identifying consensus emerging from discussion of aggregate information drawn from multiple sources, including interviews, focus groups, and survey-based measures from broad representative samples. Such an approach recognizes that sometimes it is those individuals who are outside of the organization's culture but who have benefited from in-depth knowledge of the culture through various means that can best articulate the nature of the culture.

Scoring, benchmarks, and interpretation. Various proprietary approaches to scoring cultural assessment instruments exist, and there are numerous ways to present the data. How the data are interpreted will therefore be dependent on such scoring protocols. Some consulting firms (e.g., Denison Consulting) report the relative standing of one organization compared to others on the individual dimensions (i.e., a norm-referenced approach). So, a company might be at the 90th percentile on one dimension and the 30th percentile on another. Standardized scores can be difficult to interpret, however, if the actual dimension scores are not reported. In other words, an organization can receive a relatively low percentile score even when their raw score is relatively high if other organizations tend to score highly on that dimension. In addition, as we described previously when discussing the interpretation of raw dimension scores, organizations tend to assume the lowest scores are where their efforts should be focused, but those areas may not be the most critical in terms of leading to key outcomes. The issue is the same for benchmarked scores; a focus on the lowest percentile scores may not be appropriate unless there is clear evidence that those dimensions are related to external criteria of interest.

Stakeholders invariably ask whether a particular diagnostic finding that emerges from a survey administration is good (or bad), and that request can rarely be ignored. It may be obvious but one significant drawback to a norm-referenced approach is that the score can only have meaning with reference to the specific sample of companies in the benchmark database. So, on balance, we see value in reporting norm-referenced data, but we think the wisest course of action is to report both raw and comparative (or benchmark) data, as is common practice in employee opinion survey practice that assesses morale, employee attitudes, or employee engagement.

Ideal versus current states. An alternative approach commonly used by practitioners is to consider the gaps between the organization's current state and its ideal state by directly comparing where the organization is with reference to the cultural dimensions relative to where stakeholders believe it should be. In the case study by Cameron (2008) presented above, the stakeholders provided both current and future state assessments of corporate culture. This is an approach commonly used by practitioners, with the largest gaps indicating areas where action may be appropriate. Gap analysis, as this is called, is a particularly convenient way to evaluate the significance of the culture data profiled on different dimensions and may replace the need for benchmarks. Most importantly, identifying the largest gaps allows discussion to be targeted toward the appropriate transformation efforts that may be required, particularly when the dimensional content focuses on specific behaviors or processes. From a practical standpoint, the most difficult task is ensuring that the "future state" data is relevant and valid, since asking about the ideal state of the organization presumes some level of knowledge that may not be available or even relevant to certain stakeholder groups.

Despite their convenience, gap or difference scores have been criticized on both measurement and interpretive grounds. Schneider and White (2004) highlighted these in the context of service quality, contrasting perception measures versus those based on the difference between experience and expectations (not dissimilar to desired future state). The major criticism of such difference scores is that expectations of what should be true for a setting and/or what people see as the ideal state are invariably elevated—people want the best or close to it. As such, what "should be" or what would be "ideal" serve more or less as a constant when calculating the difference score, and this paradoxically makes the result less reliable than the plain old perception data. Based on the academic evidence, one might never collect such "should" or "ideal" data, but executives appreciate seeing gap scores because they seem to tangibly reveal what requires attention. Because the gaps identified reflect the perspective of the relevant stakeholders who were asked the questions in the first place, one issue is whether the gaps are perceived similarly across known or suspected subsets of employees—management versus labor, different functional groupings, or even different demographic identity groups. The degree to which the existence of such subcultures is salient and/or requires identification is addressed next.

Identifying organizational subcultures. Quantitative approaches to measuring culture have the particular advantage of providing a clear basis by which different units or groups can be compared along dimensions of interest. In the Baker (2007) BP investigation, the survey responses about safety were compared across refineries to identify any differences in the results. Identifying such differences could lead stakeholders to question whether the presence of subcultures is good or bad. As noted by Martin (2002), in discussions of subcultures, it is typical to focus on the conflict between them, and thus the presence of subcultures is viewed as a source of tension in organizations. Nevertheless, the existence of subcultures can also provide benefits to organizations. For example, Boisnier and Chatman (2003) discussed how subcultures could allow a strong organizational culture to retain sufficient flexibility to adapt to changing environments. The contradictory values in play can thus allow for both the stability and coordination within, say, a functional department of the company—accounting versus advertising, for example—while allowing for creativity and innovation. This speaks to the logic of the CVF but expressed as variability across subcultures as opposed to variability within a single culture.

To the practitioner, the issue is one of determining whether the identifiable heterogeneity in perspectives gathered through quantitative analysis is attributable to differences across subcultures or to random variance in the data. This can be informed with latent class modeling techniques (Nylund et al., 2007), although we are not aware if this method has been applied to the identification of organizational subcultures. Subsequent questions to be asked include whether subgroups so identified are meaningful and whether subgroup differences moderate the relationship between culture and organizational performance in a specific instance (see Chapter Five for an extended discussion of subcultures).

Measuring leaders versus diagnosing cultures. At the beginning of this chapter, we noted that stakeholder views of culture, climate, leadership, and strategy go hand-in-hand, and at numerous points, we have emphasized the important role of leaders in influencing the culture and climate of the organization. In fact, in Chapter Six, we noted the importance of leadership in creating an organization's context, and how people interpret that context is a common thread to both the culture and climate perspectives. In addition, we emphasized Schein's (2010) primary embedding mechanisms (see Chapter Five, Table 5.1) for how organizations can move their organizations in the direction needed to meet their strategic goals. Because leaders play such a critical role in an organization's culture, it is possible that the measurement of culture can be addressed in some respects merely through leadership assessment. From a practitioner perspective, this raises the questions of whether both leader assessment and culture diagnosis are necessary and what the trade-offs might be in implementing a leader-focused assessment versus an organizationally focused diagnostic. For example, it seems reasonable to ask whether an intervention focused on building leadership competencies aligned with organizational values would be sufficient or perhaps the most critical step in the cultural diagnostic/change process. Indeed, the measures of group and organization-level safety climate measures developed by Zohar and Luria (2005) begin with the stem "My direct supervisor . . ." or "Top management in this company . . ." Although the measurement of culture can be addressed to some extent through leadership assessment, we believe that the two should be distinct. As practitioners evaluate an organizational context and make decisions about how best to proceed, we think the following principles may be helpful with regard to the roles of leader assessment, cultural inquiry, and how leaders interface with culture:

- A focus on leader competencies will help guide actions and development planning on culture change. The role of the leader is significant; what the leader does to provide the resources, rewards, motivation, and talent during organizational change is critical to both creating the strategic climate and sustaining the desired culture.
- Leadership actions contribute to, but are not the sole determinants of, employee behavior in organizations. The limited research on the relationship between leadership and organizational culture (see Chapter Five) shows that other factors besides proximal leadership actions need to be assessed in relative contribution to culture and culture change. In practice, this means asking the question as to how others in the organization, and not just leaders, support and facilitate the kinds of strategically relevant behaviors required.
- Changes in leader behavior are typically a precursor to creating culture change. Therefore, leaders who are not adaptable as identified through leadership assessment are not suitable for leading larger culture change. As Schein (2011) put it, climates can only be created by leaders "in what circumstances that apply" (p. xii). Context will determine both boundary conditions (who will be effective and how) and lag effects (how long will the change take). When the demands of the situation do not match the skills of the current leaders, then either those leaders need to be able to change, or they may not be the best candidates to lead the change

that is required. Even Steve Jobs was forced to leave Apple when Apple needed to be run by a manager and not just an inspirational design genius. This puts the practitioner in an awkward position to be sure, so it is best to be aware at the outset of this possibility as an outcome of the cultural inquiry.
- Efforts by *some* leaders to change their behavior to be more in line with a desired culture and strategy, even if successful, may not be sufficient for that culture to change. We unfortunately know little about what constitutes a critical mass of leaders who themselves have to change to effect organizational culture change, and little about which (if any) functional leaders are the most critical to bringing about change. Based on our experience and our knowledge of relevant research literatures, we suggest first that those who have the authority to dispense valuable resources are most critical since the goals that receive the most resources send a clear message about the culture. Second, as a total organizational issue, there is a need for functional integration of the new strategy, which means that heads of functional units must be aligned to produce the strength of culture required for change to occur. Third, customer-contact staff must be aligned to the strategic priorities, so their leaders must be part of the critical mass.
- The leadership focus needs to address not only a cultural change relative to a specific strategic goal but also the foundational elements of the culture that simultaneously balance the flexibility for change and the stability necessary for the organization as a whole to retain what is good and useful (Jonas, Fry, & Srivastra, 1990). Therefore, cultural inquiry should take into account the leadership capabilities required across the broad range of cultural demands in a given situation.
- Leaders affect culture and climate at different levels and in different ways. At the executive level, leaders can influence culture primarily through various forms of symbolic behavior (Hartnell & Walumbwa, 2011); even the allocation of scarce resources can be viewed as quite symbolic. At the unit level, leaders can more directly influence the climate of the work group because they have control over day-to-day interactions with those who do the work. It is clear, then, that any intervention with the goal of producing change must be evaluated for the level of culture that will be affected, and then be aligned with the level of leadership involved to yield maximum effectiveness
- The most effective leaders are those who empower their subordinates as change agents, creating influence through others. Thus, the focus of leader development should not only be on competencies that directly relate to leading change but also include the competency to lead others in the change process (Zaccaro, 1996).

Conclusion. There are many issues to take into account when conducting a quantitative cultural inquiry. Perhaps the best take-home message is that such an inquiry should not be undertaken without a thorough diagnosis of the goals to be reached, an in-depth review of the options that are available, and a systematic articulation of how the approach to be used is linked to the ultimate goals of the process. Taking the time and resources to address such issues during a cultural inquiry will come back several-fold in the potential benefits to the organization.

BLENDING QUALITATIVE AND QUANTITATIVE CULTURAL INQUIRY: A CASE EXAMPLE

Having now outlined the issues to be considered in conducting both qualitative and quantitative cultural inquiries, we now turn to how the two methods might be combined. It is our view that blends of these two approaches hold great value. In Chapter Four, we characterized the pros and cons of qualitative and quantitative approaches; the beauty of a blended approach is that it allows for the weaknesses of one approach to be counterbalanced by the strengths of the other approach. We do not go into the particulars of qualitative or quantitative approaches here to avoid redundancy with the qualitative and quantitative sections in previous chapters, but instead focus on issues that should be taken into account when attempting to optimally blend the two. In addition, we provide an illustration of our own experiences in putting these ideas into action.

One weakness of quantitative approaches that we regularly see and that is often highlighted by qualitative researchers is that the description of culture that is created by the practitioner through the diagnostic process is both structured and bounded by survey content and thus represents the implicit assumptions of the practitioner. What we less often see pointed out is that qualitative approaches are also not independent of the language and experiences of the person observing the culture. Thus, whether inquirers are using quantitative, qualitative, or blended approaches, they should be aware that their background and experiences affect the decisions made and the amount of structure imposed throughout the inquiry process.

Another issue is the ordering of the methods used. As we mentioned in Chapter Four when discussing methods for conducting culture research, the practitioner can start with a qualitative approach followed by quantitative (Reichers & Schneider, 1990), start with a quantitative approach followed by qualitative (Schein, 2000), or alternate back and forth in an iterative fashion (Sackmann, 2001). The benefit of starting with a qualitative approach is that it can inform the practitioner about the issues that are most salient for organizational members and should be included in the organizational survey, as well as ensure that the survey is worded in the language of organizational insiders. The benefit of starting with a quantitative approach is that a survey can help identify the issues that are most important based on the feedback of all organizational members, and then focus groups and interviews can be used to gain clarification and additional insights about those issues and why they exist. An alternating approach may be ideal but is also the most involved, expensive, and time-consuming. Thus, each situation should be evaluated to determine what approach will be the best fit and provide the inquirer with the best information to move forward with organizational change efforts.

It is now hopefully clear that the practical study of culture in large organizations is a complex undertaking. The problems that emerge include (1) the presence of subcultures and the level of access to SMEs to accurately portray those subcultures; (2) the sheer footprint of a large organization, placing significant demands on consultant availability and the corresponding need to involve an entire research team rather than a single consultant or two; (3) the practical barriers to accessing SMEs; and (4) the need to balance and accommodate varying and even conflicting data from different sources. It is unlikely to find a single case study that fully exemplifies best practices addressing each of these challenges, but a research effort led by two of the authors (Macey and Schneider) as part of a consulting assignment provides a glimpse into grappling with these practical issues.

The effort described here began when one of the consultants was contacted by an executive (who we will call the executive sponsor) who had been tasked with conducting a culture assessment. By way of context, the company was a key player in an industry that could be characterized as an oligopoly but also by significant volatility. As the consultants initially understood events, the concern for organizational culture was not brought about by any particular precipitating event, but rather the general interest of the executive team in identifying human cultural factors that might affect competitive advantage. Thus, when the effort began, the charter for the research effort was not fully articulated and only emerged from a series of pre-project conversations and early observations about the culture as the project unfolded.

Armed with comprehensive knowledge of the organization gathered through several years of survey research, the consultants met with the executive sponsor of the project and created a protocol for use in subsequent interviews with other senior executives within the organization. Some questions from the protocol included the following:

1. What are the distinguishing characteristics of the company's culture, those things that make the company unique when compared to other companies? How has this contributed to the company's success?
2. What has been lost over the years? What has changed for the better?
3. When choices have to be made, what gets the highest priority? Why?
4. How do people celebrate when things are going well?
5. How freely is feedback given? What gets someone ignored?
6. What is most important for new people to learn about the company to be successful there?

As is typically the case, the consultants did not immediately gain easy access to senior executives. Cultural inquiry is a sensitive topic, and despite the working knowledge of the company and relationships with some of its executives, it was nonetheless essential to establish credibility with the sponsor to ensure continuing support. Working through the interview protocol with the sponsor created the opportunity to build personal familiarity and to create the necessary level of comfort and credibility. Most importantly, these conversations also helped to more fully create the working charter for the cultural inquiry, although it continued to evolve throughout the early phases of the project.

The interviews were then conducted over a several week period, reflecting the difficulties in scheduling senior executives because of their prior commitments, travel schedules, etc. All interviews were conducted in the offices of either C-suite level executives or members of the senior management team reporting directly to them. Parenthetically, it is worth noting that one of the most important messages a consultant needs to convey is respect for the time of those interviewed both by creating an agenda for the meeting at the beginning of the interview and then progressing efficiently through the protocol. We have invariably found that a demonstrated respect for the executive's time typically results in extended conversations beyond those times originally scheduled—as was the case here. From a process perspective, we found it important to follow up each interview with an immediate review of interview notes, filling in details as needed and planning for any modifications to the protocol. Typically, these interviews were not recorded given the sensitivity of the topic and the need to ensure confidentiality. While perhaps also obvious, it is worth mentioning that the interview protocol was a living document that necessarily changed, although it was important not to lose sight of the original plan.

As the interviews proceeded, the authors began to recognize that the culture of the organization was viewed quite differently at the C-suite level when compared to the characterizations gathered from the management layer immediately below. The differences were not subtle, so a series of focus groups was subsequently conducted across the many geographically dispersed locations in the country. It is worth noting that the choice to conduct a series of focus groups as opposed to further individual interviews was driven by cost and efficiency considerations.

The use of focus groups necessitated expanding the consulting team and highlights one difficulty in conducting such a cultural diagnosis: the need to create an orientation mechanism by which the background information essential to the study can be shared within the consulting team. There is often a unique vocabulary and frame of reference used to describe events and parties within an organization, and without considerable familiarity with that vocabulary there is risk to the quality of data that can be gathered through both direct interviews and focus groups. The focus group interviews were similar to the individual interview protocols, but the frame of reference for these larger employee groups was different. Some examples of the questions used to foster conversation were as follows:

1. What makes the company unique? What makes it different from other places you have worked? What one thing typifies the company for you?
2. What is it about the company that is important to preserve?
3. When difficult decisions are made, what do others in the company truly value and believe?
4. What types of things do people typically get recognized or rewarded for? What tends to get ignored?
5. Are there certain kinds of roles in the company that seem to be more highly valued? Less valued?

Importantly, questions such as these are not as useful for gathering the breadth of information that is needed as they are for starting the conversation and ensuring that the energy of the people in the room is maintained and focused on the topic at hand. Obviously, it is essential to frame the introduction to focus group meetings just as it is to frame the individual conversations with sponsors, executives, or others. The protocol used by the consultants was standardized and used as a point of departure for all focus group meetings.

Simultaneous to the collection of focus group data, a sample of employees in the organization completed the DOCS. Combined with the existing qualitative and quantitative data gathered through the regular employee opinion survey process, the now larger consulting team was faced with the task of synthesizing and providing an integrated perspective on all of these data. The synthesis was prepared both in narrative form and in data displays used to synthesize the evaluations. Two key observations regarding this synthesized reporting are worth noting. First, the ratings were consensus judgments resulting from discussion of all data and observations by the entire consulting team. Differences of opinion were few but where they did exist, they were resolved through discussion within the team. Of 11 dimensions that were used to characterize the culture, complete consensus was obtained on 10. The report indicated the one minor issue where there was a difference of opinion within the consulting team. Second, the team provided its judgment as to the direction in which the culture was seen as shifting. That is, the entire pattern of data was examined with respect to where the culture was seen as moving according to the observations provided by interview and focus group participants as well as whatever supporting or corroborating survey data were available.

At the end of the project, the consulting team provided three separate reports to the executive sponsor and delivered an in-person presentation to the chief human resources officer and the chief executive officer. First, the executive interviews were summarized in a form to ensure individual anonymity. A second summary report was provided based on the focus group interviews. The third and most important report represented the synthesis of the data from the individual interviews, the focus groups, the DOCS surveys, and the existing relevant qualitative and quantitative data from the earlier employee surveys. One particular value of the approach to integrated reporting was that each consensus view of the consulting team could be supported by multiple qualitative and quantitative data sources. Thus, the report provided to the organization was specific in detail, characterized by the supporting observations that led to the consensus ratings. Purely as a practical matter, the investment of time in coming to consensus within the team resulted in a consulting deliverable that was well received because it both acknowledged the views of the executive team but also was grounded in multiple data points that served to foster credibility of the effort and acceptance of the results. All told, the individual interviews, the focus groups, and the culture survey had been completed within approximately two months, with reporting and feedback within a third month.

On a final note related to the theme of blending qualitative and quantitative methods, the particular mix used here was driven by the opportunity as it presented itself. Sponsors have ideas, too, about what kind of diagnosis will work in their context, the sense of urgency to the diagnosis, and the available resources to complete the research. Thus, a greater emphasis on qualitative research would have been outside reasonable boundaries, while a greater emphasis on quantitative techniques would have not provided the necessary voice to the executive team. A different mix of the imperatives driving this research may very easily have led to a different blend of techniques.

SUMMARY OF KEY POINTS TO CONSIDER IN CONDUCTING A CULTURAL DIAGNOSIS

We have described the rationale for conducting a cultural diagnosis and addressed the different strategies available to the practitioner for conducting this form of applied research. Ultimately, the choice of approach depends on what information is needed and how it is to be used. As a summary of the key issues we have highlighted in this chapter, we therefore offer the following discussion points to guide the relevant choices:

1. A specific charter for the cultural inquiry is essential. There are a number of reasons why cultural inquiry is relevant to the practitioner and the sponsoring stakeholders. Whether driven by a precipitating event or sense of gap between desired and end states, executives know that culture is both a lever and a potential hindrance to achieving their objectives. Any ambiguity in stakeholders' interpretation or understanding of organizational culture results in part from a lack of precision in the words used to describe culture as well as the lack of a clear specification of what they are trying to achieve.
2. Both qualitative and quantitative approaches to cultural inquiry have merit. Ideally, the practitioner will choose elements of both approaches to ensure that the sponsor's objectives are met. In fact, unless the practitioner chooses to execute an "out of the box" survey, some elements of a qualitative approach are likely essential. Qualitative approaches have particular value for working inductively and for describing the culture in indigenous terms. Quantitative approaches have the particular strength of permitting differentiation and comparison, in addition to lending themselves better to explorations of culture strength.
3. The dimensions or themes that are chosen to describe organizational culture should be articulated in a way that has meaning to stakeholders; because culture is a shared phenomenon, the inquiry should produce a work product that conveys that which is shared. This is not a matter of choosing qualitative versus quantitative approaches to cultural diagnosis, but one of choosing the language with which to describe the culture

and/or climate. The choice of framework has implications for how the cultural description will be interpreted by stakeholders.
4. The practitioner should carefully consider who would provide the evaluative frame of reference for the cultural description or observations. Some methods are inherently evaluative by the nature of the dimensions or themes that are reported. Other methods are descriptive and perhaps neutral with respect to any criterion of effectiveness.
5. Convenience and availability of benchmarks can be an important consideration in choosing an approach to cultural inquiry. However, there are trade-offs in choosing particular methods. Certain quantitative approaches are based on standardized frameworks that use unique terminology and proprietary perspectives. These standardized approaches benefit from significant conceptual thinking and even empirical research regarding linkages with organizational effectiveness criteria. One benefit of such approaches that may seem most attractive is the availability of benchmark information. However, the choice to use these models must be weighed against the benefit of describing culture in the language of the people who work there.
6. Although benchmark information may be helpful to have, cultural diagnosis does not *require* a specific external reference point. Qualified stakeholders can evaluate whether the culture as diagnosed is consistent with strategic intent; however, in such a case the link to organizational effectiveness is implicit in the judgment of the stakeholder. The subjectivity inherent in such evaluations can be hidden in the nomenclature used to describe culture or embedded in the metrics (e.g., what is "favorable" in a survey result). The practitioner should be cognizant of these implicit assumptions and articulate them in discussions with stakeholders.
7. The practitioner should guide stakeholders through the process of thinking about how the cultural description can be interpreted and who is qualified for making that evaluation. The choice of measurement operations is important because the evaluative aspect of cultural diagnosis is challenging. Who is to say that the culture is sufficiently innovative? Or too bureaucratic? Comparison to external benchmarks seemingly sidesteps that problem but only if it is assumed that the comparison organizations are appropriate and that the relationship between cultural dimensions and organizational effectiveness is consistent across organizations. As a first step in the process, the practitioner should consider how various outcomes of a cultural inquiry might be interpreted and translated into next steps or at least discussion points with the relevant stakeholders. Any lack of clarity around this point suggests that rethinking the approach may be warranted.
8. The practitioner should consider the pattern of results in its entirety. What is unique to a culture that translates to organizational effectiveness may not be captured or articulated in individual dimension scores, but rather, in the mix or configuration of elements that create the uniqueness of that culture. Using a typology approach by profiling across dimensions may be a powerful tool for capturing that uniqueness. Cultures are not easily diagnosed and defined, and the simplification achieved through dimensions may be inadequate to direct stakeholders' attention to the balance that exists among cultural elements.

9. The existence of subcultures should be anticipated. This has implications for who should be involved in the cultural inquiry as to both the depth and breadth of the process. Particular consideration should be given to different hierarchical levels within the organization.
10. Leadership assessments may be a valuable supplement to a cultural inquiry, but they should not be considered a replacement for it. Instead, the cultural inquiry should provide information on the leadership competencies required for both creating the foundational culture for change and for driving the change itself. Leadership assessment can then be used to determine the strengths and weaknesses of the current leadership team for accomplishing the organization's change goals.

The practitioner has the choice of not one but many tools available for conducting a cultural inquiry. We have stressed throughout this chapter that the charter or purpose of the inquiry is what should drive those choices, taking into account the tradeoffs that invariably make it difficult to determine what is best. Our methods provide an approximation to what we understand the culture to be, and within practical constraints, the best approach is likely to embrace a combination of different strategies as we have discussed here.

NOTES

1. A very interesting and readable book by Duhigg (2012) described how habits (closely related to what we call climate and culture) dictate our individual and organizational behavior. He detailed the research at the neuropsychological level about why habits form and how they govern our lives—and are so difficult to change.
2. The response scale used in the OCAI is referred to as an ipsative measure (ipse = s/he or him or herself), in contrast to normative data, which have an external frame of reference.
3. The Mayflower Group is a consortium of companies that share a set of items for use in their employee survey processes. Because numerous companies are involved (typically 25–40 companies) the database can be used by companies to provide comparisons between themselves and other companies through a process called benchmarking (see Johnson, 1996, for more information).
4. Note that the choice of a consensus-building process for responding to the survey obviates the possibility of measuring culture strength directly because the "score" for the evaluation process is a consensus (not average) rating.

CHAPTER
8

Summary and Conclusion

Our reviews of the organizational climate and organizational culture constructs have covered a great deal of ground, with many important historical, conceptual, research, and practical details for each of these topics. This chapter recaps our journey through these literatures, summarizing the major conclusions in one place. We understand this is potentially dangerous because, on one hand, so many interesting issues will not be covered here, and on the other hand, readers who have just made their way through the rest of the book may not find much new in this final chapter. Despite these concerns, we hope that a presentation of the key points all in one place will prove to be a useful reference—and interested readers can return to issues of special import to them in the full chapters. So, in what follows, we first discuss organizational climate, then organizational culture, and then the integration of the two that we suggest is the most useful way to proceed in the future. We close with implications for practitioners and directions for future research on the topics of organizational climate, organizational culture, and their integration.

ORGANIZATIONAL CLIMATE

The history of the organizational climate construct is traced to the research of Lewin, Lippitt, and White (1939) on the effects of leadership on groups of 10-year-old boys performing various activities like model airplane construction. One of their key findings was that the different leadership styles (autocratic, democratic, or laissez-faire) produced different "social climates" or "atmospheres" in the groups. Their focus on a specific type of climate, on the group as a whole as the level of analysis, and on the influential role of the leader laid important groundwork for future climate research.

The period from the Lewin and colleagues (1939) study through the mid-1960s marks the first era in the history of organizational climate. Researchers during this time displayed a growing interest in the ways employees experienced the environment, especially the social environment, of organizations. Climate was but one of several labels used to describe that experienced environment, with other terms like atmosphere (Fiedler, 1962; Leavitt, 1958; Lewin et al., 1939; Likert, 1961; McGregor, 1960), character (Buchele, 1955; Gilmer, 1961), and even culture (Argyris, 1958; Fleishman, 1953; Katz & Kahn, 1966; Schein, 1965) also in the mix. Nevertheless, climate was the term that gained widespread acceptance, and it became synonymous with the way the organizational environment was experienced by employees. Other work that was particularly influential early on was that of Fleishman (1953) on leadership climate, Argyris (1957) on human relations climate, and McGregor (1960) on managerial climate. These authors discussed specific kinds of climates and emphasized the role of leaders in creating them. They were also very interested in the implications of an organization's climate for its effectiveness. These themes continue to this day.

Interest in the organizational environment was part of a larger movement focusing on more macro issues at higher levels of analysis during the 1960s, and a rise in empirical research marked the beginning of a new era for the climate construct. With Tagiuri and Litwin's (1968) compilation of papers on climate from a conference at Harvard, and empirical research by Litwin and Stringer (1968) and Schneider and Bartlett (1968, 1970), interest in climate by organizational researchers reached new levels, and efforts to clarify the nature and measurement of the construct became a collective priority. Hellriegel and Slocum (1974) provided an influential review of the explosion of climate research that took place in the late 1960s and early 1970s, classifying climate research into three categories: (1) climate as an independent variable, emphasizing studies exploring links to job satisfaction and, to some extent, job performance; (2) climate as an intervening variable, exploring ways it mediated the effects of such variables as leadership and human relations training programs on satisfaction and performance; and (3) climate as a dependent variable, including the effects of structural variables on climate perceptions as well as the role of organizational development interventions on changes in climate.

As empirical research on organizational climate exploded, critiques of climate research became common—there was more to pick on! Most notable and influential were critiques by Guion (1973), Johannesson (1973), and James and Jones (1974). Replies came in the form of reviews of the climate research by authors such as Hellriegel and Slocum (1974), Schneider (1975b), and Payne and Pugh (1976). One primary critique concerned the lack of clarity regarding climate as an attribute of the individual or the organization (Guion, 1973), which forced climate researchers to think more clearly about the level of analysis in their research (Hellriegel & Slocum, 1974) and to distinguish between psychological climate at the individual level of analysis and organizational climate at the organizational level of analysis (James & Jones, 1974). A second critique concerned the presumed overlap between climate and job attitudes, especially job satisfaction (e.g., Johannesson, 1973). In response, scholars such as Schneider (1975b) and Payne, Fineman, and Wall (1976) emphasized the conceptual difference between descriptions and evaluations of the work environment, and researchers like LaFollette and Sims (1975) and Schneider and Snyder (1975) empirically demonstrated the distinction between climate and satisfaction. The resulting conceptual and empirical clarity, along with the work on levels of analysis, resulted in acceptance of the distinction between the description of the work environment as climate and the affect/evaluation associated with attitudes. A third critique of climate research involved the inconsistent findings when climate was used as an independent variable in studies of job performance (Hellriegel and Slocum, 1974). Schneider (1975b) responded that most climate measures were so broad that one would not necessarily expect them to predict specific organizational outcomes, and compounding this issue was that the level of analysis was frequently neither clearly conceptualized nor communicated. As a result, he called for research for climate with a focus on specific strategic goals linked to the outcomes of interest, and for improved understanding of the appropriate level of analysis for climate as well as outcomes.

The work responding to the critiques of climate research laid the foundation for the contemporary era of climate research, in which considerable progress on central issues in climate research have been made around (1) a definition of organizational climate that is useful both in theory and practice, (2) the levels of analysis issue, (3) the focus of climate research, (4) climate strength and other boundary conditions of the relationship between climate and outcomes, and (5) the antecedents of climate and the mediators of climate's relationship with outcomes.

Defining Organizational Climate

One of the most important accomplishments in contemporary climate research has been clarification of the definition of climate. We identified five key themes that capture current thinking and are included as part of the definition:

- *Theme 1:* Organizational climate emerges through numerous mechanisms including leadership, communication, training, and so forth
- *Theme 2:* It is not the mechanisms that are climate but rather the experiences those produce and the meaning attached to them
- *Theme 3:* Organizational climate is a property not of individuals but of units/organizations; it is based on shared experiences and shared meaning

- *Theme 4:* Shared experiences and the meaning attached to them emerge from natural interaction in units/organizations; climate is shared in the natural course of work and the interactions happening at and surrounding work
- *Theme 5:* Organizational climate is not an affective evaluation of the work environment—it is not satisfaction—but rather a descriptive abstraction of people's experiences at work and the meaning attached to them.

Based on these themes, our definition of climate is:

> *Organizational climate is the shared meaning organizational members attach to the events, policies, practices, and procedures they experience and the behaviors they see being rewarded, supported, and expected.*

This definition has both conceptual and practical usefulness. Conceptually it elucidates the many issues that yield experiences and serve as a basis for shared meaning attached to those experiences. From an applied perspective, it informs practitioners that the measurement of climate must include many practices, policies, procedures, etc., for the measure to capture the wide range of experiences that yield the climate of interest, and this range of experiences can become the foci for organizational change.

The Levels of Analysis Issue

Our focus in this book has been on organizational climate and not psychological climate. This focus, however, brings with it measurement challenges, including how to measure a unit-level (team, group, organization) phenomenon based on the perceptions of individual employees. The development of norms around writing climate items, aggregating individual-level data to represent a higher-level unit and demonstrating within-unit agreement represent a major accomplishment of climate research.

On the issue of item writing for example, Glick (1985) noted that climate items to be aggregated should be written so that respondents refer to what they observe in the unit and not to their personal experiences (what Chan, 1998, called the referent-shift model). For example, the item "I am treated with consideration by my supervisor" would be inappropriate for aggregation to represent a unit-level score for leadership. A more appropriate item would be "Our work group supervisor treats us with consideration." Meta-analytic work on justice climate by Whitman, Caleo, Carpenter, Horner, and Bernerth (2012) has verified the stronger validity for scales using the unit as the referent.

With regard to aggregation itself, Guion (1973) had proposed that unless there was 100% agreement for people in a unit, the unit score would be meaningless. Later discussions on this topic recognized that perfect agreement was unlikely to occur, but methods for assessing adequate levels of agreement were needed (James, 1982). In contemporary climate research, it is most common to report several different statistics to support aggregation, including $r_{WG(j)}$, ICC(1), and ICC(2). Although presenting adequate statistical support for aggregation is necessary, it is also important for researchers to make clear theoretical arguments for their level of analysis. Research on the climates of units and/or organizations brings with it many specific issues with which researchers must grapple (LeBreton & Senter, 2008), but the last several decades have brought tremendous progress in this area and contributed to extensive multilevel thinking and research throughout the fields of industrial/organizational psychology and organizational behavior (e.g., Klein & Kozlowski, 2000).

Molar Versus Focused Climate Research

Research on organizational climate can be divided into two major approaches: molar climate and focused climate. The goal of the molar climate approach is essentially to capture the entirety of the organizational environment, and as such, typically assesses a wide variety of dimensions, including conflict, job challenge, leader support, and workgroup friendliness (adapted from Jones & James, 1979). Such assessments can be thought of as measuring a climate for well-being. Our review of this literature indicated that although there were inconsistencies in relationships with outcomes, such a climate has demonstrated some usefulness as a foundation for more strategically focused climates. That is, creating a general positive environment for employees is an important first step in focusing employees' actions on achieving strategic goals.

The most common approach to studying climate at this writing is the focused climate approach, derived from Schneider's (1975b) proposal that a climate "for something" would avoid many of the critiques of the climate construct and should increase its predictive validity. The earliest work on focused climates involved service (Schneider, Parkington, & Buxton, 1980) and safety (Zohar, 1980), but so many different types of climate now exist in the literature that we (e.g., Schneider, Ehrhart, & Macey, 2011a) have begun to distinguish between climates that are focused on the organization's strategic performance-related outcomes (or strategic climates) and those that are focused on processes internal to the organization (or process climates). In both cases, the policies, practices, and procedures specific to the focus of interest are emphasized, but process climates (such as justice and diversity) likely play a similar role as molar climate in creating a positive organizational environment that forms the foundation for strategic climates (such as service and safety).

Climate Strength and Other Boundary Conditions

Until the past decade or so, research on organizational climate emphasized the direct effects of climate level on outcomes. So, for instance, the mean level of service climate was shown to predict customer experiences (Schneider & White, 2004), mean levels of safety climate were shown to predict injury rates (Zohar, 2000) and accidents (Zohar & Luria, 2005), and so on. As the field has developed, climate has been studied in a number of new and interesting ways, including looking at not only mean levels of climate, but within-unit variability in climate perceptions (or climate strength).

Climate strength has most commonly been studied as a moderator of the relationship between climate level and outcomes, such that the relationship is predicted to be stronger when the climate is stronger (e.g., Schneider, Salvaggio, & Subirats, 2002). However, as research on climate strength has accumulated, researchers are increasingly interested in what makes a climate strong (Bowen & Ostroff, 2004). Research indicates, for example, that higher levels of unit diversity (Colquitt, Noe, & Jackson, 2002), unit social interaction (González-Romá, Peiró, & Tordera, 2002), or leadership focus on the strategic outcome of interest (Schneider et al., 2002) result in higher levels of climate strength. The research on climate strength has also been of considerable practical value, emphasizing the importance of a focus from many vantage points in the organization on the outcome of interest if those outcomes are to be achieved (Bowen & Ostroff, 2004). An interesting finding is this regard is that in Schneider et al. (2002), high variability within bank branches on service climate was reflected in high variability in reports by bank branch customers about their customer experiences.

Climate strength is not the only moderator that has been studied in climate research. As climate research has matured, researchers have begun to identify the boundary conditions on strategic climate—strategic outcome links. For example, Ehrhart, Witt, Schneider, and Perry (2011) found that the level of internal service that those who work with customers receive from support systems outside the unit moderated the service climate—customer experience link across units. Thus, relevant variables outside the unit of interest can be conceptualized and studied as potential moderators because the climate–outcome link might not be the same regardless of the context. As another example, Mayer, Ehrhart, and Schneider (2009) showed that the degree of customer contact unit employees have acted as a moderator of the relationship between service climate and customer satisfaction with a more positive service climate only being important when customer contact was high. So establishing a service climate may be more critical for some types of services than others. Research on such boundary conditions is critical because focused climates take a great deal of time and energy to build, and it is important that those resources are not wasted and that other features of the context are in place to ensure that the optimal benefits of the climate can be achieved.

Antecedents and Mediators

We have said that climate serves as a framework of meaning shared by people in settings and that they behave in ways that reflect that meaning.

In this way climate is not the proximal antecedent of a strategic outcome of interest, but instead the proximal antecedent of some intervening or mediating behavior. For example, Schneider, Ehrhart, Mayer, Saltz, and Niles-Jolly (2005) found that customer-focused organizational citizenship behavior (OCB) served as a mediator of the service climate—customer experience link. We would propose that strategically relevant behavior might serve as a mediator of such relationships in numerous settings, although we would add that it is important that people in settings have the competencies to enact those behaviors that the climate suggests are important. They also must be motivated; research on safety climate by Neal and Griffin (2006) suggests that the way climate elicits increased strategically relevant behavior is by increasing employees' motivation to perform such behaviors.

Climate itself has also been studied as a mediator of the relationship between other organizational variables and organizational effectiveness. From the earliest days of climate research and thinking (e.g., Fleishman, 1953; Lewin et al., 1939; McGregor, 1960), leaders have been described as playing a critical role in creating climates, such that climate acts as a mechanism through which leaders have their influence. One of the key findings on the relationship between leadership and organizational climate has been to demonstrate that focused leadership (i.e., that specifically addresses the strategic outcome of interest) is more strongly related to a focused climate than general leadership behaviors (Hong, Liao, Hu & Jiang, 2013). Thus, being supportive of employees may be useful in laying the foundation for a focused climate, but behaviors that clearly communicate and role model what the strategic priorities of employees should be are required to specifically build a focused climate. In the same way, research has shown that a number of other HR and support processes serve as a foundation for focused climates (Salanova, Agut, & Peiró, 2005; Schneider, White, & Paul, 1998; Wallace, Popp, & Mondore, 2006), but when those processes are focused on a specific strategic outcome of interest, their relationship with the focused climate will be stronger (Hong et al., 2013). Thus the picture emerges that general leadership and HR processes lay the groundwork for a focused climate, but focused leadership and HR processes are still needed to ensure that the focused climate is established and subsequently that the specific employee behaviors desired by the organization are performed, ultimately leading to strategic outcomes.

ORGANIZATIONAL CULTURE

Pettigrew's *Administrative Science Quarterly* article in 1979 marks the beginning of contemporary scholarly interest in the topic of organizational culture. Pettigrew formally introduced the anthropological study of cultures to the organizational research literature, in stark contrast to the individually focused psychological research of the time on organizational climate. Factors that enhanced the effect of the Pettigrew article and that contributed to the rise in interest in culture included increased focus on the issues of the organizational environment and organizational behavior by both academics and consultants, as well as the attribution of Japan's success in quality manufacturing to differences in organizational culture. Nevertheless, it became apparent early on that there was little agreement among academics about what the culture construct was, and scholars studied different facets of it using different methodologies. The levels of analysis issue that had dominated climate research for more than a decade was not an issue in the culture literature, however, because it was implicitly accepted that organizational culture permeated the entire organization.

Understanding Organizational Culture

The primary distinction among approaches to understanding culture has been between those who wrote of culture as something organizations *have* versus those who considered culture as something organizations *are* (Smircich, 1983). From the organizations *have* cultures perspective, culture is treated as a variable that affects important organizational outcomes, and thus the goal is often to change culture to achieve results that are more functional. As such, research from this perspective tends to align with the goals and concerns of organizations' upper management. From the organizations *are* cultures perspective, culture captures the totality of individuals' experiences in organizations, with a particular emphasis on the creation of meaning through the symbolism derived from various behavioral experiences and structural perceptions workers have in and of their organizations. The goal of research from this perspective is to provide thorough descriptions of what happens in an organization as a unique setting and, in many cases, to represent the views of those who have less power in the organization (Alvesson, 2002).

A second important framework for understanding culture was proposed by Martin (1992, 2002). She described three general perspectives that have been used in describing organizational culture. The integration perspective presumes and describes culture in terms of consensus and consistency that characterizes the whole; the differentiation perspective emphasizes inconsistencies and allows for the possibility of subcultures within the organization within which there is consensus; and the fragmentation perspective focuses on ambiguities in the organization's culture where there is tension and differences in perspective. Although there is not complete consensus around these three perspectives (particularly with regard to whether it makes sense to study ambiguity as culture), in her more recent writings, Martin (2002) has proposed that all three perspectives can exist simultaneously. Thus, there are likely facets of culture for which there is strong agreement across the organization, other facets for which there are clear subcultures (e.g., by occupation or level), and other facets of culture for which there is no consensus.

Defining Organizational Culture

In light of the various conceptualizations of organizational culture, it is not surprising that a multitude of definitions for the construct have been proposed. For instance, many researchers have proposed that culture is shared, while others have emphasized the parts of culture that are not shared. Some have described culture as stable while others have focused on how culture is always changing and evolving. And some have talked about how cultures are what make organizations unique; while others have pointed out how cultures that are supposedly "unique" have many commonalities with other "unique" cultures. Nevertheless, based on our review and previous key reviews of the culture literature (e.g., Alvesson, 2002; Martin, 2002; Ott, 1989; Schein, 1991, 2010; Trice & Beyer, 1993), we conclude that there is considerable consensus that culture is shared; is stable; has depth; is symbolic, expressive, and subjective; is grounded in history and tradition; is transmitted to new members; provides order and rules to organizational existence; has breadth; is a source of collective identity and commitment; and is unique. Although no definition captures all of these elements, perhaps the most commonly cited definition of culture and the one on which we relied the most is that of Schein (2010, p. 18) in which he described organizational culture as "a pattern of shared basic assumptions learned by [an organization] as it solved its problems of external adaptation and internal integration, which has worked well enough to be considered valid and, therefore, to be taught to new members as the correct way to perceive, think, and feel in relation to those problems."

Culture is typically conceptualized as having multiple layers that are distinguished by how accessible the cultural information is, particularly to outsiders. The outer layers, or artifacts, are easily accessible and include a variety of cultural forms, including practices, language, narratives, and symbols (Trice & Beyer, 1993). The challenge with this outer layer is that the meaning of these artifacts is unclear and can actually have quite different meanings in different organizations. The next layer of culture described by Schein (2010) is espoused values. This level captures the statements by management about what the organization's core values are. These espoused values tend to be aspirational and may or may not represent the actual values of employees or be consistent with management or employee behavior (i.e., their enacted values). To better understand the true culture of the organization, according to Schein (2010), one must go to the deepest level of culture, or the underlying assumptions. Over time, as the organization finds success in operating within the artifacts and espoused values, these yield taken-for-granted assumptions about how the organization should function, to the point that insiders may not even be aware of the assumptions they hold. Of course, it is very difficult to access this level of cultural information, and not all methods for cultural inquiry will be able to do so. At the same time, to fully understand the organization and its culture, this information is critical, so a consideration of ways to study culture is useful.

Studying Organizational Culture

The methods for studying culture can be grouped into two broad categories: qualitative and quantitative. Those using an organizations *are* cultures approach tend to use qualitative methods, and those using an organizations *have* cultures approach tend to use quantitative methods. Of course, such broad categorizations and general statements oversimplify some of the nuance, including the range of qualitative methods used by researchers and examples of research that cross over the typical alignment between the culture conceptualization and method (e.g., approaching culture from an organizations *have* cultures conceptualization but using qualitative methods as in Peters & Waterman, 1982).

There are a number of pros and cons associated with the use of qualitative versus quantitative methods. For instance, qualitative research can provide rich and detailed information from an insider's perspective that can shed light on the deeper layers of culture, but it is less useful for comparing one organization's culture to another. In addition, the time and expense associated with qualitative efforts usually prevent the inclusion of a broad sample of organizational members. In contrast, quantitative research is better suited to comparing cultures and examining the relationship between culture assessments and measures of effectiveness, and using quantitative surveys permits many employees across the organization an opportunity to give their input. With quantitative approaches, however, it is difficult to judge whether the questions being asked are appropriate or relevant in a particular setting, and these approaches are more limited as a vehicle for studying the deepest levels of culture.

Clearly, the best way to take advantage of the strengths of each approach is to use both. Such an approach could begin with focus groups to determine the issues that should then be the focus of a broader organization-wide survey, or it could start with a survey that is followed with focus groups or interviews to clarify the meaning behind the survey findings. There are other possibilities to consider that alternate back and forth between the two methods, but the main point is that more is to be gained by combining the methods than by using only one.

Organizational Culture Development

As one begins to decipher an organization's culture, a critical issue is how and why the culture developed the way it did. The literature has identified a number of influences on organizational culture, but likely none has been discussed more than the founder. As emphasized by Schein (1983, 2010), founders brings their assumptions and beliefs about how the business should be run to the initial establishment of the organization. They communicate those assumptions and beliefs, through primary embedding mechanisms, which include what they pay attention to and measure, how they react to crises, how they allocate resources, the behaviors they role model, what behaviors they reward, and the criteria they use for selection and promotion. These are reinforced through secondary mechanisms, such as the organizational structure, procedures, rites and rituals, the design of the space, stories, and formal statements. Altogether, these mechanisms send messages about the founder's assumptions and values, and over time, they become the assumptions and values at the core of the organization's culture and are established as the normative way things are done in the organization.

Besides the founder, other factors influence the development of an organization's culture. One is the learning process that occurs as the organization encounters success (Schein, 1985, 2010). As the assumptions and values of the founder and initial members are met with positive results, those results serve to reinforce that how the organization is operating is the right way to go about its business, including both how it addresses issues of internal coordination and external adaptation (Schein, 2010). Other influences on organizational culture include the national culture in which the organization is based (there are main effects for national as well as organizational culture; House, Hanges, Javidan, Dorfman, & Gupta, 2004), the organization's industry and its competitors (less competition yields less innovation and change and more stability; Ott, 1989), the occupational and professional subcultures that characterize a company (e.g., physicians vs. nurses in hospitals; Gregory, 1983; Schein, 1996), the stage of an organization's life cycle (younger organizations can change rapidly while older organizations are more fixed in the ways they function; Schein, 2010), or even the kinds of people who are attracted to and who stay with an organization (firms in an industry that emphasize mass-produced services attract and retain different personalities than those that emphasize customization; Schneider, 1987). With so many factors influencing culture through such various mechanisms, there is no doubt that the development of culture is complex and should be treated as such.

Organizational Culture Maintenance

In addition to the attraction and retention of specific kinds of people, another important element in the maintenance of culture concerns the socialization processes by which newcomers learn about the culture of the organization—how to think about the organization and how to feel about the organization. Socialization has been a central issue in the organizational culture literature, as it helps explain how culture remains surprisingly stable even as new individuals enter the organization—the new learn from the old. From the newcomer's perspective, the primary underlying mechanism that is operating during socialization is uncertainty reduction, such that newcomers reduce the anxiety and ambiguity that comes from entering a new setting because the socialization process yields understanding of the new rules and norms. From the organization's perspective, the sooner new employees can "get up to speed" and function effectively within the culture, the more efficient and productive they will be.

The research literature on socialization is quite mature, although the topic of organizational culture is often not an explicit focus of that research. There is ample literature on the stages employees go through to transition from outsiders to full members (Ashforth, Sluss, & Harrison, 2007), the tactics used by organizations for socialization and the extent to which they are institutionalized versus individualized (Jones, 1986), and the proactive role newcomers play in their own socialization (Bindl & Parker, 2010). One additional topic in the socialization literature that is particularly important from an organizational culture perspective involves the sources of information used by newcomers during socialization. Although it is tempting to think of socialization as a formal process that is tightly controlled by management, which is only true for some sources of cultural information, other sources are more informal, potentially more helpful, and not necessarily aligned with the "official" company line (Cooper-Thomas & Anderson, 2006).

Organizational Culture and Organizational Effectiveness

Part of the interest in understanding culture development and maintenance is to provide the underpinnings to the link between organizational culture and organizational effectiveness. In fact, much of the energy around the topic of organizational culture in the early 1980s was because practitioners saw culture change as a way to improve their organization's performance, and to understand foci for change one had to understand how the organization became what it was. Over time, some empirical evidence has accumulated demonstrating that a more positive culture is significantly linked with a variety of measures of organizational effectiveness (see reviews by Hartnell, Ou, & Kinicki, 2011; Sackmann, 2011; Wilderom, Glunk, & Mazlowski, 2000). Although the idea that organizational culture is linked to organizational performance is not controversial in and of itself, some have questioned whether research can demonstrate such a complex relationship without reducing it to oversimplified terms (e.g., Pettigrew, 1990; Siehl & Martin, 1990). In our view, research on the relationship between culture and organizational performance would benefit from models that are more complex. Thus, it would be more theoretically interesting and practically useful to better understand how and why specific aspects of culture and/or specific types of culture are related to specific outcomes, along the lines of the competing values framework (CVF; Hartnell et al., 2011), for example.

One of the clear challenges to demonstrating a direct relationship between culture and organizational performance is that cultures under investigation may not be best captured by a general overall culture representing, in Martin's (2002) terminology, the integrated view of culture. When organizations have strong subcultures, in line with Martin's (2002) differentiation perspective, then the direct relationship between "the" organizational culture and performance may not exist. There is no doubt that subcultures exist in most organizations, but the point of contention is whether such subcultures should be the focus of investigation versus those cultural issues that are shared across the entire organization. Unfortunately, there are no easy answers, and the reality is that each organization varies in the extent to which it is defined by an overall culture versus subcultures, and even then, there may be variability depending on the organizational performance issue of interest (e.g., employee turnover rates for the organization as a whole vs. new pharmaceuticals emerging from research and development).

Tightly coupled with the idea of subcultures is the idea of culture strength, in that organizations with strong subcultures are less likely to have a strong overall culture. The most common way that culture strength is conceptualized is in terms of agreement, although culture strength has also been conceptualized in terms of how strongly or deeply members identify with the values and beliefs in the culture, or how aligned the various elements of the culture are with each other (Louis, 1985; Saffold, 1988). The early literature on culture strength presumed that stronger cultures were more effective perhaps because qualitative studies of culture associated strong cultures with more positive outcomes. Although in general it may be better to have a strong culture than a weak culture, the presence of a strong culture does not mean that the particular culture is the best fit for success in the environment (Kotter & Heskett, 1992; Sørensen, 2002). In fact, strength may be a barrier to change (Sathe, 1985). One exception is an adaptive culture in which the core values are risk-taking, flexibility, and innovation, and the general belief is that the organization must constantly be changing and improving (Kotter & Heskett, 1992). A strong culture of this sort should make the organization better able to adapt to the challenges it confronts and change as needed.

Organizational Culture Change

In the organizational culture literature, a key question is whether culture changes, and if so, whether that change can be managed. Most of the literature on organizational culture emphasizes its stability (Ott, 1989; Schein, 2010); the fact that the culture persists despite changes in the environment or to the people within it is one of the defining elements of culture. At the same time, cultures do change, but the issue is whether leaders can change culture in purposeful ways to be more in alignment with what they desire. The opinions on this issue are quite varied. Some have argued that leaders can have little to no effect on culture (Alvesson & Berg, 1992; Martin & Siehl, 1983), whereas others have implied that culture can rather easily be manipulated by management (e.g., Tichy, 1982; Turnstall, 1983). In our view, the question of whether culture can change is best viewed from a contingency perspective, such that there are times when leadership has the opportunity to have a strong influence on organizational culture, and other times when such efforts are unlikely to have tangible effects. For example, an important contingency is the organization's stage in its life cycle, with change being more likely and thus possible earlier in the life cycle and generally more difficult once the organization has matured (Burke, 2011; Schein, 2010).

Whatever the case may be, one thing is clear—culture change is not an easy or straightforward enterprise. Leaders should be clear on the numerous other competing influences on the culture (e.g., national culture, industry), be aware of when the circumstances are right for change (e.g., when there is a sense among employees that change is necessary for the organization to survive), and be focused on the specific outcomes they wish to achieve so that all can observe the connections between the changes attempted and the end goals. Perhaps most notably, and as emphasized by Schein (2010), leaders should be very targeted in their attempts to change culture. The initial focus should be on the issue that is being addressed, the problem that needs to be fixed, and the goal of the effort that is desired. Then leaders must ensure that they understand the implications of the organization's existing culture for their change efforts, including which aspects of the culture may be leveraged to support the change effort, which features of the culture are important to retain, and which may be obstacles for the change process.

INTEGRATING ORGANIZATIONAL CLIMATE AND CULTURE

A goal of this book and some of our other writing on climate and culture (Schneider, Ehrhart, & Macey, 2011b, 2013) has been to set the stage for and introduce ways of integrating across two constructs that have emerged from such different academic disciplines. The relationship between organizational climate and culture is not straightforward; although the two concepts are both focused on the work environment that employees experience in their organizations, and there is some overlap in the content that is addressed by the two constructs, there are also clear, and sometimes deep, differences. Contributing to the complexity in understanding the relationship between climate and culture is the variability in how the constructs are conceptualized and studied in their essentially separate literatures. Nevertheless, we have attempted to clarify and encourage stronger relationships between the two in the hope that each literature can profit from the strengths of the other so that there will be more integration of the two constructs in both research and practice.

Common Ground

The commonalities between climate and culture begin with how both constructs take a macro perspective in attempting to understand the cumulative effect of organizational functioning on employees, including both local level and higher-level effects on how people behave in their organizations. There is also an emphasis on the shared experiences of employees, whether across the entire organization or some smaller work unit (climate) or subculture (culture) of it. Both constructs emphasize the meaning that is created by various artifacts (in culture research) or policies, practices, and procedures (in climate research); in other words, it is not just what happens in the organization that matters, but how employees make sense of those events and react to them that is critical. Both literatures emphasize the role of leaders in creating and/or changing the climate or culture. In addition, both literatures address the concept of strength and acknowledge that there may not be complete agreement about climate/culture, nor may the elements within the climate/culture always align with each other. Finally, the idea that climate/culture has important consequences for organizational effectiveness is critical to theory and practice in both areas.

Different Ground

There are critical differences between the two literatures as well. Organizational climate developed in a psychological tradition that has tended to emphasize quantitative methods; organizational culture has anthropological roots and has traditionally emphasized qualitative methods. The scope of organizational culture is vast, and some would argue that there is little that would not be considered cultural in organizational life; the scope of organizational climate has evolved to be narrower, especially within the focused climate literature. Organizational culture includes deep layers that capture taken-for-granted assumptions employees make about their work; organizational climate focuses on what is in employee's conscious awareness as they experience their work environments. Because of its depth and breadth, culture is very difficult to change; although climate is not easy to change, it is more malleable than culture. Finally, the climate literature has developed the idea that the climate can have a specific focus, whether it is strategic outcomes or internal processes; organizational culture researchers have generally not been inclined to investigate what aspects or foci of culture are most pertinent to achieve particular strategic outcomes.

Learning and Integrated Grounds

Lessons to be learned. Building on these differences and looking forward to the future of both topics, there are a number of lessons that each literature could learn from the other. By examining how culture has been studied and written about, climate researchers might be more likely to focus on how climate develops and changes over time, to understand the possible foundations of climate in the history of the organization as it developed, to take into account a broader variety of variables that act as a source of climate information for employees, to investigate how climate gets passed on to new employees through on-boarding and formal job training, to seek a better understanding of how the external environment influences climate, to integrate qualitative methods into their research designs, and to inject more of the passion and richness that employees experience as part of climate.

For culture researchers seeking to learn from the progress that has been made in the climate literature, more emphasis on understanding how culture is manifested in organizational performance would be beneficial; the development of a more strategic outcome focus would likely improve validity for culture assessments; the introduction of more complexity (e.g., mediators and moderators) for how culture relates to effectiveness would be realistic; utilizing statistical methods for understanding agreement/strength and subcultures in organizations would be methodologically useful; and attempts to better address the concerns of managers, particularly by aligning with literatures on leader emergence and effectiveness, would prove beneficial in increasing the relevancy, acceptance, and effect of work on organizational culture to practitioners.

Integrated research efforts. In our opinion, the progress along the lines of integration has been surprisingly limited despite the rich history of the two constructs. Nevertheless, three recent frameworks may help push the fields forward toward more integration. The first is our own "climcult" framework (Schneider et al., 2011b), in which we emphasize how culture can both provide a foundation for strategic climates and create an environment that improves the attraction, socialization, and retention of key talent. Foundational to the climcult model is the idea that climate and culture are reciprocally related and thus build on each other, and yet seem to have relatively independent effects on unique aspects of organizational effectiveness. That is, culture seems to be reflected more often in well-being and commitment and OCB and turnover, while climate is reflected in more specific strategic goal accomplishments. A second and conceptually related framework is that of Ostroff, Kinicki, and Muhammad (2012). In their framework, culture is objectively manifested in the policies, practices, and procedures that form the foundation for climate, and the culture and climate work together to influence employees' attitudes and behaviors, which then ultimately affect organizational performance. The third approach is from Zohar and Hofmann (2012). Their model is unique in characterizing climate as *enacted* values and priorities, which are then contrasted with the cultural *espoused* values to provide insight into the assumptions and core values that make up the deepest layers of culture.

These three integrated models provide a very useful starting point for a more complete understanding of what an integrated approach to culture and climate might yield. They inform us that the two constructs are unique but also intertwined in their effect on employees and outcomes. They generally show the deeper layers of culture as the foundation for strategic climates, while acknowledging the potential reciprocal relationship between the two. They shed light on a number of possible mechanisms to explain the effects of both culture and climate on organizational performance. And finally, they emphasize the importance of alignment among climate, the various layers of culture, leadership, and the actual policies and practices in organizations. By taking an integrative perspective and developing strategic climates that are aligned with the values and assumptions of the culture, it is our argument that organizations can provide a sustained competitive advantage that will be difficult for others to beat.

IMPLICATIONS FOR PRACTICE

Although our discussion of organizational climate and culture has implied a number of practical steps to be taken, we wanted to be explicit about some of them here. First, we review issues we raised concerning culture diagnosis in Chapter Seven and then summarize comments we made throughout the book on the usefulness of the climate and culture concepts to understanding organizations in practice.

Cultural Inquiry

A critical issue for practitioners is organizational change, but the first step toward organizational change is a diagnosis of the existing culture, or cultural inquiry. Some of the reasons for cultural inquiry involve specific events like: (1) a major production failure, a lawsuit, or even a merger; (2) a need for change in the strategic goals of the organization; and/or (3) management deciding it simply wants information about where it stands so that it can better leverage its culture for success. Cultural inquiry offers several options for assessment and the choice of the assessment approach has implications for the type and validity of information that is obtained. Thus, such issues as the dimensions of culture to be assessed, how the questions are asked and the scale that is used for responding, and the extent to which the items in a survey are descriptive versus evaluative will affect the interpretation of the data. In addition, decisions about who will participate in the inquiry will have an effect on data interpretation and the acceptance of the results. It follows that a key question is whether qualitative and/or quantitative approaches will be used; our view is that the ideal option is to mix qualitative and quantitative methods when conducting a cultural inquiry.

Existing qualitative approaches include Appreciative Inquiry (Hammond, 1996), Cooperative Inquiry (Heron & Reason, 2006), and Narrative Inquiry (Clandinin & Connelly, 2000), all of which involve working with employees individually or in groups to gather information on their experiences in the organization. The goal is rich inquiry with regard to not just what is wrong with the organization, but its strengths as well, and particularly on how those strengths can be built upon to achieve future goals. How such qualitative data are coded, and by whom, are important considerations, and this is especially true when such data are gathered from groups of respondents.

There are a number of existing options available for using quantitative methods in a cultural inquiry. Some of these include the Organizational Culture Assessment Instrument (OCAI; Quinn & Cameron, 2011), the Denison Organizational Culture Survey (DOCS; Denison & Neale, 2000), the Organizational Culture Inventory® (OCI; Cooke & Szumal, 1993), and the Organization Culture Profile (OCP; O'Reilly, Chatman, & Caldwell, 1991). There are also climate-based alternatives, which can be particularly useful for developing customized alternatives focused on the organization's specific policies, practices, and procedures that are in place vis-à-vis strategic priorities; see the independent review panel's report on the explosion at one of BP's Texas refineries for an example (Baker, 2007).

Issues that need to be considered with regard to the choice of a survey include the extent to which an instrument focuses on a strategic goal or target of interest, the processes or styles that typify an organization, and the values that employees in an organization hold (especially compared to the values management espouses). A focus on culture dimensions (like in the DOCS or the OCP) is useful for identifying specific issues that may be targeted in organizational change efforts, whereas a focus on typologies (as in the OCAI) highlights how the interdependent parts of the organization work together to create a whole (and may be more in line with how executives talk and think about their organizations).

The presentation of data is also an issue, with some consulting firms preferring percentiles against benchmark data, others providing percentages of respondents in terms of raw scores (percent agreeing at various scale points), and others using profiles of dimension scores. The point is that there are a variety of options for the ways in which data will be presented, and practitioners would do well to know that these options exist. Finally, one advantage of survey approaches is that they allow statistical analyses to be conducted to identify subcultures. Therefore, the inquirer may want to look for instruments that provide or readily allow for such an analysis.

Organization Change

There are additional practical implications for our discussion of climate and culture as an organization thinks about attempting to change. One critical issue is what to change, and particularly whether culture change should be attempted at all. The literature is replete with warnings about the difficulties of changing culture, leading some to recommend avoiding it if possible. For instance, Schein (2010) has argued that the focus should be on improving performance and solving particular problems, and that cultural inquiry is necessary to better understand what aspects of the culture can be leveraged and which ones may be barriers to meeting those goals. Actually trying to change the culture should be attempted only if necessary.

Another issue to consider is whether the climate or the culture should be the focus of a change effort. We would argue that a focus on the policies, practices, and procedures that are the basis for both process- and outcome-focused climates may be more fruitful. Of course, changing a practice here or there will not change the climate; a new climate can only be created by creating a system of aligned and reinforcing policies, practices, and procedures and maintaining it over time through what is rewarded, supported, and expected. Once progress has been made on that front, and it becomes apparent to employees that management is serious about a specific strategic imperative and the changes are beneficial for organizational performance, the old assumptions will begin to break down and be replaced by new assumptions, yielding culture change.

If this process sounds easy and straightforward, then we have been misleading, because it is anything but. Nevertheless, we hold that climate change and the culture change that follows are possible if leadership has carefully identified the processes that must be aligned to create the new climate, is consistent in its implementation of the new policies and procedures, and is willing to persevere through the pains of change that will inevitably occur.

ORGANIZATIONAL CLIMATE AND CULTURE: A RESEARCH AGENDA

We close the book with a listing of what we see as some of the most compelling areas for future research on organizational climate and culture separately, and on the integration of the two. We begin with what we see as some important and interesting areas for organizational climate:

- Research on multiple climates. Kuenzi and Schminke (2009) have been the strongest advocates of the simultaneous study of multiple climates. This may include studying molar climates and focused climates simultaneously, or examining multiple focused climates (such as process

climates as the foundation for strategic climates, or the interaction among multiple focused climates).
- Research on climate profiles. Although the application of profiles/typologies is common in the culture literature, they have generally not been applied to climate research (see Schulte, Ostroff, Shmulyian, & Kinicki, 2009, for an exception).
- Research on how climate (including level and strength) operates simultaneously across multiple levels of analysis. Zohar and Luria (2005) provided a wonderful example of how this can be done for safety climate.
- Research on the mediating mechanisms through which climate has its effects. Work along these lines has grown, but there is still much to be done.
- Research on the moderators of climate's outcomes. Some research has shown how the effects of climate may vary in different contexts, but more work is needed.
- Research clarifying when climate strength matters and when it does not. There are mixed findings for climate strength as a moderator of the effects of climate level and research is needed to better understand why this is the case.
- Research clarifying the role of leadership in creating an organization's climate. This should include how the relevant leadership behaviors may vary for molar versus focused climates, or across levels of analysis.
- Research on how leadership and climates simultaneously emerge in complex organizations. This issue is in line with the growing body of research on network dynamics and their effect on organizational effectiveness outcomes such as adaptability, creativity, and learning (Uhl-Bien, Marion, & McKelvey, 2007).
- Research on climate formation and development. We do not know much about the sources of climate nor about the factors that affect their development and change over time.
- Research on climate interventions. There is very little work on interventions specifically developed to change strategic organizational climates (for two exceptions, see Aarons, Ehrhart, & Dlugosz, 2012; and Zohar & Luria, 2003). Such interventions would give organizations very practical tools to help them build the climates necessary to achieve their strategic goals.
- Research that blends quantitative and qualitative methods. Climate research tends to be quantitative, but some issues could be clarified and richness added by complementing quantitative methods with qualitative approaches.
- Research on the effects of the external environment on organizational climate. Studies should address how such issues as national culture or industry have direct or moderating effects on climate.

Next, we turn to the topics that may be worth pursuing in future research in the area of organizational culture:

- Research on multiple sources of culture (e.g., the founder, industry, and national culture). Research could assess the relative effects of various sources and how the strength of those effects changes over time.
- Research on socialization at the organizational level. Although research on socialization has blossomed, most of it has focused on the individual

Summary and Conclusion

level of analysis; future research could address how differences in socialization processes across organizations are associated with aspects of organizational culture.
- Research on the mediators of culture's relationship with organizational performance. There are likely many mechanisms that explain how culture has its effects, but we do not know enough about what those are.
- Research on moderators of culture's effects on organizational performance. We need to know more about the conditions under which culture is likely to have its strongest and weakest effects.
- Research on the specific aspects of culture that are related to specific performance outcomes. Research should move beyond studying the general relationship between culture and outcomes and clarify which aspects of culture are most important for which aspects of performance (e.g., Hartnell et al., 2011, on the CVF).
- Research integrating the idea of an overall culture and subcultures. Organizations likely have some aspects of their culture that are shared across most employees and others that differ across subcultures; research should empirically investigate such multilevel differences.
- Research applying statistical techniques to demonstrate the presence of subcultures and assessing the cultural strength. It is not that such research does not exist, but it is not as common as it should be.
- Research on other types of culture strength besides agreement. Louis (1985) and Saffold (1988) have clarified some of these possibilities, but little research exists on them and particularly how they operate simultaneously.
- Research on different types of cultural alignment. The concept of alignment is critical to understanding organizational culture, but the various ways of thinking about it and its implications for performance have been underexplored in empirical research.
- Research on stability and change in culture. Research could address what aspects of culture are most likely to remain stable and which are most likely to change at different points in the organization's life cycle.
- Research blending qualitative and quantitative methods. Too often culture research only takes advantage of one or the other, thus missing insights that could be gained from including both.

Finally, we summarize a number of directions for future research that integrates aspects of both organizational climate and culture:

- Research on how organizational culture forms a foundation for organizational climate. Multiple models suggest that beliefs and values are important for climate, but little research exists on the topic.
- Research on the independent outcomes of culture and climate. Some outcomes may be best predicted by culture and others by climate; integrative research could tease those apart.
- Research on how cultural variables affect climate. Research could investigate such cultural topics as rites of passage, dress, or myths and stories within a climate framework.
- Research on socialization as it relates to climate. Socialization is typically under the domain of culture, but we need to know the possible variety of ways it applies to how employees learn about their organization's climate as well.

- Research on the strategic focus of culture. This could involve studying the aspects of culture related to specific strategic climates, which aspects of culture provide a foundation for what types of strategic climates, or simply how dimensions of culture predict specific strategic outcomes.
- Research on how climate change affects culture and vice versa. The processes are likely interconnected but distinct.

CONCLUSION

We have come a long way since the late 1930s when empirical research on the human aspects of the organizational environment was just beginning. Since then, researchers from both the organizational climate and organizational culture traditions have made unique contributions to our understanding of the complexities associated with organizations as human systems. In both climate and culture traditions there has been great excitement surrounding the pursuit of theory and data, especially when the methods and approaches have proven valuable to both the understanding and prediction of important group and organizational outcomes. By bringing these two traditions together, having them learn from each other, and integrating their insights, the future of both fields will be bright indeed, and the organizations that researchers and practitioners serve will figuratively and literally profit.

REFERENCES

Aarons, G.A., Ehrhart, M.G., & Dlugosz, L.R. (2012, April). Maximizing a strategic climate for the implementation of evidence-based practice. In M.G. Ehrhart (Chair), *Focused organizational climates: New directions and new possibilities*. Symposium conducted at the 27th annual conference of the Society for Industrial and Organizational Psychology, San Diego, CA.

Aarons G.A., & Sawitzky A.C. (2006a). Organizational climate partially mediates the effect of culture on work attitudes and staff turnover in mental health services. *Administration and Policy in Mental Health and Mental Health Services Research, 33*(3), 289–301.

Aarons G.A., & Sawitzky A.C. (2006b). Organizational culture and climate and mental health provider attitudes toward evidence-based practice. *Psychological Services, 3*(1), 61–72.

Abbey, A., & Dickson, J.W. (1983). R&D work climate and innovation in semiconductors. *Academy of Management Journal, 26,* 362–368.

Abrahamson, E. & Fombrun, C.J. (1994). Macrocultures: Determinants and consequences. *Academy of Management Review, 19*(4), 728–755.

Aldenderfer, M.S., & Blashfield, R.K. (1984). *Cluster analysis*. Beverly Hills, CA: Sage.

Aldrich, H.E., & Ruef, M. (2006). *Organizations evolving* (2nd ed.). Thousand Oaks, CA: Sage.

Allen, N.J., & Meyer, J.P. (1990). The measurement and antecedents of affective, continuance, and normative commitment to the organization. *Journal of Occupational Psychology, 63,* 1–18.

Alvesson, M. (1993). *Cultural perspectives on organizations*. Cambridge, England: Cambridge University Press.

Alvesson, M. (2002). *Understanding organizational culture*. London: Sage.

Alvesson, M. (2011). Organizational culture: Meaning, discourse, and identity. In N.M. Ashkanasy, C.P.M. Wilderom, & M.F. Peterson (Eds.), *Handbook of organizational culture and climate* (2nd ed., pp. 11–28). Thousand Oaks, CA: Sage.

Alvesson, M., & Berg, P.O. (1992). *Corporate culture and organizational symbolism*. New York: de Gruyter.

Alvesson, M. & Sveningsson, S. (2008). *Changing organizational culture: Cultural change work in progress*. New York: Routledge.

Anderson, N.R., & West, M.A. (1998). Measuring climate for work group innovation: Development and validation of the team climate inventory. *Journal of Organizational Behavior, 19,* 235–258.

Andrews, J.D.W. (1967). The achievement motive in two types of organizations. *Journal of Personality and Social Psychology, 6,* 163–168.
Angle, H.L., & Perry, J.L. (1986). Dual commitment and labor–management relationship climates. *Academy of Management Journal, 29*(1), 31–50.
Argyris, C. (1957). *Personality and organization.* New York: Harper & Bros.
Argyris, C. (1958). Some problems in conceptualizing organizational climate: A case study of a bank. *Administrative Science Quarterly, 2,* 501–520.
Ashford, S.J., & Black, J.S. (1996). Proactivity during organizational entry: The role of desire for control. *Journal of Applied Psychology, 81*(2), 199–214.
Ashforth, B.E. (1985). Climate formation: Issues and extensions. *Academy of Management Review, 10,* 834–847.
Ashforth, B.E., Sluss, D.M., & Harrison, S.H. (2007). Socialization in organizational contexts. In G.P. Hodgkinson & J.K. Ford (Eds.), *International review of industrial and organizational psychology* (Vol. 22, pp. 1–70). Sussex, England: Wiley.
Ashkanasy, N.M., Broadfoot, L.E., & Falkus, S. (2000). Questionnaire measures of organizational culture. In N.M. Ashkanasy, C.P.M. Wilderom, & M.F. Peterson (Eds.), *Handbook of organizational culture and climate* (pp. 131–146). Thousand Oaks, CA: Sage.
Ashkanasy N.M., Wilderom, C.P.M., & Peterson, M.F. (Eds.). (2000a). *Handbook of organizational culture and climate.* Thousand Oaks, CA: Sage
Ashkanasy N.M., Wilderom, C.P.M., & Peterson, M.F. (2000b). Introduction. In N.M. Ashkanasy, C.P.M. Wilderom, & M.F. Peterson (Eds.), *Handbook of organizational culture and climate* (pp. 1–18). Thousand Oaks, CA: Sage.
Ashkanasy, N.M., Wilderom, C.P.M., & Peterson, M.F. (Eds.). (2011). *Handbook of organizational culture and climate* (2nd ed.). Thousand Oaks, CA: Sage.
Baer, M., & Frese, M. (2003). Innovation is not enough: Climates for initiative and psychological safety, process innovations, and firm performance. *Journal of Organizational Behavior, 24,* 45–68.
Bajdo, L., & Dickson, M.W. (2001). Perceptions of organizational culture and women's advancement in organizations: A cross-cultural examination. *Sex Roles, 45,* 399–414.
Baker, J.A. (2007). *The report of the BP US refineries independent safety review panel.* New York: CCPS.
Balthazard, P.A., Cooke, R.A., & Potter, R.E. (2006). Dysfunctional culture, dysfunctional organization: Capturing the behavioral norms that form organizational culture and drive performance. *Journal of Managerial Psychology, 21,* 709–732.
Barley, S.R. (1991). Semiotics and the study of occupational and organizational culture. In P.J. Frost, L.F. Moore, M.R. Louis, C.C. Lundberg, & J. Martin (Eds.), *Reframing organizational culture* (pp. 39–54). Newbury Park, CA: Sage.
Barling, J., Loughlin, C., & Kelloway, E.K. (2002). Development and test of a model linking safety-specific transformational leadership and occupational safety. *Journal of Applied Psychology, 87,* 488–496.
Barnard, C.I. (1938). *The functions of the executive.* Cambridge, MA: Harvard University Press.
Barney, J.B. (1986). Organizational culture: Can it be a source of sustained competitive advantage? *Academy of Management Review, 11,* 656–665.

References

Barney, J.B. (1991). Firm resources and sustained competitive advantage. *Journal of Management, 17*, 99–120.

Barney, J.B., & Arikan A.M. (2001). The resource-based view: Origins and implications. In M.A. Hitt, R.E. Freeman, & J.S. Harrison (Eds.), *Handbook of strategic management* (pp. 124–188). Oxford, UK: Blackwell Publishers.

Bartunek, J.M., & Moch, M.K. (1991). Multiple constituencies and the quality of working life: Intervention at FoodCom. In P.J. Frost, L.F. Moore, M.R. Louis, C.C. Lundberg, & J. Martin (Eds.), *Reframing organizational culture* (pp. 104–114). Newbury Park, CA: Sage.

Bass B.M. (1960). *Leadership, psychology, and organizational behavior*. New York: Harper.

Bass, B.M. (1965). *Organizational psychology*. Boston, MA: Allyn & Bacon.

Bass, B.M., & Bass, R. (2008). *The Bass handbook of leadership* (4th ed.). New York: Free Press.

Bass, B.M., Waldman, D.A., Avolio, B.J., & Bebb, M. (1987). Transformational leadership and the falling dominoes effect. *Group & Organization Management, 12*(1), 73–87.

Bauer, T.N., Bodner, T., Erdogan, B., Truxillo, D.M., & Tucker, J.S. (2007). Newcomer adjustment during organizational socialization: A meta-analytic review of antecedents, otucomes, and methods. *Journal of Applied Psychology, 92*, 707–721.

Bell, N.E., & Staw, B.M. (1989). People as sculptors versus sculpture: The roles of personality and personal control on organizations. In M.B. Arthur, D.T. Hall, & B.S. Lawrence (Eds.), *Handbook of career theory* (pp. 232–251). Cambridge, UK: Cambridge University Press.

Benne, K.D., Bradford, L.P., & Lippitt, R. (1964). The laboratory method. In L.P. Bradford, J.R. Gibb, & K.D. Benne (Eds.), *T-group theory and laboratory method: Innovation in re-education* (pp. 15–44). New York: John Wiley & Sons.

Bennis, W.G., Benne, K.D., & Chin, R. (Eds.) (1961). *The planning of change: Readings in the applied behavioral sciences*. New York: Holt, Rinehart, and Winston.

Beres, M.E., & Portwood, J.D. (1979). Explaining cultural differences in the perceived role of work: An intranational cross-cultural study. In G.W. England, A.R. Negandhi, & B. Wilpert (Eds.), *Organizational functioning in a cross-cultural perspective* (pp. 139–173). Kent, OH: Kent State University Press.

Berson, Y., Oreg, S., & Dvir, T. (2008). CEO values, organizational culture and firm outcomes. *Journal of Organizational Behavior, 29*, 615–633.

Beus, J.M., Bergman, M.E., & Payne, S.C. (2010). The influence of organizational tenure on safety climate strength: A first look. *Accident Analysis and Prevention, 42*, 1431–1437.

Beus, J.M., Payne, S.C., Bergman, M.E., & Arthur, W. Jr. (2010). Safety climate and injuries: An examination of theoretical and empirical relationships. *Journal of Applied Psychology, 95*, 713–727.

Beyer, J.M., Hannah, D.R., & Milton, L.P. (2000). Ties that bind: Culture and attachment to organizations. In N.M. Ashkanasy, C.P.M. Wilderom, & M.F. Peterson (Eds.), *Handbook of organizational culture and climate* (pp. 323–338). Thousand Oaks, CA: Sage.

Bindl, U.K., & Parker, S.K. (2010). Proactive work behavior: Forward-thinking and change-oriented action in organizations. In S. Zedeck (Ed.), *APA handbook of industrial and organizational psychology* (Vol. 2, pp. 567–598). Washington, DC: American Psychological Association.

Blau, P.M. (1964). *Exchange and power in social life.* New York: John Wiley & Sons.

Bliese, P.D. (1998). Group size, ICC values, and group level correlations: A simulation. *Organizational Research Methods, 1,* 355–373.

Bliese, P.D. (2000). Within-group agreement, non-independence, and reliability: Implications for data aggregation and analyses. In K.J. Klein & S.W.J. Kozlowski (Eds.), *Multilevel theory, research and methods in organizations: Foundations, extensions, and new directions* (pp. 349–381). San Francisco, CA: Jossey-Bass.

Bliese, P.D. (2006). Social climates: Drivers of soldier well-being and resilience. In A.B. Adler, C.A. Castro, & T.W. Britt (Eds.), *Military life: The psychology of serving in peace and combat: Vol. 2. Operational stressors* (pp. 213–234). Westport, CT: Praeger Security International.

Bliese, P.D. & Halverson, R.R. (1998). Group consensus and psychological well-being: A large field study. *Journal of Applied Social Psychology, 28,* 563–580.

Blumer, H. (1969). *Symbolic interactionism: Perspective and method.* Englewood Cliffs, NJ: Prentice-Hall.

Boglarsky, C.A., & Kwantes, C.T. (2004). *Ideal and actual culture: How different is too different?* Presented at the 65th Annual Conference of the Canadian Psychological Association, St. John's, Newfoundland, Canada.

Boisnier, A., & Chatman, J. (2003). Cultures and subcultures in dynamic organizations. In E. Mannix & R. Petersen (Eds.), *The dynamic organization* (pp. 87–114). Mahwah, NJ: Lawrence Erlbaum.

Bowen, D.E. & Ostroff, C. (2004). Understanding HRM–firm performance linkages: The role of the "strength" of the HRM system. *Academy of Management Review, 29,* 203–221.

Bradford, L.P. (1964). Membership and the learning process. In L.P. Bradford, J.R. Gibb, & K.D. Benne (Eds.), *T-group theory and laboratory method: Innovation in re-education* (pp. 190–215). New York: John Wiley & Sons.

Bradford, L.P., Gibb, J.R., & Benne, K.D. (1964a). *T-group theory and laboratory method: Innovation in re-education* (pp. 190–215). New York: John Wiley & Sons.

Bradford, L.P., Gibb, J.R., & Benne, K.D. (1964b). Two educational innovations. In L.P. Bradford, J.R. Gibb, & K.D. Benne (Eds.), *T-group theory and laboratory method: Innovation in re-education* (pp. 1–14). New York: John Wiley & Sons.

Brannen, M.Y., & Kleinberg, J. (2000). Images of Japanese management and the development of organizational culture theory. In N.M. Ashkanasy, C.P.M. Wilderom, & M.F. Peterson, (Eds.), *Handbook of organizational culture and climate* (pp. 387–400). Thousand Oaks, CA: Sage.

Brodbeck, F.C., Hanges, P.J., Dickson, M.W., Gupta, V., & Dorfman, P.W. (2004). Societal culture and industrial sector influences on organizational culture. In R.J. House, P.J. Hanges, M. Javidan, P.W. Dorfman, & V. Gupta (Eds.), *Culture, leadership, and organizations: The GLOBE study of 62 societies* (pp. 654–668). Thousand Oaks, CA: Sage.

References

Brown, R.D., & Hauenstein, N.M.A. (2005). Interrater agreement reconsidered: An alternative to the r_{WG} indices. *Organizational Research Methods, 8*, 165–184.

Brown, R.L., & Holmes, H. (1986). The use of a factor-analytic procedure for assessing the validity of an employee safety climate model. *Accident Analysis & Prevention, 18*(6), 455–470.

Buchele, R.B. (1955). Company character and the effectiveness of personnel management. *Personnel, 31*, 289–302.

Burke, M.J., Borucki, C., & Hurley, A. (1992). Reconceptualizing psychological climate in a retail service environment: A multiple stakeholder perspective. *Journal of Applied Psychology, 77*, 717–729.

Burke, M.J., Chan-Serafin, S., Salvador, R., Smith, A., & Sarpy, S.A. (2008). The role of national culture and organizational climate in safety training effectiveness. *European Journal of Work and Organizational Psychology, 17*, 133–152.

Burke, M.J., Finkelstein, L.M., & Dusig, M.S. (1999). On average deviation indices for estimating interrater agreement. *Organizational Research Methods, 2*, 49–68.

Burke, R.J. & Descza, E. (1982). Preferred organizational climates of type A individuals. *Journal of Vocational Behavior, 21*(1), 50–59.

Burke, W.W. (2011). *Organization change: Theory and practice* (3rd ed.). Thousand Oaks, CA: Sage.

Burke, W.W., & Litwin, G.H. (1992). A causal model of organizational performance and change. *Journal of Management, 18*(3), 523–545.

Cable, D.M., Aiman-Smith, L., Mulvey, P.W., & Edwards, J.R. (2000). The sources and accuracy of job applicant's beliefs about organizational culture. *Academy of Management Journal, 43*(6), 1076–1085.

Cameron, K.S. (2008). A process for changing organizational culture. In T.G. Cummings (Ed.), *Handbook of organizational development* (pp. 429–446). Thousand Oaks, CA: Sage.

Cameron, K.S., & Ettington, D.R. (1988). The conceptual foundations of organizational culture. In J.C. Smart (Ed.), *Higher education: Handbook of theory and research* (Vol. 4, pp. 356–396). New York: Agathon.

Cameron, K.S., & Freeman, S.J. (1991). Cultural congruence strength and type: Relationships to effectiveness. In R.W. Woodman & W.A. Pasmore (Eds.), *Research in organizational change and development* (Vol. 5, pp. 23–58). Greenwich, CT: JAI Press.

Cameron, K.S., & Quinn, R.E. (1999). Diagnosing and changing organizational culture: Based on the competing values framework. Reading, MA: Addison-Wesley.

Cameron, K.S., & Quinn, R.E. (2011). *Diagnosing and changing organizational culture: Based on the competing values framework* (3rd ed.). San Francisco, CA: Wiley.

Campbell, J.P., Dunnette, M.D., Lawler, E.E., III, & Weick, K.E. (1970). *Managerial behavior, performance, and effectiveness.* New York: McGraw-Hill.

Carr, J.Z., Schmidt, A.M., Ford, J.K., & DeShon, R.P. (2003). Climate perceptions matter: A meta-analytic path analysis relating molar climate, cognitive and affective states and individual level work outcomes. *Journal of Applied Psychology, 88*, 605–619.

Cartwright, D. & Zander, A. (Eds.) (1960). *Group dynamics: Research and theory* (2nd ed.). New York: Harper & Row.

Cawsey, T. (1973, April). *The interaction of motivation and environment in the prediction of performance potential and satisfaction in the life insurance industry in Canada*. Paper presented at the Sixteenth Annual Meeting of the Midwest Academy of Management, Chicago, IL.

Chan, D. (1998). Functional relations among constructs in the same content domain at different levels of analysis: A typology of composition models. *Journal of Applied Psychology, 83*, 234–246.

Chan, L.L., Shaffer, M.A., & Snape, E. (2004). In search of sustained competitive advantage: the impact of organizational culture, competitive strategy and human resource management practices on firm performance. *The International Journal of Human Resource Management, 15*(1), 17–35.

Chao, G.T., O'Leary-Kelly, A.M., Wolf, S., Klein, H.J., & Gardner, P.D. (1994). Organizational socialization: Its content and consequences. *Journal of Applied Psychology, 79*(5), 730–743.

Chatman, J. (1991). Matching people and organizations: Selection and socialization in public accounting firms. *Administrative Science Quarterly, 36*, 459–484.

Chatman, J.A., & Jehn, K.A. (1994). Assessing the relationship between industry characteristics and organizational culture: How different can you be? *Academy of Management Journal, 37*(3), 522–553.

Chen, G., & Bliese, P.D. (2002). The role of different levels of leadership in predicting self- and collective efficacy: Evidence for discontinuity. *Journal of Applied Psychology, 87*(3), 549–556.

Christian, M.S., Bradley, J.C., Wallace, J.C., & Burke, M.J. (2009). Workplace safety: A meta-analysis of the roles of person and situation factors. *Journal of Applied Psychology, 94*, 1103–1127.

Christie, R., & Merton, R.K. (1958). *Procedures for the sociological study of the values climate of medical schools.* New York: Columbia University, Bureau of Applied Social Research.

Chuang, C-H., & Liao, H. (2010). Strategic human resource management in service context: Taking care of business by taking care of employees and customers. *Personnel Psychology, 63*, 153–196.

Clandinin, D.J., & Connelly, F.M. (2000). *Narrative inquiry: Experience and story in qualitative research*. San Francisco: Jossey-Bass.

Clark, B. (1970). *The distinctive college: Antioch, Reed, and Swathmore*. Chicago: Aldine.

Clark, B. (1972). The organizational saga in higher education. *Administrative Science Quarterly, 17*, 178–184.

Cole, M.S., & Bedeian, A.G. (2007). Leadership consensus as a cross-level contextual moderator of the emotional exhaustion-work commitment relationship. *Leadership Quarterly, 18*(5), 447–462.

Colquitt, J.A., Noe, R.A., & Jackson, C.L. (2002). Justice in teams: Antecedents and consequences of procedural justice climate. *Personnel Psychology, 58*, 83–109.

Colquitt, J.A., Zapata-Phelan, C.P., & Roberson, Q.M. (2005). Justice in teams: A review of fairness effects in collective contexts. In J.J. Martocchio (Ed.), *Research in personnel and human resources management* (Vol. 24, pp. 53–94). Oxford, UK: Elsevier.

Cooil, B., Aksoy, L., Keiningham, T.L., & Marytott, K.M. (2009). The relationship of employee perceptions of organizational climate to business-unit outcomes: An MLPS approach. *Journal of Service Research, 11*, 277–294.

Cooke, R.A., & Rousseau, D.M. (1988). Behavioural norms and expectations: a quantitative approach to the assessment of organisational culture. *Group and Organization Studies, 13*, 245–273.

Cooke, R.A., & Szumal, J.L. (1993). Measuring normative beliefs and shared behavioral expectations in organizations: The reliability and validity of the organizational culture inventory. *Psychological Reports, 72*, 1299–1330.

Cooke, R.A., & Szumal, J.L. (2000). Using the organizational culture inventory to understand the operating culture of organizations. In N.M. Ashkanasy, C.P.M. Wilderom, & M.F. Peterson (Eds.), *Handbook of organizational culture and climate* (pp. 147–162). Thousand Oaks, CA: Sage.

Cooper-Thomas, H.D., & Anderson, N. (2006). Organizational socialization: A new theoretical model and recommendations for future research and HRM practices in organizations. *Journal of Managerial Psychology, 21*(5), 492–516.

Cox, T.H., Jr. (1993). *Cultural diversity in organizations: Theory, research, and practice*. San Francisco, CA: Berrett-Koehler.

Crant, J.M. (2000). Proactive behavior in organizations. *Journal of Management, 26*(3), 435–462.

Cropanzano, R., & Mitchell, M.S. (2005). Social exchange theory: An interdisciplinary review. *Journal of Management, 31*, 874–900.

Dansereau, F., & Alutto, J.A. (1990). Level-of-analysis issues in climate and culture research. In B. Schneider (Ed.), *Organizational climate and culture* (pp. 193–236). San Francisco, CA: Jossey-Bass.

Dansereau, F., Alutto, J., & Yammarino, F. (1984). *Theory testing in organizational behavior: The varient approach*. Englewood Cliffs, NJ: Prentice-Hall.

Dastmalchian, A. (2008). Industrial relations climate. In P. Blyton, N. Bacon, J. Fiorito, & E. Heery (Eds.), *Sage handbook of industrial relations* (pp. 548–571). Thousand Oaks, CA: Sage.

Davey, K.M., & Symon, G. (2001). Recent approaches to the qualitative analysis of organizational culture. In C.L. Cooper, S. Cartwright, & P.C. Earley (Eds.), *The international handbook of organizational culture and climate* (pp. 123–142). New York: Wiley.

Dawson, J.F., González-Romá, V., Davis, A., & West, M.A. (2008). Organizational climate and climate strength in UK hospitals. *European Journal of Work and Organizational Psychology, 17*, 89–111.

Deal, T.E., & Kennedy, A.A. (1982). *Corporate cultures: The rites and rituals of corporate life*. Reading, MA: Addison-Wesley.

Dean, A. (2004). Links between organizational and customer variables in service delivery: Evidence, contradictions, and challenges. *International Journal of Service Industry Management, 15*, 332–350.

Dedobbeleer, N., & Béland, F. (1991). A safety climate measure for construction sites. *Journal of Safety Research, 22*(2), 97–103.

Denison, D.R. (1990). *Corporate culture and organizational effectiveness*. New York: Wiley.

Denison, D.R. (1996). What *is* the difference between organizational culture and organizational climate? A native's point of view on a decade of paradigm wars. *Academy of Management Review, 21*, 619–654.

Denison, D.R. (2001). Organizational culture: Can it be a key lever for driving organizational change? In C.L. Cooper, S. Cartwright, & P.C. Earley (Eds.),

The international handbook of organizational culture and climate (pp. 347–372). New York: Wiley.

Denison, D. R., Haaland, S., & Goelzer, P. (2003). Corporate culture and organizational effectiveness: Is there a similar pattern around the world? *Advances in Global Leadership, 3,* 205–227.

Denison, D. R., & Mishra, A. K. (1995). Toward a theory of organizational culture and effectiveness. *Organization Science, 6,* 204–223.

Denison, D. R., & Neale, W. (2000). *Denison organizational culture survey.* Ann Arbor, MI: Denison Consulting.

Denison, D. R., Nieminen, L., & Kotrba, L. (2012). Diagnosing organizational cultures: A conceptual and empirical review of culture effectiveness surveys. *European Journal of Work and Organizational Psychology.* DOI: 10.1080/1359432X.2012.713173.

Deutsch & Shea, Inc. (1958). Company Climate and Creativity. New York, NY.

Dickson, M. W., Aditya, R. N., & Chhokar, J. S. (2000). Definition and interpretation in cross-cultural organizational culture research: Some pointers from the GLOBE research program. In N. M. Ashkanasy, C. P. M. Wilderom, & M. F. Peterson (Eds.), *Handbook of organizational culture and climate* (pp. 447–464). Thousand Oaks, CA: Sage.

Dickson, M. W., Resick, C. J., & Hanges, P. J. (2006). When organizational climate is unambiguous, it is also strong. *Journal of Applied Psychology, 91*(2), 351–364.

Dieterly, D., & Schneider, B. (1974). The effect of organizational environment on perceived power and climate: A laboratory study. *Organizational Behavior and Human Performance, 11,* 316–337.

Dietz, J., Pugh, S. D., & Wiley, J. W. (2004). Service climate effects on customer attitudes: An examination of boundary conditions. *Academy of Management Journal, 47,* 81–92.

Downey, H. K., Hellriegel, D., Phelps, M., & Slocum, J. W. (1974). Organizational climate and job satisfaction: A comparative analysis. *Journal of Business Research, 2,* 233–248.

Downey, H. K., Hellriegel, D., & Slocum, J. W. (1975). Congruence between individual needs, organizational climate, job satisfaction and performance. *Academy of Management Journal, 18*(1), 149–155.

Dragoni, L. (2005). Understanding the emergence of state goal orientation in organizational work groups: The role of leadership and multi-level climate perceptions. *Journal of Applied Psychology, 90,* 1084–1095.

Drexler, J. A. (1977). Organizational climate: Its homogeneity within organizations. *Journal of Applied Psychology, 62,* 38–42.

Duhigg, C. (2012). *The power of habits: Why we do what we do in life and business.* New York: Random House.

Dunnette, M. D. (1962). Personnel management. *Annual Review of Psychology, 13,* 285–314.

Dunnette, M. D. & Campbell, J. P. (1966). Identification and enhancement of managerial effectiveness: Part VI. Conclusions, implications and research recommendations. Greensboro, NC: Richardson Foundation Survey Report.

Duxbury, L. & Grover, L. (2011). Exploring the link between organizational culture and work-family conflict. In N. M. Ashkanasy, C. P. M. Wilderom, &

M. F. Peterson (Eds.), *Handbook of organizational culture and climate* (2nd ed., pp. 271–290). Thousand Oaks, CA: Sage.

Dyer, W. G. (1985). The cycle of cultural evolution in organizations. In R. H. Kilmann, M. J. Saxton, & R. Serpa (Eds.), *Gaining control of the corporate culture* (pp. 200–209). San Francisco: Jossey-Bass.

Eden, D. (2003). Self-fulfilling prophecies in organizations. In J. Greenberg (Ed.), *Organizational behavior: The state of the science* (2nd ed., pp. 91–122). Mahwah, NJ: Erlbaum.

Ehrhart, K. H., Witt, L. A., Schneider, B., & Perry, S. J. (2011). Service employees give as they get: Internal service as a moderator of the service climate–service outcomes link. *Journal of Applied Psychology, 96*(2), 423–431.

Ehrhart, M. G. (2004). Leadership and procedural justice climate as antecedents of unit-level organizational citizenship behavior. *Personnel Psychology, 57*, 61–94.

Ehrhart, M. G., & Raver, J. L. (in press). The effects of organizational climate and culture on productive and counterproductive behavior. In B. Schneider & K. Barbera (Eds.), *Oxford handbook of organizational climate and culture: Antecedents, consequences, and practice*. New York: Oxford University Press.

Eisenberger, R., Huntington, R., Hutchison, S., & Sowa, D. (1986). Perceived organizational support. *Journal of Applied Psychology, 71*, 500–507.

Erdogan, B., & Bauer, T. N. (2010). Differentiated leader–member exchanges: The buffering role of justice climate. *Journal of Applied Psychology, 95*(6), 1104–1120.

Etzioni, A. (1961). *A comparative analysis of complex organizations*. New York: Free Press.

Evan, W. M. (1963). Indices of the hierarchical structure of industrial organizations. *Management Science, 9*, 468–477.

Evan, W. M. (1968). A system model of organizational climate. In R. Tagiuri & G. H. Litwin (Eds.), *Organizational climate: Explorations of a concept* (pp. 110–124). Boston, MA: Harvard University.

Everitt, B. S., Landau, S., Leese, M., & Stahl, D. (2011). *Cluster analysis* (5th ed.). Chichester, UK: John Wiley & Sons.

Feldman, D. C. (1981). The multiple socialization of organization members. *Academy of Management Review, 6*, 309–318.

Feldman, M. S. (1991). The meanings of ambiguity: Learning from stories and metaphors. In P. J. Frost, L. F. Moore, M. R. Louis, C. C. Lundberg, & J. Martin (Eds.), *Reframing organizational culture* (pp. 145–156). Thousand Oaks, CA: Sage.

Fey, C., & Denison, D. R. (2003). Organizational culture and effectiveness: Can an American theory be applied in Russia? *Organization Science, 14*, 686–706.

Fiedler, F. E. (1962). Leader attitudes, group climate, and group creativity. *The Journal of Abnormal and Social Psychology, 65*(5), 308–318.

Field, G., & Abelson, M. (1982). Climate: A reconceptualization and proposed model. *Human Relations, 35*, 181–201.

Fiol, M., Hatch, M. J., & Golden-Biddle, K. (1998). Organizational culture and identity: What's the difference anyway? In D. Whetten & P. Godfrey, (Eds.),

Identity in organizations: Developing theory through conversations (pp. 56–59). Thousand Oaks, CA: Sage.
Fisher, C.D. (1986). Organizational socialization: An integrative review. In K. Rowland & G. Ferris (Eds.), *Research in personnel and human resource management* (Vol. 4, pp. 101–145). Greenwich, CT: JAI Press.
Fitzgerald, L.F., Drasgow, F., Hulin, C.L., Gelfand, M.J., & Magley, V.J. (1997). Antecedents and consequences of sexual harassment in organizations: A test of an integrated model. *Journal of Applied Psychology, 82*(4), 578–589.
Flamholtz, E.G., & Randle, Y. (2011). *Corporate culture: The ultimate strategic asset*. Palo Alto, CA: Stanford University Press.
Flanagan, J.C. (1954). The critical incident technique. *Psychological Bulletin, 51*, 327–358.
Fleishman, E.A. (1953). Leadership climate, human relations training and supervisory behavior. *Personnel Psychology, 6*, 205–222.
Flynn, F.J., & Chatman, J.A. (2001). Strong cultures and innovation: Oxymoron or opportunity? In C.L. Cooper, S. Cartwright, & P.C. Earley (Eds.), *The international handbook of organizational culture and climate* (pp. 263–287). New York: Wiley.
Forehand, G.A. (1963). Assessment of innovative behavior. Partial criteria for the assessment of executive performance. *Journal of Applied Psychology, 47*, 206–213.
Forehand, G.A. (1968). On the interaction of persons and organizations. In R. Tagiuri & G.H. Litwin (Eds.), *Organizational climate: Explorations of a concept* (pp. 65–82). Boston, MA: Harvard University.
Forehand, G.A., & Gilmer, B. v. H. (1964). Environmental variation in studies of organizational behavior. *Psychological Bulletin, 62*, 361–382.
Frederiksen, N.O. (1966). Some effects of organizational climates on administrative performance. *Research memorandum RM-66-21*. Washington, DC: Educational Testing Services.
Frederiksen, N., Jensen, O., & Beaton, A.E. (1972). *Prediction of organizational behavior*. New York: Pergamon.
Friedlander, F., & Greenberg, S. (1971). Effect of job attitudes, training, and organizational climate on performance of the hardcore unemployed. *Journal of Applied Psychology, 55*, 287–295.
Friedlander, F., & Margulies, N. (1969). Multiple impacts of organizational climate and individual value systems upon job satisfaction, *Personnel Psychology, 22*, 171–183.
Frost, P.J., Moore, L.F., Louis, M.R., Lundberg, C.C., & Martin, J. (1985a). An allegorical view of organizational culture. In P.J. Frost, L.F. Moore, M.R. Louis, C.C. Lundberg, & J. Martin (Eds.), *Organizational culture* (pp. 13–25). Beverly Hills, CA: Sage.
Frost, P.J., Moore, L.F., Louis, M.R., Lundberg, C.C., & Martin, J. (Eds.). (1985b). *Organizational culture*. Beverly Hills, CA: Sage.
Frost, P.J., Moore, L.F., Louis, M.R., Lundberg, C.C., & Martin, J. (Eds.) (1991). *Reframing organizational culture*. Newbury Park, CA: Sage.
Gardner, B. (1945). *Human relations in industry*. Homewood, IL: Irwin.
Geertz, C. (1973). *The interpretation of cultures*. New York: Basic Books.
Gelfand, M.J., Nishii, L.H., & Raver, J.L. (2006). On the nature and importance of cultural tightness-looseness. *Journal of Applied Psychology, 91*(6), 1225–1244.

Gellerman, S.W. (1959). The company personality. *Management Review, 48,* 60–76.

Gellerman, S.W. (1960). *People, problems, and profits: The uses of psychology in management.* New York: McGraw-Hill.

George, J.M., & James, L.R. (1993). Personality, affect, and behavior in groups revisited: Comment on aggregation, levels of analysis, and a recent application of within and between analysis. *Journal of Applied Psychology, 78,* 798–804.

Georgopoulos, B.S. (1965). Normative structure variables and organizational behavior. *Human Relations, 18,* 115–170.

Gerhart, B. (2009). How much does national culture constrain organizational culture? *Management and Organization Review, 5*(2), 241–259.

Gerstner, Jr., L.V. (2002). *Who says elephants can't dance? Leading a great enterprise through dramatic change.* New York: HarperCollins.

Gettman, H.J., & Gelfand, M.J. (2007). When the customer shouldn't be king: Antecedents and consequences of sexual harassment by clients and customers. *Journal of Applied Psychology, 92,* 757–770.

Ghiselli, E.E. (1939). All or none versus graded response questionnaires. *Journal of Applied Psychology, 23,* 405–413.

Gibb, J.R. (1964). Climate for trust formation. In L.P. Bradford, J.R. Gibb, & K.D. Benne (Eds.), *T-group theory and laboratory method: Innovation in reeducation* (pp. 279–309). New York: John Wiley & Sons.

Gillespie, M.A., Denison, D.R., Haaland, S., Smerek, R., & Neale, W.S. (2008). Linking organizational culture and customer satisfaction: Results from two companies in different industries. *European Journal of Work and Organizational Psychology, 17,* 112–132.

Gilmer, B. v. H. (1960). Industrial psychology. *Annual Review of Psychology, 11,* 323–350.

Gilmer, B. v. H. (1961). *Industrial Psychology.* New York: McGraw-Hill.

Gilmer, B. v. H. (1966). *Industrial Psychology* (2nd ed.). New York: McGraw-Hill.

Glick, W.H. (1985). Conceptualizing and measuring organizational and psychological climate: Pitfalls of multilevel research. *Academy of Management Review, 10,* 601–610.

Glick, W.H. (1988). Response: Organizations are not central tendencies: Shadowboxing in the dark, round 2. *Academy of Management Review, 13,* 133–137.

Glisson C., & Green P. (2006). The effects of organizational culture and climate on the access to mental health care in child welfare and juvenile justice systems. *Administration and Policy in Mental Health, 33*(4), 433–448.

Glisson, C., & James, L.R. (2002). The cross-level effects of culture and climate in human service teams. *Journal of Organizational Behavior, 23*(6), 767–794.

Glisson, C., Schoenwald, S.K., Kelleher, K., Landsverk, J., Hoagwood, K.E., Mayberg, S., & Green, P. (2008). Therapist turnover and new program sustainability in mental health clinics as a function of organizational culture, climate, and service structure. *Administration and Policy in Mental Health and Mental Health Services Research, 35*(1), 124–133.

Gonzalez, J.A., & DeNisi, A.S. (2009). Cross-level effects of demography and diversity climate on organizational attachment and firm effectiveness. *Journal of Organizational Behavior, 30,* 21–40.

González-Romá, V., Fortes-Ferreira, L., & Peiró, J.M. (2009). Team climate, climate strength and team performance. A longitudinal study. *Journal of Occupational & Organizational Psychology, 82*(3), 511–536.

González-Romá, V., Peiró, J.M., & Tordera, N. (2002). An examination of the antecedents and moderator influences of climate strength. *Journal of Applied Psychology, 87*, 465–473.

Gordon, G.G. (1991). Industry determinants of organizational culture. *Academy of Management Review. 18*, 396–415.

Gordon, G.G., & DiTomaso, N. (1992). Predicting corporate performance from organizational culture. *Journal of Management Studies, 29*, 783–798.

Gregory, B.T., Harris, S.G., Armenakis, A.A., & Shook, C.L. (2009). Organizational culture and effectiveness: A study of values, attitudes, and organizational outcomes. *Journal of Business Research, 62*, 673–679.

Gregory, K. (1983). Native-view paradigms: Multiple culture and culture conflicts in organizations. *Administrative Science Quarterly, 28*, 359–376.

Griffin, A.E., Colella, A., & Goparaju, S. (2000). Newcomer and organizational socialization tactics: An interactionist perspective. *Human Resource Management Review, 10*(4), 453–474.

Griffin, M.A., & Neal, A. (2000). Perceptions of safety at work: A framework for linking safety climate to safety performance, knowledge, and motivation. *Journal of Occupational Health Psychology, 5*(3), 347–358.

Grizzle, J.W., Zablah, A.R., Brown, T.J., Mowen, J.C., & Lee, J.M. (2009). Employee customer orientation in context: How the environment moderates the influence of customer orientation on performance outcomes. *Journal of Applied Psychology, 94*(5), 1227–1242.

Guion, R.M. (1973). A note on organizational climate. *Organizational Behavior and Human Performance, 9*, 120–125.

Gundry, L.K., & Rousseau, D.M. (1994). Critical incidents in communicating culture to newcomers: The meaning is the message. *Human Relations, 47*, 1063–1087.

Gutek, B.A. (1995). *The dynamics of service: Reflections on the changing nature of customer/provider interactions.* San Francisco: Jossey-Bass.

Gutek, B.A. (2000). Service relationships, pseudo-relationships, and service encounters. In Schwartz, T.A., & Iacobucci, D. (Eds.), *Handbook of services marketing and management* (pp. 371–380). Thousand Oaks, CA: Sage.

Hall, D., & Lawler, E. (1969). Unused potential in research development organizations. *Research Management, 12*, 339–354.

Halpin, A.W., & Croft, D.B. (1963). *The organizational climate of schools.* Chicago: Midwest Administration Center of the University of Chicago.

Hammond, S.A. (1996). *The thin book of appreciative inquiry.* Plano, TX: Thin Book Publishing.

Hand, H., Richards, M., & Slocum, J. (1973). Organizational climate and the effectiveness of a human relations training program. *Academy of Management Journal, 16*, 185–195.

Harrell, T.W. (1953). Industrial psychology. *Annual Review of Psychology, 4*, 215–238.

Harrison, D.A., Newman, D.A., & Roth, P.L. (2006). How important are job attitudes? Meta-analytic comparisons of integrative behavioral outcomes and time sequences. *Academy of Management Journal, 40*, 305–325.

Hartnell, C.A., Ou, A.Y., & Kinicki A. (2011). Organizational culture and organizational effectiveness: A meta-analytic investigation of the competing values framework's theoretical suppositions. *Journal of Applied Psychology, 96*, 677–694.

Hartnell, C.A., & Walumbwa, F.O. (2011). Transformational leadership and organizational culture: Toward integrating a multilevel framework. In N.M. Ashkanasy, C.P.M. Wilderom, & M.F. Peterson (Eds.), *Handbook of organizational culture and climate* (2nd ed., pp. 515–537). Thousand Oaks, CA: Sage.

Hatch, M.J. (1993). The dynamics of organizational culture. *Academy of Management Review, 18*, 657–693.

Hatch, M.J. (2000). The cultural dynamics of organizing and change. In N.M. Ashkanasy, C.P.M. Wilderom, & M.F. Peterson (Eds.), *Handbook of organizational culture and climate* (pp. 245–260). Thousand Oaks, CA: Sage.

Hatch, M.J., & Schultz, M. (1997). Relations between organizational culture, identity, and image. *European Journal of Marketing, 31*, 356–365.

Hatch, M.J., & Schultz, M. (2000). Scaling the Tower of Babel: Relational differences between identity, image, and culture in organizations. In M. Schultz, M.J. Hatch, & M.H. Larsen (Eds.), *The expressive organization: Linking identity, reputation, and the corporate brand* (pp. 13–35). Oxford, UK: Oxford University Press.

Hellriegel, D., & Slocum, J.W., Jr. (1974). Organizational climate: Measures, research, and contingencies. *Academy of Management Journal, 17*, 255–280.

Henderson, D.J., Wayne, S.J., Shore, L.M., Bommer, W.H., & Tetrick, L.E. (2008). Leader-member exchange, differentiation, and psychological contract fulfillment: A multilevel examination. *Journal of Applied Psychology, 93*(6), 1208–1219.

Herdman, A.O., & McMilan-Capehart, A. (2010). Establishing a diversity program is not enough: Exploring the determinants of diversity climate. *Journal of Business and Psychology, 25*, 39–53.

Heron, J., & Reason, P. (2006). The practice of co-operative inquiry: Research 'with' rather than 'on' people. In P. Reason & H. Bradbury (Eds.), *Handbook of action research* (pp. 179–188). Thousand Oaks, CA: Sage.

Hicks-Clarke, D., & Iles, P. (2000). Climate for diversity and its effects on career and organizational attitudes and perceptions. *Personnel Review, 29*, 324–346.

Hofmann, D.A., & Mark, B. (2006). An investigation of the relationship between safety climate and medication errors as well as other nurse and patient outcomes. *Personnel Psychology, 59*, 847–869.

Hofmann, D.A., Morgeson, F.P., & Gerras, S.J. (2003). Climate as a moderator of the relationship between leader-member exchange and content specific citizenship: Safety climate as an exemplar. *Journal of Applied Psychology, 88*, 170–178.

Hofmann, D.A., & Stetzer, A. (1996). A cross-level investigation of factors influencing unsafe behaviors and accidents. *Personnel Psychology, 49*, 307–339.

Hofmann, D.A., & Stetzer, A. (1998). The role of safety climate and communication in accident interpretation: Implications for learning from negative events. *Academy of Management Journal, 41*, 644–658.

Hofstede, G. (1980). *Culture's consequences: International differences in work-related values*. Beverly Hills, CA: Sage.

Hofstede, G. (1991). *Cultures and organizations: Software of the mind*. London: McGraw-Hill.

Hofstede, G., & Peterson, M.F. (2000). Culture: National values and organizational practices. In N.M. Ashkanasy, C.P.M. Wilderom, & M.F. Peterson (Eds.), *Handbook of organizational culture and climate* (pp. 401–414). Thousand Oaks, CA: Sage.

Holland, J.L. (1997). *Making vocational choices* (3rd ed.). Odessa, FL: PAR.

Hong, Y., Liao, H., Hu, J., & Jiang, K. (2013). Missing link in the service profit chain: A meta-analytic review of the antecedents, consequences, and moderators of service climate. *Journal of Applied Psychology, 98*, 237–267.

House, R.J., Hanges, P.J., Javidan, M., Dorfman, P.W., & Gupta, V. (2004). *Culture, leadership, and organizations: The GLOBE study of 62 societies*. Thousand Oaks, CA: Sage.

House, R.J., & Rizzo, J.R. (1972). Toward the measurement of organizational practices: Scale development and validation. *Journal of Applied Psychology, 56*, 388–396.

Hovland, C.I., Janis, I.L., & Kelley, H.H. (1953). *Communication and persuasion*. New Haven, CT: Yale University Press.

Howe, J.G. (1977). Group climate: An exploratory analysis of construct validity. *Organizational Behavior & Human Performance, 19*(1), 106–125.

Hudson, P. (2007). Implementing safety culture in a major multi-national. *Safety Science, 45*, 697–722.

Jackofsky, E.F., & Slocum, J.W. (1988). A longitudinal study of climates. *Journal of Organizational Behavior, 9*, 319–334.

Jaques, E. (1951). *The changing culture of a factory*. New York: Dryden Press.

James, L.A., & James, L.R. (1989). Integrating work environment perceptions: Explorations into the measurement of meaning. *Journal of Applied Psychology, 74*, 739–751.

James, L.R. (1982). Aggregation bias in estimates of perceptual agreement. *Journal of Applied Psychology, 67*, 219–229.

James, L.R., Choi, C.C., Ko, C.H.E., McNeil, P.K., Minton, M.K., Wright, M.A., & Kim, K. (2008). Organizational and psychological climate: A review of theory and research. *European Journal of Work and Organizational Psychology, 17*, 5–32.

James, L.R., Demaree, R.G., & Wolf, G. (1984). Estimating within-group interrater reliability with and without response bias. *Journal of Applied Psychology, 69*, 85–98.

James, L. R., James, L. A., & Ashe, D. K. (1990). The meaning of organizations: The role of cognition and values. In B. Schneider (Ed.), *Organizational climate and culture* (pp. 40–84). San Francisco, CA: Jossey-Bass.

James, L.R., & Jones, A.P. (1974). Organizational climate: A review of theory and research. *Psychological Bulletin, 81*, 1096–1112.

James, L.R., Joyce, W.F., & Slocum, J.W. (1988). Comment: Organizations do not cognize. *Academy of Management Review, 13*, 129–132.

James, L.R., & Tetrick, L.E. (1986). Confirmatory analytic tests of three causal models relating job perceptions to job satisfaction. *Journal of Applied Psychology, 71*, 77–82.

Jermier, J.M., Slocum, J.W., Fry, L.W., & Gaines, J. (1991). Organizational subcultures in a soft bureaucracy: Resistance behind the myth and façade of an official culture. *Organization Science, 2*, 170–194.

Johannesson, R. (1973). Some problems in the measurement of organizational climate. *Organizational Behavior and Human Performance, 10*, 118–145.

Johnson, R.H. (1996). Life in the consortium: The Mayflower Group. In A.I. Kraut (Ed.), *Organizational surveys: Tools for assessment and change* (pp. 285–309). San Francisco: Jossey-Bass.

Johnston, H.R., Jr. (1976). A new conceptualization of source of organizational climate. *Administrative Science Quarterly, 21*, 95–103.
Jonas, H.S., Fry, R.E., & Srivastva, S. (1990). The office of the CEO: Understanding the executive experience. *Academy of Management Executive, 4*, 36–67.
Jones, A.P., & James, L.R. (1979). Psychological climate: Dimensions and relationships of individual and aggregated work environment perceptions. *Organizational Behavior and Human Performance, 23*, 201–250.
Jones, G.R. (1986). Socialization tactics, self-efficacy, and newcomers' adjustments to organizations. *Academy of Management Journal, 29*, 262–279.
Joyce, W.F., & Slocum, J.W. (1982). Climate discrepancy: Refining the concepts of psychological and organizational climate. *Human Relations, 35*, 951–972.
Joyce, W.F., & Slocum, J.W. (1984). Collective climate: Agreement as a basis for defining aggregate climate in organizations. *Academy of Management Journal, 27*, 721–742.
Jung, T., Scott, T., Davies, H.T.O., Bower, P., Whalley, D., McNally, R., & Mannion, R. (2009). Instruments for exploring organizational culture: A review of the literature. *Public Administration Review, 69*, 1087–1096.
Kaplan, R.S., & Norton, D.P. (2001). *The strategy focused organization: how balanced scorecard companies thrive in the new business environment*. Boston, MA: Harvard Business Publishing Corporation.
Katz, D., & Kahn, R.L. (1966). *The social psychology of organizations*. New York: Wiley.
Katz, D., & Kahn, R.L. (1978). *The social psychology of organizations* (2nd ed.). New York: Wiley.
Katzell, R.A. (1957). Industrial psychology. *Annual Review of Psychology, 8*, 237–268.
Keenan, A., & Newton, T.J. (1984). Frustration in organizations: Relationships to role stress, climate, and psychological strain. *Journal of Occupational Psychology, 57*, 57–65.
Keith, N., & Frese, M. (2011). Enhancing firm performance and innovativeness through error management culture. In N.M. Ashkanasy, C.P.M. Wilderom, & M.F. Peterson (Eds.), *Handbook of organizational culture and climate* (2nd ed., pp. 137–157). Thousand Oaks, CA: Sage.
Kendall, W.E. (1956). Industrial psychology. *Annual Review of Psychology, 7*, 197–232.
Kerr, S., & Jermier, J.M. (1978). Substitutes for leadership: Their meaning and measurement. *Organizational Behavior and Human Performance, 22*, 375–403.
Ketchen, D.J., Jr., Thomas, J.B., & Snow, C.C. (1993). Organizational configurations and performance: A comparison of theoretical approaches. *Academy of Management Journal, 36*, 1276–1313.
King, E.B., de Chermont, K., West, M., Dawson, J.F. & Hebl, M.R. (2007). How innovation can alleviate negative consequences of demanding work contexts: The influence of climate for innovation on organizational outcomes. *Journal of Occupational and Organizational Psychology, 80*, 631–645.

Klein, K.J., Bliese, P.D., Kozlowski, S.W.J., Dansereau, F., Gavin, M.B., Griffin, M.A., Hofman, D.A., James, L.R., Yammarino, F.J., & Bligh, M.C. (2000). Multilevel analytic techniques: Commonalities, differences, and continuing questions. In K.J. Klein & S.W.J. Kozlowski (Eds.), *Multilevel theory, research, and methods in organizations: Foundations, extensions, and new directions* (pp. 512–553). San Francisco: Jossey-Bass.

Klein, K.J., Conn, A.B., Smith, D.B., & Sorra, J.S. (2001). Is everyone in agreement? An exploration of within-group agreement in employee perceptions of the work environment. *Journal of Applied Psychology*, 86, 3–16.

Klein, K.J., Conn, A.B., & Sorra, J.S. (2001). Implementing computerized technology: An organizational analysis. *Journal of Applied Psychology*, 86, 811–824.

Klein K.J., & Kozlowski, S.W.J. (Eds.). (2000). *Multilevel theory, research, and methods in organizations: Foundations, extensions, and new directions*. San Francisco: Jossey-Bass.

Kopelman, R.E., Brief, A.P., & Guzzo, R.A. (1990). The role of climate and culture in productivity. In B. Schneider (Ed.), *Organizational climate and culture* (pp. 282–318). San Francisco: Jossey-Bass.

Kossek, E.E., & Zonia, S.C. (1993). Assessing diversity climate: A field study of reactions to employer efforts to promote diversity. *Journal of Organizational Behavior*, 14, 61–81.

Kotrba, L.M., Gillespie, M.A., Schmidt, A.M., Smerek, R.E., Ritchie, S.A., & Denison, D.R. (2012). Do consistent corporate cultures have better business performance? Exploring the interaction effects. *Human Relations*, 65, 241–262.

Kotter, J.P., & Heskett, J.L. (1992). *Corporate culture and performance*. New York: Free Press.

Kozlowski, S.W.J., & Doherty, M.L. (1989). An integration of climate and leadership: Examination of a neglected issue. *Journal of Applied Psychology*, 74, 546–553.

Kozlowski, S.W.J., & Hattrup, K. (1992). A disagreement about within-group agreement: Disentangling issues of consistency versus consensus. *Journal of Applied Psychology*, 77, 161–167.

Kozlowski, S.W.J., & Hults, B.M. (1987). An exploration of climates for technical updating and performance. *Personnel Psychology*, 40, 539–563.

Kozlowski, S.W.J., & Klein, K.J. (2000). A multilevel approach to theory and research in organizations: Contextual, temporal, and emergent processes. In K.J. Klein & S.W.J. Kozlowski (Eds.), *Multilevel theory, research, and methods in organizations: Foundations, extensions, and new directions* (pp. 3–90). San Francisco: Jossey-Bass.

Krefting, L.A., & Frost, P.J. (1985). Untangling webs, surfing waves, and wildcatting: a multiple-metaphor perspective on managing organizational culture. In P.J. Frost, L.F. Moore, M.R. Louis, C.C. Lundberg, & J. Martin (Eds.), *Organizational culture* (pp. 155–168). Beverly Hills, CA: Sage.

Kreiner, G.E. (2011). Organizational identity: Culture's conceptual cousin. In N.M. Ashkanasy, C.P.M. Wilderom, & M.F. Peterson (Eds.), *Handbook of*

organizational culture and climate (2nd ed., pp. 463–480). Thousand Oaks, CA: Sage.
Krippendorff, K. (1971). Communication and the genesis of structure. *General Systems, 16,* 171–185.
Kuenzi, M., & Schminke, M. (2009). Assembling fragments into a lens: A review, critique, and proposed research agenda for the organizational work climate literature. *Journal of Management, 35,* 634–717.
Kwantes, C.T., & Dickson, M.W. (2011). Organizational culture in a societal context: Lessons from GLOBE and beyond. In N.M. Ashkanasy, C.P.M. Wilderom, & M.F. Peterson (Eds.), *Handbook of organizational culture and climate* (2nd ed., pp. 494–514). Thousand Oaks, CA: Sage.
LaFollette, W.R., & Sims, H.P., Jr. (1975). Is satisfaction redundant with climate? *Organizational Behavior and Human Performance, 10,* 118–144.
Lance, C.E., Butts, M.M., & Michels, L.C. (2006). The sources of four commonly reported cutoff criteria: What did they really say? *Organizational Research Methods, 9,* 202–220.
Latham, G.P. (2007). *Work motivation: History, theory, research and practice.* Thousand Oaks, CA: Sage.
Lawler, E.E., Hall, D.T., & Oldham, G.R. (1974). Organizational climate: Relationship to organizational structure, process and performance. *Organizational Behavior and Human Performance, 11*(1), 139–155.
Leana, C.R., & Barry, B. (2000). Stability and change as simultaneous experiences in organizational life. *Academy of Management Review, 25*(4), 753–759.
Leavitt, H.J. (1958). *Managerial psychology: An introduction to individuals, pairs, and groups in organizations.* Chicago: University of Chicago Press.
Leavitt, H.J. (1965). Applied organizational change in industry: Structural, technological and humanistic approaches. In J. March (Ed.), *Handbook of Organizations* (pp. 1144–1170). Chicago: Rand McNally.
Leavitt, H.J., & Bass, B.M. (1964). Organizational psychology. *Annual Review of Psychology, 15,* 371–398.
LeBreton, J.M., & Senter, J.L. (2008). Answers to twenty questions about inter-rater reliability and interrater agreement. *Organizational Research Methods, 11,* 815–852.
Lee, S.K.J., & Yu, K. (2004). Corporate culture and organizational performance. *Journal of Managerial Psychology, 19,* 340–359.
Levine, E.L. (2010). Emotion and power (as social influence): Their impact on organizational citizenship and counterproductive individual and organizational behavior. *Human Resource Management Review, 20*(1), 4–17.
Lewin, K. (1951). *Field theory in social science.* New York: Harper & Row.
Lewin, K., Lippitt, R., & White, R.K. (1939). Patterns of aggressive behavior in experimentally created "social climates." *Journal of Social Psychology, 10,* 271–299.
Li, A., & Cropanzano, R. (2009). Fairness at the group level: Justice climate and intraunit justice climate. *Journal of Management, 35,* 564–599.
Liao, H., & Chuang, A. (2004). A multilevel investigation of factors influencing employee service performance and customer outcomes. *Academy of Management Journal, 47,* 41–58.

Liao H., & Chuang A. (2007). Transforming service employees and climate: A multilevel multi-source examination of transformational leadership in building long-term service relationships. *Journal of Applied Psychology, 92*, 1006–1019.
Liao, H., & Rupp, D.E. (2005). The impact of justice climate and justice orientation on work outcomes: A cross-level multifoci framework. *Journal of Applied Psychology, 90*, 242–256.
Likert, R. (1961). *New patterns of management*. New York: McGraw-Hill.
Likert, R. (1967). *The human organization*. New York: McGraw-Hill.
Lindell, M., & Brandt, C. (2000). Climate quality and climate consensus as mediators of the relationship between organizational antecedents and outcomes. *Journal of Applied Psychology, 85*, 331–348.
Litwin, G.H. (1968a). Climate and behavior theory: An environmental perspective on theories of individual and organizational behavior. In R. Tagiuri & G.H. Litwin (Eds.), *Organizational climate: Explorations of a concept* (pp. 35–61). Boston, MA: Harvard University.
Litwin, G.H. (1968b). Climate and motivation: An experimental study. In R. Tagiuri & G.H. Litwin (Eds.), *Organizational climate: Explorations of a concept* (pp. 169–190). Boston, MA: Harvard University.
Litwin, G.H., & Stringer, R.A. (1968). *Motivation and organizational climate*. Cambridge, MA: Harvard Business School, Division of Research.
Löfgren, O. (1982). Kulturbygge och kulturkonfrontattion ('Culture building and culture confrontation'). In U. Hannerz, R. Liljeström, & O. Löfgren (Eds.) *Kultur och medvtande*. Stockholm: Akademilitteratur.
Lord, R.G., & Hanges, P.J. (1987). A control systems model of organizational motivation: Theoretical development and applied implications. *Behavioral Science, 32*, 161–178.
Louis, M.R. (1980). Surprise and sense making: What newcomers experience in entering unfamiliar organizational settings. *Administrative Science Quarterly, 25*, 226–250.
Louis, M.R. (1983). Organizations as culture-bearing milieux. In L.R. Pondy, P.J. Frost, G. Morgan & T.C. Dandridge (Eds.), *Organizational symbolism* (pp. 39–54). Greenwich, CT: JAI Press.
Louis, M.R. (1985). An investigator's guide to workplace culture. In P.J. Frost, L.F. Moore, M.R. Louis, C.C. Lundberg, & J. Martin (Eds.), *Organizational culture* (pp. 73–93). Beverly Hills, CA: Sage.
Louis, M.R. (1990). Acculturation in the work place: Newcomers as lay ethnographers. In Schneider, B. (Ed.), *Organizational climate and culture* (pp. 85–129). San Francisco: Jossey-Bass.
Louis, M.R., Posner, B.Z., & Powell, G.N. (1983). The availability and helpfulness of socialization practices. *Personnel Psychology, 36*, 857–866.
Lundberg, C.C. (1985). On the feasibility of cultural intervention in organizations. In P.J. Frost, L.F. Moore, M.R. Louis, C.C. Lundberg, & J. Martin (Eds.), *Organizational culture* (pp. 169–185). Beverly Hills, CA: Sage.
Lundberg, C.C. (1990). Surfacing organisational culture. *Journal of Managerial Psychology, 5*(4), 19–26.

Lundby, K., Lee, W.C., & Macey, W.H. (2012). Leadership essentials to attract, engage, and retain global human talent. In W. H. Mobley, Y. Wang, & M. Li (Eds.), *Advances in global leadership* (Vol. 7, pp. 251–270). Bingly, UK: Emerald Group Publishing.

Luria G. (2008). Climate strength—How leaders form consensus. *Leadership Quarterly, 19*, 42–53.

Macey, W.H., Schneider, B., Barbera, K.M., & Young, S.A. (2009). *Employee engagement: Tools for analysis, practice, and competitive advantage*. New York: Wiley-Blackwell.

Mannix, E.A., Thatcher, S., & Jehn, K.A. (2001). Does culture always flow downstream? Linking group consensus and organizational culture. In C.L. Cooper, S. Cartwright, & P.C. Earley (Eds.), *The international handbook of organizational culture and climate* (pp. 289–306). New York: Wiley.

Markus, K.A. (2000). Twelve testable assertions about cultural dynamics and reproduction of organizational change. In N.M. Ashkanasy, C.P.M. Wilderom, & M.F. Peterson (Eds.), *Handbook of organizational culture and climate* (pp. 297–308). Thousand Oaks, CA: Sage.

Martin, J. (1985). Can organizational culture be managed? In P.J. Frost, L.F. Moore, M.R. Louis, C.C. Lundberg, & J. Martin (Eds.), *Organizational culture* (pp. 95–98). Beverly Hills, CA: Sage.

Martin, J. (1992). *Cultures in organizations: Three perspectives*. New York: Oxford University Press.

Martin, J. (2002). *Organizational culture: Mapping the terrain*. Thousand Oaks, CA: Sage.

Martin, J., Feldman, M.S., Hatch, M.J., & Sitkin, S.B. (1983). The uniqueness paradox in organizational stories. *Administrative Science Quarterly. 28*, 438–453.

Martin, J., & Frost, P.J. (1996). The organizational culture war games: A struggle for intellectual dominance. In S.R. Clegg, C. Hardy, & W.R. Nord, (Eds.), *Handbook of organizational studies* (pp. 599–621). Thousand Oaks, CA: Sage.

Martin, J., Frost, P.J., & O'Neill, O.A. (2006). Organizational culture: Beyond struggles for intellectual dominance. In S. Clegg, C. Hardy, T. Lawrence, & W. Nord (Eds.), *Sage handbook of organizational studies* (2nd ed., pp. 725–753). Thousand Oaks, CA: Sage.

Martin, J., & Siehl, C.J. (1983). Organizational culture and counterculture: An uneasy symbiosis. *Organizational Dynamics, 12*, 52–64.

Martin, J., Sitkin, S.B., & Boehm, M. (1985). Founders and the elusiveness of a cultural legacy. In P.J. Frost, L.F. Moore, M.R. Louis, C.C. Lundberg, & J. Martin (Eds.), *Organizational culture* (pp. 99–124). Beverly Hills, CA: Sage.

Martin, J., Su, S., & Beckman, C. (1997). Enacting shared values—Myth or reality? A context-specific values audit. Research Paper Number 1469. Stanford, CA: Stanford University Graduate School of Business.

Mayer, D.M., Ehrhart, M.G., & Schneider, B. (2009). Service attribute boundary conditions of the service climate—customer satisfaction link. *Academy of Management Journal, 52*, 1034–1050.

Mayer, D.M., & Kuenzi, M. (2010). Exploring the "black box" of justice climate: What mechanisms link justice climate and outcomes? In E. Mullen, E. Mannix, & M. Neale (Eds.), *Research on managing groups and teams: Fairness* (Vol. 13, pp. 331–346). London: Elsevier Science Press.

Mayer, D.M., Kuenzi, M., & Greenbaum, R.L. (2009). Making ethical climate a mainstream management topic: A review, critique, and prescription for the empirical research on ethical climate. In D. De Cremer (Ed.), *Psychological perspectives on ethical behavior and decision making* (pp. 181–213). Greenwich, CT: Information Age Publishing.

Mayer, D.M., Kuenzi, M., Greenbaum, R., Bardes, M., & Salvador, R. (2009). How low does ethical leadership flow? Test of a trickle-down model. *Organizational Behavior and Human Decision Processes, 108*(1), 1–13.

Mayer, D.M., Nishii, L.H., Schneider, B., & Goldstein, H.W. (2007). The precursors and products of fair climates: Group leader antecedents and employee attitudinal consequences. *Personnel Psychology, 60*, 929–963.

Mayhew, B.H. (1980). Structuralism versus individualism: Part 1, shadowboxing in the dark. *Social Forces, 59*, 335–375.

Mayo, E. (1933). *The human problems of industrial civilization*. New York: Macmillan.

Mayo, E. (1945). *The social problems of industrial civilization*. Boston: Harvard University, Graduate School of Business Administration.

McDonald, P. (1991). The Los Angeles Olympic Organizing Committee: Developing organizational culture in the short run. In P.J. Frost, L.F. Moore, M.R. Louis, C.C. Lundberg, & J. Martin (Eds.), *Reframing organizational culture* (pp. 26–38). Newbury Park, CA: Sage.

McGregor, D.M. (1960). *The human side of enterprise*. New York: McGraw-Hill.

McKay, P.F., Avery, D.R., Liao, H., & Morris, M.A. (2011). Does diversity climate lead to customer satisfaction? It depends on the service climate and business unit demography. *Organization Science, 22*, 788–803.

McKay, P.F., Avery, D.R., & Morris, M.A. (2008). Mean racial-ethnic differences in employee sales performance: The moderating role of diversity climate. *Personnel Psychology, 61*, 349–374.

McKay, P.F., Avery, D.R., & Morris, M.A. (2009). A tale of two climates: Diversity climate from subordinates' and managers' perspectives and their role in store unit sales performance. *Personnel Psychology, 62*, 767–791.

Mead, J.H. (1934). *Mind, self, and society*. Chicago: University of Chicago Press.

Meek, V.L. (1988). Organizational culture: Origins and weaknesses. *Organization Studies, 9*(4), 453–473.

Meglino, B.M., Ravlin, E.C., & Adkins, C.L. (1989). A work values approach to corporate culture: A field test of the value congruence process and its relationship to individual outcomes. *Journal of Applied Psychology, 74*(3), 424–432.

Meglino, B.M., Ravlin, E.C., & Adkins, C.L. (1991). Value congruence and satisfaction with a leader: An examination of the role of interaction. *Human Relations, 44*(5), 481–495.

Meindl, J.R. (1990). On leadership: An alternative to the conventional wisdom. In B.M. Staw & L.L. Cummings (Eds.), *Research in organizational behavior* (Vol. 12, pp. 159–203). Greenwich, CT: JAI Press.

Meindl, J.R. (1993). Reinventing leadership: A radical, social psychological approach. In J.K. Murnighan (Ed.), *Social psychology in organizations* (pp. 89–118). Englewood Cliffs, NJ: Prentice Hall.

Meindl, J.R. (1995). The romance of leadership as a follower-centric theory: A social constructionist approach. *Leadership Quarterly, 6*(3), 329–341.

Meindl, J.R., & Ehrlich, S.B. (1987). The romance of leadership and the evaluation of organizational performance. *Academy of Management Journal, 30*(1), 91–109.

Meindl, J.R., Ehrlich, S.B., & Dukerich, J.M. (1985). The romance of leadership. *Administrative Science Quarterly, 30*, 78–102.

Meyer, H.H. (1968). Achievement motivation and industrial climates. In R. Tagiuri & G.H. Litwin (Eds.), *Organizational climate: Explorations of a concept* (pp. 151–166). Boston, MA: Harvard University.

Meyer, R.D., & Dalal, R.S. (2009). Situational strength as a means of conceptualizing context. *Industrial and Organizational Psychology: Perspectives on Science and Practice, 2*, 99–102.

Meyer, R.D., Dalal, R.S., & Bonaccio, S. (2009). A meta-analytic investigation into the moderating effects of situational strength on the conscientiousness–performance relationship. *Journal of Organizational Behavior, 30*, 1077–1102.

Meyer, R.D., Dalal, R.S., & Hermida, R. (2010). A review and synthesis of situational strength in the organizational sciences. *Journal of Management, 36*, 121–40.

Meyerson, D.E. (1991a). Acknowledging and uncovering ambiguities in cultures. In P.J. Frost, L.F. Moore, M.R. Louis, C.C. Lundberg, & J. Martin (Eds.), *Reframing organizational culture* (pp. 254–270). Newbury Park, CA: Sage.

Meyerson, D.E. (1991b). "Normal" ambiguity? A glimpse of an occupational culture. In P.J. Frost, L.F. Moore, M.R. Louis, C.C. Lundberg, & J. Martin (Eds.), *Reframing organizational culture* (pp. 131–144). Newbury Park, CA: Sage.

Miceli, M.P., & Near, J.P. (1985). Characteristics of organizational climate and perceived wrongdoing associated with whistle-blowing decision. *Personnel Psychology, 38*(3), 525–544.

Michael, J.A. (1961). High school climates and plans for entering college. *Public Opinion Quarterly, 25*, 585–595.

Michaelis, B., Stegmaier, R., & Sonntag, K. (2010). Shedding light on followers' innovation implementation behavior: The role of transformational leadership, commitment to change, and climate for initiative. *Journal of Managerial Psychology, 25*, 408–429.

Michela, J.L., & Burke, W.W. (2000). Organizational culture and climate in transformations for quality and innovation. In N.M. Ashkanasy, C.P.M. Wilderom, & M.F. Peterson (Eds.), *Handbook of organizational culture and climate* (pp. 225–244). Thousand Oaks, CA: Sage.

Miller, D. (1990). *The Icarus paradox: How exceptional companies bring about their own downfall.* New York: Harper Business.

Miller, V.D., & Jablin, F.M. (1991). Information seeking during organizational entry: Influences, tactics, and a model of the process. *Academy of Management Review, 16*, 92–120.

Miner, J.B. (2002). *Organizational behavior: Foundations, theories and analyses.* New York: Oxford.

Mischel, W. (1968). *Personality and assessment.* New York: Wiley.

Mischel, W. (1973). Toward a cognitive social learning reconceptualization of personality. *Psychological Review, 80*, 252–283.

Moliner, C., Martínez-Tur, V., Peiró, J.M., Ramos, J., & Cropanzano, R. (2005). Relationships between organizational justice and burnout at the work-unit level. *International Journal of Stress Management, 12*(2), 99–116.

Mor Barak, M.E., Cherin, D.A., & Berkman, S. (1998). Organizational and personal dimensions of diversity climate: Ethnic and gender differences in employee perceptions. *Journal of Applied Behavioral Science, 31*, 82–104.

Moran, E.T., & Volkwein, J.F. (1992). The cultural approach to the formation of organizational climate. *Human Relations, 45*, 19–47.

Morgan, G. (1986). *Images of organization*. Newbury Park, CA: Sage.

Morgan, G. (2006). *Images of organization* (3rd ed.). Thousand Oaks, CA: Sage.

Morrison, E.W. (1993). Newcomer information seeking: Exploring types, modes, sources, and outcomes. *Academy of Management Journal, 36*(3), 557–589.

Mossholder, K.W., Bennett, N., & Martin, C.L. (1998). A multilevel analysis of procedural justice context. *Journal of Organizational Behavior, 19*, 131–141.

Muchinsky, P.M. (1976). An assessment of the Litwin and Stringer organization climate questionnaire: An empirical and theoretical extension of the Sims and LaFollette study. *Personnel Psychology, 29*, 371–392.

Muchinsky, P.M. (1977). Organizational communication: Relationships to organizational climate and job satisfaction. *Academy of Management Journal, 20*(4), 592–607.

Mumford, M.D., Marks, M.A., Connelly, M.S., Zaccaro, S.J., & Reiter-Palmon, R. (2000). Development of leadership skills: Experience and timing. *Leadership Quarterly, 11*, 87–114.

Naumann, S.E., & Bennett, N. (2000). A case for procedural justice climate: Development and test of a multilevel model. *Academy of Management Journal, 43*, 881–889.

Neal, A., & Griffin, M.A. (2006). A study of the lagged relationships among safety climate, safety motivation, safety behavior, and accidents at the individual and group levels. *Journal of Applied Psychology, 91*, 946–953.

Nelson, D.L., & Quick, J.C. (1991). Social support and newcomer adjustment in organizations: attachment theory at work? *Journal of Organizational Behavior, 12*(6), 543–554.

Newman, D.A., & Harrison, D.A. (2008). Been there, bottled that: Are state and behavioral work engagement new and useful construct 'wines'? *Industrial and Organizational Psychology: Perspectives on Science and Practice, 1*, 31–35.

Newman, D.A., & Sin, H.P. (2009). How do missing data bias estimates of within-group agreement?: Sensitivity of SD_{WG}, CV_{WG}, $r_{WG(J)}$, $r_{WG(J)}^*$, and ICC to systematic nonresponse. *Organizational Research Methods, 12*, 113–147.

Nishii, L.H., & Mayer, D.M. (2009). Do inclusive leaders help to reduce turnover in diverse groups? The moderating role of leader–member exchange in the diversity to turnover relationship. *Journal of Applied Psychology, 94*(6), 1412–1426.

Nylund, K.L., Asparouhov, T., & Muthén, B. (2007). Deciding on the number of classes in latent class analysis and growth mixture modeling: A Monte Carlo simulation study. *Structural Equation Modeling: A Multidisciplinary Journal, 14*, 535–569.

Odiorne, G.S. (1960). Company growth and personnel administration. *Personnel, 37*, 32–41.

Ogbonna, E., & Harris, L.C. (1998). Managing organizational culture: Compliance or genuine change? *British Journal of Management, 9*, 273–288.

Ogbonna, E., & Harris, L.C. (2002). Organizational culture: A ten year, two-phase study of change in the UK food retailing sector. *Journal of Management Studies, 39*, 673–706.

Ogbonna, E., & Wilkinson, B. (1990). Corporate strategy and corporate culture: The view from the checkout. *Personnel Review, 19*(4), 9–15.

O'Reilly, C.A., & Chatman, J.A. (1996). Culture as social control: Corporations, cults and commitment. In B.M. Staw & L.L. Cummings (Eds.), *Research in organizational behavior* (Vol. 18, pp. 157–200). Greenwich, CT: JAI Press.

O'Reilly, C.A., Chatman, J., & Caldwell, D.F. (1991). People and organizational culture: A profile comparison approach to assessing person-organization fit. *Academy of Management Journal, 34*, 487–516.

Ostroff, C. (1993). The effects of climate and personal influences on individual behavior and attitudes in organizations. *Organizational Behavior and Human Decision Processes, 56*, 56–90.

Ostroff, C., Kinicki, A.J., & Muhammad, R.S. (2012). Organizational culture and climate. In N.W. Schmitt & S. Highhouse (Eds.), *Handbook of psychology, Vol. 12: Industrial and organizational psychology* (2nd ed., pp. 643–676). Hoboken, NJ: Wiley.

Ostroff, C., Kinicki, A.J., & Tamkins, M.M. (2003). Organizational culture and climate. In W.C. Borman, D.R. Ilgen, & R.J. Klimoski (Eds.), *Handbook of psychology, Vol. 12: I/O psychology* (pp. 565–593). New York: Wiley.

Ostroff, C., & Kozlowski, S.W.J. (1992). Organizational socialization as a learning process: The role of information acquisition. *Personnel Psychology, 45*(4), 849–874.

Ott, J.S. (1989). *The organizational culture perspective.* Pacific Grove, CA: Brooks-Cole.

Ouchi, W.G. (1981). *Theory Z: How American business can meet the Japanese challenge.* Reading, MA: Addison-Wesley.

Ouchi, W.G. & Wilkins, A.L. (1985). Organizational culture. *Annual Review of Sociology, 11*, 457–483.

Pacanowsky, M.E., & O'Donnell-Trujillo, N. (1983). Organizational communication as cultural performance. *Communications Monographs, 50*(2), 126–147.

Pace, C.R. (1963). *College and university environment scales: Technical manual.* Princeton, NJ: Educational Testing Service.

Pace, C.R. (1968). The measurement of college environments. In R. Tagiuri & G.H. Litwin (Eds.), *Organizational climate: Explorations of a concept* (pp. 129–147). Boston, MA: Harvard University.

Pace, C.R., & Stern, G.G. (1958). An approach to the measurement of psychological characteristics of college environments. *Journal of Educational Psychology, 49*(5), 269–277.

Parker, C.P., Baltes, B.B., Young, S.A., Huff, J.W., Altmann, R.A., LaCost, H.A., & Roberts, J.E. (2003). Relationships between psychological climate perceptions and work outcomes: A meta-analytic review. *Journal of Organizational Behavior, 24*, 389–416.

Parkington, J.J., & Schneider, B. (1979). Some correlates of experienced job stress: a boundary role study. *Academy of Management Journal, 22*(2), 270–281.

Parsons, T. (1951). *The social system.* Glencoe, IL: Free Press.

Pascale, R., & Athos, A. (1982). *The art of Japanese management.* London: Penguin.

Patterson, M.G., West, M.A., Shackleton, V.J., Dawson, J.F., Lawthom, R., Maitlis, S., Robinson, D.L., & Wallace, A.M. (2005). Validating the organizational climate measure: Links to managerial practices, productivity, and innovation. *Journal of Organizational Behavior, 26,* 379–408.

Payne, R.L. (2000). Climate and culture: How close can they get? In N.M. Ashkanasy, C.P.M. Wilderom, & M.F. Peterson (Eds.), *Handbook of organizational culture and climate* (pp. 163–176). Thousand Oaks, CA: Sage.

Payne, R.L. (2001). A three dimensional framework for analyzing and assessing culture/climate and its relevance for cultural change. In C.L. Cooper, S. Cartwright, & P.C. Earley (Eds.), *The international handbook of organizational culture and climate* (pp. 107–122). New York: Wiley.

Payne, R.L., Fineman, S., & Wall, T.D. (1976). Organizational climate and job satisfaction: A conceptual synthesis. *Organizational Behavior and Human Performance, 16,* 45–62.

Payne, R.L., & Mansfield, R. (1973). Relationships of perceptions of organizational climate to organizational structure, context, and hierarchical position. *Administrative Science Quarterly, 18,* 515–526.

Payne, R.L., & Pheysey, D.C. (1971). G.G. Stern's Organizational Climate Index: A reconceptualization and application to business organizations. *Organizational Behavior and Human Performance, 6,* 77–98.

Payne, R.L., & Pugh, D.S. (1976). Organizational structure and climate. In M.D. Dunnette (Ed.), *Handbook of industrial and organizational psychology,* (pp. 1125–1173). Chicago: Rand McNally.

Pelz, D.C., & Andrews, F.M. (1966). *Scientists in organization: Productive climates for research and development.* New York: Wiley.

Peters, T.J., & Waterman, R.H. Jr. (1982). *In search of excellence.* New York: Harper & Row.

Pettigrew, A.M. (1979). On studying organizational cultures. *Administrative Science Quarterly, 24,* 570–581.

Pettigrew, A.M. (1987a). Introduction: Researching strategic change. In A.M. Pettigrew (Ed.), *The management of strategic change* (pp. 1–13). Oxford, UK: Blackwell.

Pettigrew, A.M. (Ed.) (1987b). *The management of strategic change.* Oxford, UK: Blackwell.

Pettigrew, A.M. (1990). Organizational climate and culture: Two constructs in search of a role. In B. Schneider (Ed.), *Organizational climate and culture* (pp. 413–434). San Francisco: Jossey-Bass.

Phillips, N., & Hardy, C. (2002). *Discourse analysis.* Thousand Oaks, CA: Sage.

Porter, L.W. (1966). Personnel management. *Annual Review of Psychology, 17,* 395–422.

Powell, G.N., & Butterfield, D.A. (1978). The case for subsystem climates in organizations. *Academy of Management Review, 3*(1), 151–157.

Pritchard, R.D., & Karasick, B. (1973). The effects of organizational climate on managerial job performance and job satisfaction. *Organizational Behavior and Human Performance, 9,* 126–146.

Probst, T. (2004). Safety and insecurity: Exploring the moderating effect of organizational safety climate. *Journal of Occupational Health Psychology, 9,* 3–40.

Probst, T., Brubaker, T., & Barsotti, A. (2008). Organizational under-reporting of injury rates: An examination of the moderating effect of organizational safety climate. *Journal of Applied Psychology, 93,* 1147–1154.

Pugh, S.D., Dietz, J., Brief, A.P., & Wiley J.W. (2008). Looking inside and out: The impact of employee and community demographic composition on organizational diversity climate. *Journal of Applied Psychology, 93*, 1422–1428.

Pugh, D.S., & Hickson, D.J. (1972). Causal inference and the Aston studies. *Administrative Science Quarterly, 17*(2), 273–276.

Quinn, R.E., & Kimberly, J.R. (1984). Paradox, planning, and perseverance: Guidelines for managerial practice. In J.R. Kimberly & R.E. Quinn (Eds.), *Managing organizational transitions* (pp. 295–313). Homewood, IL: DowJones-Irwin.

Quinn, R.E., & Rohrbaugh, J. (1983). A special model of effectiveness criteria: Toward a competing values approach to organizational analysis. *Management Science, 29*, 363–377.

Quinn, R.E., & Spreitzer, G.M. (1991). The psychometrics of the competing values culture instrument and an analysis of the impact of organizational culture on quality of life. In R.W. Woodman, & W.A. Pasmore (Eds.), *Research in organizational change and development* (Vol. 5, pp. 115–142). Greenwich, CT: JAI Press.

Rafferty, A.E., & Jimmieson, N.L. (2010). Team change climate: A group-level analysis of the relationships among change information and change participation, role stressors, and well-being. *European Journal of Work and Organizational Psychology, 19*, 551–586.

Rafferty, A.E., Jimmieson, N.L., & Armenakis, A.A. (2013). Change readiness: A multilevel review. *Journal of Management, 39*, 110–135.

Ravasi, D., & Schultz, M. (2006). Responding to organizational identity threats: Exploring the role of organizational culture. *Academy of Management Journal, 49*, 433–458.

Ray, R., & Sanders, E. (2008). AHP cultural transformation: Driving positive organizational change. *OD Practitioner, 40*, 410–416.

Reger, S.J.M. (2006). *Can two rights make a wrong? Insights from IBM's tangible culture approach.* Upper Saddle River, NJ: IBM Press.

Reichers, A.E., & Schneider, B. (1990). Climate and culture: An evolution of constructs. In B. Schneider (Ed.), *Organizational climate and culture* (pp. 5–39). San Francisco: Jossey-Bass.

Roberson, Q.M. (2006a). Justice in teams: The activation and role of sensemaking in the emergence of justice climates. *Organizational Behavior and Human Decision Processes, 100*, 177–192.

Roberson, Q.M. (2006b). Justice in teams: The effects of interdependence and identification on referent choice and justice climate strength. *Social Justice Research, 19*, 323–344.

Roberson, Q.M., & Colquitt, J.A. (2005). Shared and configural justice: A social network model of justice in teams. *Academy of Management Review, 30*, 595–607.

Roberson, Q.M., Sturman, M.C., & Simons, T.L. (2007). Does the measure of dispersion matter in multilevel research? A comparison of the relative performance of dispersion indexes. *Organizational Research Methods, 10*(4), 564–588.

Roberson, Q.M., & Williamson, I.O. (2012). Justice in self-managing teams: The role of social networks in the emergence of procedural justice climates. *Academy of Management Journal, 55*, 685–701.

Roethlisberger, F.J. (1941). *Management and morale*. Cambridge, MA: Harvard University Press.
Roethlisberger, F.J., & Dickson, W.J. (1939). *Management and the worker*. Boston: Harvard School.
Rouiller, J.Z., & Goldstein, I.L. (1993). The relationship between organizational transfer climate and positive transfer of training. *Human Resource Development Quarterly, 4*, 377–390.
Rousseau, D.M. (1990a). Assessing organizational culture: The case for multiple methods. In B. Schneider (Ed.), *Organizational climate and culture* (pp. 153–192). San Francisco: Jossey-Bass.
Rousseau, D.M. (1990b). Normative beliefs in fund-raising organizations: Linking culture to organizational performance and individual responses. *Group & Organizational Studies, 15*, 448–460.
Rupp, D.E., Bashshur, M., & Liao, H. (2007a). Justice climate: Consideration of source, target, type, specificity, and emergence. In F. Dansereau & F.J. Yammarino (Eds.), *Research in multi-level issues* (Vol. 6, pp. 439–459). Oxford, UK: Elsevier.
Rupp, D.E., Bashshur, M., & Liao, H. (2007b). Justice climate past, present, and future: Models of structure and emergence. In F. Dansereau & F.J. Yammarino (Eds.), *Research in multi-level issues* (Vol. 6, pp. 357–396). Oxford, UK: Elsevier.
Russell, S.V., & McIntosh, M. (2011). Organizational change for sustainability. In N.M. Ashkanasy, C.P.M. Wilderom & M.F. Peterson (Eds.), *Handbook of organizational culture and climate* (2nd ed., pp. 393–411). Thousand Oaks, CA: Sage.
Sackmann, S.A. (1991). Uncovering culture in organizations. *Journal of Applied Behavioral Science, 27*(3), 295–317.
Sackmann, S.A. (2001). Cultural complexity in organizations: The value and limitations of qualitative methodology and approaches. In C.L. Cooper, S. Cartwright, & P.C. Earley (Eds.), *The international handbook of organizational culture and climate* (pp. 143–163). New York: Wiley.
Sackmann, S.A. (2011). Culture and performance. In N.M. Ashkanasy, C.P.M. Wilderom, & M.F. Peterson (Eds.), *Handbook of organizational culture and climate* (2nd ed., pp. 188–224). Thousand Oaks, CA: Sage.
Saffold, G.S. (1988). Culture traits, strength, and organizational performance: Moving beyond "strong" culture. *Academy of Management Review, 13*, 546–558.
Saks, A.M., & Ashforth, B.E. (1997). Organizational socialization: Making sense of the past and present as a prologue for the future. *Journal of Vocational Behavior, 51*(2), 234–279.
Salanova, M., Agut, S., & Peiró, J.M. (2005). Linking organizational resources and work engagement to employee performance and customer loyalty: The mediation of service climate. *Journal of Applied Psychology, 90*, 1217–1227.
Salas, E., Priest, H.A., Stagl, K.C., Sims, D.E., & Burke, C.S. (2007). Work teams in organizations: A historical reflection and lessons learned. In L. Koppes (Ed.), *Historical perspectives in industrial and organizational psychology* (pp. 407–440). Mahwah, NJ: Lawrence Erlbaum Associates.
Salvaggio, A.N., Schneider, B., Nishii, L.H., Mayer, D.M., Ramesh, A., & Lyon, J.S. (2007). Manager personality, manager service quality orientation, and service climate: Test of a model. *Journal of Applied Psychology, 92*, 1741–1750.

Sarros, J.C., Gray, J., Dentsten, I.L., & Cooper, B. (2005). The organizational culture profile revisited and revised: An Australian perspective. *Australian Journal of Management, 30*, 159–182.
Sathe, V. (1983). Implications of corporate culture: A manager's guide to action. *Organizational Dynamics, 12*(4), 4–23.
Sathe, V. (1985). *Culture and related corporate realities.* Homewood, IL: Irwin.
Sathe, V., & Davidson, E.J. (2000). Toward a new conceptualization of culture change. In N.M. Ashkanasy, C.P.M. Wilderom, & M.F. Peterson (Eds.), *Handbook of organizational culture and climate* (pp. 279–296). Thousand Oaks, CA: Sage.
Schall, E., Ospina, S., Godsoe, B., & Dodge, J. (2004). *Appreciative narratives as leadership research: Matching method to lens.* In D.L. Cooperrider and M. Avital (Eds.), *Advances in appreciative inquiry, Vol. 1: Constructive discourse and human organization* (pp. 147–170). Oxford, England: Elsevier Science.
Schaubroeck, J.M., Hannah, S.T., Avolio, B.J., Kozlowski, S.W.J., Lord, R.G., Treviño, L.K., Dimotakis, N., & Peng, A.C. (2012). Embedding ethical leadership within and across organization levels. *Academy of Management Journal, 55*, 1053–1078.
Schein, E.H. (1965). *Organizational psychology.* Englewood Cliffs, NJ: Prentice-Hall.
Schein, E.H. (1983). The role of the founder in creating organizational culture. *Organizational Dynamics, 12*(1), 13–28.
Schein, E.H. (1985). *Organizational culture and leadership.* San Francisco: Jossey-Bass.
Schein, E.H. (1990). Organizational culture. *American Psychologist, 45*, 109–119.
Schein, E.H. (1991). What is culture? In P.J. Frost, L.F. Moore, M.R. Louis, C.C. Lundberg, & J. Martin (Eds.), *Reframing organizational culture* (pp. 243–253). Newbury Park, CA: Sage.
Schein, E.H. (1992). *Organizational culture and leadership* (2nd ed.). San Francisco: Jossey-Bass.
Schein, E.H. (1996, Fall). Three cultures of management: The key to organizational learning. *Sloan Management Review*, 9–20.
Schein, E.H. (2000). Sense and nonsense about culture and climate. In N.M. Ashkanasy, C.P.M. Wilderom, & M.F. Peterson (Eds.), *Handbook of organizational culture and climate* (pp. xxiii–xxx). Thousand Oaks, CA: Sage.
Schein, E.H. (2004). *Organizational culture and leadership* (3rd ed.). San Francisco: Jossey-Bass.
Schein, E.H. (2010). *Organizational culture and leadership* (4th ed.). San Francisco: Jossey-Bass.
Schein, E.H. (2011). Preface. In N.M. Ashkanasy, C.P.M. Wilderom, & M.F. Peterson (Eds.), *Handbook of organizational culture and climate* (2nd ed., pp. xi–xiii). Thousand Oaks, CA: Sage.
Schmidt, F.L., & Hunter, J.E. (1977). Development of a general solution to the problem of validity generalization. *Journal of Applied Psychology, 62*(5), 529–540.
Schnake, M.E. (1983). An empirical assessment of the effects of affective response in the measurement of organizational climate. *Personnel Psychology, 36*, 791–807.
Schneider, B. (1970). Relationships between various criteria of leadership in small groups. *Journal of Social Psychology, 82*, 253–261.
Schneider, B. (1972). Organizational climate: Individual preferences and organizational realities. *Journal of Applied Psychology, 56*, 211–217.

Schneider, B. (1973). The perception of organizational climate: The customer's view. *Journal of Applied Psychology, 57*, 248–256.
Schneider, B. (1975a). Organizational climate: Individual preferences and organizational realities revisited. *Journal of Applied Psychology, 60*(4), 459–465.
Schneider, B. (1975b). Organizational climates: An essay. *Personnel Psychology, 28*, 447–479.
Schneider, B. (1985). Organizational behavior. *Annual Review of Psychology, 36*, 573–611.
Schneider, B. (1987). The people make the place. *Personnel Psychology, 40*, 437–453.
Schneider, B. (1994). HRM-a service perspective: Toward a customer-focused HRM. *International Journal of Service Industry Management, 5*, 65–76.
Schneider, B. (2000). The psychological life of organizations. In N.M. Ashkanasy, C.P.M. Wilderom, & M.F. Peterson (Eds.), *Handbook of organizational culture & climate* (pp. xvii–xxi). Thousand Oaks, CA: Sage.
Schneider, B., & Bartlett, C.J. (1968). Individual differences and organizational climate, I: The research plan and questionnaire development. *Personnel Psychology, 21*, 323–333.
Schneider, B., & Bartlett, C.J. (1970). Individual differences and organizational climate, II: Measurement of organizational climate by the multitrait-multirater matrix. *Personnel Psychology, 23*, 493–512.
Schneider, B., & Bowen, D.E. (1985). Employee and customer perceptions of service in banks: Replication and extension. *Journal of Applied Psychology, 70*, 423–433.
Schneider, B., & Bowen, D.E. (1995). *Winning the service game*. Boston, MA: Harvard Business School Press.
Schneider, B., Bowen, D.E., Ehrhart, M.G., & Holcombe, K.M. (2000). The climate for service: Evolution of a construct. In N.M. Ashkanasy, C.P.M. Wilderom, & M.F. Peterson (Eds.), *Handbook of organizational culture and climate* (pp. 21–36). Thousand Oaks, CA: Sage.
Schneider, B., Ehrhart, M.G., & Macey, W.A. (2011a). Organizational climate research: Achievements and the road ahead. In N.M. Ashkanasy, C.P.M. Wilderom, & M.F. Peterson (Eds.), *Handbook of organizational culture and climate* (2nd ed., pp. 29–49). Thousand Oaks, CA: Sage.
Schneider, B., Ehrhart, M.G., & Macey, W.A. (2011b). Perspectives on organizational climate and culture. In S. Zedeck (Ed.), *APA handbook of industrial and organizational psychology: Vol. 1. Building and developing the organization* (pp. 373–414). Washington, DC: American Psychological Association.
Schneider, B., Ehrhart, M.G., & Macey, W.A. (2012). A funny thing happened on the way to the future: The focus on organizational competitive advantage lost out. *Industrial and Organizational Psychology: Perspectives on Science and Practice, 5*, 96–101.
Schneider, B., Ehrhart, M.G., & Macey, W.A. (2013). Organizational climate and culture. *Annual Review of Psychology, 64*, 361–388.
Schneider, B., Ehrhart, M.G., Mayer, D.M., Saltz, J.L., & Niles-Jolly, K. (2005). Understanding organization-customer links in service settings. *Academy of Management Journal, 48*, 1017–1032.

References

Schneider, B., & Hall, D.T. (1972). Towards specifying the concept of work climate: A study of Roman Catholic Diocesan priests. *Journal of Applied Psychology, 56*, 447–455.

Schneider, B., Macey, W.H., Lee, W.C., & Young, S.A. (2009). Organizational service climate drivers of the American Customer Satisfaction Index (ACSI) and financial and market performance. *Journal of Service Research, 12*, 3–14.

Schneider, B., Parkington, J.J., & Buxton, V.M. (1980). Employee and customer perceptions of service in banks. *Administrative Science Quarterly, 25*, 252–267.

Schneider, B., & Reichers, A.E. (1983). On the etiology of climates. *Personnel Psychology, 36*, 19–39.

Schneider, B., Salvaggio, A.N., & Subirats, M. (2002). Climate strength: A new direction for climate research. *Journal of Applied Psychology, 87*, 220–229.

Schneider, B., & Snyder, R.A. (1975). Some relationships between job satisfaction and organizational climate. *Journal of Applied Psychology, 60*, 318–328.

Schneider, B., Wheeler, J.K., & Cox, J.F. (1992). A passion for service: Using content analysis to explicate service climate themes. *Journal of Applied Psychology, 77*, 705–716.

Schneider, B., & White, S.S. (2004). *Service quality: Research perspectives*. Thousand Oaks, CA: Sage.

Schneider, B., White, S.S., & Paul, M.C. (1998). Linking service climate and customer perceptions of service quality: Test of a causal model. *Journal of Applied Psychology, 83*, 150–163.

Schulte, M., Ostroff, C., Shmulyian, S., & Kinicki, A. (2009). Organizational climate configurations: Relationships to collective attitudes, customer satisfaction, and financial performance. *Journal of Applied Psychology, 94*, 618–634.

Schwartz, H., & Davis, S. 1981. Matching corporate culture and business strategy. *Organizational Dynamics, 10*(1), 30–38.

Schyns, B., & Van Veldhoven, M. (2010). Group leadership climate and individual organizational commitment: A multilevel analysis. *Journal of Personnel Psychology, 9*(2), 57–68.

Seashore, S.E. (1954). *Group cohesiveness in the industrial work group*. Ann Arbor, MI: Institute for Social Research.

Sells, S.B. (1964). Personnel management. *Annual Review of Psychology, 15*, 399–420.

Selznick, P. (1957). *Leadership in administration*. New York: Harper & Row.

Shamir, B. (1995). Social distance and charisma: Theoretical notes and an exploratory study. *Leadership Quarterly, 6*, 19–47.

Shanahan, J.G., Qu, Y., & Wiebe, J. (2006). *Computing attitude and affect in text: Theory and applications*. Dordrecht, Netherlands: Springer.

Siehl, C. (1985). After the founder: An opportunity to manage culture. In P.J. Frost, L.F. Moore, M.R. Louis, C.C. Lundberg, & J. Martin (Eds.), *Organizational culture* (pp. 125–140). Beverly Hills, CA: Sage.

Siehl, C., & Martin, J. (1988). Measuring organizational culture: Mixing qualitative and quantitative methods. In M. Jones, M. Moore, & R. Snyder (Eds.), *Inside organizations: Understanding the human dimension* (pp. 79–104). Newbury Park, CA: Sage.

Siehl, C., & Martin J. (1990). Organizational culture: A key to financial performance? In B. Schneider (Ed.), *Organizational climate and culture* (pp. 241–281). San Francisco: Jossey-Bass.

Simons, T., & Roberson, Q. (2003). Why managers should care about fairness: The effects of aggregate justice perceptions on organizational outcomes. *Journal of Applied Psychology, 88*, 432–443.

Sims, H. P., & LaFollette, W. (1975). An assessment of the Litwin and Stringer organization climate questionnaire. *Personnel Psychology, 28*(1), 19–38.

Skinner, B. F. (1938). *The behavior of organisms: An experimental analysis*. New York: Appleton-Century.

Smircich L. (1983). Concepts of culture and organizational analysis. *Administrative Science Quarterly, 28*, 339–358.

Smircich, L. (1985). Is the concept of culture a paradigm for understanding organizations and ourselves? In P. Frost, L. Moore, M. R. Louis, C. C. Lundberg, & J. Martin (Eds.), *Organizational culture* (pp. 55–72). Beverly Hills, CA: Sage.

Smircich, L., & Calás, M. B. (1987). Organizational culture: A critical assessment. In F. M. Jablin, L. L. Putnam, K. H. Roberts, & L. W. Porter (Eds.), *Handbook of organizational communication* (pp. 228–263). Beverly Hills, CA: Sage.

Smith, P. C., Smith, O. W., & Rollo, J. (1974). Factor structure for blacks and whites of the job descriptive index and its discriminations of job satisfactions among three groups of subjects. *Journal of Applied Psychology, 59*, 99–100.

Snijders, T. A. B., & Bosker, R. J. (1999). *Multilevel analysis: An introduction to basic and advanced multilevel modeling*. Thousand Oaks, CA: Sage.

Solomon, E. E. (1986). Private and public sector managers: An empirical investigation of job characteristics and organizational climate. *Journal of Applied Psychology, 71*, 247–259.

Sørensen, J. B. (2002). The strength of corporate culture and the reliability of firm performance. *Administrative Science Quarterly, 47*, 70–91.

Sowinski, D. R., Fortmann, K. A., & Lezotte, D. V. (2008). Climate for service and the moderating effects of climate strength on customer satisfaction, voluntary turnover, and profitability. *European Journal of Work and Organizational Psychology, 17*, 73–88.

Spell, C. S., & Arnold, T. J. (2007). A multi-level analysis of organizational justice climate, structure, and employee mental health. *Journal of Management, 33*, 724–751.

Spitzmuller, M., & Ilies, R. (2010). Do they [all] see my true self? Leader's relational authenticity and followers' assessments of transformational leadership. *European Journal of Work and Organizational Psychology, 19*(3), 304–332.

Stern, G. G. (1967). *People in context: The measurement of environmental interaction in school and society*. Syracuse, NY: Syracuse University.

Stern, G. G. (1970). *People in context: Measuring person-environment congruence in education and industry*. New York: Wiley.

Stogdill, R. M. (1968). *Leadership: A survey of the literature. I. Selected topics*. Greensboro, NC: Smith Richardson Foundation.

Sutton, R. I., & Rafaeli, A. (1988). Untangling the relationships between displayed emotions and organizational sales: The case of convenience stores. *Academy of Management Journal, 31*(3), 461–487.

References

Tagiuri, R. (1968a). The concept of organizational climate. In R. Tagiuri & G.H. Litwin (Eds.), *Organizational climate: Explorations of a concept* (pp. 11–32). Boston, MA: Harvard University.

Tagiuri, R. (1968b). Executive climate. In R. Tagiuri & G.H. Litwin (Eds.), *Organizational climate: Explorations of a concept* (pp. 225–241). Boston, MA: Harvard University.

Tagiuri, R., & Litwin, G.H. (Eds.). (1968). *Organizational climate: Explorations of a concept*. Boston: Harvard University.

Tangirala, S., & Ramanujam, R. (2008). Employee silence on critical work issues: The cross level effects of procedural justice climate. *Personnel Psychology, 61,* 37–68.

Tichy, N.M. (1982). Managing change strategically: The technical, political, and cultural keys. *Organizational dynamics, 11*(2), 59–80.

Tracey, J.B., Tannenbaum, S.I., & Kavanaugh, M.J. (1995). Applying trained skills on the job: The importance of the work environment. *Journal of Applied Psychology, 80,* 239–252.

Trice, H.M. (1991). Comments and discussion. In P.J. Frost, L.F. Moore, M.R. Louis, C.C. Lundberg, & J. Martin (Eds.), *Reframing organizational culture* (pp. 298–308). Newbury Park, CA: Sage.

Trice, H.M., & Beyer, J.M. (1993). *The cultures of work organizations*. Englewood Cliffs, NJ: Prentice-Hall.

Tsui, A.S., Wang, H., & Xin, K.R. (2006). Organizational culture in China: An analysis of culture dimensions and culture types. *Management and Organizational Review, 2,* 345–376.

Tsui, A.S., Zhang, Z-X., Wang, H., Xin, K.R., & Wu, J.B. (2006). Unpacking the relationship between CEO leadership behavior and organizational culture. *Leadership Quarterly, 17,* 113–137.

Turner, B. (1971). *Exploring the industrial subculture*. London: Macmillan.

Turnstall, W.B. (1983). Cultural transition at AT&T. *Sloan Management Review, 25*(1), 1–12.

Uhl-Bien, M., Marion, R., & McKelvey, B. (2007). Complexity leadership theory: Shifting leadership from the industrial age to the knowledge era. *Leadership Quarterly, 18,* 298–318.

Van Gennep, A. (1908/1960). *Rites of passage*. Chicago: University of Chicago Press (original work published 1908).

Van Maanen, J. (1976). Breaking in: Socialization to work. In R. Dubin (Eds.) *Handbook of work, organization and society* (pp. 67–130). Chicago: Rand McNally.

Van Maanen, J. (1988). *Tales of the field: On writing ethnography*. Chicago: University of Chicago Press.

Van Maanen, J. (1991). The smile factory: Work at Disneyland. In P.J. Frost, L.F. Moore, M.R. Louis, C.C. Lundberg, & J. Martin (Eds.), *Reframing organizational culture* (pp. 58–76). Newbury Park, CA: Sage.

Van Maanen, J., & Barley, S.R. (1984). Occupational communities: Cultural control in organizations. In L.L. Cummings & B.M. Staw (Eds.), *Research in organizational behavior* (Vol. 6, pp. 287–365). Greenwich, CT: JAI Press.

Van Maanen, J., & Barley, S.R. (1985). Cultural organization: Fragments of a theory. In P.J. Frost, L.F. Moore, M.R. Louis, C.C. Lundberg, & J. Martin (Eds.), *Organizational culture* (pp. 31–54). Beverly Hills, CA: Sage.

Van Maanen, J., & Schein, E.H. (1979). Toward a theory of organizational socialization. In B.M. Staw (Ed.), *Research in organizational behavior* (Vol. 1, pp. 209–264). Greenwich, CT: JAI Press.

Verbeke, W., Volgering, M., & Hessels, M. (1998). Exploring the conceptual expansion within the field of organizational behaviour: Organizational climate and organizational culture. *Journal of Management Studies, 35*(3), 303–329.

Victor, B., & Cullen, J.B. (1987). A theory and measure of ethical climate in organizations. In W.C. Frederick (Ed.), *Research in corporate social performance and policy* (Vol. 9, pp. 51–71). Greenwich, CT: JAI Press.

Victor, B., & Cullen, J.B. (1988). The organizational bases of ethical work climates. *Administrative Science Quarterly, 33*, 101–125.

Virtanen, T. (2000). Commitment and the study of organizational climate and culture. In N.M. Ashkanasy, C.P.M. Wilderom, & M.F. Peterson (Eds.), *Handbook of organizational culture and climate* (pp. 339–354). Thousand Oaks, CA: Sage.

Viteles, M.S. (1932). *Industrial psychology*. New York, NY: Norton.

Vroom, V.H., & Maier, N.R.F. (1961). Industrial social psychology. *Annual Review of Psychology, 12*, 413–446.

Wallace, J.C., Johnson, P.D., Mathe, K., & Paul, J. (2011). Structural and psychological empowerment climates, performance, and the moderating role of shared felt accountability: A managerial perspective. *Journal of Applied Psychology, 96*(4), 840–850.

Wallace, J.C., Popp, E., & Mondore, S. (2006). Safety climate as a mediator between foundation climates and occupational accidents: A group-level investigation. *Journal of Applied Psychology, 91*, 681–688.

Wallace, S.R., & Weitz, J. (1955). Industrial psychology. *Annual Review of Psychology, 6*, 217–250.

Walsh, B.M., Matthews, R.A. Tuller, M.D., Parks, K.M., & McDonald, D.P. (2010). A multilevel model of the effects of equal opportunity climate on job satisfaction in the military. *Journal of Occupational Health Psychology, 15*, 191–207.

Walumbwa, F.O., Hartnell, C.A., & Oke, A. (2010). Servant leadership, procedural justice climate, service climate, employee attitudes, and organizational citizenship behavior: A cross-level investigation. *Journal of Applied Psychology, 95*, 517–529.

Walumbwa, F.O., Peterson, S.J., Avolio, B.J., & Hartnell, C.A. (2010). Relationships of leader and follower psychological capital, service climate, and job performance. *Personnel Psychology, 63*(4), 937–963.

Way, S.A., Sturman, M.C., & Raab, C. (2010). What matters more? Contrasting the effects of job satisfaction and service climate on hotel food and beverage managers' job performance. *Cornell Hotel Quarterly, 51*, 379–397.

Weber, K., & Dacin, M.T. (2011). The cultural construction of organizational life: Introduction to the special issue. *Organization Science, 22*, 287–298.

Weber, Y. (1996). Corporate culture fit and performance in mergers and acquisitions. *Human Relations, 49*, 1181–1202.

Weick, K.E. (1985). The significance of corporate culture. In P.J. Frost, L.F. Moore, M.R. Louis, C.C. Lundberg, & J. Martin (Eds.), *Organizational culture* (pp. 381–390). Thousand Oaks, CA: Sage.

Welsch, L.P., & LaVan, H. (1981). Inter-relationships between organizational commitment and job characteristics, job satisfaction, professional behavior, and organizational climate. *Human Relations, 34*(12), 1079–1089.

Whetten, D.A. (2006). Albert and Whetten revisited: Strengthening the concept of organizational identity. *Journal of Management Inquiry, 15*, 219–234.

Whitman, D.S., Caleo, S., Carpenter, N.C., Horner, M.T., & Bernerth, J.B. (2012). Fairness at the collective level: A meta-analytic examination of the consequences and boundary conditions of organizational justice climate. *Journal of Applied Psychology, 97*, 776–791.

Whyte, W.F. (1943). *Street corner society*. Chicago: University of Chicago Press.

Whyte, W.F. (1948). *Human relations in the restaurant industry*. New York: McGraw-Hill.

Wilderom, C.P.M., Glunk, U., & Mazlowski, R. (2000). Organizational culture as a predictor of organizational performance. In N.M. Ashkanasy, C.P.M. Wilderom, & M.F. Peterson (Eds.), *Handbook of organizational culture and climate* (pp. 193–209). Thousand Oaks, CA: Sage.

Wiley, J.W. (1996). Linking survey results to customer satisfaction and business performance. In A.I. Kraut (Ed.), *Organizational surveys: Tools for assessment and change* (pp. 350–369). San Francisco: Jossey-Bass.

Wiley, J.W. (2010). *Strategic employee surveys: Evidenced-based guidelines for driving organizational success*. San Francisco, CA: Jossey-Bass.

Wiley, J.W., & Brooks, S.M. (2000). The high-performance organizational climate: How workers describe top-performing units. In N.M. Ashkanasy, C.P.M. Wilderom, & M.F. Peterson (Eds.), *Handbook of organizational culture and climate* (pp. 177–191). Thousand Oaks, CA: Sage.

Woodman, R.W., & King, D.C. (1978). Organizational climate: Science or folklore? *Academy of Management Review, 3*, 816–826.

Workday, Inc. (2012). Form S-1 registration statement. Retrieved from http://www.sec.gov/Archives/edgar/data/1327811/000119312512375787/d385110ds1.htm

Xenikou, A., & Simosi, M. (2006). Organizational culture and transformational leadership as predictors of business unit performance. *Journal of Managerial Psychology, 21*(6), 566–579.

Yagil, D. (2008). *The service providers*. New York: Palgrave Macmillan.

Yammarino, F.J., & Dansereau, F. (2011). Multilevel issues in organizational culture and climate research. In N.M. Ashkanasy, C.P.M. Wilderom, & M.F. Peterson (Eds.), *Handbook of organizational culture and climate* (2nd ed., pp. 50–76). Thousand Oaks, CA: Sage.

Yang, J., Mossholder, K.W., & Peng, T.K. (2007). Procedural justice climate and group power distance: An examination of cross-level interaction effects. *Journal of Applied Psychology, 92*, 681–692.

Zaccaro, S.J. (1996). *Models and theories of executive leadership: A conceptual/empirical review and integration*. Alexandria, VA: U.S. Army Research Institute for the Behavioral and Social Sciences.

Zaccaro, S.J. (2001). *The nature of executive leadership: A conceptual and empirical analysis of success*. Washington, DC: APA Books.

Zohar, D. (1980). Safety climate in industrial organizations: Theoretical and applied implications. *Journal of Applied Psychology, 65*, 96–102.

Zohar, D. (2000). A group level model of safety climate: Testing the effect of group climate on microaccidents in manufacturing jobs. *Journal of Applied Psychology, 85*, 587–596.

Zohar, D. (2002). The effects of leadership dimensions, safety climate, and assigned priorities on minor injuries in work groups. *Journal of Organizational Behavior, 23*(1), 75–92.

Zohar, D., & Hofmann, D.A. (2012). Organizational culture and climate. In S.W.J. Kozlowski (Ed.), *The Oxford handbook of industrial and organizational psychology* (pp. 643–666). Oxford, UK: Oxford University Press.

Zohar, D., & Luria, G. (2003). The use of supervisory practices as leverage to improve safety behavior: A cross-level intervention model. *Journal of Safety Research, 34,* 567–577.

Zohar, D., & Luria, G. (2004). Climate as social-cognitive construction of supervisory safety practices: Scripts as proxy of behavior patterns. *Journal of Applied Psychology, 89,* 322–333.

Zohar, D., & Luria, G. (2005). A multi-level model of safety climate: Cross-level relationships between organization and group-level climates. *Journal of Applied Psychology, 90,* 616–628.

Zohar, D., & Tenne-Gazit, O. (2008). Transformational leadership and group interaction as climate antecedents: A social network analysis. *Journal of Applied Psychology, 93,* 744–757.

AUTHOR INDEX

Italicized numbers refer to names in tables or figures.

Aarons, G. A. 196, 302
Abbey, A. 87
Abelson, M. *61*
Abrahamson, E. 170
Adkins, C. L. 174
Agut, S. 91, 113, 212, 289
Aiman-Smith, L. 158
Aksoy, L. 91
Aldenderfer, M. S. 216
Aldrich, H. E. 148, 150, 183
Allen, N. J. 158
Altmann, R. A. 71
Alutto, J. A. 74
Alvesson, M. 4, 7, 117–18, 120–9, *128*, 131–4, 148, 153, 164, 167, 177, 187–8, 190–1, 196, 205–6, 214, 217, 290–1, 296
Anderson, N. 159–60, 294
Anderson, N. R. 87
Andrews, F. M. 28, 85–6
Andrews, J. D. W. 36
Angle, H. L. *61*
Argyris, C. 15–19, 23, 32–3, 60, 65–6, 70, 72, 85, 119, 196, 284
Arikan, A. M. 225
Armenakis, A. A. 165, 238
Arnold, T. J. 107
Arthur, W. Jr. 93
Ashe, D. K. 66
Ashford, S. J. 159
Ashforth, B. E. 60, *61*, 156–7, 155, 294
Ashkanasy, N. M. 6–7, 69, 117, 123, *142*, 143, 196, 214, 242, 262, 265
Asparouhov, T. 216

Athos, A. G. 121–2, 150, 161
Avery, D. R. 87, 97
Avolio, B. J. 91, 112, 214

Baer, M. 87, 109
Bajdo, L. 165
Baker, J. A. 259–63, 269, 272, 300
Baltes, B. B. 71
Balthazard, P. A. 254–5
Barbera, K. M. 84, 236
Bardes, M. 112
Barley, S. R. 136, 149, 154, 168, 170–1, 173
Barling, J. 93, 112
Barnard, C. I. 26
Barney, J. B. 225–7
Barry, B. 182
Barsotti, A. 93
Bartlett, C. J. *38*, 40–3, *42*, 62, 79–80, *81*, 108, 284
Bartunek, J. M. 169
Bashshur, M. 95
Bass, B. M. 31, 70, 112, 191
Bass, R. 191
Bauer, T. N. 94–5, 156, 158
Beaton, A. E. *38*, 43–5, 65
Bebb, M. 112
Beckman, C. 168
Bedeian, A. G. 104
Béland, F. 92
Bell, N. E. 158–9
Benne, K. D. 27–8, 178
Bennett, N. 87, 94–5, 99
Bennis, W. G. 178
Beres, M. E. 154

Berg, P. O. 117–18, 120–4, 129, 164, 167, 187–8, 196, 205–6, 214, 217, 296
Bergman, M. E. 100
Berkman, S. 87, 93, 96
Bernerth, J. B. 73, 286
Berson, Y. 191
BeShears, R. S. 132
Beus, J. M. 93, 100
Beyer, J. M. 7, 117–18, 121–3, 131, 133, 135, 138–9, 146, 148, 150, 152, 155–6, 158, 170–2, 174, 180, 196, 212, 291
Bindl, U. K. 158–9, 294
Black, J. S. 159
Blashfield, R. K. 216
Blau, P. M. 219
Bliese, P. D. 74–5, 78, 87, 99
Blumer, H. 67
Bodner, T. 156
Boehm, M. 148
Boglarsky, C. A. 263
Boisnier, A. 272
Bommer, W. H. 104
Bonaccio, S. 108
Borucki, C. 82
Bosker, R. J. 78
Bowen, D. E. 6, *61*, 87, 90, 100, 105, 108–9, 199, 214, 288
Bower, P. 242
Bradford, L. P. 27–8, 86
Bradley, J. C. 93
Brandt, C. 99, 101–2
Brannen, M. Y. 150
Broadfoot, L. E. *142*, 242, 262, 265
Brodbeck, F. C. 150, 152
Brooks, S. M. 69
Brown, R. D. 74
Brown, R. L. 92
Brown, T. J. 108–9
Brubaker, T. 93
Buchele, R. B. 26–7, 284
Burke, C. S. 14
Burke, M. J. 74, 82, 93, 109–10
Burke, R. J. *61*
Burke, W. W. 40, 48, 69, 80, 161, 178, 206, 230, 243, 296
Butterfield, D. A. 51, 58, 66

Butts, M. M. 75
Buxton, V. M. 60, *61*, 89, 287

Cable, D. M. 158
Calás, M. B. 117
Caldwell, D. F. 256, 300
Caleo, S. 73, 286
Cameron, K. S. 125, 131, 134, 175, 181, 187, 206, 249–51, *250*, 264, 268–71, 300
Campbell, J. P. 32, 35–7, 43, 66, 79–80, *81*
Carpenter, N. C. 73, 286
Carr, J. Z. 71
Cartwright, D. 19, 178
Cawsey, T. 57
Chan, D. 72–3, 99
Chan, L. L. 165
Chan-Serafin, S. 109–10
Chao, G. T. 159
Chatman, J. A. 125, 133, 177, 256, 258, 264, 272, 300
Chen, G. 87
Cherin, D. A. 87, 96
Chin, R. 178
Choi, C. C. 68
Christian, M. S. 93
Christie, R. 28, 85
Chuang, A. 91
Clandinin, D. J. 245, 300
Clark, B. 118
Cole, M. S. 104
Colella, A. 159
Colquitt, J. A. 87, 94–5, 99–102, 288
Conn, A. B. 46, 68, 111
Connelly, F. M. 245, 300
Connelly, M. S. 112
Cooil, B. 91
Cooke, R. A. 165, 254, *255*, 300
Cooper, B. 258
Cooper-Thomas, H. D. 159–60, 294
Cox, J. F. 212, 248
Cox, T. H., Jr. 96
Crant, J. M. 159
Croft, Don 28–9, 43, 49
Cropanzano, R. 87, 95, 219
Cullen, J. B. *61*, 87

Author Index

Dacin, M. T. 9
Dalal, R. S. 98, 108
Dansereau, F. 243
Dastmalchian, A. 87
Davey, K. M. 125, 141
Davidson, E. J. 230
Davies, H. T. O. 242
Davis, A. 101–2
Davis, S. 134
Dawson, J. F. 87, 101–4
Deal, T. E. 7, 122, 151, 161, 175, 179, 187, 206, 243
Dean, A. 91
de Chermont, K. 87
Dedobbeleer, N. 92
DeLorean, J. 169
Demaree, R. G. 74
DeNisi, A. S. 97
Denison, D. R. 7, 129–30, *130*, 140, 161–2, 164–5, 167, 176, 196, 198, 201, 203, 207, 212, 214, 216–19, 251–3, *252*, 300
Dentsten, I. L. 258
Descza, E. *61*
DeShon, R. P. 71
Deutsch and Shea, Inc. 30
Dickson, J. W. 87
Dickson, M. W. 103, 132, 150–1, 165
Dickson, W. J. 12, 26, 118, 154
Dieterly, D. *38*
Dietz, J. 105–7
Dimotakis, N. 214
DiTomaso, N. 176
Dlugosz, L. R. 302
Dodge, J. 244–5
Doherty, M. L. *62*, 111
Dorfman, P. W. 103, 150–1, 293
Downey, H. K. *38*, 54–5
Dragoni, L. 111–12
Drasgow, F. 87
Drexler, J. A. *39*, 52, 58
Duhigg, C. 281
Dukerich, J. M. 148
Dunnette, M. D. 31–2, 35–7, 66
Dusig, M. S. 74
Duxbury, L. 214
Dvir, T. 191
Dyer, W. G. 190

Eden, D. 210
Edwards, J. R. 158
Ehrhart, K. H. 106, 288
Ehrhart, M. G. 1, 4–6, 14, 71, 87, 90, 94–5, 106, 111–12, 114, 143, 200, 209, 211, 214, 219–20, *220*, 287–9, 296, 302
Ehrlich, S. B. 148
Eisenberger, R. 210
Erdogan, B. 94–5, 156
Ettington, D. R. 125, 131, 134, 175, 206
Etzioni, A. 154
Evan, W. M. 33–5, 52, 65, 98, 119, 196
Everitt, B. S. 216

Falkus, S. *142*, 242, 262, 265
Feldman, D. C. 159
Feldman, M. S. 134, 174
Fiedler, F. E. 27, 284
Field, G. *61*
Fineman, S. 51, 54, 285
Finkelstein, L. M. 74
Fiol, M. 172
Fisher, C. D. 159
Fitzgerald, L. F. 87
Flamholtz, E. G. 181, 240, 242, 262, 264
Flanagan, J. C. 246
Fleishman, E. A. 14–15, 24, 27, 30, 41, 65, 79, 85, 110, 119, 196, 284, 289
Flynn, F. J. 177
Fombrun, C. J. 170
Ford, J. K. 71
Forehand, G. A. 20–3, 27, 31, 33–4, 46, 53, 59, 64, 66
Fortes-Ferreira, L. 99
Fortmann, K. A. 101–2
Frederiksen, N. O. *38*, 43–5, 56, 65–6, 86, 116
French, J. R. P., Jr. 26
Frese, M. 87, 109, 214
Friedlander, F. *38*, 43, 56
Frost, P. J. 4, 117–18, 122–4, 126, 129, 133, 137, 140–1, 145, 155, 167, 172, 180, 190, 214, 217

Fry, L. W. 170
Fry, R. E. 274

Gaines, J. 170
Gardner, B. 118
Gardner, P. D. 159
Geertz, C. 67
Gelfand, M. J. 87, 151
Gellerman, S. W. 36, 119–20
George, J. M. 74, 76–8
Georgopoulos, B. S. 26, 36
Gerhart, B. 150
Gerras, S. 93
Gerstner, L. V., Jr. 234
Gettman, H. J. 87
Ghiselli, E. E. 11
Gibb, J. R. 27–8
Gillespie, M. A. 164–5, 251, 253
Gilmer, B. v. H. 20–3, 30–1, 33, 46, 53, 59, 64, 66, 119, 284
Glick, W. H. 60, *61–2*, 67, 71–2, 286
Glisson, C. 73, 165, 196, 256
Glunk, U. 162, 294
Godsoe, B. 244–5
Golden-Biddle, K. 172
Goldstein, H. W. 111
Goldstein, I. L. 87
Goldstein, J. W. 94
Gonzalez, J. A. 97
González-Romá, V. 99–102, 288
Goparaju, S. 159
Gordon, G. G. 151–2, 176
Gouldner, A. 178
Gray, J. 258
Green, P. 165, 196, 256
Greenbaum, R. L. 87, 112
Greenberg, S. *38*, 56
Gregory, B. T. 165–6, 169, 215, 251, 293
Griffin, A. E. 159
Griffin, M. A. 92–3, 114, 289
Grizzle, J. W. 108–9
Grover, L. 214
Guion, R. M. 50–2, 54–6, 59, 68, 70, 73–4, 85, 99, 284, 286
Gundry, L. K. 246, 248
Gupta, V. 103, 132, 150–1, 293
Gutek, B. A. 106–8

Haaland, S. 165, 251
Hall, D. T. *38*, 48–9, *49*, 56
Halpin, A. 28–9, 43, 49
Halverson, R. R. 99
Hammond, S. A. 245, 300
Hand, H. *38*
Hanges, P. J. 103, 150–1, 206, 293
Hannah, D. R. 135
Hannah, S. T. 214
Hardy, C. 124
Harrell, T. W. 30
Harris, L. C. 207, 231
Harris, S. G. 165
Harrison, D. A. 56, 72
Harrison, S. H. 156–7, 294
Hartnell, C. A. 91, 162, *163*, 191, 214, 251, 266–7, 274, 294–5, 303
Hatch, M. J. 134, 137–8, 172, 180, 183, 231
Hattrup, K. 74
Hauenstein, N. M. A. 74
Hebl, M. R. 87
Hellriegel, D. *38*, 49–51, 53–6, 58, 80, 82, 105, 284–5
Helms Mills, J. C. 133
Henderson, D. J. 104
Herdman, A. O. 87, 97
Hermida, R. 98, 108
Heron, J. 245, 300
Heskett, J. L. 161, 175–7, 191, 207, 211, 236, 243, 295
Hessels, M. 131
Hicks-Clarke, D. 96
Hickson, D. J. 46
Hoagwood, K. E. 165, 196
Hofmann, D. A. 44, 92–4, 106, 116, 196, 200, 205, 209, 211, 222–4, *223*, 231, 298–9
Hofstede, G. 7, 150–1
Holcombe, K. M. 6, 214
Holland, J. L. 111, 151, 171, *172*
Holmes, H. 92
Hong, Y. 91, 112, 212, 289
Horner, M. T. 73, 286
House, R. J. *38*, 103, 151, 164, 293
Hovland, C. I. 230
Howe, J. G. *39*
Hu, J. 91, 289
Hudson, P. 215

Author Index

Huff, J. W. 71
Hulin, C. L. 87
Hults, B. M. *61*, 87
Hunter, J. E. 41
Huntington, R. 210
Hurley, A. 82
Hutchison, S. 210

Iles, P. 96
Ilies, R. 104

Jablin, F. M. 159
Jackson, C. L. 87, 288
Jacofsky, E. F. *61–2*
Jacque, E. 118
James, L. A. *62*, 66, 72, *81*, 83
James, L. R. 22, 49–54, 60, *61–2*,
  66–8, 70–4, 76–8, *81*, 81–3, 256,
  284–7
Janis, I. L. 230
Javidan, M. 103, 151, 293
Jehn, K. A. 174, 256
Jensen, O. *38*, 43–5, 65
Jermier, J. M. 170, 216, 236
Jiang, K. 91, 289
Jimmieson, N. L. 101, 238
Johanneson, R. E. 50, 54–6, 284–5
Johnson, R. H. 253
Johnston, H. R., Jr. 58
Jonas, H. S. 274
Jones, A. P. 22, 49–54, 60, *61*, 68, 70,
  81, *81*, 284–5, 287
Jones, G. R. 158, 294
Joyce, W. F. *61–2*, 67
Jung, T. 242

Kahn, R. L. 19, 23, 25–6, 88, 98, 120,
  136, 154, 182, 196, 284
Kaplan, R. S. 235
Karasick, B. W. *38*, 45–6, *46*, 57, 64–6
Katz, D. 19, 23, 25–6, 88, 98, 120,
  136, 154, 182, 196, 284
Katzell, R. A. 30
Kavanaugh, M. J. 87
Keenan, A. *61*
Keiningham, T. L. 91
Keith, N. 214
Kelleher, K. 165, 196
Kelley, H. H. 230

Kelloway, E. K. 93, 112
Kelman, H. 178
Kendall, W. E. 30
Kennedy, A. A. 7, 122, 151, 161, 175,
  179, 187, 206, 243
Kerr, S. 236
Ketchen, D. J., Jr. 268
Kim, K. 68
Kimberly, J. R. 162
King, D. C. 52
King, E. B. 87
Kinicki, A. J. 84, 162, *163*, 196,
  220–2, *221*, 242, 294, 298, 302
Klein, H. J. 159
Klein, K. J. 46, 68, 73, 75–6, 111, 114,
  287
Kleinberg, J. 150
Ko, C. H. E. 68
Kopelman, R. E. 218
Kossek, E. E. 96
Kotrba, L. M. 164–5, 215, 251, 253
Kotter, J. P. 161, 175–7, 191, 207, 211,
  236, 243, 295
Kozlowski, S. W. J. 46, *61–2*, 73–4, 76,
  87, 111, 159–60, 214, *223*, 287
Krefting, L. A. 133, 145, 155, 180,
  190
Kreiner, G. E. 172
Krippendorf, K. 67
Kuenzi, M. 4, 9, 71, 87–8, 95, 98, 107,
  112, 116, 125, 215, 301–2
Kwantes, C. T. 150–1, 263

LaCost, H. A. 71
Lafferty, J. C. *255*
LaFollette, W. R. *39*, 54–7, 285
Lance, C. E. 75
Landau, S. 216
Landsverk, J. 165, 196
Latham, G. P. 37
LaVan, H. *61*
Lawler, E. E., III 26, 32, 35–7, *38*,
  48–9, *49*, 56, 66
Leana, C. R. 182
Leavitt, H. J. 16–17, 31, 49, 284
LeBreton, J. M. 74–5, 77, 287
Lee, J. M. 108–9
Lee, S. K. J. 165, 177, 256, 268
Lee, W. C. 91, 258

Leese, M. 216
Lewin, K. 13–14, 16, 21, 27, 32, 59, 66, 69–70, 72, 79, 85, 110, 178, 283–4, 289
Lezotte, D. V. 101–2
Li, A. 95
Liao, H. 91, 94–5, 97, 107, 289
Likert, R. 19–20, 23, 26, 31–2, 49, 60, 111, 120, 284
Lindell, M. 99, 101–2
Lippitt, R. 13–14, 27, 178, 283
Litwin, G. H. 33–5, 37–41, *38–9*, 43, 48–9, 53, 64–6, 79–80, *81*, 111, 119, 218, 284
Löfgren, O. 153
Lord, R. G. 206, 214
Loughlin, C. 93, 112
Louis, M. R. 122–3, 128–9, 134, 141, 155, 157, 160, 170, 174, 188–90, 201, 295, 303
Lundberg, C. C. 122–3, 136, 188, *188*, 236
Lundby, K. 258
Luria, G. 44, 78, 93–4, 99–103, 113, 209, 259, 273, 288, 302
Lyon, J. S. 111

McDonald, D. P. 87, 156
Macey, W. H. 1, 4–5, 65, 71, 84, 87, 91, 190, 200, 211, 219–20, *220*, 236, 258, 276, 287, 296
McGregor, D. 16–19, 23–4, 32, 41, 60, 65–6, 70, 72, 79, 85, 110–11, 178, 284, 289
McIntosh, M. 214
McKay, P. F. 87, 96–7, 107, 109, 217
McKelvey, B. 302
McMilan-Capehart, A. 87, 97
McNally, R. 242
McNeil, P. K. 68
Magley, V. J. 87
Maier, N. 31
Mannion, R. 242
Mannix, E. A. 174
Mansfield, R. *38*, 46–8, *47*
Margulies, N. *38*, 43
Marion, R. 302
Mark, B. 94, 106
Marks, M. A. 112

Markus, K. A. 180, 183, 197
Martin, C. L. 94
Martin, J. 4, 7, 117–18, 122–4, 126–9, 131–7, 140–1, 143–4, 148, 161, 164, 167–70, 172, 174, 182–3, 187, 190, 199, 206–7, 214, 216–17, 272, 290–1, 294–6
Martinez-Tur, V. 87
Marytott, K. M. 91
Matthews, R. A. 87
Mayberg, S. 165, 196
Mayer, D. M. 14, 87, 90, 94–5, 104, 106–7, 111–12, 220, 288–9
Mayhew, B. H. 67
Mayo, E. 12, 26
Mazlowski, R. 162, 294
Mead, J. H. 67
Meek, V. L. 187
Meglino, B. M. 174
Meindl, J. R. 148
Merton, R. 28, 85, 178
Meyer, H. H. 34–5
Meyer, J. P. 158
Meyer, R. D. 98, 108
Meyerson, D. E. 123, 140, 174
Miceli, M. P. *61*
Michael, J. A. 28
Michaelis, B. 87
Michela, J. L. 69, 230
Michels, L. C. 75
Miller, D. 149
Miller, V. D. 159
Mills, A. J. 133
Milton, L. P. 135
Miner, J. B. 124
Minton, M. K. 68
Mischel, W. 98, 108
Mishra, A. K. 161–2, 167, 216
Mitchell, M. S. 219
Moch, M. K. 169
Moliner, C. 87
Mondore, S. 93, 113, 289
Moore, L. F. 122–3
Moran, E. T. 218, 230
Mor Barak, M. E. 87, 96
Morgan, G. 130, 179, 184, 190–1, 193
Morgeson, F. 93
Morris, M. A. 87, 97
Morrison, E. W. 159

Author Index

Mossholder, K. W. 94–5
Mowen, J. C. 108–9
Muchinsky, P. M. 39
Muhammad, R. H. 196, 220–2, *221*, 298
Mulvey, P. W. 158
Mumford, M. D. 112
Murray, H. 28
Muthén, B. 216

Naumann, S. E. 87, 94–5, 99
Neal, A. 92–3, 114, 289
Neale, W. S. 165, 201, 207, 251, 300
Near, J. P. *61*
Nelson, D. L. 160
Newman, D. A. 56, 75, 78
Newton, T. J. *61*
Nieminen, L. 165, 251
Niles-Jolly, K. 14, 90, 220, 289
Nishii, L. H. 94, 104, 111, 151
Noe, R. A. 87, 288
Norton, D. P. 235
Nylund, K. L. 216, 268, 272

Odiorne, G. S. 31
O'Donnell-Trujillo, N. 125
Ogbonna, E. 207, 231
Oldham, G. R. *38*, 48–9, *49*
O'Leary-Kelly, A. M. 159
O'Neill, O. A. 4, 117–18, 123–4
Oreg, S. 191
O'Reilly, C. A. 125, 133, 207, 256, *256–7*, 258, 300
Ospina, S. 244–5
Ostroff, C. 81–2, 84, 87, 100, 159–60, 196, 199, 211, 220–2, *221*, 242, 288, 298, 302
Ott, J. S. 69, 123, 131, 133, 135–6, 140, 146–7, 150–1, 158, 180, 196, 206, 291, 293, 295
Ou, A. Y. 162, *163*, 294
Ouchi, W. G. 117, 121–2, 141, 150, 161

Pacanowsky, M. E. 125
Pace, C. R. 28, 34, 59, 73, 86
Parker, C. P. 71
Parker, S. K. 158–9, 294
Parkington, J. J. 60, *61*, 89, 108–9, 287

Parks, K. M. 87
Parsons, T. 154, 178
Pascale, R. T. 121–2, 150, 161
Patterson, M. G. 82, *83*, 261
Paul, M. C. 84, 209, 289
Payne, R. L. *38*, 46–8, *47*, 51–2, 54–5, 58–9, 80–1, 99, 104, 127, 174–5, 181, 197, 201, 284–5
Payne, S. C. 93, 100
Peiró, J. M. 87, 91, 99, 113, 212, 288–9
Pelz, D. C. 28, 85–6
Peng, A. C. 214
Peng, T. K. 95
Perry, J. L. *61*
Perry, S. J. 106, 288
Peters, T. J. 119, 122, 161, 292
Peterson, M. F. 6–7, 69, 117, 143, 150–1, 196, 214
Peterson, S. J. 91
Pettigrew, A. 76–7, 79, 117–21, 130, 139, 166, 197, 289–90, 294
Phelps, M. *38*, 54
Pheysey, D. C. *38*
Phillips, N. 124
Popp, E. 93, 113, 289
Porter, L. W. 31
Portwood, J. D. 154
Posner, B. Z. 160
Potter, R. E. 254
Powell, G. N. 51, 58, 66, 160
Priest, H. A. 14
Pritchard, R. D. *38*, 45–6, *46*, 57, 64–6
Probst, T. 93–4
Pugh, D. S. 46, 51–2, 58, 80–1, 284
Pugh, S. D. 97, 105–6

Qu, Y. 248
Quick, J. C. 160
Quinn, R. E. 82, 162, 181, 187, 249–51, *250*, 264, 268, 300

Raab, C. 91
Rafaeli, A. 143
Rafferty, A. E. 101, 238
Ramanujam, R. 95
Ramesh, A. 111
Ramos, J. 87

Randle, Y. 181, 240, 242, 262, 264
Ravasi, D. 172
Raver, J. L. 114, 151, 209
Ravlin, E. C. 174
Ray, R. 270
Reason, P. 245, 300
Reger, S. J. M. 184, *185–6*
Reichers, A. E. 6, 33, 60, *61*, 66–7, 71, 80, 84, 141, 143, 196, 203, 205, 218, 229, 275
Reiter-Palmon, R. 112
Resick, C. J. 103
Richards, M. *38*
Ritchie, S. A. 164
Rizzo, J. R. *38*
Roberson, Q. 94–5, 100, 104
Roberts, J. E. 71
Roethlisberger, F. J. 12, 26, 118, 154
Rohrbaugh, J. 82, 162, 249
Roth, P. L. 56
Rouiller, J. Z. 87
Rousseau, D. M. 69, 135, 137–8, 141, 196, 246, 248, 254
Ruef, M. 148, 150, 183
Rupp, D. E. 94–5, 107
Russell, S. V. 214

Sackmann, S. A. 139, 141, 143, 162, 166–7, 214, 275, 294
Saffold, G. S. 164–5, 167, 174–5, 201, 295, 303
Saks, A. M. 155
Salanova, M. 91, 113, 212, 289
Salas, E. 14
Saltz, J. L. 14, 90, 220, 289
Salvador, R. 109–10, 112
Salvaggio, A. N. 99, 111, 288
Sanders, E. 270
Sarpy, S. A. 109–10
Sarros, J. C. 258
Sathe, V. 123, 134, 136, 158, 175, 177, 230, 295
Sawitzky, A. C. 196
Schall, E. 244–5
Schaubroeck, J. M. 214
Schein, E. H. 2, 7, 23–5, 70, 116, 119–20, 123, 127, 131–7, 140–1, 143, 146–9, *147*, 154, 157, 161, 170, 175, 177, 180–2, 189–90, 192–3, 197, 201–2, 204–7, 209–11, 217, 224, 229–31, 235, 237–8, 243, 247, 269, 273–5, 284, 291, 293, 295–6, 301
Schmidt, A. M. 71, 164, 251
Schmidt, F. L. 41
Schminke, M. 4, 71, 87–8, 98, 107, 116, 125, 215, 301–2
Schnake, M. E. *61*
Schneider, B. 1, 3–6, 14–16, 21, 33, *38*, 40–3, *42*, 45, 49, 51–8, 60, *61*, 62, 66–8, 70–1, 79–80, *81*, 84–91, 94, 99, 101, 105–9, 111–14, 141, 143, 152–3, 171–2, 189–90, 196–7, 199–200, 202–3, 205–7, 209, 211–12, 214–15, 218–20, *220*, 229–30, 236, 248, 271, 275–6, 284–5, 287–9, 293, 296, 298
Schoenwald, S. K. 165, 196
Schulte, M. 84, 242, 268, 302
Schultz, M. 172
Schwartz, H. 134
Schyns, B. 87
Scott, T. 242
Seashore, S. E. 26
Sells, S. B. 31
Selznick, P. 118
Senter, J. L. 74–5, 77, 287
Shaffer, M. A. 165
Shanahan, J. G. 248
Shmulyian, S. 84, 242, 302
Shook, C. L. 165
Shore, L. M. 104
Siehl, C. 135–6, 148, 161, 164, 167, 169, 187, 189–90, 206–7, 216, 294, 296
Simons, T. 94–5
Simons, T. L. 104
Simosi, M. 165, 256
Sims, D. E. 14
Sims, H. P. *39*, 54–7
Sin, H. P. 75, 78
Sitkin, S. B. 134, 148
Skinner, B. F. 11
Slocum, J. W., Jr. *38*, 49–51, 53–6, 58, 60, *61–2*, 67, 80, 82, 105, 170, 284–5

Sluss, D. M. 156–7, 294
Smerek, R. E. 164–5, 251
Smircich, L. 117, 125, 128, 130, 139, 144, 161, 187–8, 290
Smith, A. 109–10
Smith, D. B. 46
Smith, P. C. 56
Snape, E. 165
Snijders, T. A. B. 78
Snow, C. C. 268
Snyder, R. A. *38*, 54–5, 57, 80, 285
Solomon, E. E. *61*
Sonntag, K. 87
Sørensen, J. B. 164, 176–7, 215, 295
Sorra, J. S. 46, 68, 111
Sowa, D. 210
Sowinski, D. R. 101–2
Spell, C. S. 107
Spitzmuller, M. 104
Spreitzer, G. M. 251
Srivastva, S. 274
Stagl, K. C. 14
Stahl. D. 216
Staw, B. M. 158–9
Stegmaier, R. 87
Stern, G. 28, 73
Stetzer, A. 92
Stogdill, R. 14
Stringer, R. A. 34–5, 37–41, *38–9*, 43, 49, 53, 64–6, 79–80, *81*, 111, 119, 218, 284
Sturman, M. C. 91, 104
Su, S. 168
Subirats, M. 99, 288
Sutton, R. I. 143
Sveningsson, S. 188, 190
Symon, G. 125, 141
Szumal, J. L. 165, 254, 300

Tagiuri, R. 28, 33–5, 64–6, 85, 284
Tamkins, M. M. 220
Tangirala, S. 95
Tannenbaum, S. I. 87
Tenne-Gazit, O. 93–4, 100, 111–12
Tetrick, L. E. *61*, 68, 104
Thatcher, S. 174
Thomas, J. B. 268
Tichy, N. M. 187, 296

Tordera, N. 288
Tracey, J. B. 87
Treviño, L. K. 214
Trice, H. M. 7, 117–18, 121–3, 127, 131, 133, 135, 138–9, 146, 148, 150, 152, 155–6, 158, 170–2, 174, 180, 196, 212, 291
Truxillo, D. M. 156
Tsui, A. S. 191, 268
Tucker, J. S. 156
Tuller, M. D. 87
Turner, B. 118
Turnstall, W. B. 134, 187, 296

Uhl-Bien, M. 302

Van Gennep, A. 156
Van Maanen, J. 131, 149, 153–4, 156–7, 168–71, 173
Van Veldhoven, M. 87
Verbeke, W. 131
Victor, B. *61*, 87
Virtanen, T. 69
Viteles, M. S. 17
Volgering, M. 131
Volkwein, J. F. 218, 230
Vroom, V. H. 31

Waldman, D. A. 112
Wall, T. D. 51, 54, 285
Wallace, J. C. 93, 113, 289
Wallace, S. R., Jr. 30
Walsh, B. M. 87
Walumbwa, F. O. 91, 94–5, 191, 274
Wang, H. 191, 268
Waterman, R. H., Jr. 119, 122, 161, 292
Way, S. A. 91
Wayne, S. J. 104
Weber, K. 9
Weber, Y. 237
Weick, K. E. 32, 35–7, 66, 235
Weitz, J. 30
Welsch, L. P. *61*
West, M. 87
West, M. A. 87, 101–2
Whalley, D. 242
Wheeler, J. K. 212, 248

Whetten, D. A. 124
White, R. K. 13–14, 66, 283, 287
White, S. S. 84, 209, 271, 289
Whitman, D. S. 73, 286
Whyte, W. F. 118
Wiebe, J. 248
Wilderom, C. P. M. 6–7, 69, 84, 117, 143, 162, 165, 167, 176, 196, 214, 294
Wiley, J. W. 69, 91, 105–6
Wilkins, A. L. 117, 141
Wilkinson, B. 207
Williamson, I. O. 100
Witt, L. A. 106, 288
Wolf, G. 74
Wolf, S. 159
Woodman, R. W. 52
Workday, Inc. 238
Wright, M. A. 68
Wu, J. B. 191

Xenikou, A. 165, 256
Xin, K. R. 191, 268

Yagil, D. 91
Yammarino, F. 74, 243
Yang, J. 95, 107
Young, S. A. 71, 84, 91, 236
Yu, K. 165, 177, 256, 258, 268

Zablah, A. R. 108–9
Zaccaro, S. J. 112, 274
Zander, A. 19
Zapata-Phelan, C. P. 95
Zhang, Z.-X. 191
Zohar, D. 44, 60, *61*, 78, 92–4, 99–103, 111–13, 116, 196, 200, 205, 209, 211, 222–4, 223, 231, 259, 273, 287–8, 298–9, 302
Zonia, S. C. 96

SUBJECT INDEX

Figures/tables/photos/illustrations are indicated by an *italicized number*.

absenteeism 52, 95, 101
accidents 92–3, 109, 113, 114, 259
accumulated learning 235–6
adaptability 163, 177, 182, 256; in the DOCS 164, 207, 251–2
adaptive cultures *166*, 177, 191–2, 243
adhocracy 162–3, 249–51, 268–9
AD index *see* average deviation index
Administrative Science Quarterly 118, 123, 289–90
Agency Climate Questionnaire *42*
aggregation: 73–8, 286–7; climate strength and 99, 102; statistics 75–7; within-group agreement and 74
aggression 13, 15
agreement 59, 99; interrater 74; statistics 75, 78, 286–7; variability in 75, 77–8, 102; within-group 74, 77; within-unit 75, 77–8, 99, 286; *see also* climate strength; culture strength
AIG 240
alignment 221–2, 225, 231, 299; focused climates and 86–7; goal 161; organizational climate and 15–16, 105, 228; organizational culture and 166, 175, 234–5, *303*; strength and 98, 201–2; of talent management 240
ambiguity, in culture 126–7
analysis: cluster 170, 216; content 248; narrative 248; qualitative 247–8; *see also* levels of analysis
Annual Review of Psychology 1, 30–1

anthropology 3, 67, 123, 204
APA Handbook of Industrial and Organizational Psychology 1
Appreciative Inquiry 244–5, 300
artifacts 21, 119, 132, 135–7, *221*; penetration 175; the competing values framework and 163
The Art of Japanese Management: Applications for American Executives (Pascale & Athos) 121
ASA model *see* Attraction-Selection-Attrition model
assumptions 3–4; alignment and 202; ASA model and 153; change and 177, 183, 229–31; competitive advantage and 226; culture strength and 173–5; CVF and *163*; effectiveness and 202; of founders 146–7; hybrid research design and 143; of management 17–19, 24; organizational climate and 205, 209, 218, 229–31; of organizational culture 125, 132, 135–7, 149, 182, 220–4; organizational culture definition and 2, 134; socialization and 154–5
Aston Studies 46
atmosphere 25, 284; group 27; organizational climate and 13, 17–20; psychological 45, 65
attitudes: A factor and 56, 72; change in 230; diversity climate and 96; justice climate and 95, 107; organizational culture and 162–4, 166; as outcomes of organizational

349

climate 82, 84, 110, 221–2; overlap with organizational climate 41, 54–6, 69, 85, 285; psychological climate and 72; service climate and 91–2
Attraction-Selection-Attrition (ASA) model 16, 45, 67, 152–3, 171–2
autonomy 36, 46, 80–3, 162, 163
average deviation (AD) index 74
awareness 132, 205, 297

basic assumptions *see* assumptions
behavioral norms *see* norms
behavior patterns: as a layer of organizational culture 136–7; OCI and 254;
beliefs *see* values
benchmarks 130, 270–1, 280, 300; DOCS and 253; OCAI and 250
BOCI *see* Business Organizational Climate Index
boundary conditions: organizational climate 105–8, 287–8; organizational culture 164–5, 273; *see also* moderation
BP 215, 259–60, 272
branding 239, 260–1
breadth: culture strength and 175; of organizational culture 133; of organizational climate research 209–10; of organizational culture *versus* organizational climate 204–5
bundles 66, 228, 267; of attributes 54, 198; of resources 225, 227
bureaucracy 161
bureaucratic culture 191
burnout: climate for 87
Business Organizational Climate Index (BOCI) 47

Can Two Rights Make a Wrong? (Reger) 184–6
Carnegie Foundation 118–19
causality 84, 90, 229–30
CEO *see* chief executive officer
change 40; adaptive cultures and *166*, 177, 191–2; assumptions and 177, 183, 229–31; in attitudes 230; bases for 236–9; climate strength and 35, 98; competitive advantage and 227; culture strength and 177, 184; CVF and *163*; in goals 237–8; leadership and 21, 184–92, 229–31, 273–4, 296; life cycles and 180–3, 188–90; organizational climate 16–17, 35, 39, 73, 206, 211, 229–31, 301–2; organizational culture 120, 129–32; 178–92, 229–31, 273–4, 295–6, 301; readiness 237–8; subcultures and 183–4, 189–90; symbolism and 184, 190–1; values and 191–2
change information climate 101
character 20–1, 26–7, 31, 34, 65
chief executive officer (CEO) 112, 191
citizenship *see* organizational citizenship behavior
clan culture 122, 162–4, 249–51; 266–7
climate consensus 99; *see also* climate strength
climate–outcome relationships 113; boundary conditions 105–8
climate *see* climate strength; burnout, climate for; change information climate; defensive climate; diversity climate; emotional climate; equal opportunity climate; ethical climate; focused climates; goal-oriented climate; human relations; implementation climate; industrial relations, climate for; initiative, climate for; innovation climate; justice climate; leadership climate; managerial climate; molar climate; organizational climate; process climates; productive climates; psychological safety, climate for; safety climate; service climate; sexual harassment, climate for; social climate; strategic climates; subclimates
climate strength 98–105, 115, 199, 201; aggregation and 99, 102; as boundary condition 287–8; change and 35, 98; climate level and 102–3; conflict and 98–9;

Subject Index

dispersion and 72, 99, 104; diversity and 100; focus groups and 104; future research agenda 104, 302; group cohesiveness and 98, 100; justice climate and 94–5, 99–102; leadership and 100; leadership climate and 99; as a moderator 77, 99, 100–2, 288; molar climate and 99; multilevel 103; nonlinear relationships 101, 102, 104; outcomes of 100–1; predictors of 100; qualitative research and 104, 212; safety climate and 99, 103; service climate and 99, 101; standard deviation 201; varying findings for 101–3
climate variability 103; *see also* climate strength
climcult framework 219–20, 298–9
cluster analysis 170, 216
College Characteristics Index 28
commitment 56; clan culture and 251; climate strength and 101; CVF and 163; involvement and 162; OCP and 258; organizational climate and 82, 95, 107; organizational culture and 121, 125, 133; socialization and 158
communication: CVF and 163; focus groups and 247; leader 112; networks 94; organizational climate and 27–8, 31, 65; organizational culture and 242; socialization tactics and 158
company personality *see* personality
competing values framework (CVF) 162–4, 214, 266–9; DOCS and 251–2; OCAI and 249–51; OCM and 82; organizational life cycles and 181
competitive advantage 122, 225–9, 265
complexity: organizational climate and 22, 94, 105, 106; organizational culture and 145–6, 164, 215; social 226–8
computational linguistics 248
conflict: climate strength and 98–9; in mergers and acquisitions 237; molar climate and 80–1, 287; organizational climate and 34, 35, 39–40, 41–2; organizational culture and 126–7; role 89; among subcultures 126, 174, 272
consistency: in the DOCS 164, 215, 251–2; organizational culture and 126, 161, 222
constructive cultures: OCI and 254–6; 266–7
context 23; individuals *versus* 198–9; macro view of 198; meaning of 199–200; organizational climate and 47–8; procedural justice 94
cooperation 13, 110; molar climate and 81–3
Cooperative Inquiry 244–5, 300
critical incidents 246, 248
cultural diagnosis 184, 190, 236–9, 272–4; considerations 279–81; *see also* cultural inquiry
cultural dynamics model 137, 231
cultural forms 137–8
cultural inquiry 233–4; blending qualitative and quantitative 243–4, 275–9; charter for 269, 276, 279; focus of 263–9; focus groups in 247–8, 269–70, 275, 277–8; interviews 245–7, 275–7; key points to consider in 279–81; leadership assessments and 272–4, 281; measurement framework for 241–4; mergers and acquisitions and 237; precipitating events leading to 237; qualitative approaches to 244–9, 275–9; quantitative approach to 249–79; reasons for 236–9, 299; subcultures and 246–7; talent management and 239–41
cultural manifestations 126, 192; *see also* cultural forms
cultural penetration 174–5
culture *see* adaptive culture; bureaucratic culture; clan culture; constructive cultures; culture strength; defensive culture; error management culture; ethical culture; feeder culture; informal culture; innovative culture; market

culture; national culture; negative culture; organizational culture; safety culture; subcultures; work-family culture
culture embedding mechanisms 147, 181, 229–30; organizational climate and 201, 210–11
culture strength 173–8, 243, 295, 303; alignment and 201–2; breadth and 175
customer orientation 101, 108–9, 264
customer retention 89–90
customer satisfaction: diversity climate and 97; justice climate and 94–5; minority representation and 107; molar climate and 84–5; OCI and 254–5; service climate and 90–2, 101, 105–6, 114, 207; text analytics and 248
customer service 84–5, 90, 207
CVF *see* competing values framework

data: aggregation 73–8, 286–7; ideal *versus* future state 271–2; missing 75, 78; narrative 248; qualitative analysis of 247–8; structures, nested 75–6, 78
defensive climate 28, 34, 86
defensive culture: OCI and 254–6
Denison Consulting 253, 270
Denison Organizational Culture Survey (DOCS) 207, 251–3, 260, 263–4, 278
Department of Energy 174
development: capability 252–3; leader 274; organizational 178, 237, 270; organizational climate 211; organizational culture 145–53, 181, 211, 292–3; subculture 170
differentiation 126, 129, 131, 216; cultural evolution and 182–3; culture strength and 173–4; functional/occupational 181–2; of subcultures and 168–9, 247
Disneyland 169–70
dispersion models 72, 99, 104
diversity 214; cultural 96; gender 97; justice climate and 100; programs 97; racial 97; *see also* diversity climate

diversity climate 87–9, 96–7, 106–7, 109, 205, 217
DOCS *see* Denison Organizational Culture Survey

education: climate research in 28–30; subcultures and 170–2
effectiveness 4, 224–5; benchmarks and 280; boundary conditions and 105–8, 164–5; competitive advantage and 225–6; culture strength and 175–8; CVF and 162–4, 251, 266–7; foundation issues and 113; innovation and 109; justice climate and 73, 95; leadership and 19, 110; leadership climate and 15; managerial 32, 35–7; measurement of 165; in negative cultures 165; organizational climate and 2, 11–12, 45–6, 58, 72, 114, 202; organizational culture and 2–3, 122, 124–5, 160–8, 202, 213–15, 294–5; organizational culture change and 192, 274; organizational culture measures and 260; service climate and 105
emotional climate 87
employees: attitudes 84–5, 92, 162–4, 166; attributions made by 18; concern for 41, 82–4; engagement 56; interdependence 106; lower-level 104, 126–7; motivation 19, 23, 39, 289; performance 48, 91, 101, 113; satisfaction 90, *163*, 251; socialization of 41, 153–60, 210; support 84–5; surveys 91, 253, 271, 278; well-being 82, 162, 214, 219
enacted values: espoused values *versus* 135, 205, 223–5, 231, 291, 298–9; organizational climate and 200, 209, 222–3
engagement 56; service climate and 91, 113
environment 32, 36–7, 39, 198–9 218–9, 284–5; career 171; external 105, 175, *188*, 210–11, 302; internal 33, 45, 218; organizational climate and 54–5, 60, 66, 68,

Subject Index

70–1, 81–2; organizational culture and 119–20, 149–52, 260; school 28–30
equal opportunity climate 87
error management culture 214
espoused values 135–6, 182, 238, 291–2; enacted values *versus* 135, 205, 223–5, 231, 291, 298–9
ethical climate 87–9
ethical culture 214–15
evolution: of culture 121, 180–3, 187, 229
executive leadership 112; *see also* executives
executives: CEO 112, 191; competent 15; human resource 240; interviewing 246, 247, 277; organizational culture and 191, 234–6, 274; personality of 21; as sponsors 236, 276, 278; strategic focus and 234–5; subclimate 35; subculture 170–1; talent management and 239–40
experiences: awareness and 205; meaning and 2, 65–6, 69; member 148–9; organizational climate as abstraction of 2, 68; shared 66–8, 132, 200, 245; sharedness in 199; up-ending 156
external adaptation 2, *130*, 134, 148–9, 175, 209, *223*

feeder culture 170
financial performance 4; climate strength and 101; CVF and 162–4; diversity climate and 97; linkage research and 165; molar climate and 84; organizational culture and 214; service climate and 91–2
fit 21; ASA and 152; with company personality 120; cultural 175, 240, 258, 268; with environment 50, 109, 175–6, 188, 207; person-organization 258; socialization and 158; with organizational climate 38, 210; with strategy 239; talent management and 240
focused climates 34–5, 57, 60–2, 85–98, 206–7; alignment and 86–7;

categories of 87–8; change and 301; climate strength and 99; focused cultures *versus* 214–15; items 86; leadership and 90, 111–12; molar climate and 113–14, 202, 287; multiple 301–2; narrowness of 205; outcomes and 86, 107–8; process 87–8; strategic 87–8
focused leadership 90, 111–12
focus groups 205, 247–8, 269–70; 277–8, 292; climate strength and 104
formal organization 15–16
foundation issues 84–5, 90, 113–14; cultural diagnosis and 262–3
founder: influence on organizational culture 121, 146–8, 200–1, 293; values 147–8, 152–3, 181, *221*
fragmentation 126–7, 131, 182–3, 199, 216; culture strength and 173–4
frame of reference 72, 96, 130, 258; evaluative 246, 280; for focus groups 277–8
functionalism 125, 141, 202

gap analysis 271–2
gender diversity 97
General Electric 30–1, 184
General Motors (GM) 169
general psychological climate (PCg) 72, 82–3
gestalt 66, 73, 87, 115, 201–2, 206, *223*, 227
Gestalt psychology 3, 66, 200
Glacier Metal Works 118
GLOBE study 103, 150, 152
goals: alignment of 161; changes in 237–8; managerial climate and 19; orientation 111; strategic 84, 207, 210, 222, 234–5; Theory X and 18; Theory Y and 18
goal-oriented climate 111
groups: agreement within 74, 77; atmosphere 13, 27, 66; climate 27; climate strength 103; cohesion 94; cohesiveness 98; effective 18–19; identification 95, 100; interviews 143, 247; norms 24, 120, 159;

power distance 95, 107; processes 53, 83; size 74; social interactions within 100; *see also* focus groups
habits 281
Handbook of Organizational Culture and Climate (Ashkanasy, Wilderom & Peterson) 1, 69, 143, 196, 214
Hawthorne studies 12, 154
hierarchy 162–4, 249–51; culture strength and 174; at Disneyland 169; justice climate and 95; organizational climate and 47–8, 57, 58, 82
historical penetration 175
history: organizational climate and 209, 227–8; of organizational climate 11–62, 283–5; organizational culture and 118–25, 132–3, 139, 202, 209, 226
HR *see* human resources
human relations: orientation 14; training 24, 50
human relations climate 15, 85
human resources (HR): climate strength and 100; focused climate and 289; service climate and 91–2; talent management and 240
The Human Side of Enterprise (McGregor) 17
Human Synergistics 254–6
hybrid research design 143, 168, 170
hybrids 189, 240

IBM 184, 234
ICC *see* intraclass correlations
identity: climate strength and 100; organizational culture and 124, 133, 172; racial/ethnic 217
implementation climate 111, 114
individuals: climate as attribute of 51–2; context *versus* 198–9; differences 11–12, 37, 70, 108–9; level of analysis 16, 48, 57–8; level of climate 68, 70–2; performance 40–1, 45, 108; preferences 258
indoctrination, systematic 24
Industrial and Organizational Psychology: Perspectives on Science and Practice 1
industrial/organizational (I/O) psychology 3, 5, 19, 37, 119; *Annual Review of Psychology* and 30–1; competitive advantage and 228; ICC and 74
Industrial Psychology (Gilmer) 20–2
industrial relations: climate for 87
industry *221*; effects on organizational culture 151–2, 226; organizational climate and 302; volatility 176–7, 215
informal culture 16, 119
information: processing 206; sources 159–60
inimitability: competitive advantage and 226–8
initiative: climate for 87, 109
injuries 92–3, 106, 109
innovation: culture strength and 177; CVF and 162–4, 250–1; implementation climate and 114; moderator variables and 109–10; organizational culture and 207, 230, 262, 268–9; perceived organizational climate and 27; rules *versus* 43–5, 86; socialization 158; task completion and 24–5
innovation climate 31, 44, 87–8, *223*
innovative culture 191
inquiry *see* cultural inquiry
In Search of Excellence: Lessons from America's Best-Run Companies (Peters & Waterman) 122
integration 126–7, 182; climate strength and 101; functional 274; internal 2, *130*, 134, 148–9, 175, 209, *223*; of organizational culture with organizational climate 5, 196–7, 217–25, 296–9
internal service 106, 209, 288
interpretation: of the OCAI 251; of quantitative culture measures 262, 264–6, 270–1
interrater agreement 74
interrater reliability 74
interviews 245–47, 275–7
intraclass correlations (ICC) 74–8, 286–7

involvement: in the DOCS 251–2; molar climate and 82; organizational culture and 162
I/O psychology *see* industrial/organizational psychology

Japan 121–2, 150, 160–1
JDI *see* job descriptive index
job descriptive index (JDI) 54–6
job design 24, 83
job performance 49–50, 91, 284–5
job satisfaction: justice climate and 94–5; overlap with climate 54–6, 85; service climate and 90–2
Journal of Applied Behavioral Science 178
justice climate 73, 87–8, 94–6, 107; climate strength and 99–102; distributive 94–5, 107; leadership and 111; procedural 94–5, 107

language: cultural forms and 138; cultural inquiry and 244, 248, 275, 279–80
latent class modeling 216, 268, 272
LBDQ *see* leadership behavior description questionnaire
leader-member exchange (LMX) 93–5, 104
leader personality 94, 111
leadership 65; assessment 272–4, 281; autocratic 13; behavior 14–15, 111, 191, 273–4; character and 27; charismatic 112, 191; climate strength and 100, 104; competencies 273–4, 281; cross-cultural 103; culture embedding mechanisms and 147, 201; democratic 13; differences by organizational level 112–13; directive 15; dispersion models and 104; executive 112; focused 90, 111–12, 289; focused climate and 111–12; justice climate and 94; laissez-faire 13; molar climate and 81, 83, 112; motivation and 19–20; OCAI and 249; OCI and 254, 270; organizational climate change and 229–31; organizational climate and 24, 39–40, 53, 65, 110–13, 200–1, 219–21, 302; organizational culture and 24, 122, 200–1, 219–21, 234–6, 237; organizational culture as substitute for 235–6; organizational culture change and 184–92, 229–31, 273–4, 296; role of 200–1, 302; safety climate and 93, 111–12, 209; servant 91, 94, 111; service 90, 112; service climate and 84, 90–1, 111–12; social climate and 13–14; strategic climates and 15; styles 112, 283–4; training 14–15, 24; transactional 93; transformational 91, 93, 100, 104, 111–12, 191; values of 191–2, 229
leadership behavior description questionnaire (LBDQ) 14, 41
leadership climate 14–15, 30–1, 85, 87, 99, 110–13
Leadership, Psychology, and Organizational Behavior (Bass) 70
learning 11; accumulated 235–6; exploratory 177; integrating organizational culture and organizational climate 298–9; from organizational climate research 213–17; organizational culture development and 148–9, 293; from organizational culture research 208–13; socialization and 155–6, 159–60
Least Preferred Coworker (LPC) 27
levels of analysis 16, 46; climate strength and 103; in diversity climate 96; individual 16, 48, 57–8, 68, 72–3, 222; learning from organizational climate research on 216–17; measurement of organizational climate and 51–2, 72–9, 286–7; multiple 77–8, 103, 224, 302; organizational 51, 59, 66, 103, 222; in service climate 89–92; subclimates and 21–2; theoretical justification for 77; unit 72, 77–8, 98, 199, 224, 286–7
life cycles: organizational culture change and 183, 188–90; organizational culture and 180–2, 303

Life Styles Inventory 254
linkage research 91, 165
LMX *see* leader-member exchange
longitudinal research 114, 120, 211, 243
LPC *see* Least Preferred Coworker

malleability, of organizational culture *versus* organizational climate 206
The Management of Strategic Change (Pettigrew) 121
managerial climate 18–19, 41, 85, 110–11
managerialists 124, 167
Managerial Psychology (Leavitt) 16–17
market culture 162–4, 249–51
marketing 54; of organizational culture 121–2
Mayflower Group 253, 281
meaning: of artifacts 135–6, 222; molar climate and 85; organizational climate and 2–3, 54, 65–9, 199–200, 206; organizational culture and 120–1, 132, 162, 180, 199–200; personal 162; psychological climate and 71–2; shared 33, 66, 69, 79, 199–200, 220; symbolic 126, 136, 138, 184, 192
measurement 20; of climate strength 102–3; of culture strength 176–8; in early climate research 15, 27–9, 34, 39–43, 47; framework, for cultural inquiry 241–4; ipsative 258, 267, 281; of leadership 272–4; of molar climate 60, 81–3; objective 36, 52–3, 165; of organizational climate 57, 72–9, 200; of organizational climate *versus* job attitudes 54–6; of organizational effectiveness 165; profile shapes and 242–3; quantitative, of organizational culture 167–8, 249–61; of safety climate 92, 259, 273; of service climate 89, 212; specificity of 73
mediation: focused climates and 88, 113; organizational climate and 110–14, 215, 222, 288–9, 302; organizational culture and 166–7, 215, 222, 303; safety climate and 92–3, 113–14; service climate and 90–1, 111, 113–14
mergers and acquisitions 184, 190, 237
mission: in the DOCS 251–2; organizational culture and 162
moderation: climate strength and 99–105, 302; culture strength and 176–7; diversity climate and 96–7, 107, 109; justice climate and 95, 107; organizational climate and 27, 36, 40, 108–10, 215, 288–9, 302; organizational culture and 166–7, 215, 272, 303; safety climate and 93, 103, 106, 109–10; service climate and 92, 105–6, 108–9
molar climate 60, 79–85, 205, 222; attitudes and 85; climate strength and 99; as climate for well-being 82–4; dimensions of *81*; dimensions in profile 84–5; early research on 79–80; focused climate *versus* 202, 287; foundation issues and 84–5, 88, 113–14; future research on 301–2; items 86; leadership and 81, 83, 112; measurement 60, 81–3; narrowness of 205; organizational culture and 203, 209; process climates and 88; taxonomies of 80–2; validity of 113
motivation 23, effects of leadership on 19, 40, 112, 273; manager's theories about 17–18; organizational climate and 37–40, 114; organizational culture and 161; patterns of 87–8; safety 92–3, 114
Motivation and Organizational Climate (Litwin & Stringer) 37–40

Narrative Inquiry 244–5, 300
narratives: analysis 248; cultural inquiry and 245, 248; cultural forms and 138; data 247
national culture 150–1, 164, 210–11, 293; industry *versus* 152
negative culture 165–6

Subject Index

networks: communication 22, 94; effects of 302; friendship 94; social 95-6, 100
newcomers 246, 293-4; fit and 258; organizational culture and 132-3; socialization of 153-60
norms 24-6, 223; organizational climate and 36, 45, 114; organizational culture and 16, 119-20, 128, 137, 249, 254-6; socialization and 153-4, 159

OB *see* organizational behavior
objective measures 36, 52-3, 165
OCAI *see* Organizational Culture Assessment Instrument
OCB *see* organizational citizenship behavior
occupational subcultures 170-2
OCDQ *see* Organizational Climate Description Questionnaire
OCI *see* Organizational Culture Inventory
OCM *see* Organizational Climate Measure
OCP *see* Organizational Culture Profile
OD *see* organizational development
Ohio State Leadership projects 14
organizational behavior (OB) 5, 19, 37, 70; growth of 118-19; strategic management and 123
organizational change *see* change
organizational citizenship behavior (OCB) 114, 298; customer-focused 90; justice climate and 94-5, 107; safety climate and 93-4; service climate and 90-2, 114
organizational climate: as abstraction of experiences 2, 68; aggression and 13, 15; alignment and 15-16, 105, 201-2, 228; antecedents of 110-14, 288-9; articles on *38-9, 61-2;* ASA model and 16, 45, 67; assumptions and 205, 209, 218, 229-31; attitudes, overlap with 41, 54-6, 69, 85, 285; attitudinal outcomes of 82, 84, 110, 221-2; awareness of 205, 297; boundary conditions 105-8, 287-8; breadth of 204-5, 209-10; as a bundle of attributes 54; for burnout 87; causality and 84, 90, 229-30; change 16-17, 35, 39, 73, 206, 211, 229-31, 301-2; change information 101; climcult framework and 219-20, 298-9; commitment and 82, 95, 107; communication and 27-8, 31, 65; competitive advantage and 225-9; complexity and 22, 94, 105, 106; conceptualizing 33-4; configuration of 23, 34, 54, 84-5; conflict and 34, 35, 39-40, 41-2; consensus 99; context and 47-8; critiques of 50-9, 284-5; culture embedding mechanisms and 201, 210-11; CVF and 82; data aggregation and 76; defensive 28, 34, 86; definition of 1-3, 33-4, 44-5, 64-70, 114-15, 285-6; development 211, 302; dimensions of *42, 46, 47, 49, 81, 83;* dispersion and 72, 99, 104; effectiveness and 2, 11-12, 45-6, 58, 72, 114, 202; effects of 35; emotional 87; enacted values and 200, 209, 222-3; environment and 54-5, 60, 66, 68, 70-1, 81-2; equal opportunity 87; ethical 87-9; fit and 38, 210; formation of 302; future research on 301-4; as a gestalt 66, 73, 87, 115, 201-2, 206, *223,* 227; goal-oriented 111; hierarchy and 47-8, 57, 58, 82; history and 209, 227-8; history from 1939 to mid-1960s 12-32, 283-4; history from 1960s to early-1970s 32-50, 284; history in 1980s 60-2; history in the mid-1970s 50-9, 284-5; human relations 15, 85; implementation 111, 114; for industrial relations 87; industry 302; for initiative 87, 109; innovation and 24-5, 43-5; integration with organizational culture 5, 196-7, 217-25, 296-9; interventions 302; job satisfaction overlap with 54-6, 85; lack of consensus in ratings of 58-9; lack

of uniqueness of 53-4; leadership and 24, 39-40, 53, 65, 110-13, 200-1, 219-21, 302; learning from organizational culture research 208-13; learning from research on 213-17; levels of analysis and 51-2, 72-9, 286-7; malleability of 206; meaning of 2-3, 54, 65-69, 199-200, 206; measurement of 15, 27-9, 34, 39-43, 47, 57, 72-9, 200; mediation and 110-14, 215, 222, 288-9, 302; models of 220, 221, 223; moderation and 27, 36, 40, 108-10, 215, 288-9, 302; motivation and 37-40, 114; multiple 301-2; across multiple levels of analysis 302; norms and 36, 45, 114; organizational culture differentiated from 203-8, 297; organizational culture similarities with 197-203, 297; outcomes of 2, 34-5, 46, 48-50, 56-8, 71, 222; passion and 212-13; perceptions of 19, 27, 47-8, 113, 220-4; performance and 55-8; perspective on 41-2; practical implications of 299-301; productive 28, 85; profiles 29, 302; for psychological safety 109; qualitative research on 115-16, 211-12, 302; quantitative measures of 259-61; quantitative research on 32; referent for 29, 72-3, 90, 95-6, 286; relevancy of 217; richness and 212-13; satisfaction and 43, 45-6, 48, 54-6, 68; sense-making and 200; for sexual harassment 87; social 13-14; socialization and 41, 210, 303; strategic focus of 206-7; structure and 46-8, 67; summary of 283-9; survey items 29, 46, 52, 72; symbolic interactionism and 67; technical updating 87; themes in 64-8, 285-6; training and 65, 73; for trust formation 28, 86; turnover and 55, 57; typologies and 302; unit-level behavior and 114; validation 52-3; variability 103; see also climate strength; diversity climate; focused climates; innovation climate; justice climate; leadership climate; managerial climate; molar climate; process climates; safety climate; service climate; strategic climates; subclimates

Organizational Climate Description Questionnaire (OCDQ) 29, 43

Organizational Climate Measure (OCM) 82; dimensions of 83

organizational culture 117-18; adaptive 166, 177, 191-2, 243; adhocracy 162-3, 249-51, 268-9; alignment and 166, 175, 234-5, 303; ambiguity in 126-7; anthropology and 3, 123, 204; artifacts of 21, 119, 132, 135-7, 221; ASA model and 152-3; assumptions 2, 125, 132, 134-7, 149, 182, 220; attitudes and 162-4, 166; attributes of 131-4; awareness of 132, 135, 205; behavior patterns and 136-7; boundary conditions 164-5, 273; breadth of 133, 204-5; bureaucratic 191; bypass 165; causality and 229-30; change 120, 129-32; 178-92, 229-31, 273-4, 295-6, 301; change, bases for 236-9; clan 122, 162-4, 249-51; 266-7; climcult framework and 219-20, 298-9; collective learning and 148-9; commitment and 121, 125, 133; communication and 242; competitive advantage and 122, 225-9, 265; complexity and 145-6, 164, 215; conceptualizations of 125-30, 290-1; conflict and 126-7; constructive 254-6; 266-7; cultural dynamics model of 137, 231; CVF and 162-4, 214, 249-50, 266-7, 268-9; defensive 254-6; definition of 1-3, 119-21, 130-4, 291-2; depth of 132; development of 145-53, 181, 211, 292-3; diagnosing 236-9, 272-4, 279-81; differentiation perspective of 126, 129, 131, 216; dimensions of 127-8, 263-4, 266-7; effectiveness and 2–3, 122, 124–5, 160–8, 202, 213–15, 294–5; embedding mechanisms 147, 181, 201, 210–11, 229–30; emergence of 145–53; employee well-being and 162, 214, 219; enacted values and 223–5; environment and 119–20, 149–52, 260; error management 214; espoused values and 135–6, 182, 205, 223–5, 238, 291–2; ethical 214–15; evolution of 121, 180–3, 187, 229; executives and 191, 234–6, 274; external adaptation and 2, *130*, 134, 148–9, 175, 209, *223*; financial performance and 214; fit with 175, 240, 258, 268; focused 214–15; forms of 137–8, 291; founder influences on 121, 146–8, 152–3, 181, 200–1, 293; future research on 302–4; hierarchy 162–4, 249–51; history and 118–25, 132–3, 139, 202, 209, 226; hybrid research design 143, 168; identity and 124, 133, 172; individual preferences and 258; industry effects on 151–2, 226; informal 16, 119; innovation and 207, 230, 262, 268–9; innovative 191; integration with organizational climate 5, 196–7, 217–25, 296–9; integration perspective of 126–7, 182; internal integration and 2, *130*, 134, 148–9, 175, 209, *223*; involvement and 162; issues that constitute 185–6; layers of 223–4; leadership and 24, 122, 200–1, 219–21, 234–6, 237; learning from organizational climate research 213–17; learning from research on 208–13; levels of 135–7; levels of analysis and 216–7; leveraging of 238–9; life cycles and 180–3, 189–90; maintenance 293–4; malleability of 206; market 162–4, 249–51; marketing of 121–2; meaning and 120–1, 132, 162, 180, 199–200; mediation and 166–7, 215, 222, 303; mergers and acquisitions and 184, 190; metaphors for conceptualizing 127–8; methods for studying 138–44, 292; mission and 162; models of *220, 221, 223*; moderation and 166–7, 215, 272, 303; molar climate and 203, 209; motivation and 161; negative 165–6; newcomers and 132–3; norms and 16, 119–20, 128, 137, 249, 254–6; organizational climate differentiated from 203–8, 297; organizational climate similarities with 197–203, 297; outcomes and 2–3, 125, 155, 165–7, 214–5, 303–4; penetration of 174–5; perceptions of 175; performance and 129–30, 161–7, 202, 214–15, 237, 303; perpetuation of 153–60; persistence of 183–4; practical implications of 299–301; in practice 130; process climates and 209; profiles 264–9; qualitative research on 123, 139–44, 167–8, 182, 204; quantitative measures of 249–61; quantitative research on 139–44, 167–8, 215–6, 303; relevancy of 129–30, 217; research categories 140–1; rigidity of 179; rules and 133, 161, 179; safety 215, 259–60; sense-making and 132; sharedness of 131, 175, 199; socialization and 132–3, 153–60, 210, 293–4, 302–3; sociology and 3; stability of 131–2, 180–3; strategic climates and 209, 219–20, 223, 304; strategic focus of 206–7, 304; structure and 26, 120, 174; summary of 289–96; supportive 191; surveys of 140–3, 249–61, 300; of sustainable organizations 214; symbolism in 120–2, 126, 132, 134; three-perspective theory of 127; transmission of 132–3; turnover and 298; typologies 263–9, 280; uncertainty reduction and 155; uniqueness of 133–4, 139, 190; work-family 214; *see also* cultural inquiry; culture strength; subcultures

Organizational Culture Assessment Instrument (OCAI) 249–51, 260, 263–4, 267, 269–70, 281
Organizational Culture Inventory (OCI) 254–6, 260, 266–7, 270
Organizational Culture Profile (OCP) 207, 256–61, 264, 266–7, 268
organizational development (OD) 178, 237, 270
Organizational Dynamics 146
organizational effectiveness *see* effectiveness
Organizational Psychology (Schein) 23–5, 70, 120
organizational structure *see* structure
outcomes 229, 303–4; of climate strength 99–101; of cultural inquiry 236, 243, 280; CVF and 266–7; diversity climate and 96–7; DOCS and 253; focus on 206–7; focused climate and 86–8, 107–8, 113; justice climate and 94–5; mediation and 114, 215; moderation and 215, 302; molar climate and 84–5; OCAI and 251; OCI and 254–5; OCP and 258–9; organizational climate and 2, 34–5, 46, 48–50, 56–8, 71, 222; organizational culture and 2–3, 125, 155, 165–7, 214–5, 303–4; organizational culture change and 190; process-focused climate and 88; psychological climate and 71; reciprocal relationships with 224; safety climate and 92–4, 106; service climate and 89–92; *see also* climate–outcome relationships

passion 212–13
PCg *see* general psychological climate
perceptions: diversity climate and 96–7; homogeneity of 22, 59; individual 22, 45, 54–5, 71, 96; justice climate and 94–6; objective measures *versus* 52–3; of organizational climate 19, 27, 47–8, 113, 220–4; of organizational culture 175; safety climate and 93; service climate and 89; of service

quality 89–90, 214; shared 168–9, 174–5, 199, 205–6, 209; variability in 98–9
performance: climate strength and 101, 104; culture strength and 175–7, 258–9; CVF and 162–4; diversity climate and 96–7; drivers 255–6; evaluation 15; individual 36, 40–1, 45, 51, 108, 203; job 49–50, 91, 284–5; managerial 35–7; measurement of 165; organizational 25, 114, 162–5, 175–7; organizational climate and 55–8; organizational culture and 129–30, 161–7, 202, 214–15, 237, 303; sales 96–7; service 91–2; team 95; *see also* financial performance
personality: Big Five 111; company 36, 119–20; leader 94, 111; need-press model of 28; types, in occupational subcultures 171–2
The Planning of Change: Readings in the Applied Behavioral Sciences (Bennis, Benne & Chin) 178
positive reinforcement 230
practices, cultural forms and 138
PriceWaterhouseCoopers Consulting 184
problem solving 20; external adaptation and 148–9
procedural justice climate *see* justice climate
process climates 87–9, 102, 106–7; as foundations for strategic climates 88–9, 220, 287; organizational culture and 209
productive climates 28, 85
productivity: Hawthorne studies and 12
product tangibility 106
profiles 217, 242–3, 300; climate 29, 302; cultural 263–9; molar climate 84–5; *see also* typologies
Psychological Bulletin 22
psychological climate 18, 20–2, 51–2, 60, 70–2, 221; dimensions of 81; general 72, 82–3; job attitudes and 72; satisfaction and 68

Subject Index

psychological penetration 174
psychological safety: climate for 109

Q-sort 256–8
qualitative research 4; climate strength and 104, 212; on organizational climate 115–16, 211–12, 302; on organizational culture 123, 139–44, 167–8, 182, 204; on organizational subcultures 169; pros and cons of 142; see also cultural inquiry
quantitative research 4; on organizational climate 32; on organizational culture 139–44, 167–8, 215–6, 303; pros and cons of 142; see also cultural inquiry
questions: for cultural inquiry focus groups 277–8; for cultural inquiry interviews 276; for measuring organizational climate 72; OCAI 249–50

rareness: competitive advantage and 226–7
referent: for organizational climate items 29, 72–3, 90, 95–6, 286
referent-shift consensus model 73, 286
recruitment 240
reinforcement: collective learning and 148–9; mechanisms 147, 201; positive 230; schedules 11
relevancy, of organizational culture research 129–30, 217
research: in education 28–30; future 104, 301–4; history of organizational culture 118–25; hybrid designs of 143, 168, 170; integrated 298–9; learning from organizational culture 208–13; linkage 91, 165; longitudinal 114, 120, 211, 243; mixed methods 215–16; organizational culture, categories of 140–1; survey 215–16; symbolism in 120–1; see also qualitative research; quantitative research
resource-based theory of organizations 225–9

resources 225–7; allocation of 147, 274; organizational 91, 113
response rates: within-unit 74–5, 78
return on assets 109, 258–9
return on investment (ROI) 108, 176
richness 212–13, 302
rites of passage 156
ROI see return on investment
role stress 83; service climate and 89–90, 108
rules 21; cultural manifestations and 138; innovation versus 43–4, 86; organizational culture and 133, 161, 179
rWG(j) metric 74–5, 77, 286–7; see also agreement

safety climate 23, 60–2, 92–4, 223; climate strength and 99, 103; leadership and 93, 111–12, 209; measures of 92, 259, 273; mediation and 92–3, 113–14; moderation and 93, 103, 106, 109–10; organizational citizenship behavior and 93–4; outcomes 92–4, 106; strategic climates and 87–8
safety culture 215, 259–60
safety training 92, 109–10, 259
sales 90–1, 96–7, 253
sample size, within-unit 78
satisfaction 68; climate strength and 101; employee 90, 163, 251 (see also job satisfaction); justice climate and 94–5, 107; organizational climate and 43, 45–6, 48, 54–6, 68; psychological climate and 68; service climate and 90–1; of subordinates 19; see also customer satisfaction
school environments 28–30
scientist-practitioner model 3
scoring: cultural inquiry and 270–1; of the OCAI 250–1; sentiment 248
Securities and Exchange Commission 238
selection 11–12, 23–4, 40–1, 240; see also Attraction-Selection-Attrition (ASA) model

sense-making: justice climate and 100; organizational climate and 200; organizational culture and 132; subcultures and 170
service climate 60–2, 87, 89–92; climate strength and 99, 101; customer satisfaction and 90–2, 101, 105–6, 114, 207; diversity climate and 97, 107, 109; foundation issues and 84, 90, 113; HR and 91–2; internal service and 106, 288; job satisfaction and 90–2; leadership and 84, 90–1, 111–12; measures 89–90, 212; mediation and 90–1, 111, 113–14; moderation and 92, 105–6, 108–9; organizational citizenship behavior and 90–2, 114; strategic climates and 87–8
service orientation 89, 108, 111
service performance 91–2
service quality 91, 106, 202, 214; customer perceptions of 89–90, 214; gap scores and 271–2; molar climate and 84, OCI and 254–5
service relationships 106–8
sexual harassment: climate for 87
shared meanings 33, 66, 69, 79, 199–200, 220
sharedness: culture strength and 175; in experiences 199; of organizational culture 131
Silicon Valley 169
SIOP *see* Society for Industrial and Organizational Psychology
situational strength 98, 108
situational variables 30, 34, 36
situations 11–12, 36, 40–1, 60; interaction of person and 43; organizational 53; social 25, 119–20
SMEs *see* subject matter experts
social climate 13–14
social exchange 112, 219
social interactions: meaning and 67; shared 71; climate strength and 100
social networks *see* networks
socialization 24–6, 153–60; culture strength and 175; definition of 153–4; fit and 158; individual proactive 158–9; innovation and 158; learning during 155–6, 159–60; norms and 153–4, 159; occupational subcultures and 171; organizational climate and 41, 210, 303; organizational culture and 132–3, 210, 293–4, 302–3; stages of 156–7; tactics 157–8; talent management and 240; uncertainty reduction and 155
The Social Psychology of Organizations (Katz & Kahn) 25–6
Society for Industrial and Organizational Psychology (SIOP) 1
sociological penetration 174
sociology 3, 12, 67
sponsor: of cultural inquiry 236, 276, 278–9
stakeholders: adaptive cultures and 191–2; cultural inquiry and 237–8, 262, 269–72, 279–80; external 151; multiple 4, 217
statistics: aggregation 74–7; agreement 75, 78
strategic climates 15–16, 20, 23–4, 34–5, 87; boundary conditions and 106; breadth and 205; competitive advantage and 227–9; external environment and 211; focus of 214; leadership and 273; molar climates and 84–5, 113–14; organizational culture and 209, 219–20, 223, 304; process climates and 88–9; survey 259–61
strategic focus: executives and 234–5; learning from organizational climate research on 214–15; of organizational culture 304; of organizational culture *versus* organizational climate 206–7; on surveys 259–60
strategic management 123, 211
strength *see* climate strength; culture strength; situational strength
stress: climate strength and 101; role 83, 89–90, 108
structure 221; bureaucratic 52; nested data 75–6, 78; informal 21, 26, 120; loose 174; organizational climate and 46–8, 67; of qualitative data 247–8

Subject Index

subclimates 35, 199; levels of analysis and 21–2, 78
subcultures 168–73, 199; conflict among 126, 272; cultural inquiry and 246–7, 270, 272, 281; culture strength and 173–4; definition of 168; development 170; differentiation and 126–7, 131, 168–9, 290; executive 170–1; future research on 303; levels of analysis and 216; life cycle stages and 181–2; occupational 170–2; organizational culture change and 183–4, 189–90; organizational effectiveness and 164, *166*, 295; qualitative research on *142*, 169–70; quantitative research and *142*, 216, 272
subject matter experts (SMEs) 244, 246, 275–6
substitutability: competitive advantage and 226–8
supervision, global *versus* detailed 43–5, 86
supervisor-subordinate relationship 18, 66
support: items, 86; from management 111, 113; molar climate and 84–5; organizational 93
supportive culture 191
surveys 215–16; items on 29, 46, 52, 72; linkage research and 91; of organizational culture 140–3, 249–61, 300; strategic focus of 259–60; *see also* measurement
sustainable organizations: cultures of 214
symbolic interactionism 67
symbolism: cultural dynamics model and 137; cultural forms and 138; leadership and 274; in organizational culture 120–2, 126, 132, 134; of organizational culture change 184, 190–1
System 4 Management 20, 120

tactics: proactive 159; socialization 157–8
talent management 239–41
Tavistock School 118
teams 19; alignment and 234–5; climate strength and 100–2; justice climate and 94–6; performance 95; size 94, 100; stress 101
technical updating climate 87
Texas City Refinery 259
T-Groups 27–8, 86, 178
Theory X 17–18, 85, 111
Theory Y 17–18, 85, 111
Theory Z: How American Business Can Meet the Japanese Challenge (Ouchi) 121
three-perspective theory of culture 127
training: climate for transfer of 87; human relations 24, 50; leadership 14–15, 24; organizational climate and 65, 73; safety 92, 109–10, 259; socialization and 156–7
trust: clan cultures and 122, 162–3
trust formation: climate for 28, 86
turnover: fit and 258; justice climate and 94–5; linkage research and 91; organizational climate and 55, 57; organizational culture and 298; service climate and 101
typologies 263–9, 280; organizational climate and 302; *see also* profiles

uncertainty reduction 155
underlying assumptions *see* assumptions
units: agreement within 75, 77–8, 99, 102; behavior 114, 220; effectiveness 45–6, 73, 95, 110; level of analysis 72, 77–8, 98, 199, 224, 286–7; organizational citizenship behavior 94–5, 111, 114; organizational climate and 2, 66–7, 70, 72; referent 73, 95

validation: of organizational climate 52–3
validity generalization 41
value: competitive advantage and 225–8
values 137; in adaptive cultures 177; behavior patterns and 230; CEO 191; climate of 28, 85; of climate strength 302; enacted *versus*

espoused 205, 223–5, 231, 298–9; espoused 135–6, 182, 238, 291–2; founder 147–8, 152–3, 181, *221*; layers of organizational culture and 224; leader 191, 229; OCP 256–9; organizational 36; organizational cultural change and 191–2; shared 136; statements 258; *see also* competing values framework

variability: climate 103; in agreement 75, 77–8, 102; in perceptions 98–9; in within-unit response rates 74–5; in within-unit sample size 78; *see also* climate strength, culture strength, intraclass correlations

Venn diagrams 173

vision: of founders 152; of leaders 100, 121, 188

WABA analyses 74

well-being: climate for 82–4; climate strength outcomes and 101; employee 82, 162, 214, 219

work environment *see* environment

work facilitation 90, 113

work-family culture 214